HERBERT J. GANS is a professor of
sociology at Columbia University and
a senior research associate at the
Center for Policy Research. At Harvard University, Nathan Glazer is a
professor of education and sociology
and Christopher Jencks is a professor
of sociology. Joseph R. Gusfield is a
professor of Sociology at the University of California, San Diego. By rotat-
ing the managing editor's responsibilities, they shared in the editing of
this book.

ON THE MAKING OF AMERICANS:
ESSAYS IN HONOR OF DAVID RIESMAN

ON THE MAKING OF
Essays in honor of

EDITED BY

Herbert J. Gans
Nathan Glazer
Joseph R. Gusfield
Christopher Jencks

UNIVERSITY OF PENNSYLVANIA

AMERICANS ☆☆
David Riesman

PRESS / 1979

Copyright © 1979 by the University of Pennsylvania Press, Inc.
All rights reserved
Printed in the United States of America

Composition by Deputy Crown Inc., Camden, N.J.

Designed by Adrianne Onderdonk Dudden

Library of Congress Cataloging in Publication Data

Main entry under title:
On the making of Americans.

    Bibliography: p.
    CONTENTS: What is American about America?: Featherstone, J.
John Dewey and David Riesman, from the lost individual to the lonely
crowd. Gusfield, J. R. The sociological reality of America. Jencks, C.
The social basis of unselfishness. Meyersohn, R. Abundance reconsidered. Sennett, R. What Tocqueville feared. Glazer, N. Individualism and equality in the United States. Cottle, T. J. An unemployed
family. Kato, H. Development nineteenth-century style. [etc.]
    1. United States—Social conditions—20th century—Addresses, essays,
lectures. 2. National characteristics, American—Addresses, essays, lectures. 3. Minorities—United States—Addresses, essays, lectures. 4.
Riesman, David, 1909–   —Addresses, essays, lectures. I. Riesman,
David, 1909–   II. Gans, Herbert J.

HN65.052   309.1'73'092   78-65118

ISBN 0-8122-7754-6

CONTENTS

PART II.
AMERICAN INSTITUTIONS AND
SUBCULTURES—STILL CHANGING

FOREWORD
DAVID RIESMAN: AN APPRECIATION

When the intellectual history of the twentieth century is written, the social sciences, particularly in America, will play an important role. Many analysts will no doubt focus on the importance of new methodologies for most of the social sciences. Yet I doubt that it is the methodological contributors whose work will have the greatest impact. Rather, it will be those who, like David Riesman, have combined theory, probing questions, dazzling insights based on limited data, and empirical findings.

Moreover, if the humanities and social sciences, so long separate and antagonistic toward each other, converge once more, as now seems possible, the intellectual history of the twentieth century will also remember David Riesman as having helped initiate that confluence. Today, some social scientists are viewed as humanists; Riesman, however, has always combined the best of the two branches of learning. He has been a humanist in every nuance of the word since the start of his career as a lawyer and sociologist.

David Riesman's place in the history of social thought is secured by his extraordinary range and brilliance. Both these qualities are illuminated by a candor of vision—innocent in the best sense—and a spontaneity that sends him forth on quests others do not even perceive, and enables him to find links where others see only disparities. It is spontaneity of this sort that he has admired wherever he has found it, particularly in colleagues. To those in whom he sensed promise, he was and is not only kind but unusually generous.

David Riesman is not always a patient man—few productive people are. He has himself noted that his training at the Harvard Law School, his brief practice with a Boston trial law firm, his less-than-stimulating clerkship with Justice Brandeis, and his stint as Deputy Assistant District Attorney of New York all led to a questioning approach to evidence. He has rarely been prepared to accept the apparent; like Freud, about whom he has written both critically and lovingly, he is fascinated by artichokes, whose leaves must be peeled if one is to reach the heart.

As is true of all intellectual giants, it is hard to categorize Riesman's mind or work, for they cover an immense spectrum. His first academic appointment was as a professor of law at Buffalo. His first monograph —on civil liberties—called for intervention by government, a solution he would later renounce. Throughout his career there has been a subtle countercyclical quality: an impatience with the current, a quest for clues to new directions of social action as derived from social thought. But he has never been doctrinaire. His anti-Stalinism—sometimes expressed through benign satire as in "The Nylon War," a paper on parachuting American consumer goods into the USSR after the Second World War—never kept him from forming varied political alliances in opposition to the dangers of nuclear war. What may on occasion appear as contrariness is, in fact, deeply rooted in a characteristically countercyclical mode of thought.

Like other intellectual giants, he has been accused of dilettantism. But his curiosity about the social fabric in its diverse textures, which might on rare occasion lead to superficiality, has more often led him to synthesis. His ability to link history and demography, class and individual character structure, appears graphically in *The Lonely Crowd* and the related works that followed. (What a travesty on the apparatus that serves the intellectual world, that the Yale University Press published the book in a print run, as I recall, of only 1,500 copies and that few publications deigned to review it at first!)

David Riesman's writing is complex, but it is rarely obscure. One of the few utopians of our time, he always welcomed such visions of the future where he found them—for instance, in the Goodmans' *Communitas*. A lack of that vision on the part of manipulators in organizations has led him to a dim view of our present prospects.

Of all organizations none has fascinated him more than the university and college. Here again, he has run against the tide. He fought for freshness when convention was the mode, and for solidity at a time when a pablum was resulting from the determination of curricula by faddists. He has been attracted by the paradox that American institutions of higher learning, although apparently so diverse, nonetheless results in such similar outcomes for their students. He has given his time and energy to obscure colleges and universities whose members saw themselves as neglected, even benighted, while often refusing attention to the powerful and prestigious. In his work he has been intrigued by the phenomenon of the marginal; but he is never either maudlin or reflexive in his sympathies.

Eldest son of a mother from a patrician Jewish family and of a physician-father from Germany, also Jewish, who became the leading Philadelphia internist of his day and a member of the University of Pennsylvania faculty, David Riesman moved marginally in the world of Jews. Yet that marginality served him well. He gained an insight both into the people of Northeast Harbor, Maine, where so many upper-class Philadelphians summered, as did his family, and into the world of the Jew, intellectual or otherwise—a world scorned during Riesman's days as an undergraduate in chemistry at Harvard. This same marginality has given him a special understanding of bureaucracies gleaned, for example, from his period as an official of the Sperry Gyroscope Company. In this respect, his experience recalls that of Max Weber as a territorial administrator and then a hospital executive for Germany in the First World War.

As in any great marriage, the influence of his wife, the former Evelyn Thompson, has been especially significant. She is the aesthete, the gentle critic whose smile and humor could enhance the humanity David sought in his work. In a special way she—a writer at home in all arts—is also the more cosmopolitan, glorying in the delights of Paris, Florence, or London. David Riesman has an exquisite understanding of other cultures, but almost a xenophobia about traveling in them. Yet when he did go to Japan, no American cultural figure since Lafcadio Hearn was as idolized as he.

I have known David Riesman and his family all my adult life. I have heard him reflect with some impatience on letters from his father, whose namesake he was, and who urged him to follow the Latin motto "nothing human is alien to me." I never asked why he doubted that advice, which, ironically, became a ruling principle of his life. Indeed, I know of no one who has so well combined an understanding of and affection for sophisticated high culture with a taste for mass, popular culture, whether in music, literature, or the visual arts. The first evening I ever spent with him was at a classical harmonica concert.

In surveying a character and an intellect as complex as those of David Riesman, it is almost impossible to judge the impact that others have had upon him. Among the major influences, he himself would probably include his teacher, the political philosopher Carl Joachim Friedrich, with whom he once shared a dairy farm in Vermont, and his analyst Erich Fromm. No doubt he influenced them as much as they stimulated him.

David Riesman's intellectual contributions through his writing are profound. Even more profound may be his contributions as a teacher. His energy has been remarkable. Whereas Max Weber remained a professor for twenty years without meeting a class, Riesman has relished his teaching, particularly to undergraduates, both at the University of Chicago and at Harvard. Although hating meetings, he diligently attends them, afterwards preparing exhaustive notes for himself and for others. Students who worked with him have rarely remained the same. Those who studied with him found their sensitivities heightened through the experience, and, after graduating, continued to be inspired through a correspondence that was, on occasion, copious. Some of those students are represented in this *Festschrift*. Though he was not a formal teacher of my wife, Margy, and myself—we were colleagues at both Chicago and Harvard—he has taught us constantly. David Riesman is, and always will be, a teacher to us all.

Martin Meyerson

EDITORS' INTRODUCTION

Martin Meyerson's Foreword and Everett Hughes' Epilogue speak for us, and for the contributors to this book, in honoring Dave—and equally importantly, in expressing our affection for him. But our task in this *Festschrift* is to express these feelings through our work.

In planning this volume, we asked the contributors to write on subjects of their own choice, and on work they were currently doing, rather than to comment on Dave's work. The book thus deals with many subjects, just as Dave has done in his own writing. But there is also a common theme in the book, as in Dave's work, for in one way or another, all of the articles concern themselves with what is happening to America and Americans.

As a result, the papers are concerned with topical issues. Here, too, the contributors take their lead from Dave; indeed, he, more than anyone else, initiated and legitimized the idea that sociologists should be concerned with topical issues. *The Lonely Crowd* created a stir in 1950, when it was first published, not only because of its argument, but because it suggested that sociology was more than abstract grand theory or quantitative analysis. Dave's method—to apply sociological insights to issues of the time, using a combination of theory, data, and imagination—was then novel, and more than a little heretical. In the 1950s, most sociologists felt that Dave and his coauthors were not doing sociology, and while many feel the same way today, Dave's approach is now more widely—if not yet sufficiently—accepted.

The book is divided into two interrelated, but not mutually exclusive, sections. The essays of Part One are mostly about America as a whole. The first papers address themselves to issues that have preoccupied Dave, notably the relationship between the individual and society, and the possibilities of autonomy. Featherstone's essay leads off the book, because, among other things, he puts these issues into a historical context. Gusfield and, in a somewhat different way, Jencks focus on contemporary reconsiderations of individualism.

When Dave first introduced these issues, America was, at least for the middle classes with which he has been most concerned, on the road to being an abundant and affluent society. Today, however, America is once more preoccupied with scarcity, which leads Meyersohn to cast a new glance at the questions that Dave raised in his seminal article "Abundance for What?" And perhaps because scarcity is once more a widespread preoccupation, the contemporary analysis of American individualism has been accompanied by a revival of the historic debate over liberty versus equality; this issue is one topic of the papers by Sennett and Glazer. It is also addressed by Cottle, who reminds us that for poor people, the possibilities of individualism, and liberty, are blocked by economic obstacles. Kato's paper emphasizes the economic issues as well, providing some revealing comparisons between Japan and America.

The essays in Part Two are about specific American institutions and subgroups, but many are also about individualism reconsidered. Gans suggests that contemporary ethnicity is a new resolution of the conflicts between individual and group. A similar theme runs through Weiss's paper on the changing American family, while Berger comments on transformations in the nature of group relations through his comparison of suburbs and communes, and Denney does so, in a very different way, in his paper on changing forms of sociability. Trow's essay takes the discussion to the institutional level, applying Dave's long-standing concern with diversity to the pressures that impinge on the elite private university. Grant's paper on the increasing but little-noticed convergence between journalists and social scientists comes last, but if books could duplicate the circularity that often marks real life, it would also be first, for he pays silent tribute to the joining of sociology and journalism that Dave has always encouraged. Grant is, by the way, himself a former journalist, who, like Glazer and Jencks before him, collaborated with Dave on a book.

The volume ends with a bibliography of Dave's published writings that demonstrates not only his vast output over the last forty years, but also his continuing productivity in recent years. As Everett Hughes indicates, Dave never stops working, so that the bibliography will already be out-of-date when this book is published.

Sociologists sometimes treat a *Festschrift* as an indicator of the people who constitute the intellectual or social circle around the honored person, much as Kremlinologists watch official Soviet ceremonies to figure out who is in and who is out. We urge our readers to refrain from this exercise, for Dave's colleagues and circles are so numerous and so eclectic that several books would be required to contain them. Dave's own unflagging openness to new experiences has always defied attempts at closure, both social and theoretical.

The people who contributed to this book have all been part of one or more of Dave's circles, as they themselves explain briefly in their entries in the list of contributors. But there are many others who could also have contributed. Some whom we asked were not writing at the moment, or could not meet our deadline; a few sent in papers that did not meet our standards for publication. And some of the many people who have worked with Dave over the decades could not be found or were accidentally left off our lists of potential contributors. Several authors who could not be included in this volume may, however, appear in a second *Festschrift*, which is now being prepared by Martin Kilson and Orlando Patterson.

The book was edited by a serial, and joint, division of labor: serial because we circulated the "managing editorship"; joint because we all worked with the managing editor of the moment through the mails. Glazer, with Jencks, began to assemble the book; Gusfield was managing editor in the middle stage; and Gans, with Glazer, saw the book through the final stage. We are grateful to many secretaries, who typed large numbers of letters that were exchanged among editors and with contributors, and to Robert Erwin, John McGuigan, Jane Barry, and their colleagues at the University of Pennsylvania Press, who prepared the book for publication. Last but hardly least, we thank Evey Riesman, who helped us in many ways.

Part I

WHAT IS AMERICAN ABOUT AMERICA?

1

JOHN DEWEY AND DAVID RIESMAN: FROM THE LOST INDIVIDUAL TO THE LONELY CROWD

JOSEPH FEATHERSTONE

The course of American thought is sometimes pictured as a river, but this image is terribly misleading. Instead, it is a whirl of shifting polarities that have remained remarkably stable since the nineteenth century. Each thinker bucks against predecessors, but in doing so finds himself or herself riding many of the same contradictions. By now this is a commonplace of literary criticism, where the significant continuities, the dialectic of ideas and themes, and the prevailingly Romantic cast of the American mind have all been treated. Yet few have tried to extend this pattern to our understanding of social thought. This essay tries to tackle a fragment of the larger issue by looking at the way two thinkers, John Dewey and David Riesman, are involved in aspects of a dialectic. I want to show that the central polarities in the writings of each—the tension between the individual and society and between the modern and the countermodern—are part of a cluster of shared polarities, to show how each is seeking a characteristic kind of dialectical unity, a synthesis of contrary realms, a mediation of the modern and the countermodern. Both attempt to strike a particular kind of moral balance at the midpoint of the whirl of contradictions. And it is the hope for this balance, and the kind of democratic consciousness that it implies, that is one of the truly significant continuities in American thinking.

This dialectic and its continuity are especially striking in the case of Dewey and Riesman because in many respects Riesman is a rebel against the modernizing world-view of Progressive cultural radicals

3

like Thorstein Veblen and Dewey. Riesman's *Thorstein Veblen* is an extremely critical portrait, and *The Lonely Crowd* is both a continuation of lines of thought begun by Dewey and Veblen and a critique of the Progressive interpretation of American life. Riesman's running dialogue with the Progressives has a parallel in the late Richard Hofstadter's long dissent from the work of Progressive historians like Charles Beard and Frederick Jackson Turner. In each case the rebellion and the dissent are marked by a preoccupation with the issues raised by the Progressives, even though the tone of the later thinkers is light-years away from that of the Progressives. Hofstadter spoke in the complex urban accents of irony, consensus, and acceptance that marked the writing of American history after World War II; Riesman talked the new lingo of anthropology, Freud, and social science. Then, too, after the 1930s the intellectual world of the Progressives and pragmatic social thought was displaced by the European invasion of American social thought, and the new centrality of Freud, Marx, and Weber. Yet for Riesman, as for Hofstadter, the recasting of older ideas ends up looking familiar; the quarrel with the past cannot hide real and enduring continuities.

The nub of the debate between the Progressives and Riesman was the nature of true individuality in the modern world. In *The Lonely Crowd*, Riesman speaks of Dewey as a magnificent example of the kind of autonomy that was possible in the age of inner-direction. This rings true, and yet, as I want to stress here, Dewey is also in some respects the philosopher of the age of other-direction, a rebel against the solitary excesses of nineteenth-century individualism in the name of a new Progressive vision of community, cooperation, and interdependence. Riesman's ideal of autonomy in the age of other-direction is an attack, among other things, on the groupiness of Progressive social thought.

Every occupation has its hazards; those of sociology include a tendency to ahistoricism, the refusal to see the ways in which the present is a product of the past. This was not a sin *The Lonely Crowd* committed, for its most enduring parts are the broad historical accounts of the changing American character. True, like most accounts of discovery, it exaggerated the novelty of the terrain it was exploring, slighting the glacial and cumulative nature of the changes it was pointing to and ignoring signs of the old order in the new, and signs of the new in the old. But its historical instincts were good.

The occupational hazards of historians include an opposite failing:

they sometimes stretch the present so far back into the past as to make any suggestion of change implausible. Interestingly, this is now happening with interpretations of the Progressive era: a number of historians are now arguing that the outlines of our present society emerged in the Progressive years—roughly between 1880 and 1920. There is a good deal of merit in this view. For all our dazed and unending sense of change, there are indeed many respects in which we live in a traditional order whose basic political, social, and cultural agendas have remained remarkably constant. Think of the important precedents for our present society that emerged in the Progressive era: new corporate forms; the advent of political capitalism and governmental interference in the economy; mass warfare; mass consumption; the rise of universities; the spread of education to masses of people; the growth of bureaucracies, professions, and new technical strata; the beginnings of a new radical cultural consciousness among intellectuals. With the two very important exceptions of television and nuclear weapons, the basic technology of our present world was set in place in the years between 1850 and 1940. It would be foolish to deny the enormous changes that have taken place, but unwise to close our eyes to the fact that the changes took place in a settled historical context. In education, for example, almost all our debates echo the differences among the various factions of Progressive education: education for intrinsic value and play versus education as work or preparation for work; pluralism versus uniformity; and equality versus meritocracy.

This explains, in part, our fascination with the Progressives: they laid the foundations of an order that seems recognizably ours. And although Riesman believed that the changes he was chronicling were a phenomenon of the 1940s, it seems very clear that the Progressives set into motion the series of shifts in American social character that Riesman tried to describe in the phrase "other-direction." The Progressives used different terms, of course. Their search for communitarian ideals to replace what they saw as an obsolete, yet powerfully entrenched, individualism was one of the truly significant reversals in American intellectual life. America remained capitalist, and in that sense individualistic, yet many of the Progressives were collectivists of one sort or another. It was this intellectual legacy that Riesman was rebelling against in the name of his ideal of autonomy.

Like most important truths, this one requires more than one sentence for its proper utterance. To put the matter simply as a contrast between glittering abstractions—the ideal of individual autonomy, as against the ideal of community—is to miss out on the complex dialectical dance that was going on.

A PSYCHOLOGY OF MODERNITY

The dance was part of a larger dialogue that was in the end political, for Riesman, no less than Veblen and Dewey, was responding with profoundly mixed feelings to the cluster of forces we rather abstractly call "modernity," the manifold consequences of the triple industrial, scientific, and social-political revolutions of the eighteenth and nineteenth centuries. The debate on the nature of modernity was already old. Many of its key terms had been set into play by the arch-therapist of modern man, Jean Jacques Rousseau. Rousseau proposed that one's underlying response to modernization had to be moral and political. He saw historical change and the social division of labor as enemies to inner peace and psychic wholeness, and held out two possible and quite opposed utopian alternatives to modern man. One rested on an ideal of individual autonomy, and stressed the need for education, private family life, and protection of the individual from the modern world's empire of opinion, error, oppression, inequality, and greed. This was spelled out in La Nouvelle Heloise and Emile, those seminal statements of the private ideal. The other utopia was civic, political, and collective: its ideal was the city-state, where the individual found unity by merging himself with the civic unit (later the nation or party). Both rested on a critique of modernity that stressed its corroding effects on both the true, authentic self, and civic participation and community. Rousseau's passion for equality and his suspicion that technological progress would mean an immense human disaster sounded two of the key themes of the debate, and there were others as well: authority, true individuality, authenticity, the need for new institutions to redress the imbalances of modernity. Rousseau is one of the great mythmakers of modernity: it was he who laid out the dream of secular happiness that has haunted the West ever since. He is central, too, for the way he begins the quest for nature and a new social ideal that somehow marries nature and human artifice. Nature is a norm for Rousseau—the real head of hair underneath the powdered wig—and the appeal to nature and natural things underlies all subsequent revolutionary thought.

Broadly speaking, Rousseau encompasses the two main lines of argument concerning modernity, which I call the "long revolution" and the "lost community." The first sees the progress of the West since the seventeenth century as a long revolution, a march toward greater social and political equality. The other interprets modernization in terms of a vision of lost community. Proponents of the long revolution speak of gains in equality, autonomy, and the standard of living, and proponents of the lost community speak of alienation, disenchantment, the collapse of authority, and anomie, pointing to the human cost of progress.

Rousseau illustrates the important fact that the split between the two camps is essentially political, and that the underlying argument is about nature and man's place in it. The appeal away from a corrupt society to nature was and is the essence of the revolutionary appeal; the nature of nature, so to speak, was a decisive issue. The underlying question of nature and civilization was bound to be important in a society that was the product of an age of political revolution and engaged in the development of a new continent. In the nineteenth century, the themes of nature and civilization, and of the long revolution and the lost community, appeared in moods of alternating boosterism and despair over what the forces of machinery and modernization were doing to the American landscape, and, more importantly, to the American character. The counterpoised abstractions go hand in hand, and often coexist in complex terms in the same mind. One thinks of Horace Mann's fascinating mixture of a boosterish faith in progress and a worried sense that new institutions, such as schools, will have to take up the slack for the moral and social imbalances and disruptions generated by unchecked economic and technological change.

The Progressive intellectuals were thus adding their voices to an ongoing dialogue. Indeed, the central tension in the thought of Dewey and Veblen—the contrast between the face-to-face ideal of community and the ideal of technological progress—is simply another version of the contrast between the long revolution and the lost community. *The Lonely Crowd* also continues the dialogue in familiar terms, although it casts its argument in terms of Tocqueville's central preoccupation with the tension between equality and liberty as *the* issue of modernization. Riesman's guarded pluralism resembles Tocqueville's two cheers for the possibilities of a democratic polity, and Riesman draws on sociology's rich tradition of disenchantment with modernity, speaking of progress in terms of a more or less unilinear collapse of older communal institutions, such as family, religion, and ethnicity. *The Lonely Crowd*'s exploration of the psychic costs of modern equality is Tocquevillian, but also very much in line with the traditional lament for lost community. At the same time, Riesman's commitment to science and reason, his exploration of the possibilities of abundance, and his belief in individual autonomy put him squarely in the long revolution perspective. Indeed, with its nimble irony and its preference for complexity, *The Lonely Crowd* sidesteps many of the traditional weaknesses of both perspectives: it avoids the vulgar boosterism of the long revolution argument by pointing out the price of equality and progress; and for the most part it avoids the sentimental nostalgia for the past that is the chief pitfall of the lost community perspective. (Riesman speaks scornfully of the efforts of the nostalgic classes to root the masses down in stable communities.) It opposes a simple-minded class analysis of American society, pointing to the genuine pluralism that exists; yet it tends to neglect issues of inequality and power. Like so much postwar American sociology, it is a consensus document, better at explaining agreement and shared values than at accounting for conflict. It aims for some middle ground between the modern and the countermodern.

The Lonely Crowd works out these themes in the brisk manner of post war social science. Yet they seem, from the post of view of the Progressives, very nearly traditional. Dewey and Veblen were also, after all, exploring what science, technology, and the possibility of industrial abundance were doing to the American mind and character. Dewey was struggling with the idea that the old agenda of industrial class struggle might give way to a new agenda in which the decisive issues were less economic—mastering the continent, fighting over ownership and control of production—than social, questions of human cooperation and community.

THE EDUCATION OF TOM SAWYER

Of course, the Progressives saw these issues in very different terms. They were enormously impressed both by the advance of science and by the central historical fact of their time, the economic transformation of a rustic and even wild continent into one of the world's most productive industrial societies. At the height of his Progressive phase, Dewey was a booster for progress, assuming its inevitability. In the grimmer stretches of the 1920s and 1930s, he was, as he put it, more conscious of the error in mistaking the wilderness for the promised land, and he recognized that there was something good about the good old days. He never succumbed to that nostalgia for rapidly van-ishing forms of community that was such a pronounced minor chord in American thought, but his balance sheets on the consequences of modernity became more complex. To the Progressives, the main change seemed to be the revolution implied by the application of industry and science to all realms of life; and when they spoke of this impact, they usually had a mental picture of the transformation of village minds and characters into urban and metropolitan ones. Many of Dewey's Progressive works have a description of this change. Here is one from *The School and Society* (1899):

> We cannot overlook the factors of discipline and character-building in-volved [in the old order]: training in habits of order and of industry, and in the idea of responsibility, of obligation to do something, to pro-duce something in the world . . . we cannot overlook the importance for educational purposes of the close and intimate acquaintance got with nature at first hand, with real things and materials. . . . But it is useless to bemoan the departure of the good old days of children's mod-esty, reverence, and implicit obedience. . . . We must recognize com-pensations: the increase in toleration, in breadth of social judgement, the larger acquaintance with human nature, the sharpened alertness in reading signs of character and interpreting social situations, greater accuracy of adaptation to differing personalities, contact with greater commercial activities.

Whether consciously or not, Dewey's version of the changing char-acter of modern society echoes Rousseau's original diagnosis. The advent of the triple revolutions of modernity was eroding earlier forms of community at the same time that it was making older varieties of individualism obsolete. Dewey believed—especially in this phase of his thought—that the long revolution represented true Progress, but he was mindful of the whole sociological tradition and its worried account of lost community. He was also aware, as Rousseau had been, that modernity posed particular challenges to families and educational institutions. Like Americans in every generation from the Puritans on, Dewey was arguing that schools were going to have to take up the slack for other, failing social institutions weakened by economic and technological change: the family, the village, the church. Schools as surrogate communities were going to combine the advantages of the long revolution with those of the lost community. They were to restore essential countermodern aspects of life to the modernizing industrial world.

By the 1940s figures like Riesman would be less bemused by the utopian possibilities of either educational institutions or science, but Dewey's readings of the shifts in American character in his day foreshadowed some of the later speculation. In the passage just quoted there is a remarkably balanced view of the losses and gains involved in modernization—in leaving the village and small-town order for the new urban and industrial civilization. The new order was going to be more social. The old order bred character, people who would produce. The new order bred toleration and a sharpened alertness in reading signs of character. Where the village and farm regime taught you about nature—and yourself, as Emerson would have added—cities taught you about human nature. Children's "modesty" and "reverence" in the villages sound attractive, but "implicit obedience" does not. The increase in "toleration" and "breadth of social judgement" suggests the emotional openness of the new order, and its freedom from older rigidities, at the same time that a "sharpened alertness in reading signs of character and interpreting social situations" sounds calculating. Dewey ends the list with "contact with greater commercial activities," which may suggest another source of worry.

Solon Kimball and James McLellan, among other critics of Dewey, have taken this and other similar passages as evidence for his basic conservatism. They say that Progressives like Dewey were trying to preserve certain key values from the village world in the new age of industry, science, and mass organization. They press the argument too far in one direction for my taste; I see Dewey as a profoundly divided mind—a dialectical mind—but they are quite right to point out that Dewey's assessment of the strengths and weaknesses of the village order resembles that of Mark Twain. (Riesman's *Thorstein Veblen* compares Veblen to Twain, too.) One can get a picture of what Dewey wanted schools to do by imagining how he would improve the education of Tom Sawyer. Tom's mind is a warm, yet rather feckless, hodgepodge, in which Romanticism, superstition, and false gentility jostle real and enduring values, such as kindness and loyalty. It is a village mind, with village strengths and weaknesses. Huck Finn's wondering, innocent eye caught the central weakness with Protestant clarity: Tom could not tell what was false from what was true. Dewey was a convert to science, even, for a time, a zealot, as converts are notoriously wont to be. He was also worried about the future of Tom's mind and character in the new industrial and scientific world. True, a healthy dose of science would clear Tom's head of a great many foolish ideas—all the Romantic humbug he picked up from Sir Walter Scott, and the village home "truths" that resisted being changed by evidence or experience. Tom's life was full of rich, communal meanings, but one crucial set of public meanings it lacked was standards for truth: science, reflection, critical thought.

By itself, as Dewey always argued, the scientific outlook was inadequate. Its powerful abstractions would enable the Tom Sawyers of the world to—within limits—control and predict the future, to relate one kind of experience to another, but, taken alone, the powerful instrumental abstractions of science lacked Tom's feeling for the intrinsic values of the present, the tangible, the aesthetic, the communal. When it came to meaning, as compared with truth, Tom drew on a culture that was a deep personal possession, acquired through participation in the round of village life. Dewey wanted to retain this possession, but to add to the village sense of participation the discipline of scientific curiosity and a respect for facts, without which, as the Civil War had shown, minds like Tom's were vulnerable. (Like Twain, Dewey was haunted by the Civil War and the collapse of reason it represented to him.)

The village sense of engagement in life gave its inhabitants an informal education that was whole, of a piece. It went deep—Dewey admired that—but it also taught lies and, worse, offered no basis for distinguishing between lies and the truth. As a consequence, Dewey believed, the villagers' minds were full of stereotypes and prejudices against foreigners, blacks, strangers. They were haunted by ghosts; they thought stump water could cure warts. Like Tom, they were victimized by a host of what Dewey, like Veblen, regarded as "aristocratic," "feudal," and "invidious" values that made village life something a good deal short of social democracy; the village mind left the village vulnerable to frauds and demagogues, to the dukes and dauphins who prey on democratic gullibilities.

Schools were to be surrogate villages in the new metropolises. In some ways the style of education Dewey proposed for the Tom Sawyers of his era has recognizable elements of what I call a high Romantic synthesis, a blend of reason and feeling, a kind of learning that begins in children's play and evolves into apprenticeship, that teaches the supremely Romantic village reverence for concrete experience, but also a mastery of the instrumental abstractions of science and critical thought. Dewey hoped schools could combine community and science; the vividness and personal meanings of the village order would be fused with the breadth and certainty of the scientific outlook. He was proposing the characteristic American fusion ticket: a mediation between the modern and the counter-modern.

Without these surrogates for lost community, Tom and people like him might be in trouble when they left Saint Petersburg for places like Chicago. What if the new scientific rationality and the older village outlook simply coexisted in different parts of the same mind? Sharing Rousseau's horror of inner division, Dewey worried about the possibility that without a real synthesis, the cold, scientific way of knowing would destroy the arenas where a rich way of appreciating meanings flourished. Without a link to personal values and meanings, science would end up treating the world as lifeless matter, abstractions to be manipulated for any ends.

Looked at from another angle, the Progressive utopia that combined the best of the old and the new was a possible antiutopia, combining the worst. The last item on Dewey's checklist of modernity —the expansion of capitalism—suggested one force that might twist science to serve the power of wealth, not communal values. Dewey remained a meliorist all his life—things could be better, even if progress was by no means inevitable—but his final reading of the trends in his lifetime was closer to Henry Adams' forebodings than to his own earlier Progressive hopes. The challenge remained the same: how to consolidate the unparalleled material abundance, the new possibilities for cooperation, democracy, rationality, and science, and yet create in impersonal cities some form of communal and participatory modes of learning and civic action, "something of the other side of life." Dewey's Emersonian effort to fuse contraries—to reconcile the one and the many—took the form of a search for what he called a great community, which would somehow restore the lost individual. The Public and Its Problems is a utopian argument for a society committed to science, rationality, and economic progress, on the one hand, and participation and recreated face-to-face community, on the other. It is a gloomy book, for all its bland surface meliorism. Dewey plainly felt that the moral and political discipline of local publics and participation was necessary if the vast new collective apparatus being thrown up by technology was not going to be exploited by private interests. The new, smoother, more responsive social character might, at the last, serve the same old selfish ends. Perhaps a few of the older-style wolves would manipulate the herds of anxious sheep. Without communal settings, the new order might turn out to be a disaster.

There was one aspect of Tom Sawyer's world that Dewey excluded from his hopeful utopia. Tom had been raised to have a guilty conscience. The communal supports of the village had not spared its inhabitants the pain of a solitary conscience. This was an aspect of the old moral universe that Dewey was out to destroy root and branch. His hatred of the old order's rigidities and constraints rivaled that of the novelists of Main Street, the Middle Border, and country towns. Like many in his generation—perhaps especially the refugees from the provinces—Dewey opposed the old moral style, with its agonizing self-scrutiny, its fixed, unchanging notion of abstract moral principle, its cramped and rigid ideal of character, and its obsession with motives and inner purity. All of Dewey's successive psychologies, from the early idealist essays through *Human Nature and Conduct*, were, among other things, attempts to replace the dark solitude of private, individualistic conceptions of morality with a sunlit, public set of standards. Dewey wanted to replace the inner torment of Emersonian subjectivity with a social, communal, and—in Dewey's reckoning—more objective set of standards of judgment, to destroy with his ethical theories the notion that morality was mainly an affair of motives, inner responses to abstract principle. He hated the evangelical fear of counterfeit grace, the constant preaching and hypocrisy, the constant, introspective focus on inner feelings. He hated it when his mother asked him if he was right with Jesus. Instead of rhetoric and guilt, Dewey wanted ethics that focused on what really mattered: action and its visible consequences. He rejected both the utilitarian calculating machine and the old appeal to a guilty conscience because they denied the possibility of a common moral world. He wanted an ideal of character that would change in response to life, that took a conscious, experimental attitude towards experience. This was why his ethics were supremely social and communal—people had to connect, and ideals had to be grounded in real experience. The point was always to situate morality in a conscious realm accessible to others, and to public modes of reasoning, not to let it remain inside the lonely self, cut off from the common life.

ABUNDANCE AND SCARCITY

Emersonian individualism had with considerable daring proclaimed that only the individual was natural; society was artificial and corrupt. Dewey wanted to reverse this value, and many others as well, but he was continuing a dialogue on nature and civilization. Progressive cultural radicals like Dewey and Veblen found in Darwin a new source of metaphors for nature. The Progressive rediscovery of man's naturally social character was part of a complex reworking of two key polarities in the debate on modernity: the symbols of nature and civilization, and the symbols of individuality and community. Both were framed in the tensions between the poles of a third duality: abundance and scarcity.

The two faces of Darwinian evolutionary doctrine suggested two quite different lines of thought. These began to diverge in the 1880s, when a shift in the American intellectual climate began to take place. Slowly the sense grew that history was making older forms of individualism obsolete. The passing of the frontier, the new corporate institutions of capitalism, the problems of cities and immigrants, the new collective work settings for intellectuals in the universities—all these contributed to a remarkable intellectual reaction against individualism. Enormous and complex shifts in society and people's values were reflected in the vogue for German idealist philosophy. To those troubled by the spiritual implications of the march of deterministic science, or by what was called "the social issue," German philosophy's emphasis on "organic" social harmony and values that transcended materialism whispered possibilities of a reconstruction of the social order. Darwinism was crucial. Evolutionary thought had first been seized upon by figures like Spencer, who had reworked it to buttress the older values of individualism and competition. By the 1880s, however, thinkers like Ward had already begun to show how the gloomy premises of the Darwinian social imagination might be reworked to include the possibility of cooperative social evolution. If mind and society alike were products of evolution, then perhaps the social mind could direct the course of further evolution. Perhaps cooperative intelligence was the next phase in nature's design for humanity. The neo-Darwinian counterattack of James, Dewey, and Veblen converted evolution into a critique of the older materialism and argued that laissez faire and competition were atavisms. Thus, Darwinian evolutionary doctrine could stress the struggle for existence among scarce resources, in which case it sanctioned competition, or it could stress cooperation, the emergence of a social mind, and the creation of an abundant, interdependent world, in which case there was hope for the creative possibilities of evolution. Dewey was trying to take the hopes of idealist philosophy and the utopian hopes of thinkers like Henry

George and Edward Bellamy and cast them into the form of evolutionary possibilities that a naturalistic social science was making more and more plausible.

The counterattack insisted that society was man's natural realm, his second nature. It argued that the unfolding social nature of man was not in fact bound by the necessities of the old regime. The social theory of the survival of the fittest had rested on the idea that the basic fact about life was scarcity. The neo-Darwinian ideals of interdependence and cooperation suggested the possibility of a new order of abundance. Both strands of evolutionary thought were fascinated by the possibility that evolution meant a shift from older forms of individualism to newer forms of collectivism. In Dewey's youth, this had taken the form of a debate between despairing Darwinian individualists, such as Sumner, and optimistic collectivists, like Ward. Here again Riesman's great theme—the Tocquevillian tension between equality and liberty in an age of abundance—echoed the older debate.

In denying that life had to be a competitive struggle over scarce resources, the Progressive cultural radicals were questioning the idea that economic values should prevail over all others. This was not wholly new, either. There had been thin scatterings of dissent from the regime of Mammon and hard labor in the nineteenth century. Emerson and the Romantic transcendentalists insisted that man's true being lay beyond material and economic necessity, voicing a radically Protestant dissent from what is generally called the Protestant ethic; Emerson and Thoreau were individualists to a profound degree, but they, no less than Whitman, saw the dominant economic individualism of their day as a threat to the human soul. Then, too, the late nineteenth-century utopians—Bellamy, George, and Howells—based their visions on the possibility of abundance, leisure, and a shift away from economic values. Yet the Progressive intellectuals, and especially Dewey and Veblen, put the exploration of abundance and the effect of technology and science on the American character on a new intellectual footing, articulating visions, dreams, insights, and errors that would remain central to the American dialogue as it continued into the new century.

Veblen and Dewey were interested in whether technological change might mean something outside the narrow sphere of machines and profits. They believed that it would create vast shifts in society, values, and the way people felt about their daily lives. Although they sensed that there might be wrong turnings in the future, they were initially quite hopeful that change would indeed mean progress. Like most discoverers, they greatly exaggerated the significance of what they found. Veblen's notion that industrial workers and engineers would turn out to be more rational and scientific than other people did not in fact turn out to be true; nor was Dewey's faith that what he called "the method of intelligence" would come to be widely shared and applied to daily living well-founded. (It was Veblen, after all, who showed in his brilliant account of imperial Germany how scientific and prescientific modes of thought could easily be grafted together— the ease with which science and technology could be enlisted to serve barbarism.) The social psychology of industry, science, and technology anticipated by Dewey and Veblen emerged as a much more complicated, limited, and puzzling set of phenomena than they had initially expected. Dewey's Progressive intuition that science would pervade all aspects of daily thought did not come true, except that a fear of the consequences of perverted science and technology came to be a part of the mental furniture of many thoughtful Americans as the century wore on.

Yet the central insight was profound: through technology and relative abundance, Americans were going to be living in a society where, increasingly, the challenge was neither conquering nature nor producing goods, but dealing with other people. Dewey was the unconscious herald of a society in which many of the central economic roles are in what we now think of as the service sector, areas like education, which in his day still seemed fairly marginal to most observers.

INNER- AND OTHER-DIRECTION

The Progressives often thought of the social changes they were living through in terms of a shift from the village mind to the urban, industrial, scientific mind. To them, the essence of the contrast was the supposed absorption of science and technology into the everyday outlook of Americans. A variant of this was a notion that both Dewey and Veblen were fond of—a notion showing the implicit ideal of progress they both struggled to break with throughout their careers. This was the idea of a "lag," a failure of ideas, habits, and institutions to keep up with the march of science and industry. Dewey believed that somehow culture, morals, and thought had slowed down on their side of the street, while science had shot ahead. Veblen told a more dramatic story: the "lag" was actually a result of the sabotage of the productive values of industry by profit-minded businessmen.

In broad intellectual terms, however, it seems clear that the Progressives were grappling with some of the ongoing changes in social character that, decades later, Riesman and his colleagues were to think of as the shift from "inner-direction" to "other-direction." The arguments of *The Lonely Crowd* were profound and original, but they took place within the context of the earlier debates over individualism, scarcity, and abundance in the age of Darwin. Riesman was quite conscious of the European side of these debates: he sides with Godwin against Malthus, echoes Tocqueville, and incorporates John Stuart Mill by copious reference. Yet *The Lonely Crowd* was also a critical response to the intellectual world the Progressives built. Riesman was of a later intellectual generation, of course, and the biological metaphors that meant so much to the vitalistic Darwinian imagination of pragmatic sociology were missing; Riesman had a much clearer sense of how institutions and culture overlay the "natural" man. What was left of the Progressive biological emphasis was the fascination with the effect of birthrates and demography on culture, and an underlying Freudian intellectual framework, which echoed, at one cultural remove, Freud's own neo-Darwinism

Without putting it this way, the authors of *The Lonely Crowd* were attempting to describe the broad social changes that had taken place between Emerson's individualistic America and the interdependent corporate society whose foundations were being laid in the Progressive era. Like the Progressives themselves, they were searching for generic differences between past societies and American society in the modern period, for the contrast they drew between nineteenth-century inner-direction and twentieth-century other-direction was in effect an argument that all phases of American history had been beyond tradition—wholly in the modern era. Of the book's three ideal types of social character—traditional, inner-directed, other-directed—only the second and third are truly American. Traditional society was—to use a later molecular metaphor coined by Lévi-Strauss—"cool," slow to change; it demanded conformity to time-honored roles and customs, and did not bother much about the inner man or woman; its patterns of child rearing, for example, focused on outright behavior, for which the mechanism of enforcement was shame. Inner-directed society was that of Emerson's America, a world of small towns, farms, frontiers, and canal and railroad speculation, a "hot" social order undergoing extraordinary population growth, economic development, and expansion. The social character of Emersonian America was tooled for mobility— geographical and social—and the production of goods. (Dewey described the good old days: "We cannot overlook the factors of discipline and character-building . . . training in habits of order and of industry, and in the idea of responsibility, of obligation to do something, to produce something in the world. . . .") The inner-directed social order produced people equipped with an inner psychological gyroscope that would carry them through all sorts of new situations, men and women of unbending principle. Nineteenth-century Americans seem to have worked quite consciously to instill principles in children who later would travel far and light. The ideals—"work," "success," "independence," "manliness," "character"—focused internalized patterns of drives and strivings; when they left home, the children were constantly testing their self-mastery of these ideals under the watchful eye of the Emersonian conscience, what the Freudians later called the superego. The mechanism for enforcing children's— and later adults'—behavior in the inner-directed order was Dewey's old enemy, internalized guilt. Plainly the virtues dictated by the inner-directed order were those of a regime of scarcity, geared to the struggle against nature, the competition for scarce resources, and production. This was why the older virtues were menaced by Darwinism only in the area of religion. It was a production or, as we say, a "work" ethic. It was supremely an ethic for individuals bent on mastering a continent.

The other-directed character, by contrast, signaled a broad shift from nature to society, from competition to cooperation. It reflected a world in which other people, rather than the material environment, represented the chief arena to strive in. The major premise was abundance, not scarcity; in the other-directed order, consumption was a more important force in shaping social character than production. The virtues stressed were spontaneity, openness, sensitivity, and responsiveness. Instead of the inflexible gyroscope of inner-direction, a new, infinitely sensitive radar screen was installed. This was, as the critical tone of The Lonely Crowd indicated, not necessarily a change for the better. The mechanism for enforcing right behavior became the other-directed social character's diffuse anxiety and its relentless concern over the judgment of the group. The inner-directed regime was harsh, rigid, and cruel; the new order was conformist.

Thus, in theoretical terms, *The Lonely Crowd* was in some respects a critical exploration of the darker possibilities in certain of Dewey's assumptions. Dewey, too, had looked for a more cooperative social character to emerge from the interplay of abundance and technology in American life, tending to see the long-term shift in his own lifetime as a change from the old individualistic frontier, in which nature was the challenge, to the new social frontier, in which other people were the challenge. It was the tone—the sense of the meaning of these changes—that was so different in *The Lonely Crowd*. Riesman's sober, disillusioned analysis lacked the sense of hope suggested by the Progressives' phrase "social frontier."

Dewey stood in the middle of the myriads of shifts in character, institutions, and daily living that the historical analyses of *The Lonely Crowd* pointed to. There were ironies in the role. One does not normally think of Dewey as the philosopher of the age of other-direction, "peer groups," and "adjustment," because his commitment to an ideal of fulfilled individuality was as real as his Progressive insistence on the group character of all human life, but he did at times celebrate life in groups in ways that showed the Progressive blind spot toward social conformity. Like all the Progressive social theorists, Dewey had a habit of taking Emerson's oversoul and incorporating it into an idealized face-to-face community. In rebellion against the inner-directed regime, and living at the dawn of the age of organization men and lonely crowds, Dewey saw less cause than later observers to question the social ideal of the good mixer. We who have lived for some time now in the world the Progressives anticipated so optimistically have good reason to question the groupiness of Progressive educational and social thought, seeing its oppressive, conformist, and even sinister aspects. Then too, we are much more sharply aware of how the capitalist collectivism of the major industrial sectors of American life that merged in the Progressive years was, like Soviet collectivism, run for the benefit of private individuals.

Inevitably Dewey's perspectives on all these matters are quite different from ours. He had experienced the moral regime of inner-direction as harsh—"lacerating" is his word for it—and held its ideal of conscience partly responsible for the loneliness, alienation, and inner desolation of his unhappy youth. There were excellent reasons in his own past why his children were raised as stout Progressives—they called him "John"—and why both his educational thought and his psychology were in such fierce rebellion against the constraints of the older, inner-directed character. It is perhaps too much to expect a man engaged in battle with a part of his own past to give equal recognition to the constraints of the new order.

LIFE VERSUS DEATH

Veblen and Dewey were, like Riesman, "soft" technological determinists: technology set up the arena and offered the setting, without precisely dictating the culture's response. All American social thinkers veer back and forth between the proposition that man makes his fate and the notion that in some sense the material environment makes man. Veblen used Rousseau's old device—philosophical anthropology —to work out the big historical picture. In Veblen's great historical parables, the "advance" of society from peaceful cooperative savagery to militant competitive barbarism was, of course, a lapse, a fall from primitive grace. How the fall occurred is not entirely clear from Veblen's mythic accounts. It seems that the instinct of workmanship and material circumstances somehow combined to create situations where those whose work did not meet a new standard of efficiency suffered a lack of status. Yet this was a false social standard in some respects: visible success rather than true efficiency—status rather than impersonal achievement—became the criterion, and thenceforth the aim of human effort became the signs and seals of human approval rather than impersonal service to the human group. Advanced primitive cultures already showed the seeds of the emulative and invidious barbaric order, which (in Veblen's peculiar panorama of history) stretched into the era of late capitalism. Two conditions were, however, necessary for true barbarism to emerge out of savagery. Rousseau would have recognized them both: frequent change, and exposure to a shared, shifting human environment whose approval was sought. Thus, from the discipline and relative harmony of a life-giving regime shaped by the impersonal demands of nature and the natural order, Veblen shifts to a deadening world resting on the sand of human approval, the barbaric realm of fraud, chicanery, and invidious distinction.

By Riesman's day, emulation could somewhat more plausibly be divorced from outright, violent exploitation, although *The Lonely Crowd* was never trenchant when it came to issues of power and inequality in realms other than psychology. For Veblen, all forms of emulation, consumption, and display were badges of a capacity to exploit other people. Dewey agreed, saying that the Veblenian distinction between the death-dealing, barbaric values of modern business and the good, social values of "industry"—all that impersonally advanced the life-giving material requirements of the community—was central to his own thought. Dewey's critique of classical Greek philosophy, after all, was essentially a Veblenian social analysis of the defects of a point of view that denigrated working with one's hands. It could at times be an outrageous exercise in debunking, but it also pointed to real inhumanities in a slave culture afflicted with the barbaric and aristocratic graces. Veblen and Dewey were frequently wobbly on the question of power, too, but they remained convinced that all forms of consumption linked to exploitation; however disguised, the regime of capitalist business was intrinsically, essentially barbaric. Riesman, responding to a later and more subdued, a "social" capitalism, was struggling, not entirely successfully, to dispense with the older metaphors of power and inequality.

The Progressives were prophets of technology, but they were also prophets of a revival of face-to-face community. Science and community were the two poles of their outlook. A common procedure for all of them, as they shucked off their idealist skins, was to take the old idealist Absolute and assign its general characteristics to an ideal organic community. Rightly ordered, the new scientific and industrial order would be a series of small communities linked by the technology of modern communications and supported by the abundance made possible by modern industry. Late industrialism was reassembling a world order that revived the qualities of earlier community life. In a sense this was the argument in *The Lonely Crowd*, too, where there was a certain sense of historical character doubling back on a communitarian tack after an interlude of individualism.

THE QUEST FOR A NEW CULTURE

As Riesman described the society that merged in the aftermath of the Progressive era, consumption was a more important force in shaping social character than production. Of all consumer goods, the most important were human feelings. The portrait of the regime of other-direction was not attractive. In reality, the communalism that partially triumphed in America was far from life-enhancing. Riesman extended

Veblen's analysis of leisure-class consumption and invidious display into the realm of everyman, leaning hard on Veblen's penetrating insight that in a democratic society almost everybody participates in the rituals of consumption, even if only vicariously. Here the psychology was mordant in Veblen's own debunking manner, as in Riesman's gloss on the little piggies: "Today, however, all little pigs go to market; none stay home; all have roast beef, if any do; and all say 'we-we.' "

Riesman's contrast between a possible new realm of abundance and an older era of production and scarcity echoed in its way another fascinating division in the Progressive mind. Dewey and Veblen were both products of the regime of scarcity and inner-direction, in rebellion against it, and yet, like many rebels, deeply implicated in the order they were seeking to overthrow. They were hoping for a new psychology and a new culture, but, inevitably, their hopes were shaped by their past. They were, in fact, torn between the values appropriate for a scarce order demanding production and those appropriate for an age of plenty.

Veblen's insistence on the sovereign virtues of production and efficiency tied his economics firmly to the world of scarcity. The tie was not simply economic, however; it was also profoundly moral. In Veblen's parables of human history, the snake in the garden often took the form of material plenty: the surplus wealth created by technological change nourished the seeds of privilege, power, and invidious distinctions. One has the feeling that Veblen's ideal society would run on a minimal economy, close to the natural bone, so to speak, leaving some margin for humanity, but not enough to tempt it. Dewey, having a different temperament, and not being an economist in the first place, had a keener interest in the moral possibilities of abundance. Yet he too wanted the discipline of scarcity in his utopia, to temper the lush and fantastic propensities of the human imagination with the hard facts of the material universe. Whatever turned the selfish and solitary individual outward—to nature and its disciplines, or to society and its responsibilities—carried moral possibilities. The unity Dewey always sought was like Veblen's—Veblen called it "a non-reverent sense of esthetic congruity with the environment" or "the sense of communion in the environment with the generic life processes." The Progressives shared the Romantic religion of life.

Like Emerson and Whitman before him, Dewey was haunted by the possibility of a new democratic culture; implicitly, his new culture was based on abundance, and the possibility of an escape from economics. It was not something he articulated; he might have confessed to it after a couple of drinks. The new democratic culture would rest on a new psychology, which was to be vitalistic, in touch with life, expressing life, spontaneity, and the flow of feeling. The Progressives were hungry for life. Dewey's interest in children and art reflected his concern for the Emersonian ebb and flow of psychological states that was such a prominent concern of the Progressive cultural figures whom Christopher Lasch has called the new radicals. This neo-Romantic fascination with the psychology of renewal opened up many new insights into culture, personality, and education. It also, as Lasch argues, led the Progressives and many of their successors in American social thought to concentrate on altering psychological states in the search for answers to questions that were, at bottom, political. The Progressive cultural radicals showed an early tendency to assume that the new psychology being shaped by technology and abundance would simply and automatically replace the realities of the bad old order. Dewey, in particular, was for a long time uncritical of his own assumption that progress was a given on the American scene. The whole unstated Progressive vision of progress rested, in fact, on the automatic emergence of a new psychology: somehow, scientific and industrial development would make Americans more democratic, more cooperative, less guilty, and more social-minded.

Plainly Dewey's hopes for a new character and a new culture included certain elements of the regime he was rejecting. He was in an odd position. In one corner of his mind, he was one of Lasch's cultural radicals, anticipating a neo-Romantic psychology arising out of American abundance. In another, however, he was allied with Veblen in insisting on retaining purified versions of the values of the regime of scarcity: production, discipline, efficiency, hard work. He was straddling a divide between the young Progressive cultural radicals, like Randolph Bourne and Lewis Mumford, who echoed Emerson's dissent from the work ethic, and the institutional Progressives, who were aiming to install that same ethic at the center of American life in the name of the grand Progressive ideal of "efficiency." With characteristic complexity, Dewey was voting for both tickets.

Dewey's mature social thought struck a judicious balance between the Progressive social engineers' scarce-production outlook and the Progressive cultural radicals' dream of an abundance that would create a new education, a new psychology, and a humane and playful new culture serving human rather than economic priorities. Dewey's instrumentalism continued to express the Progressive ideal of efficiency; he never lost his immense scientific respect for the discipline exerted by matter itself on the vagaries of the human imagination—material reality as a check on Romantic fantasies. Dewey still believed in the scientific discipline of the future tense; pragmatic logic said the test of truth was future consequences. These emphases in Dewey expressed traditional ideals of character, discipline, and hard work. Yet this "hard" side was balanced by a "soft" side: the realm of present meaning and expression, what Emerson had called "the everlasting NOW." Instrumentalism itself was in the late years harnessed to the abundant values of the new psychology: the novel, neo-Romantic emphasis on spontaneity, play, "consummations," the almost religious quality of Dewey's reverence for shared experience and the living moment. As he grew older, in fact, more and more of Dewey's thought centered on the Emersonian present, rather than the pragmatic and technocratic future. As a new radical, concerned with a psychology of abundance, Dewey could not help showing the marks of the very long apprenticeship he had served in the house of scarcity: it was perhaps typical of his Emersonian dread of spiritual inefficiency that his defense of play, feelings, and human expressiveness focused on realms that lent themselves to intelligible, purposeful discipline: art and children's education. The Dewey School, which seemed in some respects such a good example of how the new radicalism explored the abundant possibilities of children's play and self-expression—of consumption—was also plainly meant to inculcate the older values of scarcity, production, hard work, and achievement, albeit in a new cooperative social setting. As usual the complexities of Dewey's commitments, which accounted in part for his monumental vagueness, also lent balance and proportion to his programs.

Like the utopians of the nineties, and like John Kenneth Galbraith and Riesman and the post–World War II theorists of consumption and abundance, the Progressives assumed that abundance was very nearly an achieved fact, not a vision; and like the later theorists, they generally ignored the unequal distribution of wealth and goods. The new radicals were naive in other ways, too. In his Progressive phase, Dewey uncritically accepted the changes taking place, assuming that the new technology and new corporate forms were inherently cooperative, even as he castigated the market system and the "pecuniary" economy. Unlike Veblen, he did not see that the new bounty could readily serve the business interests of a highly competitive and unequal society. The idea that technology might enhance competition or that "neutral" bureaucracies and professions could exacerbate privilege and promote new forms of inequality was beyond the Progressive ken, as was the idea that children's peers in school would threaten their moral autonomy.

Dewey stood for what might be called the activist wing of the new cultural radicals, whereas Veblen, with his taste for rural living, his mail-order-catalogue pants, his watch held on with a safety pin, and his essential despair of individual action, represented the dropouts and the hippies. Dewey's radical utopian old age was in itself an earnest argument against withdrawal. (Santayana sneered at Dewey's "new and more difficult earnestness," demanding the un-American right *not* to be a reformer.) When we are particularly annoyed by Dewey's earnest crusading, we are apt to stress the many times he fell into the Emersonian intellectual's fallacy that it is possible to change a society through words alone. Still, there was a method in his madness. Both as a complacent Progressive social engineer and as a radical utopian, Dewey believed that it was possible to introduce pieces of the possible new culture bit by bit—decent schools, for example—and so help create elements of a new order pluralistically, without a wholesale assault on the values of corporate capitalism. This was a matter of both conviction and tactics. Being a profound pluralist when it came to explaining human conduct, and a democrat in politics— and being convinced that means and ends were intertwined—he really believed in gradual, piecemeal, and pluralistic change. Then too, there were the tactical necessities inherent in operating in a reactionary business culture where the only opportunities for advocating change were provided by traditions of political rights like due process and free speech. After realizing that History was not in fact on his side—his own folly in thinking that World War I would bring about a cooperative American commonwealth taught him that progress was an illusion—Dewey was more and more deeply impressed by the odds against what Emerson had called the party of Hope: progressive change would need all the allies it could get.

Dewey saw abundance when there was only the possibility of abundance; he tended to underplay the grip of scarcity, inequality, and the forces of competition and profit on American life; he forgot, even as he traveled through what later came to be called the Third World, the Malthusian constraints that shackled the lives of most people on the planet. He talked as though ideas were going to do the job alone. He kept psychologizing his politics, the great pitfall for all the theorists of modernity who follow in Rousseau's footsteps. He was endlessly vague. His earlier Progressive assumption of progress continued to bedevil his thinking; his historical contrast between an outdated individualism and a new cooperative social character blurred many sinister aspects of the new order: especially (as Riesman noted) the groupiness of mainstream progressive education, and the way the cooperative ideas of Progressivism had been put in the service of a collectivism run for private, rather than democratic, interests. Yet the main thing Dewey said was true. The new modes of industrial organization and technology created abundance, yet invalidated personal experience, community, and the values of shared experience; profit had overcome considerations of human welfare and perverted science and technology. For all his vagueness and commitment to science, Dewey's basic message was a recognizable descendant of Emerson's: the worth of any institution, including science, was how much it enhanced human life, individually as well as collectively.

INDIVIDUALISM VERSUS INDIVIDUALITY

Dewey's dispute with Emerson and the nineteenth century was in the end an effort to rescue the ideal of individuality, to define the terms of individual fulfillment in a way that met the necessities of what he thought of as an inevitably collectivist age. He was convinced that the issue was not whether American society in the future would be individualist or collectivist; rather the choice lay between a collectivism run for private interests or a democratic collectivism run for the benefit of all. He hoped that collective democracy could find room for an ideal of individual autonomy, although there was little basis in past historical experience for the hope. Restoring individuality was in part for Dewey a matter of economics. *Individualism Old and New* is an essay on the perversion of the classical liberal ideal of individualism in a pecuniary culture; competitive individualism eclipsed true individuality under the force of oppressive inequality. This was, like R. H. Tawney's *The Acquisitive Society*, the work of a democratic socialist. In *Liberalism and Social Action* Dewey argued that classical liberalism had been quite wrong in posing an insuperable division between the individual and society. The enduring liberal values needing preservation are freedom to fulfill oneself and freedom of thought. Dewey was most sympathetic to older liberal values when they were necessary procedures for open experience in a context of associated living; he was least sympathetic to them as defenses of propertied privilege. For Dewey and Marx, effective liberty, as opposed to merely formal liberty, was a function of social conditions. For true individuality to flourish, Dewey said, liberalism must dismantle the institutions of the older individualism, particularly the regime of profit.

Thus, as he grew older, Dewey was wrestling with the problem of preserving individuality and freeing the culture from individualism. The quality of the experience offered individuals—the potential they allowed for growth—remained the test of all institutions. In *Individualism Old and New* he was trying to think about the kinds of social support needed for true individuality—an empirical social basis for the ideal—but his imagination failed him, and he could only repeat that the defense of true individuality required a radical attack on older, economic individualism. Apart from the need for economic security and planning, he left the content of the ideal blank. He also came to value legal and constitutional rights he had once derided as merely formal. The metaphysics of natural rights that had contributed to the genesis of the Bill of Rights was no longer tenable—Dewey would not alter his position on that. But he came to see—as his later praise for Jefferson showed—that a Constitutional and democratic tradition was a necessary, if by no means sufficient, precondition for a democratic socialism.

Pragmatic social science criticized the legacy of American individualism in the name of a hope for community—Dewey was always working to reverse that piece of the Emersonian heritage—but the hope itself reflected the persistence of certain Emersonian themes. Underneath Dewey's cooperative Progressive schemes for social reform lay a Romantic, Emersonian utopia that emphasized the importance of the individual's capacity to make moral and political judgments, a faith in the individual mind as the locus of rationality, and, more importantly, of moral consciousness. Dewey never spelled out his late vision of social rationality; it hovers on the fringes of the social polemics of the 1920s and 1930s, and it lies in back of the last chapter of the *Logic*, however. The vision itself—like so much of Dewey's late social thought—was a sober and matter-of-fact updating of some of the ideas of the utopians of the 1880s and 1890s, who, it turned out, had

had a permanent influence on him. Dewey's implicit ideal of social rationality, for example, probably owed a good deal to Henry George, whom he extravagantly admired. George is known today as the prophet of the single tax, one of the few reform panaceas in economic history that have not been revived from time to time. George had built up a whole social theory from one quite penetrating insight into the history of American land speculation: that land values were actually the collective creation of the community. The lots in undeveloped prairie towns were worthless until communities developed; but the history of American wealth was the story of how private developers appropriated this publicly created wealth for themselves, cashing in on what George called the unearned increment. Dewey's *Logic* takes George's parable of land, money, and power and applies it to what might be called the sociology of the validation of knowledge. Dewey treats knowledge as a cooperatively created product of human society, and describes the history of the modern era as a constant appropriation of this social product by private interests; *The Public and Its Problems* points out how private monopolies of publicly created knowledge mean the power to deceive and manipulate, and ultimately to control. As a rule, Dewey had not been comfortable with discussions of power. In his late social thought, however, the issue kept surfacing; the political use of knowledge was already problematic by the 1920s and 1930s.

Besides the ghost of Henry George, there was also the ghost of Hegel hovering over this late speculation. Dewey was groping to define an empirical, twentieth-century version of Hegelian social rationality, minus Hegel's metaphysics. He was in the line of the left Hegelians who appeal dialectically away from the status quo to Reason, insisting that the given order of things is irrational, as well as unjust. The "rationalism" of the ideal was individual, however; the locus of rationality was the individual mind. Dewey's educational thought had always stressed the ideal of a society in which an individual citizen would have some necessary knowledge of the technical and social base of the culture he or she lived in. The argument broadened to include much more than education. Sometimes it was phenomenological, with Romantic echoes of Emerson and Thoreau, as well as Hegel: unless you had the sort of unitary grasp of your civilization that, say, a Bushman or an Iroquois had, then you would be a stranger in your own culture, a divided mind, lacking a cultural possession that would make your life more of a piece. This was almost an aesthetic affair; one thinks of Veblen's visions of life-enhancing unity with the environment. There was another implication, though: unless you understood the social order (or certain essential parts of it; Dewey was vague on this point), you would not be able to exert any control over it. It would control you. Rousseau's fear that the social division of labor had opened up a Pandora's box of evils was echoed in Dewey's late social thought, which followed older Progressive threads to gloomier conclusions. Like Brandeis, Dewey was haunted by a sense of lost community and a fear that American institutions were getting too big. For a time both were Progressive social engineers—Brandeis seems even more typical of the administrative and legal Progressives than Dewey—yet both were also Emersonian conservatives, fearful for the fate of individual morality in the new order. The question, in part, was the relationship of scale and impersonality to individual judgment. Unless some institutions were of a scale to be comprehended by one man's mind, then both anticipation and moral judgment might become impossible. Dewey's old dread of secondhand experience—a Romantic Emersonian religious and moral concern—now took on political overtones. Thus, for all his commitment to institutions like schools, to science and technology, Dewey's late utopian vision of social "rationality" was in many respects an implicit Emersonian critique of the rationalized corporate social order the mainstream Progressives had built. The "rationality" of the new corporations and bureaucracies was, of course, Weberian. Weberian rationality made the institution, not the individual, the repository of rationality. The soldiers in the trenches did not have access to the big picture; that could only be seen in the war room. The workers in Taylorized factories were not supposed to know why they were doing what they were doing. In the Weberian world that began to emerge in the 1920s when "rationality" became tied to the organization, Dewey was making a utopian complaint that American society had lost the rational individual.

American social thought in the twentieth century played back and forth between many of Dewey's complex themes, even when a given writer was attempting to criticize Dewey and free himself from the intellectual and social heritage of the Progressives. *The Lonely Crowd*, for example, may be read as a somber meditation on the cultural triumph of Progressive groupiness, the pitfalls of affluence, and the miseries attendant on a new social climate. Tocqueville was right, it argued: the American disease was conformity, for which a possible, though not very hopeful, cure was a subdued and chastened ideal of autonomous individuality. C. Wright Mills, too, in many works attacked pragmatic social thought for its neglect of the dimensions of power and social class and its growing loss of critical perception. Mills and Riesman had antithetical, not to say contradictory, views of American life and institutions, and very different political commitments. The great sprawling society continued to elude a definitive portrait, as it had in Dewey's day. And yet much of the interesting social thought in the decades after Dewey's death swung between his ideals of community on the one hand, and of individual autonomy and rationality on the other. For all their opposed views of American politics, for example—Riesman's pluralism and Mills' emphasis on power elites—both Riesman and Mills echoed Dewey's concern for the fate of morals and rational individual judgment in a world of groups and Weberian rationality, where the individual lacked the big picture, where autonomy represented a consumer's choice among manipulated options, and where there were no vital publics, only lonely crowds. They continued Dewey's exploration of liberal values in an increasingly illiberal world.

Dewey's legacy is a baffling one: on the one hand it offers an Emersonian critique of all our major institutions from the point of view of their consequences for individual lives, and on the other it suggests that older ideals of individualism are not adequate to live by.

RIESMAN AND THE YEARS OF THE MODERN

Like the question of abundance, that of individualism—or, more properly, the nature of true individuality—eluded a definitive answer both in Dewey's age of the lost individual and in Riesman's era of the lonely crowd. The inquest into the strengths and weaknesses of the classic liberal tradition went on, playing back and forth between the classic themes.

One such theme, from Tocqueville, was that of voluntary association and local publics as a defense of individuality. This is something Dewey kept coming back to. Sometimes he thought of workers' control as a step toward solidarity and a sense of interdependence, but at other times he was thinking more of civic and moral neighborhoods, so to speak. He pursues the point, although it is impossible for him to free his ideas either of nostalgia or of vagueness. This appeal to community is not something one finds in *The Lonely Crowd*, with its sense that a new and complex form of political pluralism had rendered older, turf-bound and face-to-face forms of local democracy obsolete, its animus against sentimental communitarianism, and its qualified determination to march in time to the beat of modernity. Rejecting one of the two poles of Progressive thought, the ideal of community, Riesman accepts a sober version of the potential of technology, although he remains a countermodern modernizer at some level.

The debate over abundance and the nature of true individuality was, like the whole discussion of modernity, a political matter. Dewey was in the end always concerned with the moral, metaphysical, and cultural implications of democracy, and these were the issues that ultimately *The Lonely Crowd* is tackling too. It looks at them through a darker lens, of course; it is a critique of the simple Progressive defense of the people against the interests, pointing out, among other things that the people are often part of the democratic problem.

In *Thorstein Veblen* Riesman predicts that Veblen's future influence rests with the fate of what might broadly be thought of as Populism, and says that this is why one's judgment of Progressives like Veblen hinges on one's assessment of the possibilities for American culture. Both statements hold as well for Riesman's thought, which struggles with the implications for Populism, broadly speaking, and democracy posed by twentieth-century social thought. It is also a reckoning with cultural modernism, the ironic, mocking, fragmentary ideal of culture that emerged out of the collapse of bourgeois humanism. The vogue of Marx, Weber, and Freud in the post–World War II era was in part a judgment on the extent to which their perceptions of man had discredited the democratic ideal and the possibility of a democratic culture; modernism was rendering the same judgment in the realm of the arts. Riesman is divided on this question, opposing the old-fashioned Populist—even Jamesian—innocence of a figure like Dewey, and yet keeping alive, in some ironic, modernist fashion, a democratic hope.

The issue of Populism was key. We often forget that, by and large, American literary and philosophical traditions have been Populist, believing that there is a people's road to truth that is not the private possession of the learned, the rich, and the powerful. American thought in the nineteenth century tended to be Romantic and Populist. Dewey was trying to change this tradition—to translate its low, irrationalist Romanticism into a high Romantic synthesis of reason and feeling with a new dose of scientific and cultural standards. He wanted to keep its commitment to a democratic culture and to what the architect Louis Sullivan called a people's scholarship. New standards were vital because American Populism had been deeply anti-intellectual and often passionately irrational: Dewey wanted to scrap the old, dim-witted moralizing that had passed for thought in so much of the American past. He was trying to force a Romantic and Populist culture to accept the discipline of science and thought; and at the same time he was trying to reconstitute a psychology of the human imagination at its full power in a new Romantic fashion, to marry reason and feeling.

Dewey attempted to harness technology, science, and cultural standards to communal, Populist, and egalitarian ends, instead of private, elite interests. As a reformer, for example, he often found himself in opposition to the American reform tradition, which has been for the most part profoundly elitist. His was a typically complex utopian balancing act, and it did not always work. Yet a marriage of cultural standards and Populism was consistently his aim. This was the source of his quarrel with the aesthetes of the 1890s, those, like Santayana and Henry Adams, who recoiled from the vulgarity of American life into reveries of the past and dreams of aesthetic perfection. Ultimately Dewey, who had been something of a Progressive Philistine himself, came to agree with the aesthetes' indictment of American civilization —Art as Experience attacks what we now call the quality of life under a regime of profit in the name of a vision of "consummations" and a complex picture of human fulfillment—but he never abandoned his faith in the possibilities of a democratic culture. From today's perspective, Dewey's quarrel with the aesthetes—over their scorn for science and community, as well as equality and democracy—looks like a fight with the modernist mood that has reigned in many intellectual circles since the 1920s, with its ironies, its celebration of the artist's private insight as the highest good, its denial of the possibility of a democratic culture, its nihilism.

In his inimitable tone and in much of what he says, Riesman is both an aesthete and a modernist, echoing Santayan's revulsion against much of American life. Riesman's antimoralizing morality is debunking in the Freudian manner. It is Santayana, however, whose spirit hovers over the whole work. In Riesman, as in Santayana, the aesthete and the modernist are forever at war with the moralist. Often The

Lonely Crowd's defense of aristocracy and aesthetics echoes Santayana's gibes at compulsive reformism and Dewey's "difficult earnestness." Yet the dislike of herd minds, reform, and boosterism is in the service of democratic morals, as well as aristocratic aesthetics. The Lonely Crowd defends aspects of popular culture against aesthetic disdain, for example, and fights a complicated battle on several levels for whatever expands the growth of ordinary people. It might be said to be the work of an aristocratic aesthete committed to the difficult earnestness of reform, stuck with an unpromising culture, yet fascinated, as Santayana himself sometimes was, by the depths of mystery in its democratic ordinariness.

The aristocratic fish eye The Lonely Crowd cast on American culture reflected the meritocratic and anti-Populist mood of many after World War II; besides the gloom of social science and Freudian analysis, it reflected a blend of disillusionment with the proletariat as social saviors, awareness of the sloganeering in the Cold War appeal to the defense of democracy, worry about the demagogic potential of popular government, and a well-warranted revulsion against the anti-intellectualism that is indeed such an important part of American intellectual tradition. Among intellectuals, the egalitarianism of the New Deal and the war years now encountered resistance.

Science was no longer an idol. Where Dewey and Veblen had believed that science and its standards would—if done right—inevitably serve the people and the common life, this was no longer as convincing to Riesman. Like Veblen, Riesman was intent on establishing the right of the disinterested mind to theorize, to play with ideas, to mock the vulgar pragmatic truths of the crowd. This and the attack on the moral bullying of egalitarianism made The Lonely Crowd in some respects a meritocratic document, more concerned for margins for autonomous minds than anything else. On the dilemma of how to square the claims of equality against those of meritocracy, it came down firmly on the side of merit. So, of course, in his own peculiar way had Veblen, with his defense of idle curiosity and disinterested research in the universities, and his hope for soviets of experts in industry. Dewey, for his part, had rarely acknowledged the potential of organized science and expertise to undermine older formulations of democracy and equality. It seldom occurred to the Progressives that, whatever else they were doing, they were rationalizing new elites, meritocracies, professions, and bureaucracies. For all their collectivism, Veblen and Dewey both held to an older, individual-artisan ideal of research and science that bore little relation to the bureaucratic, highly political institution we might think of as Big Science today. Neither had much sense of the way organizations and bureaucracy can harness the ideal of science to their own political ends. The Progressives, like the Bolsheviks they sometimes so curiously resembled, were blind to the issues posed for equality by the new elites, just as Riesman seemed oblivious of these dangers in his implicit espousal of meritocracy. In our age, it seems plain, the tension between meritocracy and the Populist promise of equality is central again. Dewey's problem—squaring a commitment to democracy with intellectual and professional standards—remains ours. He defined the problem without solving it: for us, as for him, the question is one of balance. Without a commitment to the possibilities of a democratic and egalitarian culture, intellectual and professional endeavors usually end up rationalizing what exists. And yet the chief task of intellectuals—which they all too regularly abandon—is the defense of intellectual standards. This is a complex issue, and each intellectual generation will draw its own balance on it. Dewey and Veblen were hampered by their Populist simplicities at times, and yet it seems to me from today's perspective that much postwar scholarship, for all its rich new sense of complexity, lost something in abandoning Populism and the Progressive radicals' opposition to the regime of profit, even though maintaining a sane radicalism in subsequent years has proved to be a heartbreaking enterprise. I think Riesman has been wrong to ignore the Populist issues of equality, power, and profit that once again seem so important. The defense of democracy is not the same as the defense of corporate capitalism.

At one level, then, Riesman as an opponent of the Progressive radicals is a critic of the intellectual, cultural, moral, and psychological weaknesses in the culture's endemic Populism. Populism is the issue. And yet nothing in the whirl of American polarities is ever that straightforward, either. One befriends democracy by being its critic, after all, and under Riesman's pluralism, and his illusory hopes that the regime of play and leisure can be divorced from issues of equality, work, and the workplace, lie what seem to me two insistently democratic themes that we are not likely to get away from. One is democratic utopianism, and the other is the democratic ideal of consciousness that this utopianism serves. Both are mostly implicit in what he has to say; both temper his irony at the expense of our Populist hopes. At this level, Riesman is confessing himself a camerado of Walt Whitman, too.

UTOPIA AND CONSCIOUSNESS

Both democratic utopianism and the ideal of consciousness reflect the fact that American social thought is in the end supremely Romantic and psychological: its essential quest is for a means of renewing ordinary life. It looks for a dialectic of impulse and reality, a mediation of reason and feeling, in the interests of renewal. Like Veblen and Dewey, Riesman is essentially a psychologist. (Whatever field they are in, Americans end up doing psychology: Veblen wrote the psychology of production, consumption, and emulation; Dewey wrote a logic that was less normative logic than a map of the processes of thought; and William James wrote an entire book on religion that never talked about God at all, dwelling almost wholly on states of religious consciousness.) Riesman is a master of psychology and character; on his own ground he is unbeatable, yet he runs some of the same risks that earlier figures did. Psychology cannot cover the whole of social analysis. It is one thing to talk about the psychology induced by the market; it is another to talk about the market itself. The institutions behind the market tend to get lost in the discussion of the market orientation. Riesman points to a supreme paradox: that Americans have become a more cooperative and sympathetic people at the same time that they continue to serve institutions geared to competition and economic growth at any price. The capitalist institutions of the age of profit, competition, and inner-direction continue to dominate our national life; this is an issue that no amount of psychologizing can deal with adequately without a wider perspective on society and social institutions, as Riesman himself acknowledges in a later preface to the book. Yet with all its limitations, the psychology of *The Lonely Crowd* has endured, and its continuing appeal remains its penetration into American character and the kind of challenge to one's consciousness that living in America poses.

The utopianism is explicit in the fragmentary and puzzling last chapters of *The Lonely Crowd* and in some of Riesman's essays. All the greatest thinkers in our line are utopians, holding out for some essential mediation between the modern and the countermodern. Sometimes the tradition offers mainly rhetorical visions of unity, and sometimes the dialectical mediations of contrary realms are real and valid. The Progressives, too, were dialectical utopians. Dewey was clearly aware that he was trying to put the ideas of the utopians of the nineties, especially Henry George and Edward Bellamy, on a practical basis; Veblen was not, I suspect. Whether conscious or not, the Progressive utopias shared two important traits. One is that they represent a harmonious marriage, or mediation, of contrary realms: Dewey wanted to synthesize high Romanticism—thought and feeling—with science, democracy, and industry; Veblen wanted to fuse the skepticism and matter-of-fact discipline of the scientific mind with the amiable unassertiveness of preindustrial man, to combine the warm virtues of fraternity and abundance with the discipline of the material realm and production. In their separate ways, Dewey and Veblen wanted a blend of long revolution and lost community, a mix of modernizing and countermodern impulses. It is not altogether clear what contraries Riesman wants to unite in his utopia, but *The Lonely Crowd* clearly argues for a fusion of some of the "soft" virtues of other-direction (minus its soft vices) with certain of the "hard" disciplines of inner-direction, minus its harsh rigidities; it takes the mediating stance of figures like Dewey and applies it to the issue of, as Emerson put it, the one and the many: the problem was to avoid the anomie of the older individualism and the "adjustment" of the social world the Progressives built, to be autonomous. The utopian ideal in all cases offers a blend of nature and artifice, feeling and reason, the individual and the community, long revolution and lost community— of modern and countermodern; Veblen's industrial pastorale, Dewey's dreams of community and schools as child-gardens for the new industrial wilderness, and Riesman's images of a world of autonomy and play are all in the utopian tradition. As ideals they have the defects of the utopian tradition—its propensity to abstractness, sentimentality, empty spiritualizing—and its strengths as well, notably the utopian moral imagination's capacity to consider alternatives to the world we are given, and its hunger for a holistic portrait of human possibility. This is a consistent strain in American social thought, the belief in the possibility (not necessarily the probability) of a harmony of contrary realms, and the faith in the possibility (not necessarily the probability) that the economic order can be made to give way to a regime based on human and social priorities.

The utopianism is by its nature in some measure optimistic: Riesman's skepticism and anti-Populism mask his own version of the difficult American reform earnestness, a continuing belief in democracy that he shares with Dewey. This is apparent in his use of Freud to argue a complex case for an un-Freudian and democratic—and in the end rather Deweyan—picture of human nature as rational, productive, and loving at some basic level, and even more apparent in a final continuity he shares with the Progressives he quarreled with, a complex idea of democratic consciousness. Riesman's ideal of autonomy in the age of other-direction is, as I have said, a rebuke to the Progressive hope that community will take the place of rugged individualism. Yet these genuine disagreements with Dewey mask a common preference for a dialectical stance in which neither pole alone does justice to the actual complexity of the goal. The utopian mediation of contrary realms is very much a fusion ticket, a unity achieved out of diversity, incorporating opposites. This is its glory and its weakness. The purpose of the dialectic is a kind of moral balance that permits the exercise of a democratic consciousness. It can produce daydreams and idylls, and it can also embody true dialectical unities wrenched from the soul of a culture that lives by conflicting dualities. The individualism celebrated by our dialectical utopians from Whitman and Emerson to Dewey and Riesman is an ideal of conscious awareness. It is difficult to describe because it stands for an experimental attitude toward experience and life that is the highest value of all, the Romantic value of values.

The ideal derives intellectually from a culture that sets a high value on votes, checks, and balances—a culture that sanctions in a host of ways the divorce of authority from power, and power from truth, that promotes dissent and shifting electoral alliances. Democratic politics implies a consciousness that acts and watches, that is, in Whitman's metaphor, simultaneously in and out of the game. The Romantic, democratic consciousness stops short of ultimate commitments because the ultimate commitment, even for its socialists, is to individual awareness, consciousness. Truth and morals are, like political figures, elected for short terms of office and subject to recall and referenda. This is a commonplace of political thought, and a host of recent critics have pointed to the importance of this kind of Romantic consciousness in American literature. Now it is time to see that our traditions in social thought are also dialectical and Romantic. It is not only intellectual understanding that is sought, but a certain kind of flowering of the imagination, the psychological growth that results from a proper, mediated set of tensions between head, heart, action, and the objective world—the high Romantic psychology described by Whitman and Coleridge and updated in Dewey's *Art as Experience* and *Experience and Nature*. The enduring dialectical—Romantic—goal is openness to new experience, the determination to remain aware.

This method of mediating contraries and riding negations in the name of an independent consciousness and the high Romantic imagination is the ideal of individuality that many American thinkers have upheld, even when, like Dewey, they attacked the older style of individualism in the name of a cooperative democratic socialism. This is, for all its frequent moderation in practice, its quest for unity and balance, a radical ideal: no idea, feeling, institution, movement, or practice can ever command complete allegiance. It will be more and more critical for us to restate this in an age of antidemocratic cultural modernisms and totalitarian socialisms—especially those of us who are democrats, modernists, and socialists. Plainly this is also a risky ideal. It expresses an odd sort of American existentialism in which everything is sacrificed to the flow of the consciousness. It can at times settle for purely rhetorical unities. It can be earnest, and it can be crazy. It can seem evasive to the point of amorality, as in Emerson's pinwheels of polarities or Dewey's eternal peanut-buttery vagueness. It can rationalize indecision and solipsism. It can be tragic, as well as utopian. It can too readily sacrifice action to criticism. No one has been harsher on American democracy than its democrats: think of Emerson on the moral bankruptcy of the Jacksonian and pre-Civil War eras; Thoreau on the consequences of the division of labor and the quiet desperation of ordinary lives; Whitman on the psychic costs of individualism; Dewey on the American technological "wilderness" that divorced science and value; Riesman on the price of equality. In each case the criticism is in the service of the ideal of consciousness and the workings of the imagination, a dialectic by which assertions of belief pile up against their opposites, making a total truth of experience greater than the lesser, contending truths that make it up. In this sense, for all its disillusionment, *The Lonely Crowd* is in the grand dialectical line. We may read it today, as I do, feeling that Riesman confuses the defense of democracy with the defense of technology and capitalism, and we must wonder, as I do, whether his ideal of autonomy and consciousness can survive in a hungry, violent, and illiberal world; but the ideal of a democratic consciousness remains the basis for hopes for humanism and democracy in a collectivist age.

In this essay I have tried to describe some continuities in a debate. Inevitably an exercise of this sort focuses on one of the patterns in the carpet to the exclusion of others, and I recognize that another pattern of breaks and discontinuities can be described. I am also aware that concentrating on patterns in themselves neglects substantive issues.

The historical swing between ideals of individualism and ideals of community, for example, is clearly not dictated only by shifts in the positions of various debaters in each generation. The polarities recur and shift because they reflect a changing social reality and point to real and enduring social dilemmas that each generation faces anew, demanding fresh responses to a new social scene and novel problems. They also recur, however, because American intellectual debate takes the form of a dialectical pendulum, and not a spiral. Each generation in what I sometimes think of as the United States of Amnesia starts from scratch: we write novels, do sociology, discuss education, politics, and philosophy, as though nobody had ever done these things before, and we often do end up reversing older sets of polarities without advancing our understanding. Riesman is unusually historically-minded for an American thinker—all his theorizing is grounded in history, and his book on Veblen is an open reckoning with the Progressives—yet even he, I think, ignores the way the central images of abundance and scarcity figured in earlier thought, and how much the Progressives' rebellion against individualism shared the dialectical features of his rebellion against community. His critique of Populism is searching and novel, but it rests on a vision of utopia and an ideal of mediated consciousness and imagination that remain Romantic, and therefore classically American. In its fascination with democratic possibilities, Riesman's work resists the final implications of his skepticism and irony, and connects itself to the hopes and ideals of the writers of what F. O. Matthiessen called the American Renaissance, as well as to more sober European figures like Mill and Tocqueville. If my story has a moral, it is that Americans need to be more conscious of their traditions of thought, reform, and action, because that will help them know where they can build on past traditions and where they must strike out in wholly new directions.

My main point has not been to make morals, however, but to locate these voices in a context and show that there is, for better and for worse, an American culture we draw on when we try to think about such issues as modernity, a set of inherited intellectual lenses that both limits and focuses our vision. In describing this aspect of the culture I wanted to record a facet of what might be called our national character.

2

THE SOCIOLOGICAL REALITY
OF AMERICA:
AN ESSAY ON MASS CULTURE

JOSEPH R. GUSFIELD

In his book *The Unadjusted Girl*, the sociologist W. I. Thomas describes an elderly immigrant couple living in Brooklyn in the 1910s. After twenty years in the United States they were robbed of their savings by a young man who was their boarder. They wrote to the *Bintel Brief*, the Ann Landers column of the Yiddish press of that day, and asked the readers to help them locate the young man. They deplored the theft, but they still wanted the boarder to return, because they missed him. "He told us about America."

Whether immigrant or not, most of us also depend upon someone to tell us about America. That is what this paper is about: how we come to experience America as a real and coherent object that we can label a "society." More exactly this paper is about how some aspects of culture-producing agents, especially the mass media and the colleges, create an image of American society and how that image has significant effects. Here, too, Thomas's famous aphorism is worth stating again: "If men define situations as real, they are real in their consequences."

A parable will serve to further this introduction. While teaching an undergraduate course in social stratification some years ago, I asked a student to categorize her family by using the rubrics of W. Lloyd Warner, then fashionable in the field. When she confessed an inability to place her family on one of the six rungs of the Warnerian ladder, I probed to see if she understood the method Warner had used and the criteria for such placements. "How would you go about

41

classifying your family?" I asked. I have never forgotten her answer: "I'd ask a sociologist."

Sociology, as an educational discipline, is one voice in the chorus of mass education and mass media that serves to tell us about America. That telling is itself an act in which Americans learn a lesson of cultural anthropology. The media of mass culture depict the culture and the social structure of America. They are a significant part of the creation of the popular consciousness of what is America. This construction of the reality of American culture and society is the theme and substance of this paper.

AMERICA AS A PUBLIC EVENT

As a part of the consciousness of each American, the object "American society" is a construction of personal and vicarious experience. The "American population" cannot be experienced in a personal or direct sense; two hundred million people are beyond the capacity of direct observation. The concept is an aggregated abstraction. We have to be told about it through the work of an organization of census officials, demographers, teachers, and journalists. It is a public event, a matter of the society beyond personal experience and shared in a public broadcast and published fashion.

In this process of constructing the public event of America, mass education and the mass media are profoundly significant. That these institutions generate a shared content of public experiences is important. For the perspective of this paper, however, it is even more significant that they develop and transmit a sense of what is public rather than private; what is typical, shared, and socially organized. Not only do teachers, journalists, and entertainers inform audiences and classrooms about facts and ideas; they inform them about what the American culture and the American society are.

It is useful to call attention to what Jack Douglas refers to as "the publicity effect, the effect on the meanings of things of their being public, rather than private."[1] It is not only that public events are abstract; it is also significant that being public, they provide the recognition that others are also experiencing them. The media of mass culture portray that culture, describe it, and comment on it. They attribute to others the schemes of norms and expectations assumed to be shared and typical.

The idea of "youth culture" is a good illustration of this process. A sociological term and idea, developed by and associated with Talcott Parsons and other sociologists, it has become part of the ideas and language of the mass media and the agencies of education. It is presented as the typical experience of parents and adolescents in American society. It is what being young is like in America. "Youth culture" becomes the standard of behavior against which the personal experience of the parent or the child is now to be seen. Each member of the audience now can impute meanings and experiences that he or she may share, can anticipate and act toward events that may or may not occur. His or her individual experience is now projected against the public experience. The social organization of youth is thus upheld as a "normal" order of events and personal experience, private experience seen as typical or as abnormal. The public event of "youth" is affirmed; there *is* a typical pattern of youthful behavior in America; there *is* a youth culture and an American society.

American culture is then found both in the individual consciousness and in public statements and descriptions. There is what we think and what we do. There is also what we think others think and what we think others do. The possibility for conflict and support between these levels of consciousness and behavior has been one of the recurrent and central questions of social theory. Social scientists as diverse as Talcott Parsons, Karl Marx, and Karl Mannheim have emphasized the disposition of consciousness and social structure to become mutually supportive. Others, such as Thorstein Veblen, William Ogburn, Joseph Schumpeter, and, most recently, Daniel Bell, have focused on disjunctures between the realm of culture and the arena of behavior and social structure.

The sources of tension between culture and social structure are both general and particular. The general sources are inherent in the nature of these two sides of human life. The particular ones are unique to specific societies and historical periods. I will discuss some of the inherent sources before detailing the implications of mass culture for the contemporary era.

Inherent Sources of Tension in Social Orderliness

In its daily round of routine and crisis, human behavior is seldom perfect. Judged by transcending principles of moral right, religious impulse, or creative standards, it falls short of the purity of principle by which loyalty to authority and social structure are made legitimate. Only the most exemplary of leaders and saints are totally free from corruption. Disenchantment with the failure of human behavior to approximate the ideals of cultural prescriptions is a constant feature of social life.

One major source of dissonance is *the disparity between idealization and situational action*. Human action emerges in highly specific contexts in which values and desires are pragmatically weighed in an immediate choice of goods and evils as they are symbolized and presented in an instant case. Abstractions in the form of general principles and ethical precepts are just that—abstractions. Their relation to situated activities is problematic and not clearly specifiable from general statements. Saintliness is not common, and popular religion is not that of the literati. Repeated studies have pointed up the tenuousness of utilizing respondents' accounts of themselves or of their society as true maps to the explanation or prediction of their behavior.

In the face of concrete situations, human actors feel the tensions between ideals and the immediate realities of choice. Social institutions are thus corrupt and immoral.[2] The destruction of innocence and the birth of personal sophistication and skepticism is a persistent theme of writers depicting the passage from youth to adulthood. That the emperor has few clothes, if any, is a pervasive source of a disillusioned bitterness that corrodes the shining metal of the mystique surrounding authority.

Another source of the tension between the transcendent and the mundane arises from *the organizational character of authority*. This was central to Max Weber's analysis of charismatic leadership. The demands of daily living and fact of the death of leaders made it essential for sects, cults, revolutionary governments, and other associations founded on charismatic legitimation to routinize and develop into regularized and predictable institutions. Organizations are faced with problems of succession, custodianship, coordination, and survival that lead them to replace the rule of the extraordinary "saint" with the administrative skills of efficient and trained personnel. The humdrum and the predictable supplant the romantic, the exciting, and the unique. What remains, however, is a subterranean enchantment with the "Golden Age": a continuing critique of the organization and its authority. In short, in the process of organization, the nonrational sources of authority are weakened, and the gap between transcendent principles and organizational "realities" is widened.

Variant Sources of Tension

These sources are presented here as ubiquitous aspects of social life. A major insight of sociologists, however, has been the recognition that these tensions are greater, wider, and more salient under certain conditions, in some societies, and with some cultures. William Fielding Ogburn, for example, placed his emphasis on those particular points in history when technological change widens the gap between principles of action and the realities of new situations. Max Weber found Catholicism more tolerant of the frailities of human beings and human situations than Protestantism.

Not all social orders, institutions, or social arrangements are subject equally to the alienating force of such tensions. Some societies contain or control the tensions between transcendence and organizational structures with less deterioration of their institutional charisma. They are better able than others to retain the mystique of the elite's right to rule, the virtue of the Revolution, or the inherent and divine origin of social inequities. It was Weber's fundamental view of Western history that bureaucratic institutions do not generate legitimating mystiques; they are inimical to charisma, and they "disenchant" the world.

Joseph Schumpeter's analysis of modern capitalism is especially pertinent, both for its clarity and for its analysis of modern, scientized societies as weak sources for nonrational loyalty and allegiance. Schumpeter argued for the economic wisdom of monopoly capitalism as an instrument of wealth and mass well-being, yet he predicted the collapse of capitalist economic institutions. As he saw it, the mechanisms of the market and the development of nonmarket monopolistic business could and would continue to solve the economic problems of production and distribution with admirable effectiveness. What they could not do was cope with the dialectical consequences of capitalistic rationality and calculative logic on the nonrational, sacred, and mystical sources of loyalty to its own institutions and authority. He reasoned that the civilization of capitalism would erode the bases of its own authority and dig its grave, not with the weapons of the proletariat, but with the tools of its own logic.

Social order is an approximation, always judged lacking by ultimate principles. A major source of social disorder thus lies in the erosion of institutional support by cultural precepts. Alienation is as much a part of social life as is allegiance.

The Phenomenological Character of Authority

Perhaps an even more significant source of social order lies in the effectiveness of institutions in actually maintaining authority. We are not here referring to their effectiveness as instruments for meeting member expectations. That is important, but so frequently discussed in analyses of dissent that we have little to contribute here. Instead, we are interested in the effectiveness of maintaining allegiance as itself a source of allegiance.

One of the processes that support any social order is the belief that it exists; that violations of legal, moral, or cognitive precepts will lead to sanctions. Whatever one's own doubts about the legitimacy of institutions and authorities, their continuance is enhanced when doubters see their own internal dissent as unique and unshared. Social order is respected and adherence attained in part because that order is believed to be a matter of fact. There *really* is a consensus about morals and norms; sanctions *will* follow rebellion; actors *will* carry out their expected roles.

A degree of *pluralistic ignorance* underlies social institutions, especially in complex societies composed of diverse cultures and differentiated social levels. Each member of the group imputes to the others meanings and criteria that he himself does not share. Each, ignorant of the others, believes in a wider consensus than exists. The capacity for sudden change is thus often unrecognized until events and communication reveal less consent than appeared in public awareness.

Such pluralistic ignorance is often the basis for imputations of a greater orderliness than exists within the society. Questionnaire data of sociologists and survey research thus often tell us what respondents think about others rather than about themselves. The classic study of occupational prestige made by the National Opinion Research Center has been interpreted and studied not as the responses to individual judgments of occupations, but as judgments of what others think: the respondent's view of his society, not of himself.[3] Rather than telling the sociologist the prestige the respondent accords to a given occupation, they are actually giving their judgment of how they see others placing such occupations.

Belief in the facticity of the social order is maintained by the self-fulfilling myth of consensus. To a significant extent, social order is constructed by systems of consistent accounting used by members to convert situational actions into moral orders.[4] As long as the social order is believed to exist, seemingly inconsistent events are dealt with by a process of normalization, "explained away" through ad hoc arguments that preserve the institution.

Jack Douglas has put this perspective clearly:

> In such an uncertain and conflictful society, the belief in an absolutist set of moral rules is important not only because it is reassuring and because it helps one to control his nightmares of social chaos and violence, but also because it helps the individuals involved in political action to solve the fundamental problems of constructing order . . . the belief that a rational and ordered society is both possible and already existing gives individuals the belief that their attempts to construct social order will be successful.[5]

Disbelief in the Facticity of Social Order

The belief that social order is a fact—that others neither doubt the legitimacy of institutions nor fail to carry out roles—is not itself a stable part of social reality. Its tenuousness is accentuated by the visibility of acts that belie the assumptions of normality. Acts of deviance, defiance, and alienation, as Durkheim realized, subvert order beyond their immediate effects. Normalizing explanations and insulation from the visibility of doubts and rebellious behavior seem essential to sustain the myth of consensus. As Samuel Johnson posited for the dramatic stage, so too for societies: a "willing suspension of disbelief" keeps the social order operating. He who cries that the emperor has no clothes does commit treason.

This understanding of social order and disorder indicates that one significant source subverting institutional authority arises from those events, processes, and persons that disturb belief in the facticity of the institution, that make apparent the tenuous and problematic hold of norms, values, and beliefs within the population. Before the charisma of revolt can be affective, the charisma of established authority is peeled away.

"Creative disturbance" is just that; it creates disturbance by making the orderly account of events and expectations problematic and no longer taken for granted. The actions of people now become unreliable, unanticipated, and "absurd." New explanations and theories are required; new possibilities emerge.

The activity or action that movements of revolt and rebellion engage in takes on highly consequential significance, whatever the aims or immediate effects of the acts. Absurdity—activity unexplainable by prevailing systems of explanation—can thus have great import for diminishing the claim that authority actually governs. The "crazies," the impetuous, "left-wing adventurers," the proponents of "revolution for the hell of it" intuitively recognize this. It is not terror that loosens the bonds of authority so much as it is the sheer act of disobedience and disconformity: the audacious show of disregard for the logic, power, and morality of seemingly established, yet shaky, authority. Even the theater of the absurd operates on premises that put both literary devices and socially valid explanations in doubt.[6] Abbie Hoffman has been clear in seeing this impact of disturbance:

Why did the kids rip the hands off the clock?

I don't know. Maybe they hate time and schedules. Maybe they thought the clock was ugly. They also decorated the clock with sketches. Maybe they were having fun. When we put on a large celebration the aim is to create a liberated area. People can do whatever they want. They can begin to live the revolution even if only within a confined area. We will learn how to govern ourselves. . . . The revolutionary experience is far more than just the fighting units.[7]

In the remainder of this paper I want to advance the assertion that certain characteristics of mass culture make for a widening of the tensions between thought and action, consciousness and social structure, culture and society. They diminish cultural support for established arrangements of social authority and enhance the sense of the self as embattled in a struggle against social structure. One example of this process is in the content of education, especially in the ideas of conventional sociology. Another is instanced in the forms of cultural transmission that mass media utilize.

SOCIOLOGY AND THE SOCIAL CONSTRUCTION OF "SOCIETY"

If the nineteenth century has sometimes been linked intellectually to the "dismal science" of economics, the twentieth is better symbolized by the "science" taught by sociologists, one less sad than sanguine in its belief that the world can be reshaped and improved if the laws of human action are discovered. In the past twenty-five years, the gist of sociology may be found less in its development as an instrument of knowledge and technology than in its contribution to the popular consciousness of Americans about themselves and their America.

Robert Park is reported to have once said that sociology was at best a pedagogical exercise. That exercise is by no means inconsequential when seven million students are enrolled in higher education. Several years ago a publisher's representative said that approximately two hundred fifty thousand students were enrolled in introductory sociology courses in American colleges and universities every term. The language of sociology has leaped into public discourse: terms such as "charisma," "alienation," "ethnic," "other-directed," "power structure," and "anomic" are now part of American speech, their sources no longer in need of footnotes.

Sociological concepts and ideas provide an invitation to experience oneself as one of a group and as a person engaged in typical acts. In providing a language and a perspective that encompasses large numbers of people and a wide expanse of situations, the sociologist constructs an idealized version of reality, one firmer and more organized than is given by concentrating on the unique qualities of specific events and individual persons.

The Sociological View of America

The artist, the historian, the novelist, and the man of *belles-lettres* in the United States have often been obsessed with the phenomenon of Americanness. The sociologist is but the latest entrant into the field, although one immensely threatening to the hegemony of the humanist. As an entrant, the sociologist brings to the self-perception of the person and the social organization a distinctive emphasis on a world of group identities, loyalties, and typical situations.

Looked at reflexively, sociological conceptions are more than neutral, olympian pronouncements about an objective world. They appear as devices that actively shape the experience they are seeking to describe. As Raymond Williams wrote:

> There are in fact no masses; there are only ways of seeing people as masses. . . . The point is not to reiterate the objective conditions but to consider, personally and collectively, what these have done to our thinking.[8]

Perhaps the most important and profound impact of sociology on American popular consciousness has been to reinforce the consciousness of America as a "society." It invites us to experience America as an entity—as a consistent and patterned set of relationships. Even the diversities and differences of groups and classes are described as organized, defined, and systematized differences. They are capable of description and analysis through general concepts and propositions that characterize even the diversities as unitary, shared, and hence group experiences. Whatever else America may be, in the imagery of the sociologist, it *is*.

Studies of new nations and economically developing areas have proceeded on quite opposite assumptions. A literature on nation building (an illustrative phrase itself) and the emergence of social order has taken the creation of "social order" as itself tenuous and problematic for many areas of the world. Just the names of some of the major works in the field of "development" are instructive: *The Passing of Traditional Society; Old Societies and New States; Nation-Building*. It has even made sense for professors of Indian Studies to ask Ph.D. candidates if it is useful to talk of "India" as a subject for research.

No such doubt pervades the current sociological perspectives about America. It used to be said that the European peasant remained oblivious of the political and military events that made up the history of his "society." The wider national society was not a significant part of his experience. He lived within a small area of consciousness whose borders were tangible and immediate. Both for America and for other contemporary social aggregations, this has no longer seemed appropriate. Edward Shils has captured the sense of the self as implicated in a widened social organization:

> The new society is a mass society precisely in the sense that the mass of population has become incorporated *into* society. The center of the society . . . has extended its boundaries. Most of the population (the mass) now stands in a closer relationship to the center. . . . In previous societies, a substantial portion of the population, often the majority, were born and forever remained "outsiders."[9]

Here Shils appears to refer to two aspects of "society" in the phrase "stands in a relationship." In one meaning, he refers to tangible and active *relations* between people, as in the receipt of social security checks, enrollment in educational institutions, and voting. In another, he points to the *experience* of living in a "society"; the phenomena of the person thinking about himself or herself as living in America, perceiving the self as American, and conceptualizing the nature and character of that "society."

The implications of seeing oneself as a piece of society might also be described as a kind of Keynesianism of human behavior. Keynes replaced the emphasis of economic theory on individual enterprisers and firms with the analysis of "the economy" as an aggregate. The concept of Gross National Product is but a recent addition to the arsenal of economists' weapons. It is part of a reconstituted perception of the aggregate as the unit of analysis, a perception deeply at the foundation of sociological method.

The analogy to economics also suggests contrasts. Ideas often exist in symbiotic antagonism, each clarifying itself by its differences from the other. A great deal of sociology emerged from the polemic against classical economic theory. Intellectually, sociologists of seminal influence, like Durkheim and Marx, were critics of Benthamite utilitarianism, Ricardian individualism, and Spencerian rationalism. Politically, they attacked the doctrine of individualism as minimizing the possibilities and values of collective action in achieving social justice. For the French, individualism was a term of opprobrium, redolent of selfish greed and an anomic world.[10] In the United States, it was crucial for the sociologist to counteract the force of a heroic individualism, one that saw collective aspects of life as surmountable and even unimportant. The sociologist brought to the public arena an accent on the person as a group phenomenon: a figure of role and status, class and ethnic group, region and religion. No sociologist could subscribe to the applause that Walt Whitman gave to the self: "One's self I sing, a simple separate person."

For sociological thought, the Romantic figure of the individual in Whitman, the Renaissance man of Michelangelo, the rational man of Adam Smith, is counterpoised against the person in a social context, the artistic types of German expressionist faces or the abstracted characteristics of a "social role." This emphasis on what is typical and general has meant a preoccupation with the macroscopic rather than the situational. It has meant an emphasis on group components and institutional features, coupled with an unwillingness to analyze events as unique occurrences. The styles of sociological language are those of ideal types, in which the specifics of ambivalence, ambiguity, and doubt are minimized.

In their efforts to correct the unbalanced view of nineteenth-century individualism, sociologists compensated by the attenuation of group types. Sociology abounds in typologies through which the person can perceive his or her typicality: universalistic and particular; primary and secondary; achieved and ascribed; inner-directed and other-directed; upper, lower, and middle class.

The rhetoric of sociological polemics against nineteenth-century individualism has added up to an expansion of scene and a diminution of agent. The necessary "put down" of the individual and "build up" of the "society" provide the possibilities of self-perception through group affiliates. It is the reality of being an individual versus being a part of society that constitutes the distinctive sociological contribution to the reconsideration of the individual in the mid-twentieth century.

The Objectification of "Society"

The impact of this sociological rhetoric on self-conceptions seems to me a vital part of its cultural influence. If the "self-made man" was the American model of heroic character, the image of the American as "group product," "class character," and "institutional role" has emerged as a balance. Sociological thought has been part of the shift away from the perception of the individual as active agent and toward self-appraisal as a passive recipient of group memberships.

> . . . there is then a tendency to say that not individuals, but these larger entities, are ultimately 'responsible.' I live at a particular moment of time in the spiritual and social and economic circumstances into which I have been cast; how then can I help choosing and acting as I do? The values in terms of which I conduct my life are the values of my class, or race, or church, or civilization, or are part and parcel of my 'station'—my position in the 'social structure.'[11]

The theoretical sources of contemporary sociology derive largely from a view of society as an external, objective phenomenon in which persons are socialized and to which they adjust or rebel. Marx (especially the Marx of *Capital*) and Durkheim contributed seminally to the objectification of society as "social fact." They shared a perspective toward human behavior that looks to group characteristics and social structure to find the determining features of social situations and the possibilities for engineering social or political change.

In conceiving of social facts as external to the person, Durkheim minimized the importance and effect of individual action and choice in the composition and development of the person. *Suicide*, the model for much of sociological method in the twentieth century, was a major exercise in utilizing group variables to explain and predict aggregate and public events—group suicide rates.

Marx (of the latter-day "church") presented an equally objectified view of human behavior in the polity of Necessity. In what I always think of as the most summatory sentence of modern sociology he wrote: "It is not the consciousness of men which determines their existence but on the contrary it is their social existence which determines their consciousness."[12] Both in the *Manifesto* and in Engel's work *Socialism: Utopian and Scientific*, Marx and Engels drew the necessary conclusions. It was useless to dream dreams and construct utopias unless they were consonant with underlying structural characteristics of the society. Men can make their own history, but only at certain times and in certain ways. If they are not puppets, nevertheless, they must be mindful of the many, many strings attached.

In more recent decades a stress on the interdependence and systematic implications of events has appeared in sociological theories. These portray the individual as enmeshed in and shaped by total systems. This has especially been the case in the influential work of Talcott Parsons and in the many empirical studies that sought for "underlying causes" in the objective conditions of social structure. In his classic essay "Social Structure and Anomie," Robert Merton clearly displayed the logic and rhetoric of this analytic model. "Our primary aim," he wrote, "lies in discovering how some social structures *exert a definite pressure* upon certain persons in the society to engage in nonconformist rather than conformist conduct."[13] (*Italics added*)

The sociological self-image is detected wherever people see themselves *only* as role, as group member, as social function. I am startled and upset when people respond to a demand for justification by providing an explanation in sociological terms. Asked to justify political opinion or cultural taste, they sometimes do so by giving their class, race, religion, age, or sex, saying that "of course" they must then have such and such ideas, values, or motives; "I am as I am and that is all that I am." To transcend the social self is impossible for the socialized self to comprehend.

This objectification of society is neither liberal, radical, nor conservative. Implicit in the perspective is the view that America is a "finished" society, the "First New Nation"; hence the emphasis on the search for sources of unity, centralization, and power. In the endless arguments between the "pluralists" and their "power structure" antagonists, there is the implicit and shared assumption that power has a structure in America, whether it be one of compromise between group interests or the heavy hand of monopoly capitalism. A social organization exists, and with it is the power to move levers that shape and can shape events. Even the radical revolutionary and the conservative right-winger assume that somewhere in the confusion of events there is a pattern and a plan. Once the old order of domination is evicted, the new one can remodel or return the old furniture. For all the antagonists in this political process, society is like an apartment house, and changing landlords is a significant event, determining the interior decoration and the location of rooms.

This sociological conception of American life as an organized set of structures is implicit as well in those who adopt a romantic critique of the American life portrayed in sociological concepts. The quest for the autonomous individual has absorbed American social comment from Emerson to Riesman. Such perspectives have posited a search for a non sociological self, apart from and directing the commitment and distance of the person from social structures of role and status.[14]

In a brilliant essay, *Sincerity and Authenticity*, Lionel Trilling has described a major shift in cultural content from a concern for issues of sincerity—the fit of the self with the demands of the social structure—to a concern for authenticity—the expression of the self in opposition to the demands of the social structure.[15] The first expresses a fear that the person is not the socialized person that he pretends to be. It applauds the fit and worries about the discrepancies. The second view expresses the fear that the pretension is not the person and applauds the abdication of pretense and the expression of the "real self" as authentic.

This glorification of the authentic, found in many life-style movements today, itself assumes the sociological view of society. It is this assumption of a social structure that makes the search for authenticity necessary and problematic. The earlier emphasis on sincerity, still the touchstone for public officials, made society the problematic focus. The sociological view of society is itself a feature of the setting in which culture and society collide.

MASS CULTURE AND DRAMATIC ART

The conflict between culture and society is a part of the content of contemporary culture. It is accentuated and widened by the American media of popular culture. The large body of cultural output represented by the mass media of newspapers, movies, radio, television, and the public school is a shared part of the consciousness of much of the American population. It is in this sense of a more homogeneous populace possessing a common content of culture that mass culture represents a historical event qualitatively different from the disparate and localized cultures of America before World War I. It is through the medium of these cultural institutions that Americans most saliently share the symbols of an association of people.

The Culture of Mass Media

There is more to the process of a shared popular culture than an extension of older forms of theater, news, and art. The degree and scope of monitoring is far more extensive and intensive than has existed in other historical periods among large sectors of the population. The direct televised reports of the Vietnam War are one illustration of this. So too is the process by which issues are quickly disseminated and heroes and villains developed almost daily.

Mass Culture as an Abstraction from Situated Events

While the society is constantly monitored and events transmitted, the content of that dissemination is not the same as the full complexity of events themselves. Television, for example, gives us the selected image of the event and not the event itself.[16]

Here again the contrast is painted between the situational context of actions, where values are multiple and ethical issues of assigning priorities exist, and the cultural realms, where situations emerge in an idealized form. The mass media are artistic; they produce cultural products for an audience. The general categories and judgments are pervaded by beliefs about distant events and persons and are not checked, as activities are, by the "buzzing, booming confusion" of reality. Rather than reflections of the society, they are independent products necessarily refracting the social situations they seem to describe.

The significance of this, as well as the other characteristics of mass culture outlined above, is considerable. Appeals to cultural principle and charismatic heroes pervade popular and mass culture because they are dramatic, rather than factual. We live in the contemporary world, immersed in and surrounded by a culture of dramatic excitement. This point is central to my argument and will be expanded upon below.

The Significance of Dramatic Art in Mass Culture

Participants in mass culture act chiefly as listeners and watchers. The bulk of mass culture is artistic—drama, music, stories—material deliberately created for an audience. Even news for the mass readership is entertainment, and the reader's interest is a primary aim. In the 1930s Leo Rosten observed that Washington correspondents who hoped to be read had to report news as exciting encounters between persons rather than as duller conflicts of ideologies or institutions.[17] That need continues in all the media.

A key to the impact of mass culture is that it dramatizes events and persons. The intricate flux of human situations defies the institutional norms and cultural categories through which we perceive, arrange, and order life. The styles of action existent in institutional roles are imperfectly followed and frequently clash with other definitions of value that are part of the ambivalences of a culture. Dramatic situations, being products of artistic creation, can do precisely what social situations contradict: they can stylize events and persons and bring conflicts to definitive resolutions. To stylize is to reduce the complex and the diverse to standard categories and types and symbols. We know the good guys from the bad guys by their clothing, their language, the way they walk. We know that events described on the first page of the news have greater "seriousness" than those described in the second section. Here, as in so much of the understanding of human behavior, Kenneth Burke has given us great illumination: "The logic of symbolic resources drives towards its fullness in a universal definition."[18] It leads men to pose the situations in artistic opposites, to develop heroes and villains in a reciprocal fashion that blurs the ambivalences of realities. "The 'fragmentary' nature of the enemy thus comes to take on the attributes of an absolute."[19]

Mass culture abounds in the creation of myth and with it the development of heroes and villains; they are more interesting, more colorful, and more provocative than "reality." They are also part of the abstracting process, which limits of space, time, and spectator experience make necessary. They create a world of excitement and glamour in contrast to the prosaic and the routine.[20] Most importantly, they convey a world of clear purity, where the principles of action otherwise diffused and corrupted can be utilized and upheld. In the competition for audiences and advertising revenue, this is a crucial source of attention.

We need to look at social conflict in the light of how media of communication prestructure situations through the myths of conflict. Analysts of violent disorder in the United States during the 1960s have observed the "self-fulfilling prophecy" character of encounters between police and the black population, and police and student demonstrators. Each brings to such encounters a view of the other group as villainous and his own group as heroic. Action follows from these premises, and the ensuing reaction verifies the assumptions.[21]

The significance of the dramatic for political and social tension lies in the appeals to ultimate principle, to the transcending elements of culture as sources by which to judge actions and institutions. The hero has two sides to his demands; one is a critique of the existent institutions as villainous, and the other is a presentation of himself as the embodiment of the pure, of the principles that are already there in the traditions of the culture. The charisma of De Gaulle was not self-contained but was dependent on the drama of France in a period of declining power and glory and on the image of the general as the redeemer, the symbol of national greatness as a pure and uncorrupted impulse.

Authority is itself always subject to the attack of purity. Institutions must depend on the routine appeal to interests rather than the less reliable sentiments; charismatic qualities must be subordinated to dependable role behavior. Thus, social life is corrupt, and the hero, by his message and his manner, appears as the opposite. His very weakness can be a source of appeal if it is contrasted with the institutional authority against which he struggles.[22]

Here is how one of the news media pictures a contemporary hero:

> "Nader's gift is not one of personal mien. His narrow-lapelled, ever rumpled suits and too short sideburns make no concession to the generally young, liberal audience he addresses. What Nader radiates is pure purpose, an almost fanatical *sincerity*."[23]

The Age of the Dramatic

We live today in an era of drama and artistic excitement. The participant society of mass publics is involved with the total society in and through mass media. They exist alongside and often in conflict with the face-to-face and mediated interactions of social structures and groups. Do riots occur in New Jersey? Is the dollar sound? Is heroin use on the increase? Our involvement in these questions comes to us, to a very great extent, through artfully created events rather than personal confrontation or transmission through informal group networks.[24]

The importance of this for the development of social and political movements and for the emergence of charismatic figures lies in the necessity for actions that will become part of the mass culture, that will be reported and command attention. John McCarthy and Mayer

Zald have suggested that many social causes are today developed and advanced by small cadres of professional and otherwise skilled practitioners of the art of creating news, of giving the appearance of a vast public following.[25] The classic pattern of a movement with leaders and members may be inappropriate to this context, they maintain. Certainly the case of the Black Panthers is only one illustration of how the quest for the dramatic sense of conflict leads the media to confer "spokesman" status on those whose actions are exciting; it shows how conflict and flamboyance enable the actor to gain the attention and agenda of publics.

We are, then, asserting that the media and the popular culture they create are not solely neutral agencies, reflecting the society and its tensions. It is certainly true, as Bennett Berger maintains, that the products of mass culture are "culturally resonant"; they produce vivid responses "because they touch something vital or important (though perhaps not conscious) in the common life which they affirm, challenge, modify, or (if it is not yet conscious) create."[26] This is, of course, the case. But the forms of mass culture do more than reflect; they also refract. They define, explain, elaborate, and provide programs. They give to the vague and unspoken disturbances of their audiences "a local habitation and a name."

Mass culture accentuates the conflictful side of human society; it tends to move the awareness of events in the direction of the abstract. The inherent tensions between institutions and their grounds of legitimacy in principle are extended and reinforced.

The Disjuncture of Culture and Social Structure

Another way of viewing the importance of cultural media in modern life is found in the recognition of *the public nature of mass symbolic forms*. The public behavior of cultural forms is often sharply to be distinguished from the public behavior of institutions. While official agents of control often project a public morality more absolutist than the private, the popular arts often uphold, inform, and construct a more separate and critical morality, one that stands apart from and develops a body of description and myth in which ultimate principles conflict with each other and with the rules of social agencies and institutions.

Even the sheer monitoring of disorder and dissent, as we have suggested above, places against the belief in the facticity of order, the "reality" of dissent, criticism, and disorder. The individual finds that his imputation of conformity to others is unfounded and his own doubts are more shared than he had thought. The threat that this entails for others, for whom belief in the "reality" of the rules is significant, makes the affirmation process more essential than ever. The result is polarization—militant efforts by some to support, by others to reject, the legitimacy at the base of social order. The current "generation gap" has much of this character, each "side" feeding on the discussions and imputations in the public arena, fixing the meanings of events in an ever-wider conflict of ultimate principles.

Here we need again to consider the disjuncture described by Schumpeter between values embodied in institutions and those "free-floating" and maintained and transmitted through culture. Max Weber's view of modern society as organized, rationalized, bureaucratic, and technical has much in common with Schumpeter's view of capitalist culture. It left the modern world, for Weber, in a sad condition: "Specialists without spirit; sensualists without heart."[27] Schumpeter's judgment seems more correct. Even if Weber is right in his assessment of social organization, his is hardly a fair assessment of mass culture. Here the ultimate principles of passion, will, justice, and honor still have life. Great movies are made about Pattons, not about Eisenhowers.

Mass culture has about it the aura of the charismatic appeal to the sacred, the sentimental, and the heroic. Many of the themes recently celebrated as aspects of "counterculture" are old, traditional elements of American culture. Theodore Roszak subtitles his book on youth as a counterculture "Reflections on the Technocratic Society and its Youthful Opposition." The drama of news and popular art has continued and reinforced the basic themes of the current criticism of rationalism, technological progress, and organizational efficiency. Avid watchers of television "late shows" will find the plot of *The Graduate* repeated over and over in the movies of the past several decades, while the social structure of an industrial, bureaucratized, and organizational society based on scientific knowledge is seldom celebrated. The theme of *The Graduate* is not unique or even recent in American cultural life. It is a frequent message of the media: the race may be to the swift and the skilled, but the people of sentiment and feeling enunciate the sacred principles of the society in judgment of the workaday world. The only "culture hero" whose work provides drama, respect, and material success in the popular culture is the physician.[28]

Competent administrators, lawyers, generals, accountants, and janitors, and even physicians in routine work, are boring; neither do they uphold populistic, pietistic, and hedonistic values. The hero gains his interest from the contrast embodied in dramatic conflict against a corrupt social structure and the sacred values displayed in pure form. Mr. Deeds goes to Washington to end politics, not to win at it.

These problems of heroic virtues against routine, established roles and "systems" are, of course, often solved in different ways, with different qualifications, yet the mythic themes pose culture against social structure. Let me mention one such theme as an indication of what I mean by the culture-generating themes of social tension. One point of disjuncture is between *the alienated and the committed*. The hero must decide between giving in to the lures associated with institutional performance of tasks and the personal motives of ambition, on the one hand, and the prime importance of family, or love, or a "cause" that will impede his institutional tasks. How he solves the problem, how it is given meaning by the writers, or how compromises are developed vary, but the problem has now become publicly admissible and shared. The resolution probably will uphold the cultural values, find an acceptable compromise, or end on a note of bitterness.

What this theme assumes, however, is the very objectified view of American society that the sociological conceptions present, a rationalistic, organized set of events and relationships. Within such a world, the individual must struggle to maintain his self, not through society, but against it. The cultural media present both a view of "society" and a statement about the shared values of that "society" that place the social structure at the focus of opposition to culture. The popular culture of our times keeps alive a high level of dramatic excitement. In so doing, it accentuates the tensions inherent in the conflict between the realm of situated, everyday events and the abstractions of cultural thought. It contributes to a perception of society as a social order and a public that shares in the distrust of that order.

Weber's philosophy of history is far too fatalistic. The world of technological organization may be a disenchanted one, but the roots of enchantment do not wither. Men and women can and do examine the predicaments of history and respond to their fate. Modern society has its own characteristic means for stating and publicizing the conflicts in its operation, but we are not really in so iron a cage, nor is modern life so sterile, that Sentiment, Morality, and Honor do not retain their hold on our imagination and action.

NOTES

1. Jack D. Douglas, *American Social Order* (New York: Free Press, 1971), p. 240.

2. For this reason, a greart deal of empirical and observational sociology has a "debunking" character. It shows the discrepancy between actuality and the official or public conception of events and processes.

3. Joseph Gusfield and Michael Schwartz, "The Meanings of Occupational Prestige: Reconsideration of the NORC Scale," *American Sociological Review* 28 (1963): 265–71.

4. See the essay "Accounts," in Stanford Lyman and Marvin Scott, *A Sociology of the Absurd* (New York: Appleton-Century-Crofts, 1970). For general statements of the phenomenological perspective in sociology, see Harold Garfinkel, *Studies in Ethnomethodology* (New York: Prentice-Hall, 1967); and Jack D. Douglas, "Understanding Everyday Life," in Jack D. Douglas, ed., *Understanding Everyday Life* (Chicago: Aldine Publications, 1970); and *American Social Order*.

5. Douglas, *American Social Order*, p. 308.

6. "Once drawn into the mystery of the play, the spectator is compelled to come to terms with his experience. The stage supplies him with a number of disjointed clues that he has to fit into a meaningful pattern. . . . The time has been made to appear out of joint; the audience of the theatre of the absurd is being compelled to set it right." Martin Esslin, *The Theatre of the Absurd* (London: Eyre and Spottiswoods, 1961), p. 301.

7. Abbie Hoffman, *Revolution for the Hell of It* (New York: Dial Press, 1968), pp. 69–70.

8. Raymond Williams, *Culture and Society 1780–1950* (Garden City, N.Y.: Doubleday, Anchor Books, 1960), p. 319.

9. Edward Shils, "Mass Society and Its Culture," *Daedalus* 89 (1960): 288.

10. Steven Lukes, *Individualism* (Oxford: Basil Blackwell, 1973), pp. 3–16.

11. Isaih Berlin, *Four Essays on Liberty* (New York: Oxford University Press, 1969), pp. 63–64.

12. Karl Marx, "Critique of Political Economy," in *Capital and Other Writings* (New York: Modern Library, 1932), p. 10.

13. Robert Merton, "Social Structure and Anomie," *American Sociological Review* 3 (1938): 672.

14. An opposite view of "society" as process has often existed in sociology, though as a minor theme (Dennis Wrong, "The Over-Socialized Conception of Man in Modern Sociology," *American Sociological Review* 26 [1961]: 183–93). Recent writings of ethnomethodologists are again raising such theoretical issues, as in Harold Garfinkel's contention that conventional sociology falsely sees human beings as "cultural dopes." Cf. Garfinkel, *Studies in Ethnomethodology*.

15. Lionel Trilling, *Sincerity and Authenticity* (Cambridge: Harvard University Press, 1971); and cf. Ralph Turner, "The Real Self—From Institution to Impulse," *American Journal of Sociology* 81 (1976): 989–1017.

16. The Langs' study of the discrepancy between the event of the McArthur Day parade in Chicago and the television "coverage" illustrates the importance of reaching for dramatic affect in constructing "pseudo-events." Kurt Lang and Gladys Engel Lang, *Politics and Television* (Chicago: Quadrangle Books, 1968), chap. 2.

17. Leo Rosten, *The Washington Correspondents* (New York: Harcourt, Brace, 1937).

18. Kenneth Burke, *Permanence and Change*, 2d. rev. ed. (Indianapolis: Library of Liberal Arts, 1965), p. 292.

19. Ibid., p. 293.

20. The work of Orrin Klapp on contemporary heroes, as well as on mass culture in general, has been of profound importance. Klapp's view that much of

mass culture is an effort to balance the "banality" of contemporary existence seems unnecessarily functional. However, he provides abundant insight and evidence supporting the quest for and achievement of excitement through dramatic en- counters as central to mass culture. His analyses of hero-construction and villain-construction are similarly significant. Orrin Klapp, *Heroes, Villains and Fools* (Englewood Cliffs, N.J.: Prentice-Hall, 1962); *Symbolic Leadership* (Chicago: Aldine, 1964); *Collective Search for Identity* (New York: Holt, Rinehart & Winston, 1969).

21. Gary Marx, "Civil Disorder and the Agents of Social Control," *Journal of Social Issues* 26 (1970): 19–57; *The Kerner Report—Report of the National Advisory Commission on Civil Disorders* (New York: Bantam Books, 1968), chaps. 11, 12.

22. Klapp, *Symbolic Leadership*, esp. chap. 3.

23. *Time*, 10 May 1971, p. 18.

24. Herbert Blumer's classic account of the mass is based on this distinction between the traditional sociological view of behavior as interaction and the mass situation, in which assumptions of mutual awareness and response are absent. See Herbert Blumer, "Collective Behavior," in A. M. Lees, ed., *New Outlines of the Principles of Sociology* (New York: Barnes and Nobles, 1946), pp. 165–222; and William Kornhouser, *The Politics of Mass Society* (Glencoe: Free Press, 1959).

25. John McCarthy and Mayer Zald, *Social Movements in Modern America: Professionalization and Resource Mobilization* (Morristown, N.J.: General Learning Press, 1973).

26. Bennett Berger, *Looking for America: Essays on Youth, Suburbia and Other American Obsessions* (Englewood Cliffs, N.J.: Prentice-Hall, 1971), p. 4.

27. Max Weber, *The Protestant Ethic and the Spirit of Capitalism*, trans. Talcott Parsons (New York: Charles Scribner's Sons, 1930), p. 182.

28. David Beardslee and Donald O'Dowd, in an interesting study more than a decade ago, provided evidence for comparatively low esteem of businessmen, engineers, and lawyers among college students, and showed the concern of students with the style of life provided by an occupation and the lack of perception or approval of the work connected with it. David Beardslee and Donald O'Dowd, "Students and the Occupational World," in Nevitt Sanford, ed., *The American College* (New York: John Wiley & Sons, 1962).

3

THE SOCIAL BASIS OF UNSELFISHNESS

CHRISTOPHER JENCKS

One of the classic puzzles—perhaps *the* classic puzzle—of social theory is how society induces us to behave in ways that serve not our own private interest, but the common interest of society as a whole. Social scientists have developed a bewildering variety of vocabularies for analyzing this question, invoking concepts like "socialization," "operant conditioning," and "deterrence." In this essay I want to explore the advantages of reverting to a more primitive vocabulary. I think we can learn something by formulating the tension between public and private interests in traditional moral terms, that is, as a problem of selfishness versus unselfishness.

For these terms to be useful, however, they must be fairly precisely defined. I will describe individuals as "selfish" (or "egoistic") if (1) their subjective definition of their welfare does not include the welfare of others; or (2) their actual behavior indicates that they are not concerned with the welfare of others; or (3) their concern with the welfare of others is merely an instrumental means for promoting their own longer-term selfish ends, and ceases once these selfish ends can be more easily realized in some other way. A man with a sick business partner is thus "selfish" if (1) he does not care whether his partner recovers; or (2) he does not take obvious steps that would help his partner to recover; or (3) he only takes those steps if he believes that his partner's recovery will increase his own income. I will describe individuals as "unselfish" (or "altruistic") when they feel and act as if the long-term welfare of others is important *independent* of its effects on their own welfare.

Every motive or act falls somewhere on a spectrum between extreme selfishness and extreme unselfishness, depending on the relative weight we give our own interests and the interests of others. Most ethical theories imply that we should place the same weight on other people's interests as on our own when choosing a course of action. We should, in other words, pursue the greatest good of the greatest number, counting our own good as neither more nor less important than anyone else's. I will call this ideal "complete" unselfishness. In practice, few people live up to this "disinterested" ideal. Most of us do, however, take some account of the interests of the individuals affected by our behavior. I will call this "partial" unselfishness. In a few cases we may go to the opposite extreme, weighing other people's individual interests more heavily than our own. I will call this "extreme" unselfishness.

I will also distinguish three sources of unselfishness: empathy, community, and morality. What I will call "empathic unselfishness" derives from the fact that we "identify" with people outside ourselves. We incorporate their interests into our subjective welfare function, so that their interests become our own. As a result, our "selfish" interests are no longer synonymous with the interests of the biological organism in which our consciousness resides. When this process goes far enough, we say that we "love" the other individuals whose welfare concerns us.

What I will call "communitarian unselfishness" involves identification with a collectivity rather than with specific individuals. This collectivity can take virtually any form, but the most common examples in modern societies are probably the family, the work group, the nation-state, and the species. In each case we redefine our "selfish" interest so that it includes our subjective understanding of the interests of a larger collectivity of which we are a part. In large complex societies we usually identify at least partially with more than one such collectivity. This means that we can easily find ourselves in situations where the claims of different collectivities (for example, family and nation) conflict with one another as well as with our narrow self-interest.

Communitarian unselfishness can also take a more extreme form, at least in small homogeneous groups. In what Redfield called a "folk society," individuals identify so completely with the group to which they belong that they do not even imagine the possibility that their private interests could diverge from those of the group. By limiting imagination in this way, a society can, at least in theory, prevent individuals from even developing a sense of "self," and hence from conceiving courses of action that are "selfish" in the modern sense. While I find it hard to believe that any society is completely successful in doing this, what Tonnies characterized as "Gemeinschaft" and what Durkheim called "mechanical solidarity" both seem to assume something close to this result.

Moralistic unselfishness involves the incorporation of external moral ideals into our sense of "self." These moral ideals are usually derived from the collective culture of a larger group. For reasons I will discuss later, they usually imply that we should behave in ways that take account of other people's interests as well as our own. Once we have internalized such ideals, failure to follow them produces some sort of inner conflict (for example, between "superego" and "id"). Since such conflict is painful, we are often willing to sacrifice the interests of the id in order to quiet the superego.

These three varieties of unselfishness can lead to quite different forms of behavior. Empathy, for example, usually induces us to promote the interests of some specific individual, whereas communitarian unselfishness encourages us to promote the interests of a larger group. The two can therefore conflict. Likewise, moralistic unselfishness involves the subordination of self to some principle, the application of which may well conflict with the interests of other individuals with whom we empathize, as well as with our own selfish interests. Many of the moral dilemmas that fascinate philosophers and novelists involve precisely such conflicts between varieties of unselfishness, rather than just conflicts between selfishness and unselfishness.

All three varieties of unselfishness involve a redefinition or transformation of the self so as to incorporate "outside" elements. Once the self is transformed in this way, there is a sense in which all acts are selfish. Because of this, some cynics like to argue that unselfishness is impossible. Every voluntary act, even if it leads to death, must serve some "selfish" end, since otherwise we would not have chosen it. But such reasoning still leaves us with the problem of distinguishing behavior that takes no account of the ultimate welfare of others from behavior that is at least partially concerned with the welfare of others. Labels like "selfish" and "unselfish" allow us to make this useful distinction, which is why they persist despite efforts to get by without them.

The psychological mechanisms that lead to unselfishness also play a major role in selfish behavior. At least as ordinarily conceived, selfishness involves concern with one's own welfare *over time*. To be selfish is to be concerned not just with the welfare of the person I now am, but with the welfare of the person I will become in a day, a year, or even fifty years. Those who are indifferent to the welfare of these future selves are usually described as "irrational." The mechanisms that make us take account of the welfare of our future selves are, I think, much the same as the mechanisms that make us take account of others. One reason for altruism vis-à-vis our future selves is that we empathize with the person we will later become and anticipate how he or she will feel if we choose a given course of action. We save for our old age, for example, because we imagine what it would be like to be old and poor. If we cannot imagine this, we may not save. A second reason for altruistic acts vis-à-vis our future selves is that we have internalized the general principle that we ought to be "prudent." Not saving for our old age, for example, makes some of us feel guilty. A third, less common, reason for altruism vis-à-vis our future selves is that we identify with a larger group. ("If I get drunk tonight, I will not play well tomorrow, and that would be letting down the team.") Individuals who cannot empathize with the person they will eventually become (for example, adolescents), and who do not feel guilty when they act imprudently, are likely to act selfishly vis-à-vis their future selves.

The remainder of the essay has four parts. First, I will argue that, contrary to the claims of many influential social theorists since Hobbes, a complex society cannot survive if all its members are governed by exclusively selfish motives. Second, I will explore the effects of genetic selection on the evolution of unselfish behavior. Next, I will discuss the implications of cultural selection, which are quite different from those of genetic selection. Finally, having explored the tension between genetic and cultural selection, I will conclude with some speculations about the implications of my analysis for American society.

HOBBES AND BEYOND

Virtually all of us assume that when interests conflict, most of our neighbors will habitually place their own interest ahead of other people's. When this does not happen, we are pleasantly surprised. Most people also see this tendency toward selfishness as one of the prime sources of human misery. There are two distinct responses to this situation, one of which I will label "idealistic," the other "cynical."

Idealists respond to human selfishness by trying to reduce its prevalence. Christianity, for example, exhorts the faithful to do unto others as they would have others do unto them. Maoism urges its adherents to "serve the people" selflessly. Indeed, virtually every movement for radical social change seeks to transform not only social institutions, but also individual consciousness in such a way as to make people less selfish.

Cynics dismiss all attempts to reduce the prevalence of selfishness as "utopian." Instead, they concentrate on trying to limit the damaging consequences of pervasive selfishness. This means arranging social institutions so that the private pursuit of selfish advantage also promotes the common good. This ideal has dominated Anglo-American economic thought for the past three hundred years. Its most elegant and influential expression is probably *The Wealth of Nations*, where Adam Smith shows that under not unusual conditions, competitive markets ensure that the pursuit of private advantage will maximize economic output. The same general approach has also pervaded Anglo-American political theory. Classical liberal theorists argued that the purpose of the state was to maximize citizens' freedom to pursue their selfish ends. More recently, many democratic theorists have argued that if politicians compete for votes in the same way that merchants compete for customers, these politicians will tend to adopt policies that promote the greatest good of the greatest number. In all these visions, society is simply a machine for resolving conflicts between selfish individuals and perhaps helping them to pursue shared objectives more effectively. It is not a system for making people less selfish or even reshaping their selfish impulses.

Thomas Hobbes was the first English theorist to argue that society could be organized around entirely selfish motives. Since his *Leviathan* (1651) presages most of what has come since, it provides a convenient illustration of the problems posed by this view. *Leviathan* argues that men are driven by "a perpetual and restless desire of Power after power, that ceaseth only in Death." In the absence of some collective restraint on this "natural" impulse, such a populace would engage in a permanent "war of all against all." The result would be anarchy, in which life was, in Hobbes' most famous phrase, "solitary, poore, nasty, brutish, and short." The only way to end this war is through a contract. Whatever its form, the aim of the contract is to bring "peace." Its substance is that each citizen should forswear violence and "be contented with so much liberty against other men, as he would allow other men against himselfe."

It is clear why people agree to such a contract. Given the dangers of the war of all against all, we want to restrain others' depredations against ourselves. But having agreed to such a contract, why abide by it? From a strictly selfish viewpoint, our interest is merely to persuade *others* to abide by the contract. We have no reason for sticking to the contract ourselves unless violating it would encourage others to do the same at our expense. If we can violate the contract without detection, why not do so?

Hobbes saw only two possible reasons why men might abide by the social contract: "either a Feare of the consequence of breaking their word; or a Glory or Pride in not appearing to breake it." Pride, he argued, was seldom sufficient to ensure that individuals kept to the contract, so fear had to be the dominant motive. Fear could come in either of two varieties: fear of the "Power of Spirits Invisible" or fear of "the Power of those men they shall therein Offend." Of these two, Hobbes wrote, "though the former be the greatest Power, yet the feare of the latter is commonly the greater Feare."

Fear of detection and punishment may well suffice to enforce the social contract in small communities where nobody has much privacy and few people have dealings with strangers. Those who violate rules against prohibited forms of selfishness are likely to be detected, and once detected they can easily be punished, either formally or informally. But in a large society, where one is often dealing with strangers and where one also has a certain amount of privacy even vis-à-vis others whom one knows, we can no longer be certain that prohibited forms of selfishness will be detected. We do not usually know, for example, when someone fails to report a fire. We simply assume that the fire was unnoticed. Even when we know that someone has violated a rule, the culprit may be impossible to identify or punish. Large complex societies develop formal policing systems to deal with this problem, but this is not in itself sufficient. If *everyone* responds to privacy and anonymity by pursuing his or her selfish interests, the number of individuals who violate established norms will soon be very large. This will lower the odds that any individual "cheater" will be caught and punished, leading to a further increase in cheating. Eventually this vicious circle will lead to a collapse of the established social order and a return to the war of all against all. Policing is only feasible when violations are relatively infrequent and when the police themselves are relatively committed to the norms they enforce.

Some argue, of course, that even if only a small proportion of cheaters are caught, society can deter violations by making the penalties for cheating much larger than the potential benefits. If there is "too much" cheating, according to this view, society can always increase the severity of the penalties against those whom it catches. This changes the "expected" cost of a violation, at least in a mathematical sense. Experience suggests, however, that neither the probability nor the severity of punishment explains most of the variance in crime rates. The cleanliness of public parks does not, for example, bear much relationship to the number of police patrolling the park or the size of the fine for littering. This does not mean that deterrence is completely ineffective, but it does suggest that Hobbes' analysis of our reasons for conforming to the social contract is incomplete.

The missing element is not far to seek. We abide by the social contract partly because we have "moral" ideas. We ask not only whether acts are "prudent" or "imprudent," but whether they are "right" or "wrong." For Hobbes, moral ideas seem to reflect our anticipation of divine retribution. But if that were their main source, they should have disappeared with the rise of religious scepticism in the eighteenth century. Since this did not happen, an alternative explanation is needed. Perhaps the best is Adam Smith's *Theory of Moral Sentiments* (1759).

Smith argues that moral ideas derive from our capacity for what he calls "sympathy," or what we would now call "empathy." Because we are capable of experiencing the pleasure and pain of others, we cannot be completely selfish. Furthermore—and this is vitally important— Smith asserts that we *value* sympathy with others as an end in itself. We want to experience the pleasure and pain of others and to have them experience ours. (Even for Hobbes, one of the drawbacks of the state of nature was its being "solitary.") But in order to maintain this kind of emotional interchange with others, Smith argues, we must protect ourselves against one of its most common consequences: casual or unjust judgments of our behavior by others. We therefore develop standards of what others "ought" to think about our conduct. To do this, we try to see our behavior "objectively," that is, as others would see it. This means trying to evaluate our behavior from a perspective in which our selfish interests count no more than the interests of others. These "moral" standards are, in principle, independent of any particular individual's judgment.

The linkage between moral ideas and selflessness recurs over and over in subsequent theories. Rawls, for example, argues that we carry out the social contract not merely because we are afraid to break it, but because we are positively attracted to a "just" society, and because we feel rules are "just" if they are the rules we would agree to if we did not know our selfish interests. Our capacity to imagine such rules is, I think, inextricably tied to our ability to experience the disapproval others would express if they knew we had broken such rules. We know what others would say or feel, and we know how we would respond. Such vicarious feelings are not likely to be as strong as feelings about real events, but for most people this is a difference of degree, not of kind.

If this argument is correct, the viability of the social contract depends not just on society's capacity to inspire fear in the hearts of potential violators, but on its capacity to develop the empathic tendencies from which moral sentiments derive. If a society can do this, it can expect its members to act unselfishly at least some of the time. When we calculate the costs and benefits of a particular action, we will include not only its costs and benefits to ourselves, but also its costs and benefits to the others who populate our imagination. The weight we attach to the presumed judgments of these "significant others" may be less than the weight we attach to our own selfish judgment, but it will seldom be zero. (When it is, we judge an individual "morally deficient" or "psychopathic.") The views we impute to our imaginary others may also be quite unrealistic, but again, they are seldom completely fanciful. (When they are, we judge an individual "psychotic.")

Empathy is not, of course, the primary mechanism for enforcing the social contract on a day-to-day basis. Rather, enforcement depends on the fact that people have moral ideas. These ideas have a life of their own. They can, indeed, prevent us from acting unselfishly vis-à-vis those with whom we empathize when such actions would, at least in theory, have negative consequences for others with whom we do not empathize. When Kohlberg asks respondents whether a man should steal a drug to save his wife's life, for example, he is asking, among other things, whether they endorse a universalistic morality based on concern for anonymous others, or a particularistic morality based on empathy.

Furthermore, while the existence of moral ideas probably depends on our collective capacity for empathy, the force of these ideas in the lives of particular individuals seems to depend on many factors besides the intensity with which they empathize with others. In the caricature version of psychoanalytic theory, for example, the development of empathy depends on a warm, loving mother, while the development of moral standards depends on a powerful, punitive father. Whether for this reason or others, there are plenty of people whose behavior seems to be deeply influenced by moral ideals that demand a high level of unselfishness, but who nonetheless show little sign of participating vicariously in the pleasure or suffering of those whom their unselfishness benefits. This suggests that we should not equate cultural dynamics with psychodynamics, or assume that the logic of cultural evolution is the same as the logic of individual development.

One reason why cultural dynamics differ from psychodynamics is that patterns of behavior that are desirable from a cultural viewpoint are often undesirable from an individual perspective. It seems clear, for example, that society as a whole would be better off if the combined effect of empathy, community, and morality were to ensure that everyone always abided by the social contract. Yet we know that no society has ever come close to achieving this goal. In order to understand why this has never happened, it is helpful to look more closely at the mechanisms by which natural selection operates.

THE GENETIC TRAP

Our genetic heritage limits the likely range of human behavior in innumerable ways. Genes, for example, provide the physiological basis for empathizing with others. Physiology also ensures that we will almost always experience our own pleasure or pain more vividly than we experience the pleasure or pain of others. Humans are thus "partial empathizers." This is a quite predictable by-product of spontaneous variation and natural selection over many generations.

Consider the likely fate of a "complete empathizer." Suppose that genetic mutations occasionally produced individuals who empathized completely with the pleasures and pains of those around them. These mutants would presumably act completely unselfishly vis-à-vis everyone they encountered. If they saw a fellow human attacked by a predator, for example, they would come to the victim's aid whenever the likely benefit to the victim exceeded the likely risk to themselves. This would be a very satisfactory state of affairs if the victims were also complete empathizers, and therefore reciprocated whenever the tables were turned. But if the victims were only partial empathizers, they would often fail to reciprocate. A complete empathizer's chances of surviving and leaving altruistic progeny would therefore be less than a partial empathizer's chances of doing so. The genes that led to total empathy would therefore be subject to negative selection and would eventually be eliminated from the population.

Next consider the fate of a "nonempathizer." At first glance it might seem that natural selection would favor nonempathizers over partial empathizers, since a nonempathizer would not be likely to take any risks on behalf of others, and would therefore have a greater chance of leaving surviving offspring. There are, however, three common circumstances in which failure to take risks for others will reduce the odds that our genes will be represented in later generations. The most obvious circumstance is where the risks are taken on behalf of our own offspring. I know of no hard evidence that empathy is essential for effective parenting, but the assumption is widely shared by parents, social workers, pediatricians, and psychiatrists. If partial empathizers took better care of their offspring than nonempathizers, the genes responsible for partial empathy would gradually spread through the entire population.

A second hazard of nonempathy is its likely effect on one's behavior toward other relatives. Individuals share more of their genes with their immediate relatives than with other members of their species. Siblings, for example, share about half the genes that ordinarily vary within a species. This means that if I engage in altruistic acts that increase my siblings' chances of survival, I have a 50–50 chance of facilitating the survival of my own genes, including those that make me act altruistically. This means that there will be positive selection over time for altruistic acts that increase my siblings' chances of survival by more than twice as much as they reduce my chances of survival.[1] If altruism toward relatives depends on empathy, nonempathizers' genes may be less likely to survive over time than partial empathizers' genes.

The third problem posed by the absence of empathy is its likely effect on what Robert Trivers calls "reciprocal altruism."[2] By this he means an ongoing pattern of interaction in which I help you, then you help me, and so on. If each helpful act involves some risk to the actor but a greater benefit to the recipient, such interactions will eventually benefit both parties. Genetic selection will favor such acts in relatively small closed systems, where each party can expect the other to reciprocate, though not in large open systems, where there is a low probability that those for whom I take risks will be in a position to reciprocate or can be induced to do so. Within a small closed system, genetic selection will also favor what Trivers calls "moralistic aggression," that is, punitive behavior toward those who are not sufficiently altruistic toward me. At the same time, genetic selection will favor what Trivers labels "subtle cheating," that is, behavior that looks altruistic (and thus forestalls moralistic aggression), but that really minimizes the risk to the actor.

What Trivers calls reciprocal altruism is not really altruistic in my sense of the term; rather, it is a matter of "enlightened self-interest." But the label is not critical in the present context. The important point is that reciprocal altruism among humans seems to depend on what we ordinarily call "trust," and trust probably depends to some extent on empathy. If nonempathizers never trusted anyone, they would never engage in reciprocal altruism, and this would probably reduce their chances of leaving surviving offspring.

If the foregoing analysis is correct, we would expect genetic selection to eliminate *both* empathizers *and* nonempathizers, leaving a population composed entirely of partial empathizers. We would also expect greater empathy vis-à-vis offspring, relatives, and acquaintances with whom one has a reciprocal relationship. As a practical matter, we cannot control empathy this precisely. We do, however, seem to empathize primarily with individuals who occupy roles that are usually occupied by kin, offspring, or acquaintances, that is, those with whom we have frequent and prolonged visual contact. Rationing empathy in this way minimizes altruistic acts vis-à-vis strangers, and therefore minimizes the likelihood of unproductive risk taking.

To the extent that human behavior depends on genes, then, we expect it to be only fitfully and partially unselfish, with continuous subtle cheating by nominal adherents to the social contract and flagrant cheating by strangers, who are not part of an ongoing system that can enforce the social contract. This pattern of behavior is by no means ideal from the viewpoint of the species as a whole, since it implies that humans will often fail to help one another in circumstances where such help would increase the overall survival rate of the species.

Suppose, for example, that a committee was charged with drawing up guidelines on how we should respond when we saw someone drowning, and that the committee's sole objective was to multiply the human race as fast as possible—an admittedly tawdry goal. The committee would presumably suggest that we first estimate the number of additional offspring both we and the victim could expect if we both survived. This would presumably depend on our age, marital status, physical health, and the like. Then the committee would suggest that we estimate the likelihood of saving the victim and the likelihood of drowning ourselves if we adopted various courses of action. Finally, it would tell us to choose the course of action that maximized the number of offspring both we and the victim could expect to produce in the future, paying no attention to whether these offspring were our own or the victim's. The committee would, in short, tell us to be complete altruists.

Genetic selection would almost never favor this response. If our behavior depended entirely on our genes, and if these had been selected for optimal fitness in this specific situation (an admittedly unlikely situation), we would first determine whether the victim was a relative, an acquaintance who could be expected to help us at some future date, or a stranger. If the victim was a relative, we would attempt a rescue only if this increased the probability that our genes would be represented in future generations. This would depend on the fraction of our genes we shared with the victim, our expected fertility relative to that of the victim, and the relative risk to us and the victim of various courses of action. If our expected future fertility was the same as the victim's, we would always respond in partially rather than completely altruistic ways. Much the same logic would apply to acquaintances. We would try to rescue them only if the risk to ourselves was smaller than the combined probability that by taking this risk we would *both* save the victim *and* allow the victim to save us at some future date. Since the second contingency is never absolutely certain, we would never respond as complete altruists. Finally, if the victim was a complete stranger, genetic selection would give us no reason to attempt a rescue.

The fact that genes are passed on by individuals, not groups, thus means that genetic selection favors behavior that is far from optimal for the group. To escape this genetic trap a group must devise some way of modifying the effects of genetic selection on individual behavior.

CULTURAL SELECTION

Human behavior depends not only on genes but also on past experience. This means that we can sometimes structure other people's experience so as to alter behavior that does not work to our advantage.

In general, each of us has an interest in persuading others to act altruistically toward us. One possible way of doing this is to get others to empathize with us. Another possibility is to convince them that unless they are unselfish they will be severely punished (via moralistic aggression). Still another possibility is to get others to internalize altruistic norms, so that they punish themselves for violations. We all try to manipulate other people's behavior in such ways, but other people also resist our efforts. Unless we are larger and cleverer than the other person—as we are vis-à-vis our children—our individual efforts to manipulate others are seldom very successful.

But when the number of individuals attempting to manipulate a given person's behavior becomes large, resistance becomes increasingly difficult. This happens, for example, when a group collectively tries to manipulate the behavior of its individual members. If the group is united, it can sometimes drastically alter patterns of behavior favored by genetic selection. It can, for example, induce members of the group to sacrifice their lives for the group's welfare. It can also induce them to place more value on principles like "honor," "friendship," and "loyalty" than on survival.

All cultures engage in such collective efforts at manipulating individual behavior. But not all cultures promote the same kinds of behavior, and those with similar goals are not all equally successful in attaining them. While the range of cultural variation over the centuries is far from exhaustive, it is still impressive. This means that there has been considerable room for cultural as well as genetic selection.

While the principles of cultural selection are far from clear, a norm's chances of surviving are related to at least two factors. First, the norm must be compatible with the development of military organizations that can protect those who accept the norm. Second, for a norm to become widespread today, it must be compatible with reasonably efficient organization of economic production and distribution. This is partly because efficient economic organization provides a surplus to support military activities, and partly because it allows population growth.

One prerequisite of both military and economic efficiency, I believe, is effective inhibition of many kinds of selfishness. Let us begin with an extreme case: military combat. Members of a combat unit must be willing to risk death. If they take this risk only when they fear a court martial, they will not make a very effective unit. First, they will avoid engaging the enemy whenever possible. Then, if engagement is unavoidable, they will minimize risks to themselves individually, even when this increases the risks to other members of the unit. Such behavior will lower the unit's overall survival rate while raising the enemy's survival rate. The more nearly altruistic the members of a unit are relative to one another, the higher their overall survival rate is likely to be, and the lower the likely survival rate of the enemy.

Or consider a nation seeking to mobilize large numbers of men and machines for military defense. Such a nation must somehow persuade its citizens to abide by a rather elaborate set of rules aimed at promoting the common defense. If citizens abide by these rules only when they believe this serves their private interests, large numbers of violations will occur. Extensive policing may reduce violations, but one can only police activities if they are organized so that every participant's behavior is, in principle, "public." This requires a division of labor far less efficient than the division that would be selected if everyone could be expected to subordinate his or her private interests to the common defense without policing. Of course, no culture can make its citizens completely selfless. But even a very low level of unselfishness suffices to solve many problems, for it eliminates cheating where the private benefits are small relative to the collective costs —a very common situation.

We can formulate this general argument somewhat differently by noting that efficient organizations usually have two distinctive features. First, they coordinate the activities of many people who are virtual strangers to one another. In order to operate efficiently, a large organization must dissuade such strangers from exploiting every available opportunity for personal advantage. In cultures where taking advantage of strangers is the norm, large organizations have great difficulty imposing sanctions that are sufficient to make the organization function smoothly. This is partly because sanctions themselves are hard to implement in an unprincipled system, since the prospective victims find it easy to buy off the enforcers.

A second distinctive feature of efficient organizations is that they provide many of their members with a significant amount of individual discretion in their behavior. This means that individuals have many opportunities for subtle cheating. If all members engage in subtle cheating, the organization must reduce the amount of discretion through more extensive policing. Yet this often lowers morale and thereby encourages even more cheating in the remaining areas of discretion. This forces still further reductions in discretion, leading to further reductions in morale. This downward spiral eventually produces the GI mentality, in which everyone is completely cynical and nobody does more than absolutely necessary.

The pivotal role of unselfishness emerges in somewhat different form if one considers the social prerequisites of urbanization. Some degree of urbanization clearly enhances economic efficiency by reducing communication and transportation costs. But urbanization also increases the number of potential interactions among strangers. There is no way of policing all these potential interactions. Thus if all strangers deal completely selfishly with one another, the crime rate will be extremely high. If all opportunities for profitable crime were taken, urban life would be impossible. Society would have to revert to smaller, more physically separated communities that could police themselves internally and restrict access by strangers.

The foregoing examples suggest that cultures are likely to spread to the degree that they can inhibit individual selfishness and induce their members to abide by behavioral norms laid down by the group as a whole. But if complete subordination of individual interests to collective goals facilitates the survival and spread of cultures, why have no cultures actually achieved this end? Or to use a slightly different language, why is socialization not more effective? The answer appears to be that while cultural selection favors complete altruism, genetic selection favors limited altruism vis-à-vis kin, subtle cheating vis-à-vis acquaintances, and complete egoism vis-à-vis strangers. Powerful as culture is, it cannot fully overcome this genetic heritage.

The fact that cultural selection favors different behavior patterns from genetic selection has many complex consequences. If each selection system operated independently of the other, observed behavior would be a mixture of selfishness and unselfishness. But each selection system also tries to modify the other. Genetic selection, for example, not only encourages varieties of selfishness that are not favored by cultural selection, but encourages defensive rationalizations about the social value of such selfishness. These rationalizations then become part of the culture. Indeed, Donald Campbell interprets the bulk of twentieth-century psychotherapy in this light.[3] I would say the same about Social Darwinism and the Chicago school of economics. At the same time, however, cultural support for altruism can modify the effects of natural selection on the gene pool. In the simplest case, a culture may encourage its members to kill off individuals who are insufficiently altruistic. Genetic selection also favors this kind of moralistic aggression, but only when the benefit to specific aggressors exceeds the cost. Cultural selection may favor it even when the risks to specific aggressors are high, so long as the aggression increases the overall survival rate for the group as a whole. Cultural selection may also favor changes in breeding patterns that alter gene frequencies. If altruistic risk takers find it easier to attract or keep mates, for example, this may lead to positive rather than negative selection for altruistic risk taking.

The interpenetration of genetic and cultural selection systems also allows unusually powerful individuals or groups within a society to manipulate cultural norms so as to promote their selfish ends. Their success in doing this will be directly proportional to their capacity to persuade others that the norms in question actually promote the common good rather than the good of a particular subgroup. As a result, the culture as a whole is likely to embody a complex mix of partially contradictory norms, some of which promote the common good, some of which merely appear to promote the common good while actually promoting the interests of powerful subgroups, and some of which explicitly assert the legitimacy of individual selfishness.

It is also important to emphasize that the tension between genetic and cultural selection involves only those traits that can affect either our own chances of survival or our chances of leaving surviving offspring. This is an important limitation. Most human behavior, including unselfish behavior, has no direct effect on anyone's chances of surviving. Instead, it is directed toward enhancing the subjective well-being of individuals whose survival depends on other factors. Behavior that affects only subjective well-being is subject to genetic selection only if it is caused by underlying propensities, like empathy or guilt, that also affect an individual's chances of surviving or leaving surviving offspring. If there are forms of unselfishness that do not depend on traits that affect survival, these forms of unselfishness will not be subject to negative genetic selection.

This points to a more fundamental difficulty. While it is analytically useful to label many different forms of behavior as "selfish" or "unselfish," the use of a single label encourages the illusion that there is a single underlying trait ("unselfishness") that determines whether an individual engages in all these different forms of behavior. This seems unlikely. While I know of no systematic data on the extent to which an individual's propensity to act unselfishly in one context predicts his or her propensity to act unselfishly in other contexts, casual observation suggests that different kinds of unselfishness are only loosely related to one another. This is hardly surprising, given the multitude of motives that affect unselfish behavior. Intense empathy with another individual, strong identification with a larger group, and a strong propensity to follow universalistic rules need not arise in the same individuals. Furthermore, none of these three sources of unselfishness is itself a unitary trait. Those who empathize intensely with one person may not emphathize with another, and the same holds for those who identify with one or another larger group. Even the intensity of an individual's commitment to universalistic moral rules will vary according to his or her past experience with the specific rule and the situation to which it nominally applies.

My concern in this essay is not with explaining individual behavior but with explaining differences between cultures. Again, however, we cannot simply assume that because a culture induces people to engage in one variety of unselfish behavior, it will be equally successful in getting them to engage in other varieties of unselfish behavior as well. Thus there is no guarantee that we will be able to characterize cultures as unusually successful in promoting unselfishness as a whole. Furthermore, even if we could characterize cultures in this way, there is no guarantee that historical selection will favor cultures that promote unselfishness in general. Rather, historical selection is likely to favor those forms of unselfishness that contribute to military and economic success. It may be quite indifferent to other forms of unselfishness, even though they contribute in important ways to the subjective well-being of those who participate in the culture.

UNSELFISHNESS IN AMERICA

Almost twenty years ago Gabriel Almond and Sidney Verba asked American, British, West German, Italian, and urban Mexican adults, "Would you say that most people are more inclined to help others, or more inclined to look out for themselves?" This is a strong question. To give an "altruistic" response one must believe—or claim to believe—that the world is composed primarily of complete, rather than just partial, altruists. This seems highly unlikely. Nonetheless, 31 percent of all Americans asserted that helping others was more common than selfishness. This proportion was lower in the other four countries: 28 percent in Great Britain, 15 percent in both West

Germany and urban Mexico, and a mere 5 percent in Italy.⁴ Many social psychologists interpret respondents' answers to questions like this as a projective measure of the respondent's own motives. But it also seems likely that answers to these questions are to some extent affected by reality. Rather than automatically treating national differences in perceived selfishness as reflecting different perceptions of the same underlying reality ("human nature"), we must therefore consider the possibility that respondents are describing different realities, simply because they live in different countries. We must, in other words, entertain the hypothesis that Americans are less selfish in their dealings with one another than the residents of England, West Germany, Italy, or urban Mexico.

The only systematic attempt to test this hypothesis seems to be Roy Feldman's comparative data on Boston, Paris, and Athens.⁵ When dealing with compatriots, Bostonians were more likely than Parisians or Athenians to give directions to a stranger, mail a letter for a stranger, and return change that a stranger left in a store. Residents of the three cities were equally unlikely to falsely claim money found on the ground by an unknown compatriot, and cab drivers in the three cities were equally unlikely to cheat a compatriot. When the stranger was a foreigner, however, the results were less consistent. Bostonians were more willing than Athenians or Parisians to give directions to a foreigner, but were less willing to mail letters and return change to foreigners.

It is hard to trace the apparently greater unselfishness of the Americans vis-à-vis their compatriots to distinctively American cultural values. American culture has never placed great emphasis on the bonds that link people to one another, or on obligations of any sort. Whereas the French revolutionaries proclaimed liberty, equality, and fraternity as coequal goals, the Americans were almost exclusively concerned with liberty and paid virtually no attention to fraternity. This ideology has persisted. When Tocqueville sought to characterize the Americans of 1830, he said, "They owe nothing to any man; they expect nothing from any man. They acquire the habit of always considering themselves as standing alone."⁶ Yet as Tocqueville emphasized, these same Americans created an extraordinary number of voluntary associations—associations that are seldom viable if every member calculates his self-interest narrowly and refuses to contribute more than he personally gets back from his efforts. It may therefore be the case that individualism was more an ideology than a way of life even in the 1830s.

As an ideology, however, individualism has persisted down to the present day. We continue to give liberty priority over fraternity. Indeed, the very word "fraternity" sounds alien to most Americans. When I have asked students to define it, they have been nonplussed. Likewise, when I have asked them to define "community," they have almost all assumed that this was a strictly geographic concept. They do not seem to have even a basic vocabulary for discussing the ties that bind us all together, much less a developed ideology regarding the importance of these ties. They find Adam Smith's notion that we value empathy as an end in itself quite startling, though they often accept its validity after some discussion. Nor is this kind of individualism confined to the middle classes. The ideal of working-class "solidarity," for example, plays a far smaller role in the rhetoric of the American labor movement than in that of most European ones.

The primacy of liberty over fraternity in American ideology is also apparent in our attitudes toward equality. Liberty and fraternity are "ultimate" goods. We value them as ends in themselves. Equality, in contrast, is usually valued as a means for promoting either liberty or fraternity. A country committed to fraternity rejects inequality when it divides people from one another and leads the more advantaged to treat the less advantaged as if they were not fully human. A country committed to liberty, in contrast, rejects inequality when it places unacceptable limits on the choices available to the least advantaged.

America's concern with equality has derived largely from its concern with liberty. The War on Poverty, for example, was advertised as an effort to give the poor certain basic "rights" that other Americans already enjoyed. These rights were said to include not only a wider range of consumer choices, but legal services, medical care, and better education as well. In assessing its success in eliminating poverty, the government measured changes in the absolute standard of living of the least advantaged members of society. The fact that the purchasing power of the poorest fifth of all families rose by 51 percent between 1960 and 1970 was therefore taken as evidence that poverty had been sharply reduced during this decade.

But as Lee Rainwater and others have forcefully argued, people do not in fact experience poverty primarily as a restriction on their personal freedom. Rather, what they experience is exclusion from a social community. When a family's disposable income falls too far below that of its neighbors, the family is no longer able to participate in what Rainwater calls "socially validated" activities.[7] Its members cannot act or feel as if they were part of the same social system as their more affluent neighbors. This means that if poor people's incomes rise, but their neighbors' incomes rise even faster, the poor will not feel better off. They will feel worse off. If the poor define their poverty in such relativistic terms, the only way to eliminate it is to narrow the economic distance between the poor and the middle classes. There was some movement in this direction during the 1960s, since the incomes of the poorest fifth of all families rose from 26 to 29 percent of the national average between 1960 and 1970. But the important point is that neither the American government nor the American people defined success in these terms, or cited statistics of this kind in assessing the success of federal efforts to reduce poverty. Fraternity was not our goal.

America's persistent emphasis on personal liberty is also fundamentally at odds with cultural efforts to inhibit selfishness. Our responses to psychotherapy illustrate this point. Freud taught us that moral inhibitions were often neurotic by-products of our subjugation to parental authority in childhood, but he also argued that civilization could not survive without these inhibitions. Americans seem for the most part to have heard only the first part of this message. For us, therapy has become synonymous with personal "liberation." Both therapists and patients tend to talk as if their joint aim were simply to eliminate feelings of guilt. Some therapists even make explicit efforts to promote selfishness on the patient's part. For extreme altruists who have spent a lifetime subordinating their needs to those of the people around them, this may be essential advice. But extreme altruism is hardly the characteristic disorder of our time.

Guilt is not the only mechanism for inhibiting selfishness that a libertarian culture denigrates. Liberals also tend to be suspicious of rituals that encourage individuals to identify with larger groups, whether these be college fraternities, national corporations, or the nation itself. Such rituals conjure up images of Hitler and Nuremberg. Even empathy can be suspect unless it is restricted to individuals we have selected voluntarily, like friends and lovers. When empathy leads to a diffuse fear of the reactions of colleagues, neighbors, or other involuntary associates, we often feel that this is a sign of weakness rather than sensitivity.

If these ideological tendencies had actually shaped American behavior, urbanization and industrialization would have been almost impossible. This is an ideology suitable only for a nation of yeoman farmers, such as America was two hundred years ago. The fact is, however, that Americans have adapted remarkably successfully to the demands of large-scale organization. This seems to reflect the fact that despite our individualistic rhetoric and libertarian ideology, our actual behavior has been less selfish than that of individuals in many other societies. Indeed, I suspect that America's ideological emphasis on personal liberty derives in part from the fact that we take for granted a wide range of social and moral limitations on selfish behavior, without which personal liberty would seem far less attractive. Conversely, I suspect that the Italian Communists' emphasis on solidarity is at least in part an attempt to counterbalance a pervasive national tendency toward what Wilson and Banfield call "private-regarding" as against "public-regarding" behavior.[8] Likewise, Mao's emphasis on selflessness and asceticism in China may well reflect the fact that the Chinese Communist Party was born into a chaotic, brutalized society in which selflessness was almost unheard of. Creating even a moderately tolerable social order therefore required a drastic change in the personal behavior of millions of people, for which heroic rhetoric seemed necessary. In Japan, in contrast, the network of reciprocal obligations and group loyalties inherited from the feudal era was never completely shattered, and selfishness was never given completely free rein. As a result, there seems to have been less need for rhetorical emphasis on selflessness.[9]

If the relationship between cultural norms and actual behavior is as problematic as these observations imply, we must obviously exercise extreme caution in making inferences about historical changes in behavior from evidence regarding changes in cultural norms. Nonetheless, I am impressed by the fact that Riesman's historical analysis of American national character in *The Lonely Crowd* can also be interpreted as an analysis of the mechanisms by which American society has inhibited selfishness.

What Riesman calls "tradition-directed" societies presumably inhibited selfishness by encouraging individuals to identify more or less completely with the larger community of which they were a part. There is reason to doubt that medieval Europe, which served as Riesman's nominal model for "tradition-direction," ever fitted this picture very well. But if we take the American Indians rather than European peasants as the predecessors of the New England Puritans, the model may be applicable.

In what Riesman calls "inner-directed" societies, selfishness is no longer restrained primarily by identification with the group, but rather by the internalization of moral norms. This moral "gyroscope," as Riesman calls it, allows a group to control individual behavior to some significant extent even when the group is no longer sufficiently cohesive to prevent the individual from realizing that his or her self-interest is not synonymous with the interest of the group. This machinery works reasonably well so long as (1) the principles that an individual learns from his or her parents remain compatible with the group's collective welfare throughout the individual's lifetime; and (2) the group is willing to pay the human price required to instill such principles; and (3) the group is willing to let individuals follow these principles even when they conflict with the claims of group loyalty and empathy. But as the rate of social change accelerates, individuals must learn to regulate their behavior not by principles instilled in childhood, but by principles that are constantly modified by their peers. In Riesman's language, they need "radar" rather than a "gyroscope."

What Riesman calls "other-direction" inhibits selfishness by inducing individuals to empathize with their peers. This is not, however, a matter of empathizing directly with the individuals whom our actions affect and making their welfare our own. Rather, it is a matter of empathizing with those who might judge our behavior if they knew about it, anticipating their likely reactions, and adjusting our behavior to obtain the most favorable possible response. In many cases, of course, these adjustments are made for narrowly selfish reasons: we need other people's approval to obtain our own objectives. In Riesman's terms this is still inner-directed behavior. But when the approval of others becomes an end in itself, we move toward what he calls other-direction. And when we begin to seek the hypothetical approval of others in situations where there is little chance that they will actually know how we acted, much less pass judgment on our actions, the result is, as Riesman suggests, analogous to traditional moral inhibitions.

The correspondence between Riesman's three stages of historical development and my three mechanisms for inhibiting selfishness is obviously far from perfect. Nonetheless, the analogy does raise the question of whether the three mechanisms I have discussed for inhibiting selfishness are mutually exclusive, and whether societies move from one mode of controlling selfishness to another in some predictable sequence. My tentative answer is that while no society relies exclusively on one of these three mechanisms to the exclusion of the other two, it may still be useful to characterize different societies and different historical epochs by their dominant method of inhibiting selfish behavior. I doubt, however, that changes in these methods follow any consistent historical pattern.

It is true, for example, that a society must be extremely small in order to inhibit selfishness by preventing the development of a separate sense of self. But while complete identification with the group is only possible in very small societies, partial identification with larger groups is an important mechanism for inhibiting selfishness even in large, complex societies. Patriotism is the most obvious and perhaps the most powerful example of such group loyalty, but similar feelings are at work in many Japanese and some American corporations, where pride in being a "Hitachi man" or an "IBM man" limits propensities to self-indulgence.

Likewise, while internalized moral norms probably played a larger role in American life in the nineteenth century than they do today, I doubt that there is any necessary link between reliance on such internal norms and the early stages of an industrial revolution. The Japanese example suggests that a society can also use a combination of empathy and group identification to inhibit selfishness and facilitate the creation of large, complex organizations, placing relatively little reliance on internalized principles that are applied independently of the social context. Thus, I doubt that the relative importance of guilt, empathy, and group loyalty has any consistent relationship to a culture's overall capacity to inhibit selfishness or to sustain complex organizations.

Rigorous historical or cross-cultural analysis of these issues is, however, beyond the powers of any single individual working alone. In order to move beyond what Riesman and other students of "national character" accomplished in the 1940s and 1950s, we would have to find ways of coordinating the efforts of substantial numbers of scholars along common lines. We would, for example, have to collect much more complex and subtle attitude data from a much larger variety of nations than Almond and Verba surveyed. We would also have to link these attitudinal findings to experiments of the kind that Feldman conducted. There is virtually no chance that this will be done in the foreseeable future. Nonetheless, it seems clear, at least to me, that unselfishness is an extremely valuable and relatively scarce resource.[10] Without it, our lives would indeed be "solitary, poore, nasty, brutish, and short." Individuals with a concern for posterity should therefore devote some of their intellectual energy to figuring out how this resource can be transmitted to future generations.

NOTES

1. See W. D. Hamilton, "The Genetical Evolution of Social Behavior," *Journal of Theoretical Biology* 7 (1964): 1–52, for a full analysis of altruism among relatives.

2. Robert Trivers, "The Evolution of Reciprocal Altruism," *Quarterly Review of Biology* 46 (1971): 35–57.

3. See Donald Campbell, "On the Conflicts between Biological and Social Evolution and between Psychology and Moral Tradition," *American Psychologist* 30 (1975): 1103–26. My entire argument in this section has been heavily influenced by Campbell's analysis.

4. Gabriel Almond and Sidney Verba, *The Civic Culture* (Boston: Little, Brown, 1965), p. 213.

5. Roy Feldman, "Response to Compatriot and Foreigner Who Seek Assistance," *Journal of Personality and Social Psychology* 10 (1968): 202–14.

6. Alexis de Tocqueville, *Democracy in America* (New York: Oxford University Press, 1947), p. 44.

7. Lee Rainwater, *What Money Buys* (New York: Basic Books, 1974).

8. James Q. Wilson and Edward Banfield, "Public-Regardingness as a Value Premise in Voting Behavior," *American Political Science Review* 58 (1964): 876–87. See also Banfield's *The Moral Basis of a Backward Society* (New York: Free Press, 1961).

9. I am indebted to Ezra Vogel for suggesting this interpretation of Chinese-Japanese differences in rhetorical selflessness.

10. Gary Becker first suggested to me that we should see altruism as a scarce resource, but see also Sir Denis Robertson, *Economic Commentaries* (London: Staples Press, 1954).

4

ABUNDANCE RECONSIDERED*

ROLF MEYERSOHN

WHAT ABUNDANCE?

David Riesman's article "Abundance for What?" came out in 1958, the year that John Kenneth Galbraith published *The Affluent Society*, and a time in which the belief in America as an abundant society became so deeply engrained that it assumed the quality of myth.[1] Notice was, of course, taken that there are islands of poverty and that from time to time serious recessions erupt, but the United States was seen as prospering and flourishing and setting the pace for the rest of the world, fiscally and even culturally. The United States became the nation in whose image "underdeveloped" nations were expected to develop.

What concerned social scientists was not the existence of affluence as such but its meaning, the effect that abundance might have on the American character. David Potter, in *People of Plenty* (1954), argued that abundance made for a permissive society as scarcity made for a submissive one.[2] David Riesman was concerned that the economic surplus might have a debilitating effect on Americans, that there was a possible lack of challenge in American society, and that there was a lack of spirit in the new generation, which he called the "found generation." (Significantly, "Abundance for What?" was written at the time of the launching of Sputnik, an event that helped to shatter the American sense of omnipotence.)

* A PSC-BHE Fellowship Award enabled me to collect some of the material in this article.

Two decades later the fundamental abundance of American society has come into question. Much as the closing of the American frontier led to a shattering recognition of the geographic limits of this country, so current doubts about the infinite resources and resilience of America have been raised.

The decline of the myth of affluence comes only in part from the growing recognition of the limits of our natural resources—which had seemed limitless during the post–World War II period, when the rest of the industrialized world was still weak from war—and also only in part from the intractable problems of racial inequality and what appears to be a permanent state of high unemployment. The roots of the decline are not in the economic infrastructure of our society (which has changed little in the past twenty years), but in changes in our social interactions and in our relationship to things.

Three recent works epitomize this view: Tibor Scitovsky's *The Joyless Economy*, Staffan Burenstam Linder's *The Harried Leisure Class*, and Fred Hirsch's *Social Limits to Growth*.[3] All three are efforts by economists to deal with noneconomic components of consumer behavior. All three are written by Europeans who try to comprehend America. All three are pessimistic pictures of American society, as the titles suggest. The questions they raise—about lack of satisfaction, lack of time, lack of easy consumption—are no longer attempts to answer the question "abundance for what?" but rather, "what abundance?"

Scarcity of Satisfaction

At what point are humans ever satisfied with what they have? This question has been a fulcrum for moralizing ever since Ecclesiastes.

The eye is not satisfied with seeing,
Nor the ear filled with hearing.

Samuel Johnson, speculating in 1759 about why the pharaohs built pyramids, attributed them to a "hunger of imagination."

That hunger of imagination which preys incessantly upon life. . . .
Those who already have all that they can enjoy, must enlarge their
desires. . . . I consider this mighty structure as a monument to the insufficiency of human enjoyments.[4]

Whatever we have, we are able to imagine more, and to imagine more is very soon to want more.[5] Objects create desires, and desires create further objects. Karl Marx, in *Grundrisse*, specified the process quite directly.

> An object of art . . . creates a public sensitive to art and capable of enjoying beauty. Thus production creates not only an object for the subject but also a subject for the object.[6]

Habits are habit-forming, interests create interests, "l'appetit vient mangeant."[7] If we desire nothing but are stimulated, we might develop an appetite; on the other hand, if we already have the appetite, apparently it becomes impossible to fulfill it.

Such philosophical speculations are not at all an aspect of capitalism as such, though capitalism has made the most of the process. A market economy is well suited to stimulate and generate tastes and desires and interests that become subject for object, and object for subject.

What is new is that the "hunger of imagination" has become so widespread. Until a consumer society was developed, satiation, fatigue, or dissatisfaction could not erupt on a large scale; most people and most societies were too poor to worry about such problems. But now there is concern about diminished satisfaction as a widespread problem. "The most serious scarcity in our time . . . is a *scarcity of satisfactions*," according to Michael Kammen's recent essay "From Scarcity to Abundance—to Scarcity?"[8] It is this sentiment that Scitovsky voices in *The Joyless Economy*. He bemoans the growing pursuit of *comfort*, which in his view has driven out *pleasure*. He believes that abundance as such corrodes the spirit.

> One must be tired to enjoy resting, cold to appreciate a warm fire, and hungry in order really to enjoy a good meal.[9]

New is the belief that enjoyment is desirable but that there is a self-defeating quality in the way in which it is sought.

> We get and pay for more comfort than is necessary for the good life, and some of our comforts crowd out some of the enjoyments of life.[10]

Scarcity becomes a virtue for the pleasure it gives in its relief. Scitovsky's defense of scarcity goes beyond the ancient fear that luxury corrupts and corrodes, that, as Saint Augustine warned, "the appearance of luxury signals the onset of the death fever of civilization."[11] His view is that abundance interferes with pleasure, and that Americans do not engage in the kinds of activities that should be carried out in the service of pleasure. Instead they pursue activities in the service of comfort.

The corrosive effects of luxury are also invoked in current commentaries on and obituaries of American civilization, particularly in comparisons with the last stages of the Roman Empire. Robert Heilbroner, for example, sees a similar "deep and pervasive crisis of faith"; Thomas Kando finds a resemblance in that both societies, "when faced by the challenge of excess wealth, luxury, and time . . . responded by yielding to corruption—and ultimately lost the simple virtues that had made them great as a nation."[12]

Such explanations for the frustrations of affluence are based on rather simple conceptions of human nature: namely, that we are spoiled; that "what we previously had to struggle for now comes easily, so we appreciate it less";[13] that we have excessive expectations. But if indeed there is a scarcity of satisfaction, among the middle class in particular (presumably poor people have fewer problems of enjoyment since they are more likely to experience hunger, cold, exhaustion), it derives from elements that are not psychological; they are not even a form of "relative deprivation," which is a kind of mental trick—if you compare yourself with somebody poorer than you, you can feel better than if you compare yourself with a Rockefeller. There is, instead, a structure of dissatisfaction that derives from the *social* meanings of consumption, the result of what Peter Berger et al. have called the underinstitutionalization of the private sphere.

> More and more time is spent in private life. This shift in the "time budget" of most people has put additional strain upon the private sphere and its "solutions" to the problem of modern discontents. The search for satisfactory meanings for individuals and collective existence has become, in consequence, more frantic.[14]

On the one hand, more time is spent in the private sphere; on the other hand, there is "a shortage of institutions that firmly and reliably structure human activity"; and the result is that individuals are insufficiently protected from "having to make too many choices."[15]

Richard Sennett's *The Fall of Public Man* also attributes contemporary discontents to a shift from the public sphere to the private sphere; the growth of the private sphere resulted in part from the sterility of the public sphere. What is the end product of this shift? Narcissism.

> Narcissism is now mobilized in social relations by a culture deprived of belief in the public and ruled by intimate feeling as a measure of the meaning of reality.[16]

By providing a sociological context for individual behavior, the Bergers, Kellner, and Sennett fill in the missing element in Scitovsky's analysis. The precipitating problem for scarcity of satisfaction derives not from false expectations or from being spoiled Americans, but from the inevitable strains that come out of the absence of communal meaning and out of languishing too long in the private sphere. The result might be psychological deprivations, what Scitovsky would call "spoiled," and Sennett more accurately describes as the life of narcissism.

Scarcity of Time

"Abundance for What?" was originally presented at a symposium sponsored by the Committee for Economic Development. One of the other contributors to that symposium was Roy F. Harrod, who drew attention to a growing scarcity of free time due to the time required for the servicing and maintenance of goods. Gary Becker elaborated upon this idea when he developed a theory of time allocation that included time spent in using consumer goods.[17]

The paradox was completed by Staffan Burenstam Linder, a Swedish economist and member of Parliament, who wrote *The Harried Leisure Class*. He pointed out that with the increase in leisure goods came a decrease in leisure time, and that

> material riches of advanced societies are apparently incompatible with the superfluity of time that is characteristic of materially poor cultures.[18]

This paradox is explained by the fact that not only does shopping take time, but so does the maintenance of all the goods and acquisitions that have been accumulated. His examples of harriedness include the economic commitment to maintain and service everything from automobiles to washing machines. The time spent in shopping and maintenance is called the "shadow price" of high consumption.

This price is becoming ever higher, and the end result is a "time famine."[19] The rising "shadow price" makes the increased leisure time that Americans have gained with affluence somewhat illusory. Part of it is converted back into work to generate the income required to buy the maintenance time required for the many consumer goods; another part is "wasted" in coping with traffic jams and congestions of various sorts; and part of it is spent simply calculating how to minimize the first two forms of time expenditure.

Daniel Bell, in *The Coming of Post-Industrial Society*, writes that "Utopia thus stands confounded."

> In the post-industrial society, the multiplication of things and their rising custodial costs bring time into the calculus of allocating one's personal activities; men become enslaved to its measurement through marginal utility. . . . In the end, all time has become an economic calculus.[20]

The wide variety of time cycles that characterize human activities appear at first glance to be largely idiosyncratic, and congestion appears as a sign of poor planning—when, of course, it is a sign, as Kevin Lynch has pointed out, that people tend to want the same things at the same time.[21] Leisure activities especially are timed not because they can be carried out efficiently, but because they constitute social interaction. Beaches are emptier on a Tuesday than on a Saturday not only because more people are at work then, but also because even those who are not are unlikely to want to go to the beach by themselves.

The weekend-weekday alternation has become a periodicity as deeply ingrained as the seasons. Even for those persons to whom it does not apply, such as the retired, it appears to have its impact. Studies of airport congestion have shown that Friday evening is the most popular departure time and consequently the most congested. A large segment of Friday evening travelers could in fact travel some other time but in spite of the inconvenience choose not to. This finding testifies not to the irrationality of an ingrained habit, but rather to the stubborn fact that social interaction tends to occur when it is most convenient for all, guest as well as host.

These massive undulations of time and activities pose a dilemma. The enjoyment of leisure requires available companionship, available time, and available space, all of which contribute to the aggregate bunching imposed by the inflexibilities of scheduling and of human preferences. The solutions, both individual and societal, are varied, involving a number of different trade-offs between time and money.

For example, there are two periods of life during which the time famine is abated—among the young and among the old. Here the famine is more likely to be financial. Among youth and retirees there tends to be a shortage of work, of independence, and of responsibility, all of which are concentrated in the middle years of life. It is here that the scarcity of time is likely to be felt most keenly.

Two government officials, Fred Best and Barry Stern, have recently suggested an alteration in what they call the "linear life plan" that is, the current progression from school in youth, through work during the middle years, to retirement in the later years.[22] They present the linear life plan graphically by calculating the lifetime distribution of education, work, and leisure for the past seven decades.

Chart 1*

U.S. men's lifetime distribution of education, work and leisure by primary activity, actual 1900, 1940, 1960, 1970 and projected 1980 and 1990.

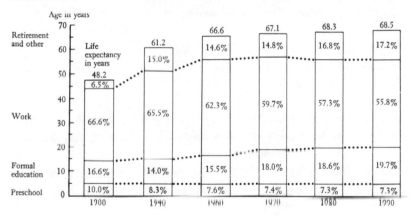

Source: Worklife expectancy figures (number of years in labor force) obtained from Howard N. Fullerton and James J. Byrne, "Length of working life for men and women, 1970," *Monthly Labor Review*, February 1976, pp. 31–33; and Howard N. Fullerton, "A table of expected working life for men, 1968," *Monthly Labor Review*, June 1971, pp. 49–54. Life expectancy figures (at birth) obtained from *Statistical Abstracts of the United States*, 1974 (Washington, Bureau of the Census, 1975), p. 55. School years (completed for persons over 25) obtained from *Digest of Educational Statistics for 1975* (Washington, U.S. Department of Health, Education, and Welfare, Office of Education, 1975), pp. 14–15. Projected figures of worklife and life expectancy from unpublished computations provided by Howard N. Fullerton, Bureau of Labor Statistics. Projected years of education are estimates derived from *Current Population Reports*, Series 20, nos. 243 and 293, and Series P-25, no. 476 (Bureau of the Census).

* From Fred Best and Barry Stern, "Education, Work, and Leisure," *Monthly Labor Review* 100 (July 1977): 4.

As Chart 1 clearly shows, the "fringes" around work are growing, and worktime is increasingly compressed. Best and Stern suggest that this clustering be broken up by the introduction of "cyclical life plans" to replace the linear life plan. They propose to redistribute some of the time currently spent in the fringes—that is, in school or in retirement—to the middle years of life, in the form of extended periods away from work for leisure or education. The result would be a life in which there is reduced schooling during youth, reduced retirement during old age, and extended periods of schooling and free time during all stages of work life.

Best and Stern suggest this alternation not so much in order to solve the problem of the scarcity of time during the middle years as to cope with the shortage of jobs for young people that, they say, could easily persist for the rest of the century.

Scarcity of Demand for Goods

In "Abundance for What?" David Riesman suggested that there is a tendency for people "once accustomed to upper-middle-class norms, to lose zest for bounteous spending on consumer goods." Instead, they will pay a premium simply to remain at their "present level of amenity and space and sanitation."[23] This thesis has recently been echoed by Fred Hirsch, who argues that this premium will in fact increase. As the general standard of living has continued to increase, Americans are no longer continuing to expand their consumption of market goods. Instead, demand increases for those goods that are ultimately unattainable for everyone. The frontier of wants is closing.

Hirsch draws a distinction between market goods and positional goods. Market goods are bought without regard to the effect that universal ownership might have on satisfaction: the enjoyment of my refrigerator is not impaired by the universal ownership of refrigerators. Positional goods, on the other hand, are those goods whose utility and satisfaction derive, to some extent, from their restricted distribution, and would be diminished if these goods were widely distributed. My enjoyment of my vacation home can be threatened by the overcrowding that would result from universal ownership. Interaction interferes.

This country, according to Hirsch, is reaching the limits of market good expansion. American consumers are now increasingly engaged in the acquisition of positional goods. This ascendancy is aggravated rather than moderated by an increase in the standard of living. Fur-

thermore, no redistribution of income can diffuse positional pre-
rogatives.

> What the wealthy have today can no longer be delivered to the rest of
> us tomorrow. [Yet] as we individually grow richer, that is what we
> expect.[24]

This is a new dilemma. Consumer interaction is itself, of course, not
new; the social, noneconomic functions of economic behavior have
been of great interest ever since Veblen. But Veblen saw conspicuous
consumption—certainly a form of social interaction revolving around
consumer choices—as a driving principle in the continuing motivation of consumers to consume. Similarly, Duesenberry's "demonstration effect" was an effort to document the impact of one consumer on
another.[25] Both conspicuous consumption and the demonstration
effect helped explain the expansion and expansiveness of consumption.
Neither concept involved any boundaries or limits to consumption;
indeed, implicit was the idea that there is an infinite supply of consumer goods and products that could become the recipients of such
largesse of attention.

Whereas Veblen and Duesenberry could consider the expansion of
the American economy and could regard "interaction effects" as a
motivating principle, Hirsch wants us to recognize the limits of the
economy, the self-defeating nature of additional consumption, the
impossibility of reaching a higher social position—if that is what our
consumption aims for—since we are locked into a relative one. Hence,
we have reached the end of affluence in the sense that the pursuit of
additional consumer goods is tantalizing but unrewarding. In the past,
through individual diligence and through mass production, consumer
goods became increasingly attainable. Positional goods cannot be made
available in that way. Hirsch's position is similar to that of the envi-
ronmentalists who have been concerned about the consequences of
the pursuit of private pleasures. For example, E. J. Mishan recently
wrote:

> Economists have not yet calculated the loss of welfare that arises when
> roads, highways, villages, parks, beaches, lakes, and resorts become so
> crowded as to cause discomfort and irritation to holiday makers and
> sportsmen. . . . As things are, many people incur heavy costs and spend
> more time traveling further afield, though with diminishing hope of
> really being able to get away, a fear which obviously reduces the value
> of their leisure activity.[26]

The costs of "being able to get away" keep growing as those who
are less able to bear them are becoming more interested in incurring

them, while those who are best able to afford them have long since incurred them—when they were less expensive.

Christopher Jencks considers other people's *time* a positional good and points out that regardless of increasing affluence, most people will never be able to acquire this luxury.

> The rich are not rich because they eat filet mignon or own yachts. Millions of people can now afford these luxuries, but they are still not "rich" in the colloquial sense. The rich are rich because they can afford to buy other people's time. They can hire other people to make their beds, tend their gardens, and drive their cars. These are not privileges that become more widely available as people become more affluent.

Even though wages rise,

> the highly paid professional will have to spend a constant percentage of his income to get a maid, a gardener, a taxi. The number of people who are "rich," in the sense of controlling more than their share of other people's time and effort, will therefore remain the same, even though consumption of yachts and filet mignon is rising.[27]

What goods and services come under the spell (if that is the word) of the concept of "positional goods"? If other people's time is included, then what is not? Hirsch suggests that economic activities of all kinds can be categorized according to their positional good element, and "most activities are not either/or but have varying positional good content, a content that may vary for different people and at different times."[28] Hence, the dynamics of positional goods are clearly double-edged. Their attractiveness rests both in the status component, the appeal they have in representing exclusivity, and in the presumed gratification derived from the activity itself—one that can be carried out without crowding, intrusion, interruption. Hirsch's concept of positional goods is based on the value placed on others' not possessing them. As demand for market goods levels off, positional goods become more widespread and therefore self-defeating.

There is a third class of goods—let's call them "critical mass goods" —that work the other way. They become more desirable and more valuable as they become more widespread; there are positive rather than negative interaction effects. For example, an American Express card becomes more useful as it is accepted more widely, and is accepted more widely as it is adopted by more consumers. Likewise the telephone, which is worthless until there is a network of users. With each additional subscriber its value increases geometrically. When telephones saturate society they are at their maximal usefulness and desirability; telephone subscribers who pay a premium to have their telephones *not* listed are attempting to convert a critical mass good to a positional good.

We have been looking at economists who have examined the current American scene in its noneconomic realms. Linder, Hirsch, and Scitovsky all follow in Veblen's footsteps in their doubt about the nature of the American character and in their belief in the eventual meaninglessness of consumer behavior (as well as in their disregard of their fellow economists). What Veblen disliked about capitalism, according to Adorno, was its waste rather than its exploitation.[29] This is probably true for Scitovsky, Linder, and Hirsch as well. But what they fail to see, unlike Veblen, is the symbolic component of consumer behavior. Veblen saw clearly that a consumer object has meaning that has little to do with the object or even its use, but is embodied in ownership itself. Further, the interaction that interested Veblen was one in which predatory, socially ambitious "grand acquisitors" (whom David Riesman called inner-directed) sought to excel. Contemporary economists describe far less bloody motives; Hirsch's positional goods involve not aggressive but "defensive acquisition," such as obtaining land to protect one's view or yet another, higher degree in case it might someday be required. They are protections against being outclassed, but a far cry from the simple, if vulgar, acquisition of status symbols.

CONCERN WITH CONFORMITY

The period during which "Abundance for What?" was written was permeated by a Biedermeier complacency, which David Riesman's work caught so brilliantly in his concern with its consequences. One of the most absorbing worries of the time was conformity—the tendency toward convergence that would standardize the American dream into a house in the suburbs, a flock of children, interest in consumption rather than production, an absence of authenticity.

There developed a critique of this constellation of values, views, and life styles that began to comment on two aspects in particular: the baby boom and the suburban expansion. Both have by now become historical; neither was "solved" in the sense that it was ever explained how the baby boom or the suburban expansion was connected to conformity, but both were eventually made irrelevant by the passage of time, by changes in life style, by the reordering of priorities. It is probably superficial to call the baby boom or the suburban expansion epiphenomenal; but they did not involve any changes in the basic power relations, in the class structure, or in the distribution of wealth. Their rise and fall could occur without rearrangement of the basic structures in society.

The pressure toward conformity had been most pressing in the political realm; in the face of a conspiratorial theory of politics fueled by McCarthy, it became necessary to demonstrate loyalty as an American. (This idea now seems remote or quaint enough to provide plot material for television and films.) In this sense, concern with conformity was part of the Zeitgeist, much as the idea of abundance was part of it. But conformity became interwoven with matters of life style in a more general sense. Lipset recently pointed out that in those days conformity was regarded as part of the American character and attributed not merely to the politics of the time but to the whole ethos.[30] And so social scientists joined journalists and other "opinion leaders" (itself a concept that grew up during the 1950s) in creating worries about conformity—rather than focusing on the vast diversity of interests, occupations, ambitions, enclaves of ethnic groups, or even on poverty in its various forms.

The Baby Boom and the Suburban Expansion

One symptom in the syndrome called conformity was the baby boom. Large families—that is, those with at least three or four children— were regarded as conforming to the norm. They spurred interest in suburban living, with houses large enough to accommodate the brood and their peers. Large families were also a symptom of conformity because they quite naturally led to concerns with issues of stability— in school, work, and society. The baby boom went beyond the presence of large numbers of children and included concern with their welfare. The center of gravity shifted from adults to children. If during the 1930s family attention centered on employment of the father, and during the 1940s on his going to war, then during the 1950s it centered on the progeny.

The boom ended some time ago, and its consequences are now making their dramatic appearances, as in the 18 May 1978 New York Times story that Levittown, Long Island, will drop seventy teachers because school enrollment is dropping to under 10,000 children, compared with an enrollment of 19,000 in 1962.

In the nation as a whole the picture is no different. Elementary school enrollment declined by 4.7 million pupils between 1970 and 1977, by 1.2 million during the past two years alone.[31] And as children go, so go the suburbs. It is too early to speak of an absolute decline in the suburban population, but the growth rate has certainly dropped markedly, from an average annual rate of 3.8 percent in the 1940s, to 2.4 percent in the 1960s, to 1.5 percent during the early part of the 1970s.[32] Once the baby boom burst and the suburban growth rate declined, concern with conformity also abated. The actual existence of conformity was never documented; nonetheless, there is something reassuring about its disappearance.

The change in migration patterns might help us understand where people are now going, even if we are unable to say with much confidence why they are doing it. If the move to the suburbs is proceeding at a reduced rate, are people then staying in cities, or are they moving to the countryside? And are suburban residents moving out? Table 1

Table 1.   Geographical Mobility in the United States,
        March 1975 to March 1977
        [Number of movers, in thousands]

Residence in 1977

Residence in 1975	Central cities	Suburbs	Nonmetropolitan areas	Total
Central cities		5,525	1,782	7,307
Suburbs	2,796		2,033	4,829
Nonmetropolitan areas	1,180	2,022		3,202
Total Movers	3,976	7,547	3,815	15,338

Note: Omitted are the following: persons who did not move during this period (73% of the population); who moved within or between cities (6.1%), suburbs (7.5%), and nonmetropolitan areas (1.0%); as well as persons who moved from abroad to the United States.

Source: The data for this table are derived from U.S. Bureau of the Census, *Current Population Reports*, Series P-20, No. 320, "Geographical Mobility: March 1975 to March 1977" (Washington, D.C.: U.S. Government Printing Office, 1978), table 1, p. 5.

provides some answers. It shows that between 1975 and 1977, over five million people moved from central cities to the suburbs but that almost that many suburbanites moved to the central cities and to the country. What is particularly significant about this population movement is the migration back to the rural areas of America. In every region except the West Coast, more persons moved from metropolitan areas (that is, central cities plus suburbs) than to them.

Reverse Migration or New Ideology?

What appeared as a mutation during the 1960s, when tiny if conspicuous counterculture groups left urban areas for the countryside, has now shown up as a statistical trend. During recent years some of the most rapid expansion in America has occurred in more remote nonmetropolitan counties. It may signify that there is a dramatic new pattern in the underlying process of urbanization. After all, for the past several centuries there has been a steady migration from countryside to urban areas. Is this movement reversing? One recent study has called the phenomenon "a clean break with the past."[33]

To be sure, there has always been a certain amount of "reverse migration" (the term itself indicates that migration has been thought of as a one-way street), particularly of persons who did not "make it" in urban areas.[34] But the present settlement of rural areas is more than that.

It is possible to compare persons who moved from city to country with those who migrated the other way. Here are some characteristics of the city-to-country movers as compared with the country-to-city movers:

1. They are older.
2. They are from higher-income groups (the trend reverses for those earning $25,000 or more annually).
3. They reflect no particular occupational pattern; occupations associated with urban life are not exempt from the ruralization trend. For every professional or executive who moved from country to city, 1.2 moved the other way.
4. More persons from suburbs than from cities moved to the country.

What are the reasons for this movement to the countryside? Both retirement migration and interest in recreation play a role. These have helped attract industries that cater to such needs and have provided additional employment opportunities. It has even been suggested that economic incentives as the primary impulse to migration may have weakened and that some nonmetropolitan in-migrants "may be inflation refugees who are more attracted by scenery than by salary."[35] No one has investigated whether the migrants to the countryside had spent their childhood there and are in that sense returning, whether they are taking a cut in pay, whether they intend to live in the country permanently, whether they were "pushed" by urban disamenities or "pulled" by some aspect of rural amenities.

The absence of research prevents us from knowing whether the migration to the countryside can be regarded as a way out of some of the dilemmas raised by abundance. The migration is clearly more than simply an extension of moving further away from the city amongst commuters. It does represent a movement out of the urbanized areas generally.

It is plausible to argue that the movers, or at least some of them, are reducing scarcities of time and satisfactions. They are avoiding some of the disamenities of urban and suburban living, such as congestion and interaction with strangers, and competition for scarce places.

The one problem that will ultimately not be solved is the demand for positional goods. The desire for living in the hinterland represents a positional good par excellence—it can remain a hinterland only so long as it is *not* desired. In the long run, if the current trend continues and expands, the hinterlands are likely to follow the path of the suburbs and yield up precisely those aspects that had made them desirable in the first place.

The countryside once before yielded up its treasures in the service of urbanity, and it became depleted of population as its youth migrated to cities in search of employment. The countryside itself became the reserve and preserve.

> By an unparalleled stroke of good fortune the countryside has begun to fall vacant just as this flight from the city assumes impressive proportions. Just at the moment when our urban civilization seems to have reached the end of its spiritual resources it miraculously acquires an inexhaustible source of strength, and acquires it by default.[36]

This acquisition "by default" might indeed constitute a new challenge and frontier, but equally likely is the eventuality that high-technology life will remake the rural landscape in the image of its urban refugees.

CONCLUSION

The concerns expressed in "Abundance for What?" continue to haunt the American middle class—the meaning of materialistic goals and objects. Their meaning has always been endowed with a mixed message, one that signifies both success and waste, but the emphasis has shifted from the one aspect to the other. In the 1950s the myth of abundance reigned supreme, and the middle class was infected by a contagion of confidence. Twenty years later the myth of scarcity has taken its place.

The 1950s produced interest in the by-products of abundance, such as leisure and life styles (exemplified by Russell Lynes's classification of taste-makers). Symbols of success were embedded in the optimism of suburbia and large families, along with their material representations (not grandiose Cadillacs but sensible station wagons). Worries centered around external threats (and their internal representations), such as the atom bomb and the Russian menace. The infrastructure was left largely unquestioned.

During the 1970s external threats have receded from consciousness, and internal ones have taken their place. The meaning of materialistic goals and objects has begun to be symbolized not by success but by waste. Waste has become for the self-conscious middle class (including many of its social scientists) what external threats had been for them in the 1950s, a sign of America's absence of power. In the past, waste had been a sign of wealth and abundance (Veblen after all immortalized the concept of "conspicuous waste"); waste has become the equivalent of sin: America's now limited resources are squandered.

Perhaps what is most striking about the 1950s as well as the 1970s— and possibly all "epochs"—is the degree of *permanence* with which beliefs about the "present" are endowed. What Simmel wrote about fashion applies:

A peculiar psychological process seems to be at work. . . . Some fashion always exists and fashion per se is indeed immortal, which fact seems to affect in some manner or other each of its manifestations, although the very nature of each individual fashion stamps it as being transitory. The fact that change itself does not change, in this instance endows each of the objects which it affects with a psychological appearance of duration.[37]

To be sure, the harriedness of today's leisure class, the joylessness of its consuming public, and the inevitability of frustration in the positional goods arena are important strains in current consumer consciousness. But their importance serves, as culture in general serves, to provide a series of preoccupations that partly hide and partly reveal the deeper fissures in the social structure.

NOTES

1. "Abundance for What?" first appeared in *Problems of U.S. Economic Development*, vol. 1 (New York: Committee for Economic Development, 1958), and was reprinted in *Bulletin of the Atomic Scientist* 14 (1958); it then appeared in *Abundance for What? And Other Essays* (Garden City, N.Y.: Doubleday, 1964), pp. 300–308.
John Kenneth Galbraith, *The Affluent Society* (Boston: Houghton Mifflin, 1958).
2. David M. Potter, *People of Plenty: Economic Abundance and the American Character* (Chicago: University of Chicago Press, 1954).
3. Tibor Scitovsky, *The Joyless Economy: An Inquiry into Human Satisfaction and Consumer Dissatisfaction* (New York: Oxford University Press, 1976); Staffan Burenstam Linder, *The Harried Leisure Class* (New York: Columbia University Press, 1970); Fred Hirsch, *Social Limits to Growth*, a Twentieth Century Fund Study (Cambridge: Harvard University Press, 1976).
4. Samuel Johnson, *The History of Rasselas, Prince of Abissinia* (London: Oxford University Press, 1971), chap. xxxii, p. 85.
5. See W. Jackson Bate, *Samuel Johnson* (New York: Harcourt Brace Jovanovich, 1977), pp. 298–300.
6. Translated from Marx-Engels-Lenin-Institut edition (Berlin: Dietz Verlag, 1953), p. 14.
7. See J. C. Flugel, " 'L'appetit vient en mangeant': Some Reflections on the Self-sustaining Tendencies," *British Journal of Psychology* 38 (1948): 171–90. Cited by Scitovsky, *The Joyless Economy*.
8. In Kenneth E. Boulding et al., *From Abundance to Scarcity*, The Hammond Lectures, Number 1 (Columbus, Ohio: Ohio State University, 1978), p. 56.
9. Scitovsky, *The Joyless Economy*, p. 71.
10. Ibid., p. 284.
11. Cited in Bate, *Samuel Johnson*, p. 300.
12. Robert L. Heilbroner, *Business Civilization in Decline* (New York: W. W. Norton & Company, 1976), p. 118; Thomas M. Kando, *Leisure and Popular Culture in Transition* (St. Louis, Missouri: C. V. Mosby, 1975), p. 204.
13. See Hirsch, *Social Limits to Growth*, p. 7.
14. Peter Berger, Brigitte Berger, and Hansfried Kellner, *The Homeless Mind: Modernization and Consciousness* (New York: Random House, 1973), p. 191.
15. Ibid., pp. 186, 187.
16. Richard Sennett, *The Fall of Public Man* (New York: Vintage Books, 1978), p. 326.
17. Gary S. Becker, "A Theory of the Allocation of Time," *Economic Journal* 65 (1965): 493–517; also see his more recent work (with G. Ghez), *The Allocation of Time and Goods over the Life-Cycle* (New York: National Bureau of Economic Research, 1975).
18. Linder, *Harried Leisure Class*, p. 103.

19. Stanley Parker, *The Sociology of Leisure* (London: George Allen & Unwin, 1976), pp. 34 ff. The term comes from Linder's *Harried Leisure Class*.

20. Daniel Bell, *The Coming of Post-Industrial Society: A Venture in Social Forecasting* (New York: Basic Books, 1973), pp. 474–75.

21. Kevin Lynch, *What Time is This Place?* (Cambridge: MIT Press, 1972), p. 72. Also see J. Anderson, "Space-Time Budgets and Activity Studies in Urban Geography and Planning," *Environment and Planning* 3 (1971): 353–68.

22. Fred Best and Barry Stern, "Education, Work, and Leisure: Must They Come in that Order?" *Monthly Labor Review* 100 (July 1977): 3–10. For a recent study suggesting that alterations in the linear life plan might be acceptable to workers, see Fred Best, "Preferences on Worklife Scheduling and Work-Leisure Tradeoffs," Monthly Labor Review 100 (June, 1978): 31–7.

23. *Abundance for What?*, p. 304.

24. Hirsch, *Social Limits to Growth*, p. 67.

25. James S. Duesenberry, *Income, Saving and the Theory of Consumer Behavior*, Harvard Economic Studies, vol. 87 (Cambridge: Harvard University Press, 1949).

26. E. J. Mishan, "The Wages of Growth," Daedalus 102 (1973): 76.

27. Christopher Jencks, *Inequality: A Reassessment of the Effect of Family and Schooling in America* (New York: Basic Books, 1972), p. 6.

28. Personal communication, 20 April 1977.

29. T. W. Adorno, "Veblen's Attack on Culture," *Studies in Philosophy and Social Science* 9 (1941): 401.

30. Seymour Martin Lipset, "Growth, Affluence, and the Limits of Futurology," Boulding et al., *From Abundance to Scarcity*, p. 76.

31. U.S. Bureau of the Census, *Current Population Reports*, Series P-20, Number 321, "School Enrollment—Social and Economic Characteristics of Students: October 1977," Advance Report (Washington, D.C.: U.S. Government Printing Office, 1978), p. 1.

32. U.S. Bureau of the Census, *Statistical Abstract of the United States: 1976*, 97th edition (Washington, D.C.: U.S. Government Printing Office, 1976), p. 16.

33. Kevin F. McCarthy and Peter A. Morrison, "The Changing Demographic and Economic Structure of Nonmetropolitan Areas in the 1970s," A Working Note prepared for the Economic Development Administration (Santa Monica: Rand, 1977). Unpublished report. See also Ervin H. Zube and Margaret J. Zube, eds., *Changing Rural Landscapes* (Amherst: University of Massachusetts Press, 1977), pp. 1–3.

34. Daniel O. Price and Melanie M. Sikes, *Rural-Urban Migration Research in the United States: Annotated Bibliography and Synthesis*, DHEW Publication No. (NIH) 75-565 (Washington, D.C.: U.S. Government Printing Office, n.d.), chap. 5.

35. McCarthy and Morrison, *The Changing Demographic Structure*, p. 72. Also see Calvin L. Beale, "Current Status of the Shift of U.S. Population to Smaller Communities." Paper presented at the annual meeting of the Population Association of America, St. Louis, 1977.

36. J. B. Jackson, "Back to the Land," in Zube and Zube, *Changing Rural Landscapes*, p. 4.

37. George Simmel, "Fashion," *American Journal of Sociology* 62 (1957): 556.

5

WHAT TOCQUEVILLE FEARED

RICHARD SENNETT

Open discussions of equality are difficult to conduct today because of a political shorthand people use. This shorthand equates critiques of equality with right-wing politics, the aspiration for equality with left-wing concerns. Tocqueville's writings on equality, in the two volumes of the *Democracy in America*, stand outside this framework. Tocqueville wrote as someone who sees demands for equality as irresistible. Unlike his aristocratic friends and family, Tocqueville did not want to hide from this force of history, or to defy it. His stand was that of a realist who accepts the inevitable and looks for how mankind can best manage with a social life it cannot avoid.

The curious, and little-remarked, thing about the critique of equality in the two volumes of the *Democracy in America* is how much Tocqueville's point of view changes from the first book to the second, which appeared five years after the first.

In the first volume, Tocqueville takes a familiar image from the past, that of mob rule, and attempts to show what a mob is like under equalitarian conditions. Tocqueville diligently tries to strip away the association of mob rule with the rule of the vulgar, the peasant, or the urban riffraff; instead he tries to show how the rule of the decent-minded majority in an equalitarian society tends to persecute the dissident. Majorities do more than express their will; they may attempt to universalize it. No one can believe unless everyone does; a minority is always a threat to a majority's faith in itself.

In the second volume, Tocqueville is no longer concerned with active majority coercion of a minority; now he is concerned with a whole society so pacified that it does not rule itself at all, but rather delegates tasks of public order to bureaucrats. Here again Tocqueville takes a familiar image from the past, that of mass stupor, and gives it a distinctive cast. He sees public stupor in equalitarian societies as produced not by sloth or moral failure, but by anxieties and frustrations in the private realm that so entrap people that they have no emotional energy left for public commitments.

In both volumes, he attempts to expound these dangers of equality without therefore concluding that equality itself is reprehensible; his concern is rather how people who grow up in equalitarian societies might avoid doing damage to themselves. Equalitarian societies face unique dangers of self-debasement, that is, of impairing the quality of action and experience; these dangers, Tocqueville believes, are counterpoised by unique claims of legitimacy unavailable to the members of societies of privilege.

Putting the dangers of equality this way jumps over the major problem, and indeed, the major weakness, of Tocqueville's thought: what is "equality"? Further, what is its relation to "democracy," a word he sometimes uses as a synonym for equality, sometimes as a consequence of it? Tocqueville's American commentator George Wilson Pierson has harsh words on this score:

> How [Tocqueville] ever allowed himself to use "democratie" in seven or eight different senses is still something of a mystery. It was his key word. To "democratie," if to anything in his book, he should have given a precise meaning. Yet he did not. The result was that it held out false promises.

Indeed, Tocqueville's thoughts on the relations of the two words "equality" and "democracy" were so unsteady that as late as 1839 he confided to John Stuart Mill that he could not decide whether to title his second volume *Democracy in America* or *Equality in America*.

WHAT TOCQUEVILLE MEANT BY "EQUALITY OF CONDITION"

Tocqueville is an inconstant and loose writer; his intentions, however, are not inconsistent. I do think one can piece together a workable, logical definition of equality from Tocqueville's writing. That definition derives from the "discovery" about equality that Tocqueville made.

Today we can think about equality in terms of two principles: *access* to resources, or *distribution* of resources. In Western capitalist societies, the principle of access is called "equality of opportunity"; in socialist societies it is called "talent utilization potential" (this barbarism comes from the Soviet planner Djumenton). The principle of equality of distribution is called in capitalist societies "equality of condition"; in socialist ones, "constant-sum redistribution." Before Tocqueville, almost all discussions of equality focused on the question of equality of access and defined the resources to be opened up as property relations or bureaucratic positions. Tocqueville was the first to emphasize the importance of constant-sum distribution—equality of condition—in terms of a wider notion of social resources.

If we think of the equalitarians of Tocqueville's parents' generation, the leaders and theorists of the revolution of 1789–1794, the radicalness of Tocqueville's emphasis comes clear. Even the Abbé de Sieyès, calling for the abolition of all private property, did not imagine the result to be a constant-sum redistribution of property in the society; differences would remain, but would no longer, the Abbé believed, arise out of an arbitrary definition of property "rights." Similarly, those who linked in the revolution the idea of equality with the cry "careers open to talent" had no notion of the interchangeability of all persons with all bureaucratic positions in society; they rather desired a new, more meritocratic hierarchy. Tocqueville is often allied with Montesquieu, but again Tocqueville's emphasis on equality as a principle of distribution has no echo in the eighteenth-century philosophe's theory of democracy; part of Montesquieu's very anxiety about democracy was that equal access to political power would be set against social and personal inequalities, and that this would create chaos.

If Tocqueville's "discovery" was of the alternative notion of equalized distribution of social resources, he did not so much declare this notion as stumble upon it. This is, I think, one of the reasons his language is so often unclear. Sometimes Tocqueville seems to be writing in the mold of past thinkers about equality, whereas in fact he means something much more radical by the term. Having come upon this definition, what was the result?

The result was a vision of society that today we would recognize through the Marxian categories infrastructure and superstructure. It would be absurd to make Tocqueville into a Marxian, but some of the

Marxian categories do help clarify Tocqueville's intent. The infra-structure Tocqueville has in mind is economic, and a political order is built upon this base; democratic politics results from an equality of conditions. What are the "conditions" Tocqueville has in mind? Here again I find comparison to Marx useful, for Tocqueville means some-thing by this word akin to the meaning Marx gave to the term "pro-duction." The equality of conditions Tocqueville envisions is an equal capacity to realize one's desires in action: one could have the same goods as other people, if one wanted them; one could have any job one wanted, if once one knows one wants it; one's traffic with others is based on the conviction that people could switch places, if they so desired. To identify the "condition" of society at its root with the possibilities of action is close to Marx's idea of production. The condi-tions of society so equalized have in turn little to do with the concept of equality of opportunity, for that implies mobility above others, it implies that the result of action will be the chance to occupy a new place in the social hierarchy. In Tocqueville's future world, hierarchy is gone, and all the possible routes of action in society are equivalent.

This infrastructure does not confound mechanical *identity* of goods possessed, services enjoyed, jobs held, with *equality*; it separates the two. What Tocqueville saw in America was the vision of a future Western world in which the realization of personal desire encountered no checks by virtue of the existence of impersonal hierarchy. What is powerful in Tocqueville's vision is that he saw, therefore, that other kinds of checks to desire, and deformation of action, would result precisely because there were no hierarchical hurdles to be overcome.

There is an untranslatable word in French that conveys the sense of this idea of equality: equality is a matter of *moeurs* ("style of ac-tion, behavior principle with moral consequences, cultural configura-tion"). Upon the *moeurs* of equality are built the political structures of society. These structures have a certain sequential pattern. From the *moeurs* of equality the people first derive a principle of legitimacy. Majority rule is legitimate; if the people are all roughly the same in condition, then what the largest number of equals want will constitute a legitimate desire. Tocqueville stresses again and again the derivation of legitimacy from equalitarian *moeurs* because he wants to explain how the conviction of a "natural" right grows up in people's minds. It does so, not because they apprehend a fundamental truth of Nature; Tocqueville's equalitarian world is no Enlightenment paradise. The people believes in itself because each man recognizes himself in all others; the stronger the sense of recognition, the more moralistic the whole. This self-confirmation is disguised as a "natural" right to majority rule.

From the conviction of legitimacy is in turn derived the machinery of democratic politics. Tocqueville usually means by "democratic" the exercising of the vote, in parliamentary situations, in voluntary organizations, in New England town meetings, and so forth. This voting machinery always brings issues to a test; the rhythm of collective action is highly formalistic. No spontaneously felt general will is spontaneously acted upon; always reality must be judged, measured, and defined through a mechanistic ritual of counting heads.

Thus the flow of force in Tocqueville's thought is from equality to a principle of legitimacy (majority rule) to democratic procedures for the majority to express its will. This flow will not reverse. You cannot start with a principle of political procedure, arrive at a principle of legitimacy, and from that create principles of equalization of action in society. As a policy matter, new modes of equality cannot be synthesized from democratic politics. If politics is the result of social conditions, not their cause, equality and democracy are not synonymous. I know Tocqueville often uses the words interchangeably, but the intent to separate them appeared even in preparatory works for the Democracy, such as the essay on religion in America, which Tocqueville wrote as he and Beaumont traveled from Manhattan to Niagara Falls. Here he put the sense of the matter as follows: leveling in society, an equality of condition, is a force that has created politics but is far beyond the power of politics subsequently to control.

We now know some of the characteristics of equality—it is a principle of distribution of action; it is prior to politics and cannot be created by political means—but what is it? In his essay on religion, Tocqueville calls it an "irresistible force," suggesting what Max Weber would later call a "world-historical idea." In the Democracy itself, Tocqueville tells us that equality is the principle of justice seeking its historical realization, but since justice is then defined as the absence of arbitrary inequality, the clarification is in fact something of a tautology. This is the analytic limit of Tocqueville's thought in the 1830s. Why equality has arisen as an historical force is never fully explained; that task will await his work on the ancien régime a decade later. The theory of equality shows where society is heading, as embodied in America in the 1830s, not why it is heading in that direction.

I think there are two ways to use the idea of equality in Tocqueville's thought. One is to treat his work as a form of deductive description; it shows us a picture of equality in a society that knows nothing of feudalism or inherited hierarchy; the author draws deductions about what Europe will look like also, once its feudal past is buried. In different ways, this was how J. S. Mill, Sainte-Beuve, and Bryce read the book. There is a second way to read the book, not contrary to the first, but one that both encompasses the advent of industrial capitalism that succeeded the Jacksonian era and Tocqueville's own more visionary purposes. This is to see Tocqueville's as a utopian critique, a critique of what today is called the postrevolutionary problem. After the old injustices are banished, after a state of justice prevails, what within the revolution will be the human problems to be faced? The moment we put aside an equation of Tocqueville's fears of equality as *per se* conservative, he can be read in this way, and I think it is in this spirit that he wished to be read: assume that the distributive problem is solved, what problems does that very solution create? This is how I should now like to present the two poles of danger Tocqueville perceived in an egalitarian society, revealed by the differences in his critique of equality in volumes one and two of the *Democracy*.

THE DANGERS OF EQUALITY

Mob rule and mass stupor are the two dangers of equality that Tocqueville sees. They are contrary in structure. The first involves the majority as an active tyrannical force, suppressing minority opinion, deviance, or nobility of individual sentiment. The second involves a whole society composed of individuals so self-absorbed, so anxiously bound up in questions of intimate life, that none can participate with real passion in impersonal affairs or politics. These anxiety-ridden individuals are content instead to leave public questions in the hands of a soft and mothering state.

The fears of mob rule and mass stupor were not newly born in Tocqueville's generation. The first has its modern intellectual roots in the doctrines of Hobbes; the second, in the writings of La Boetie on voluntary servitude. But Tocqueville's generation, barely recovered from the first great political revolution in the name of equality, on the verge of an economic revolution that would end more decisively the *ancien régime*, felt these fears intensely. People sensed a future, potential degradation of culture, but could not find the right words to explain why. Tocqueville was one of the first to find convincing words; he was the first to connect mob rule and mass stupor to conditions of equality throughout society, beyond the pale of political conditions or rights.

Tocqueville's arguments about mob rule appear in those famous chapters on the tyranny of the majority of volume one of the *Democracy*. Earlier writers who feared a mob thought of a rabble, the dregs of society, a vulgar majority, so that the question of tyranny per se became allied to the question of status. In Montesquieu, for instance, this image of majority tyranny really was an image of a just hierarchy upset, with the least worthy, who were the most numerous, having control over their betters. Tocqueville's arguments about majority tyranny do not depend on a notion of a just hierarchy upset; they are more subtle. Let us follow him step by step through the first and best known of those chapters in which he forms his own thoughts, "Tyrannie de la Majorite."

He begins with a paradox: he regards as detestable the maxim that the majority of a people has the right to do any and everything it desires, yet majority rule is the only feasible modern principle of legitimate power. To show that this paradox is not a contradiction, Tocqueville advances three explanations. The first is based on Enlightenment principles. There is a universal society called humanity, and its ruling principle is justice. Each nation is like a jury called to apply this universal justice to particular cases; like any jury, it can make mistakes. Thus, the right of majority rule is at once legitimate and limited, and

> when I refuse to obey an unjust law. . . . I appeal solely from the sovereignty of a particular group of people to the sovereignty of the human race.*

But what are the principles of this universal justice? Tocqueville does not tell us, because this first explanation is a prelude to his own theory, an obeisance to past Enlightenment thought. His theory is expressed in the second of his three responses to the paradox of legitimate but limited majority rule when he asks, "What is a majority?" He answers that a collective majority is an "individual," and this collective individual has interests and opinions like any person, equal

---

* All translations are mine, based on the definitive edition of Tocqueville's work prepared under the direction of J. P. Mayer (Paris: Gallimard, 1952–1976).

therefore to that collective individual called a minority. He poses a rhetorical question: when men join together in a collectivity, do they change their characters? Do the people become more patient, or wiser, or in any way different when they act together? To this question Tocqueville gives a firm no. That negative has great consequences. It means that he can treat the politics of society in the same terms as the psychology of an individual human being. Unlike Rousseau before him or the social psychologist Le Bon after him, Tocqueville here denies that the nature of the human being is transformed by social conditions; rather, society is a collective self.

This anthropomorphic image of collective life is what makes Tocqueville's writings in this first volume so vivid, so particular and personal, even when he is making the most sweeping generalization. Equally, it leads him to a particular concept of justice in deciding how to protect the minority person against the majority person. This concept, rendered into modern sociological jargon, is the maximization of countervailing power. There must be as many checks as possible to majority rule, in the form of complexities of interest that impede the majority from acting for the whole; these checks are created through a multidimensional set of interests, so that the majority itself is never one person, but a number of persons at the same time. Tocqueville insists that absolute pluralism cannot and should not be the result of fragmenting the majority's image of itself, for if the majority has no identity, then society will either enter into revolution or dissolve into anarchy. The principle of legitimacy (majority rule) is also a principle of order, but this order can only resist developing into tyranny if it contains contradictions within itself, so that the will of the majority is checked by the fact that those in the majority feel themselves to have several collective personalities at the same time.

Tocqueville then brings into play his third idea, which is the experience of the tyranny of the majority in an equalitarian society. Analytically, it may seem that such tyranny could appear in no other kind of society. This is not the case; in a democracy, a republic, a monarchy, or an aristocratic state, that collective person can appear, representing the dominant feelings of a majority of the citizens or subjects. The people do not have to take each other as equals to act as one to suppress dissidents or outsiders. But when they do take each other as equals, the dangers of tyranny of the majority have a special form and a special force. When a man or a group suffers from an injustice in equalitarian society, Tocqueville asks:

to whom can he appeal? to public opinion? No, that shapes the majority's will; to the legislative body? No, that represents the majority and obeys it blindly; to executive power? No, the executive is appointed by the majority and serves it as a passive instrument; to the national guard . . . to a jury . . . to [elected] judges?

The problem in a society of equal conditions is that there are few sources that would lead each man to think of himself as belonging to different kinds of majorities. He always belongs to one majority, because the economics of life are that everyone knows essentially the same conditions of action. Thus, the greater the equality of condition, the greater the potential of the majority to rule tyrannically; and under a system of absolute equality, Tocqueville concludes, "No matter how unfair or unreasonable the issue which injures you, it is necessary that you submit to it."

The formula that the greater the equality of condition the greater the possibility of tyranny is a stark one. In the face of it, Tocqueville does not abandon the idea of majority rule. Rather, he sees this danger as somewhat modifiable by purely political means, although politics can never "cure" these dangers, which arise from the same forces that cause politics to exist. He envisions a legislative body, on the model of the American Senate, which "represents the majority without being necessarily the slave of the majority's passions." A decentralized administrative apparatus is another means to tame this danger, by depriving the people of a uniform, effective instrument of enacting its will, as is a class of lawyers with such great self-regard that they refuse to be the passive servants of the people and instead, by their very pomposities and rituals, moderate the impetuousness of the people.

Finally, there appears in this vision of majority tyranny in an equalitarian society an idea that, if not dissonant with the general outlines of Tocqueville's theory, still stands apart from the logic of his main argument. Tocqueville argues that the effect of this tyranny is not merely to apply sanctions to the dissident, but also to seduce him. Everyone participates on an equal footing in society, and there is no real boundary between public life and private affairs. When, therefore, a sentiment is shared by a majority of people so that they feel as one person, the person who might feel a contrary opinion or sentiment feels also an immense pressure from this majority: by what right does he or she dissent? What makes him feel so much superior that he does not share the feelings of his equals? This peer pressure either gradually seduces him into abandoning his opinion, or forces him into exile. He is unlike the others, he does not belong, otherwise he would feel as they do.

Today we have names for this seduction: self-criticism, thought-reform, and the like. Tocqueville describes it as the spirit of courtiers extended to the whole character of a society; people assure each other that they belong by mouthing similar thoughts, equality of condition being ideologically confirmed by similarity of thought. But in his argument on majority tyranny, this observation appears in disjointed form; Tocqueville cannot really explain why the majority needs to confirm itself through pressuring dissenters into agreement, why the majority is not content with sheer domination. This problem, however, preyed upon Tocqueville's mind after he finished the first volume of the *Democracy*, and he took it up again in the second. Ultimately, in explaining the need of an equalitarian majority to absorb or expel a minority, he formulated a new notion of the dangers of equalitarian society.

Tocqueville's American biographer, Pierson, portrays the differences between the first and second volumes of the *Democracy* as changes in tone and language, the first being more concrete, the second more purely "philosophic." In the five years that elapsed between the writing of these two volumes, other observers have noted, Tocqueville was able to see the effects of bourgeois monarchy in France, with its spirit of "cultural leveling in the midst of economic differentiation" (Raymond Aron). Tocqueville, it is said, was thus disposed more and more to write about his American experiences in terms of cultural homogenization. Some commentators have explained the change of emphasis simply in terms of a change in subject; active mob tyranny is the danger of equality in equalitarian politics, but another danger appears when one comes to consider equality as a cultural phenomenon.

None of these explanations suffices, I believe, because none gives due credit to the interior strengths of Tocqueville's thought, especially his capacity for working through a problem so that by the time he arrived at the end of an idea, the beginning assumptions were transformed or reversed. Tocqueville worked through the traditional ideas of mob rule to a unique vision of majoritarian tyranny; one of the conclusions of that effort—that equalitarian societies are hungry for more than the brute domination of minority dissidents—led Tocqueville to transform traditional ideas of mass stupor into a new critique of egalitarian culture. The terms of this critique end by being largely opposed to the premises from which he began in volume one.

Probably the greatest writer on mass stupor before Tocqueville was La Boetie, a sixteenth-century French writer passionately concerned about voluntary servitude. The qualities of his thought come through in such passages as these:

> . . . so many men, so many villages, so many cities, so many nations, sometimes suffer under a single tyrant who has no other power than the power they give him; who could do them absolutely no injury unless they preferred to put up with him rather than contradict him . . . it is therefore the inhabitants themselves who permit, or rather, bring about, their own subjection, since by ceasing to submit they would put an end to their servitude. A people enslaves itself, cuts its throat . . . gives consent to its own misery, or rather, apparently welcomes it. . . . It is the stupid and cowardly who are neither able to endure hardship nor to vindicate their rights; they stop at merely longing for them, and lose through timidity the valor roused by the effort to claim their rights, although the desire to be free still remains a part of their nature.

La Boetie sees voluntary slavery as a moral condition; although such slavery is a collective phenomenon, it results from the failings of personal character. Freedom, action, and self-denial are on one side; slavery, passivity, and self-gratification on the other. Therefore, the desire to be a slave results from a desire for comfort, and comfort induces a loss of will. By the end of the second volume of the *Democracy*, Tocqueville had come to conceive of voluntary slavery as a matter of personal anxiety and discomfort, mediated by a peculiar set of social conditions. Private discontents in an egalitarian world produced a sense of disconnection from public life, a loss of interest in all that lay outside the traumas of self, and therefore a willingness to be ruled politically by an authoritarian regime. Tocqueville replaced La Boetie's indictment of voluntary slavery as moral failure with a notion of voluntary slavery as social tragedy. However, by this point he had also replaced his own earlier notion of society as a collective person with a more truly sociological idea: that society has the power to transform human character. The social psychology produced by equality of condition was an anxiety on the part of individuals about their individual worth, correlated to a loss of interest in social matters that could not be brought within the circle of that concern. The greater the anxiety equality produces about intimate life, the less those who are made anxious care about the public domain. Society renders them passive in social terms only by making them more and more unsure of themselves as individuals. This perception of an equation between private misery and public apathy, I believe, finally makes Tocqueville's work great.

The curtain opens on this tragedy in the first chapter of the second part of volume two. This chapter introduces the effects of equality on the sentiments of a people; it begins what today would be called a treatise in social psychology. As in volume one, Tocqueville declares the primacy of the social experience of equality over political experience: "equality can establish itself in society and yet be absent in the political world." A variety of political forms can be built out of equality, and now, by bringing in psychological questions of desire, Tocqueville pursues a dangerous combination. In the modern world, the desire for social equality is "ardent," while the desire for political liberty is weak. Why should this imbalance exist? Is there some correlation between the two so that the stronger the desire for social equality, the weaker the desire for political liberty? The rest of volume two is largely devoted to answering these two questions.

Tocqueville gives in this same chapter an intimation of what will come. To love liberty, to seek it out, requires a person to take risks, to deny the self, to be willing to disrupt the tranquility of intimate life. The desire for social equality is born out of contrary impulses— the desire for tangible gratification, the desire to stabilize and tranquilize family relations. The psychology of equality is that men cherish the illusion that once they are on a plane with everyone else, then they have a security that will allow them to enjoy the immediate things and people around them. Social equality is thus supposedly the means to the "sweet pleasures" of everyday existence, while liberty demands the renunciation of these pleasures. Therefore, men are more ardent in their desire for equality than in their desire for liberty.

Having set up this imbalance, Tocqueville is ready to show how the pursuit of a peaceful *vie quotidienne* gradually leads people to a state of anxiety, unrest, and pleasurelessness, while instilling in them no contrary impulse for greater liberty. He asks: what kind of person possesses the desire for peaceful intimate life, given an equality of social conditions? Tocqueville calls him an "individual," and the social condition he represents "individualism," and declares this condition a unique historical production. The character of modern individualism he brings forward by contrasting it to egoism,

a passionate and exaggerated love of oneself, which leads a person to relate everything to himself and to prefer his own needs to everything else.

Individualism is defined as

> a peaceful and moderated feeling which leads each citizen to isolate himself from the mass of his equals and to withdraw within the circle of his family and his friends. Further, having created this little society for his immediate ease, he willingly abandons the larger society to go its own way.

It is often said that the nineteenth century was the era of individualism, both in ideology and in practice. This cliche does great violence to Tocqueville's use of the word. He is not using it in the sense that the Social Darwinists would come to use it; his individualism is not a world of rugged struggle for survival, agonistic and hard, but exactly the reverse. Think again of the differences between Jacob Burckhardt's use of "individualism" to describe the modern spirit born in the Italian Renaissance and Tocqueville's usage. Burckhardt shows us men and women struggling to win praise from each other, struggling to be recognized as "individuals" because they have special qualities. This display of *virtus* is anarchic, but it involves a strong sense of community. Tocqueville shows us men and women who no longer make demands on each other, save the demand to be left alone; his individuals do not want praise for being extraordinary; they want to be just like everyone else so that no one will give them any trouble and they can, in modern argot, do their own thing.

This notion of modern individualism also changes the analytic scheme that appeared in volume one. Remember that in that volume Tocqueville represented social groups as a collective person: what is true of a single man's feelings being true of a group. But paradoxically this individualism arises only because a certain kind of group life exists: once the fantasy arises that equality of condition will give each person the opportunity to live peacefully, only then does the person desire to withdraw from his fellows, to isolate himself. Egoism is a passion that can be writ large, from single to collective cases; individualism cannot be. This personal desire to withdraw is created by a collective life in which social similarity holds out the promise that men will no longer have to delay gratifying their intimate, small-scale desires for comfort. With the theory of individualism, Tocqueville became a true social psychologist, but a paradoxical one: the emotion that modern collective life arouses is that a person can withdraw from collective life. Everyone is pretty much like oneself, so one need not worry about violation or disruption; therefore, one leaves public affairs in the hands of the state and cultivates one's own garden.

I have used the word "fantasy" to describe the basis of this individualism because it identifies Tocqueville's view of the relation of this collective psychology to collective reality in an equalitarian society. In fact, the practice of individualism does not lead to the rewards of intimate gratification; withdrawal from association with other people creates instead a ceaseless striving after pleasure. One attempts to gorge oneself on the "experiences" that are available to everyone in society, because everyone is on an equal footing of action, but one moves from experience to experience never feeling satisfied, never feeling that the immediate and concrete is "enough."

How can equality of condition produce meaningless experience, equally available to all? When Tocqueville turns his attention to the taste for material well-being in America, he answers this question in a striking way. He propounds a theory that could be called horizontal mobility. The more a society destroys hierarchic barriers to action, the more the diversity of experience occurs within a single, central band, then the more people believe they must exhaustively explore all forms of living in order to be psychologically complete. In equalitarian regimes, people are not prone to choose what they will enjoy; rather, they are prone to try to experience everything—equally at the command of all—in order to convince themselves they are "really living." Tocqueville contrasts this horizontal mobility to the deprivations of an *ancien régime* village by saying that those at the bottom of a hierarchy in a hierarchical world enjoy what is available to them while resenting at the same time the evils they presently endure; and the citizens of an equalitarian society discount the reality of their present condition and think only of the events and gratifications that they have yet to enjoy. Independently of whatever a person experiences at a given moment,

> he imagines a thousand other gratifications which death will keep him from knowing, if he does not hurry. This thought troubles him, fills him with fear and regret, and maintains his spirit in a state of incessant trepidation; at every moment he feels he is on the verge of changing his designs and his place in life.

It is exactly an equalitarian society that will arouse this restlessness, Tocqueville argues. Neither law nor custom pins a person down to a place; the concept of external necessity disappears and is replaced by demands of a more internalized sort. Out of fear of being deprived, when nothing social and hierarchic stands in the way of possible gratification, whatever one's current condition, it becomes by definition not enough.

When I first began reading Tocqueville I thought, therefore, that what he had in mind when he spoke of equality was equality of condition joined to material abundance. Unless there was more than enough to go around, how could people feel unceasingly that what they had at any moment was not enough? But I have come to take Tocqueville at his own word; the reason is that the images of anxiety in this second volume arise precisely out of the idea of an equalized plane of experience in which poeple's lives are not, however, identical reproductions of each other's. Whatever is available to be experienced must be exhaustively experienced; one has the illusion that only after this exhaustive consumption can one decide what one wants. The desire for what one has not is further genuine horizontal mobility; one does not want more in order to be better than other people. Toqueville's thought on equality and mobility is therefore contrary to that of Ortega, who saw citizens of a mass society continually and fruitlessly attempting by their goods to declare the individual superiority of their persons. In times of abundance and scarcity, for Tocqueville, the operating principle of an equalized condition is that fixed possession is meaningless from the vantage point of gratification; instead, stability seems a premature death. The result is a society of anxiety, with constant declarations of what is wrong, and no clear sense of what is to be finally desirable.

This anxiety makes itself manifest psychologically in the phenomenon of ambition. People are ceaselessly ambitious, but the scope of their ambition is petty. This narrowing occurs for two reasons. First, the ambition it is possible to harbor in an equalitarian society cannot be grand in scope; it cannot aim at domination of many others, nor at great wealth, for this would so upset the others that the majority would move inexorably to bring the strong man down. In the same measure, the quality of emotion in striving toward a goal is moderated. The man possessed of an idea, a project, is a man outcast from his fellows; and the society so socializes its members that fewer and fewer are willing to appear as pariahs who cannot explain themselves to others. There is a second reason ambition has peculiar limits in an equalitarian state. Because there are no clear hierarchies, it is difficult to pursue an idealistic project through to a long-delayed conclusion;

Tocqueville in 1840 had here in mind what modern economists call the "trade-off" between bureaucratic efficiency and organizational equality: the greater the equality, the lesser the efficiency. But delay of gratification, Tocqueville argued, was intolerable in an equalitarian order; one wants one's gratifications, one's experiences, now. Therefore, the bureaucratization of institutions on an equalitarian basis meant that people became more disposed to sacrifice those tasks that might take a long time to attain. Ambitions become smaller in order that they may be more easily realized.

Two political consequences follow from this restricted restlessness. Resistance to the state, the will to fight for the liberty felt to be absent in society, diminishes. The ambition for liberty is too demanding to be easily meshed with the more fundamental kinds of ambitions individuals in an equal society harbor; moreover, it appears to be a betrayal to the others, who are simply trying to "find themselves," "make a life for themselves," engage in "self-discovery" through increasingly trivial forms of experience. Why is this person asking us to sacrifice ourselves for a far-off goal? The demand for liberty, like any other public demand—that is, a demand not related to the individual sphere—so threatens those absorbed in the "anxious, narrow tasks of individualism" that they interpret it as a form of personal insult. The insult is that the others' retreat into their private unhappiness is called into question as meaningless. It is an ultimate psychological insult: how can one spend one's life in an endless, unrewarding struggle, and then be told such struggle is trivial, unworthy? What makes the dissenter think he is so special? This is why, Tocqueville argues, if a man in an equalitarian state calls his comrades to arms in the name of liberty, their first impulse will be to kill him.

In his discussion of the second political consequence, Tocqueville returns to the issue that bothered him in his first volume: why do equalitarian societies aim at more than the brute domination of dissidents, idealists, or critics, and instead try to reform the impulse life of these challengers so that they too feel what the majority feels? Now Tocqueville can answer that psychological problem in social psychological terms. The idea that private anxiety is meaningless is intolerable in an equalitarian society. By a perverse and tautological chain, private existence, no matter what its present pain, must be meaningful in order for the individual to detach himself from the mass; and he does so in the illusion that he can find, someday, a gratifying life in the intimate sphere. A dissenter is perceived as someone who refuses that act of detachment; behind his ideological, fraternal words is perceived a condemnation of the anxieties in the name of happiness into which the others have plunged. This dissenter must, therefore, be made to cease criticizing the public order; he must be drawn into paying obeisance to it as just in order that the very withdrawal of other individuals from public concern may be justified. We often speak today of "pressures for conformity" without thinking much about what creates them; Tocqueville's analyses of ambition and equalitarian passion were a dissection of the origin of these pressures, and his conclusion was that they arise not out of the smugness of those seeking to make the others conform, but out of their very need to validate the meaning of their individual frustrations and their sense that nothing is ever enough.

A rationalist might object at this point: but surely when people suffer long enough, when they are restless year after year, at some point they are going to stop struggling inside themselves and turn against the state, laying the cause of their unhappiness at the door of the general structures of society. Tocqueville's genius was to see why the very forces that create individualized anxiety block the translation of private unrest into political discontent. Since all are equal, individual unhappiness is a privatized failure; nobody seems unlike one, so that if one is unrealized, it is one's own fault. Indeed, if the state were disrupted, then the individual would never have the chance to make himself into a real, fulfilled person. A society of equality promotes the illusion that politics is a diversion from the primary tasks of life, which are those of giving meaning to the intimate sphere. Better to let the state handle its affairs, and to handle one's own by oneself.

"I see," Tocqueville wrote,

> a vast crowd of people, similar and equal, who revolve without repose around themselves in pursuit of petty and vulgar pleasures, pleasures from which they hope to fill up their souls. Each person, withdrawn into himself, behaves as though he is a stranger to the destiny of all the others. His children and his good friends constitute for him the whole of the human species. As for his transactions with his fellow citizens, he may mix among them, but he sees them not; he touches them, but does not feel them; he exists only in himself and for himself alone.

And if on these terms there remains in his mind a sense of family, there no longer remains a sense of society.

What does the political state look like in such a society? It is "absolute, highly articulated, regular, farseeing, and soft." It resembles a father who seeks to fixate those under his control in a condition of permanent childhood. It encourages the pursuit of gratification, and does everything in its power to aid citizens in this pursuit, but discourages any criticism of the concept of gratification itself. And thus comes Tocqueville's famous indictment,

> What I reproach equality for is not that it leads men astray in the pursuit of forbidden pleasures but rather to absorb them wholly in the pursuit of those pleasures which are allowed . . . it is likely that a kind of well-meaning materialism [matérialisme honnête] is going to be established in the world, one which will not corrupt the soul but enervate it and noiselessly unbend its springs of action.

Let us contrast this fear with the terms in which La Boetie described the dangers of mass stupor. In Tocqueville's work there is no indictment of the weakness of a contented mob of slaves; there is a mass so mystified, so deracinated by its own illusions, that it is caught in the correlated terms of private misery and public apathy. True, the pursuit of gratification is the rule of this equalitarian society, but gratification is no mere matter of passing sensual pleasure; it is more psychological, more the pursuit of "experience" in an attempt to establish a completed, individualized self. The more frustrating that pursuit, the more people are enmeshed in it; their very suffering creates commitment, deluding them more and more into seeking out an "inner" answer to what appears an "inner" problem. Those who challenge this self-slavery, even out of the best humanitarian motives of alleviating suffering, this mass seeks either to exile or to thought-reform into obedience to the public order; this coercion serves to reinforce and even give a sense of correctness to the individualism of the mass. A people so withdrawn from public concern is willing to leave to a paternal government the necessary and unpleasant task of thought-reform.

Tocqueville tells us he had only "a glimpse" that such an equalitarian danger was forming in the America of the 1830s. Today we have rather more than a glimpse of it in Solzhenitsyn's documentary writings and in the books of Hannah Arendt. But these modern echoes are not quite what they seem.

THE CONTEMPORARY DIMENSIONS OF TOCQUEVILLE'S FEARS

The premise of Tocqueville's analysis is a society of equality of condition, largely achieved. But we do not inhabit such a world. Neither in North American nor in Western Europe have differentials of possession, services, or income diminished since Tocqueville's time, nor has productive action equalized, nor do the facts of property or action show any real promise of doing so in the future. What then is it in this equalitarian critique that so illuminates the problems and discontents of nonequalitarian societies?

I think that it is a weakness in his very formulation of equality that, paradoxically, makes Tocqueville's analysis of such contemporary relevance. The emphasis of his prose, in both volumes, is on what is scholastically called the "as if predicate." Tocqueville's analysis of equality of condition relies not so much on proving that equality is in fact being established as on the belief of a people that such equality is established. People behave as if they were equal in condition. If in fact they do not move roughly within the same band of action, in order to feel that they belong to a common social order, they change their tastes, habits, and outlook to appear as if they did.

Tocqueville's writing is in this sense about an ideology of equality. One of the very distinctive marks of advanced industrial society is that such an ideology will be pervasive, even as material conditions are vastly unequal and inequitable. There is in fact a positive correlation between the belief in equality of condition and the existence of unequal conditions. Challenges to the structures of inequality are deflected in a gross way by the illusion that "fundamentally" everyone is the same. They are deflected in a more subtle way by the induction of an individualist mentality in the members of the society, so that they conceive of the responsibility for gratification and personal development as an individual matter, one that plunges them into an unending, restless search.

This is why Tocqueville's thought is especially strong in the second volume of the *Democracy*, for it is here that he brings forward the correlates of belief in equalized experience, individual responsibility for experience, and increasing detachment from the affairs of the society as a whole. The equation of privatized anxiety and public apathy we can recognize in the two great industrial nations of the modern world, the Soviet Union and the United States. In the Soviet Union, the ideology that the essential tasks of redistribution are largely accomplished is enshrined in law; if opinion studies are to be believed, it is also generally accepted in popular mythology; and completely contravened by the facts of bureaucratic hierarchy and daily behavior. In the United States, the ideology of equal opportunity is enshrined in official policy, and disbelieved by a majority of the populace as an abstract proposition. But again, if opinion studies are accurate, in ordinary life people act as if the responsibility for their satisfaction in life is an entirely individual and private affair—exactly what Tocqueville saw as a consequence of the belief in equality of condition.

If Tocqueville's writing is a picture of an ideology that partly coexists with material facts that contradict it, what are we to make of the dangers of equality he perceived? Both tyranny of the majority and individualized withdrawal are means to a goal, that of preserving the legitimacy of the equalitarian order itself: "we are one," and "leave me alone." Since supposedly the majority is making decisions in his interests, the individual enshrines himself in his private anxieties because public participation would seem to threaten the very value of "self-directed" experience. In societies of great inequality these dangers can still appear as people try to accomplish a similar goal: that of maintaining a sense of cultural coherence in the midst of economic division and political conflict. The very act of affirming the ideology of equality becomes a means of establishing a cultural identity, the tools of that affirmation being either tyrannical or self-destructive or both.

Let me return in conclusion to the point at which this essay began. In the last twenty years, many radical writers in North America and Western Europe have turned away from the classical problem in political economy of domination to attacks on inequality alone. All too often it is assumed that if social conditions can be equalized, then the problems of unjust domination will necessarily and consequently be solved. The import of Tocqueville's writing is to challenge this assumption. Once the shorthand identification of a critique of equality with a necessarily conservative critique is put aside, I believe Tocqueville's writing has a special relevance to radical enquiry. It ought to bring analyses of present-day social injustices back to their proper subject, which is, what are just social rules? The utopian vision of a restructured society becomes that of a community free of domination, including the domination of one's peers, free of the subtle and destructive tyranny that can result from a desire for personal "development" through "experience."

6

INDIVIDUALISM AND EQUALITY
IN THE UNITED STATES

NATHAN GLAZER

Two values, sometimes seen as in conflict, sometimes seen as complementary, frame discussions of American society: individualism and equality. Each has had, in the course of American history, its defenders and critics. Foreign observers have emphasized first one, and then the other, as the most marked characteristic of the new society and new polity that arose in the United States.

The distinctively American aspect of individualism is symbolized by the fact that the first use of this term recorded by the *Oxford English Dictionary* is in the English translation of Alexis de Tocqueville's great book, *Democracy in America*. Individualism, Tocqueville argued, was an inevitable consequence of democracy and equality: "I have shown," he wrote, "how it is that in ages of equality every man seeks for his opinions within himself; I am now to show how it is that in the same ages all his feelings are turned to himself alone." He was concerned to distinguish this new form of human behavior from age-old selfishness. In contrast to selfishness, he wrote, "Individualism is a mature and calm feeling, which disposes each member of the community to sever himself from the mass of his fellows and to draw apart with his family and his friends, so that after he has thus formed a little circle of his own, he willingly leaves society at large to itself." He expands upon this bare definition, to give it a social and political meaning: "As social conditions become more equal, the number of persons increases who, although they are neither rich nor powerful enough to exercise any great influence over their fellows, have nevertheless acquired or retained sufficient education and fortune to satisfy their wants. They owe nothing to any man; they acquire the habit of always considering themselves as standing alone, and they are apt to imagine that their whole destiny is in their hands."[1] It is perhaps already clear that Tocqueville was—as about so many things—of two minds about individualism. A final quotation may suggest the less pleasant face of individualism: "Democratic communities . . . are constantly filled with men who, having entered but yesterday upon their independent condition, are intoxicated with their new power. They entertain a presumptuous confidence in their own strength, and as they do not suppose they can henceforward ever have occasion to claim the assistance of their fellow creatures, they do not scruple to show that they care for nobody but themselves."[2]

This double view of individualism in the United States has persisted since. The positive image of individualism has emphasized the American as pioneer, moving out into wilderness and among savages, and making his way alone, with rifle and axe. It emphasized his indifference as pioneer to governmental controls, which on occasion meant taking the law into his own hand as vigilante to impose a minimal order on frontier society. It emphasized his insistence on his rights as an American—his right to challenge government in the courts, to challenge it through organization and electoral activity, to challenge it through referendum, initiative, and recall. Much of American society and landscape is marked by this individualism: the pattern of agricultural settlement, with its farm dwelling set alone in the midst of extensive acreage, the nearest neighbor a mile away, the nearest town a day's journey back and forth, so strikingly different from the agricultural villages of Europe. Individualism, too, marked the cities, created with checkerboard patterns so that each individual could select a standard plot, and do with it what he wished. Or, in more recent decades, it has been seen in a pattern of haphazard growth, in which each enterpreneur, as individual, managed to acquire some land and, presto, laid out, indifferent to any larger image of metropolitan form or urban design, his own development, and sold to anyone who could afford the houses. We see it, too, in the pattern of American higher education, in which entrepreneurs, individual and group, could without restraint establish institutions they called colleges or universities, and provide whatever education they could or felt necessary. In the course of American history, most of these failed. Perhaps the survivors were sturdier for all that. But we now have three thousand or so institutions of higher education in the United States, and many of them permanently teeter on the edge of bankruptcy. Or, consider the pattern of American religion, in which any church or sect may be founded, and in which undoubtedly thousands of expectant prophets and builders of churches have died disappointed. But hundreds more have succeeded, and some markedly. Consider the Church of the Latter-day saints, or Christian Science.

I have tried to give a positive picture of American individualism— its opportunity for the individual, its grant of freedom, its encouragement of diversity. But in doing so, I have undoubtedly already suggested its opposite side: the indifference to the preservation of landscape or urban form, as the pioneer—agricultural or urban—moved on from worn-out land and worn-out structures, abandoning them to start up anew on virgin territory; the indifference, too, to those who fell behind in the race. "Rugged individualism," it was called in the earlier twentieth century. "Rampant individualism," answered those who considered the victims of individualists: the industrial workers who were prevented from unionizing, often by armed force; the migrant laborers who made possible the individual farmer sitting in isolated and kingly splendor in the midst of his hundreds of acres. The negative side of individualism has been so well portrayed by American writers and is so well known that it is hardly necessary to add much. One need only read Upton Sinclair and John Steinbeck.

Individualism is in poor odor on the whole in the United States today, or rather, a certain variant of individualism: that variant that emphasizes economic freedom. In the later 1960s and early 1970s we suddenly acquired a new batch of regulatory legislation, reflecting a sharply rising concern for minorities and women, for the environment and the consumer of industrial products, and for the worker in industry and agriculture, which quite transformed the face of American industry. The American industrialist and businessman and farmer, still possibly in many respects the freest in the world, began to labor under enormous restraints that were unexpected, with consequences that we still cannot foresee. The new age of regulation followed on earlier ages of regulation, stemming out of the earlier ages of reform: The late 1880s, when we passed antitrust legislation and created an Interstate Commerce Commission to regulate the railroads; the progressive period of Theodore Roosevelt and the first term of Woodrow Wilson, when these regulatory agencies were strengthened, and a

Federal Reserve Board and a Federal Trade Commission were created; and the first two terms of Franklin D. Roosevelt, when numerous regulatory agencies were spawned, most significantly a Securities and Exchange Commission and a National Labor Relations Board. But I believe future historians will have to record the period between 1964 and 1972—that of the presidential terms of Johnson and Nixon—as the age in which federal regulation of industry, business, education, and state and local governments made its greatest and most decisive strides. In 1964 we created an Equal Employment Opportunity Commission to prevent discrimination against minorities and women in employment; in 1968 we banned discrimination in housing and renting; in 1972 universities and local governments came under the control of the Equal Employment Opportunity Commission, and stricter bans on sex discrimination in higher education were imposed. Under the influence of Ralph Nader, and with the rapid rise of consumer and environmental movements, we created agencies for automobile safety, for environmental protection, for occupational safety, for consumer product safety. The effectiveness of these and other regulatory agencies is much disputed, but it is clear that they have enormously increased the power of government to intervene in what were formerly private decisions; they have imposed a great burden of paperwork on business and local and state governments, which every presidential candidate hopes to mitigate and none, when in power, it seems, can.

They have undoubtedly helped us to move in some degree toward their espoused objectives: equality for minorities and women, protection of the environment, protection for workers and consumers. Each has also spawned great volumes of regulations, new bodies of law, worked out, as is the nature of government agencies, in pedantic and humorless detail, and often to ridiculous extremes. This development raises questions in many minds as to whether it is still reasonable to consider the United States a country in which individualism prevails, rampant or otherwise. Thus, to give some examples: under the ban on discrimination based on sex in education, a boys' choir was considered discriminatory, and so was a mother-daughter event in a school. It is now considered discriminatory for an institution of higher education to impose different regulations on men and women: any sanctions as a result of pregnancy would be considered discriminatory. So would classes in physical education that separated men and women. Apparently, requiring short hair for boys and men is also discriminatory, as is requiring skirts on girls. Many institutions of higher education in the United States are set up under religious auspices, and in some of these, at least, the upholding of traditional morality is an important part of educational objectives. However, these colleges and universities also fall under the act banning discrimination on account of sex. To date only one, the Mormon Brigham Young University, has gained an exemption, on the basis of religion, from some of the requirements enforcing the ban on discrimination on grounds of sex.

It is clear that some part of American individualism, whether we consider it "rampant" or "rugged," is under severe restraint, and there is no hope that the restraints will become anything but more severe as time goes on. But it is necessary to point out that some kinds of individualism are under restraint only because another aspect of individualism is doing quite well. This is the political aspect of individualism, in which the single individual or individuals organized in private groupings battle for what they conceive to be their rights or a better condition. I have mentioned one name as expressing this rather remarkable aspect of individualism: Ralph Nader. It is hard to imagine a figure of this type having such great influence in any other country. He is without official appointment; he has no membership organization to support him. He wrote a book, *Unsafe at Any Speed*, on the lack of safety in automobiles, and was thus almost singlehandedly responsible for a great national demand for controls on automobile design, one that has affected the daily life of Americans perhaps more directly and immediately than any other legislation one can think of. It is as a result of this legislation that every American who drives a car (and that is almost all adult Americans) will be greeted on entering his vehicle by a buzzer that can be shut off only by putting on a seat-belt. The great civil rights movement, which was responsible for our civil rights legislation, owes much to individual heroes, of whom the most prominent was Martin Luther King. The women's rights movement, which has forced government agencies implementing civil rights legislation to devote as much attention to women's rights as to the rights of blacks and other minorities for which it was written, flared up, with no official encouragement or awareness, as the result of the actions of individuals, and became the most surprising and long-lasting phenomenon of the later 1960s, unexpected, unpredicted, unheralded, but suddenly there, wielding awesome power over government, business, universities, the mass media, and changing the very language with which one talked of women—just as the civil rights movement (or rather, one wing of it) changed the language with which we described the Afro-American minority. And so too with the environmental protection movement, which, flaring up in the later 1960s, developed great power, holding up the Alaskan pipeline, the development of off-shore oil resources, the development of nuclear power. This movement of individuals was able to get significant legislation passed and to intercede in the courts against so many forms of economic development that in 1979 the United States is more subject to the mercy of foreign oil exporters than it was in 1973.

Two faces of individualism: the more rugged economic and institutional individualism of the United States, hampered and hobbled by a new kind of individualism devoted to self-realization, to the protection of the environment, to suspicion of big business and big organization, which is still pragmatic enough to have enlisted, often unwillingly, the power of big government on its side, as is possible owing to the openness of the American political process, the power of the press and the media to arouse public opinion, the access to the courts of ordinary people and nonstate organizations that enables them to affect the very administration of law.

One kind of individualism hampered by another. Henry Ford hobbled by Ralph Nader. Will it matter, and how? Obviously the two kinds of individualism have different origins, motivations, consequences. Principally, the first kind has contributed to the most marked characteristic of the modern United States, its enormous productivity, while the second clearly places some limits on how this productivity may be realized. Both kinds are suspicious of government, but both are willing to enlist it. The first kind of individualism will enlist government to protect investments overseas, to foster economic growth and profits at home. The second will enlist it to achieve what is felt to be a fairer and more just society, and is relatively indifferent to the claims of production. The second kind of individualist thinks the United States is rich enough. He sees no need to endanger beaches with oil, rivers with nuclear power plants, forests because wood and newsprint are needed. This kind of individualist is disdainful of the objectives and motivations of the economic individualist: why do we need more gadgets, he is likely to say, or really more of anything? The economic individualist has, under this assault, lost his former arrogance. Very likely his own children are to be found among the passionate defenders of consumer rights, the environment, women, and minorities. And the economic individualist is hard put to justify himself. Having praised without questioning the virtues of abundance and continuous growth, he is at a loss when the simple question is put: "why?" The intelligentsia of the country is engaged in putting this question, ever more sharply, in the schools and universities, in press and radio and television, in political forums and Congress, and in the courts, which have, it seems, routed any other claimant to make the final judgments in American society, moral and political.

The upsurge of the new individualism against the old has many explanations. Basically, there seems to have been a dramatic loss in self-confidence, or, more precisely, in confidence in the old America, from about 1963 on. There was the shock of the assassination of John F. Kennedy, and it simply could not be well enough explained to themselves by the American people. A great tragedy cannot be allowed to remain senseless; people will insist on making sense out of it. From this point of view, the assassination of Abraham Lincoln had meaning: he died because he had tried to keep the union together and free the slaves by conducting a great war against the slave-holding South, and conspirators who hated him for this killed him. But what meaning could be given to the death of John F. Kennedy? Public opinion—even enlightened public opinion—refuses to accept what seems the most reasonable explanation, as well as by far the best-documented (indeed, the only documented) one, that he was killed by a single malcontent, and insists on finding a greater meaning: he was assassinated by the "right" (Texas millionaires?), or by the left (Castro?), or by Castro because the insidious American intelligence establishment, unbeknownst to the president, had tried to assassinate Castro.

But this was only the beginning of the series of blows to American self-confidence: there was the beginning of student protest on the campus that best represented America's claim that it provides the most advanced higher education to the broadest segments of youth; the riots of blacks in America's leading cities; involvement in a disastrous and unending war. And even that was not the end. There was the wide-spreading Watergate scandal, with all its ramifications, including the shattering discovery that our nation's leaders were engaged in acts against public morality and against the law. Perhaps we have come to the end of that period, which has consumed most of three presidential terms. But the result of it was the withdrawal of faith in America's central purposes and underlying virtue by a large part of America's youth, a large part of its mass media, a substantial part of its intellectuals. The defense of American society, the American political system, American culture, became, for a while, very much a minority and suspect activity, generally conducted under attack, and almost as a guerilla operation.

We have lived through a strange period in which two American presidents and their leading advisors seem to have conducted American policy in isolation from, and with the disapproval of, the highly educated public and the elite mass media. This is not the whole story. Faith in the system seems to have continued, even if shaken and weakened, among the less educated elements and the political figures representing ordinary people. Thus the United States has developed a strange political system. Overlying the more obvious and understandable divisions between the better-off and the worse-off, the businessman and the worker, the minorities and the majority, there is now a new division, between those who are basically conservative about the American system, who do not want to see rapid change, who feel that despite the traumas of the past dozen years America has not done so badly; and those who feel quite the opposite, who see the society, culture, and polity as something like disaster areas, and who want change. The latter element is better educated, more influential in the media, and was aided in gaining electoral office by the Watergate scandal. But this creates a substantial strain in the American system in my view: a basically conservative populace now finds its leadership concentrated in more liberal and to some extent even radical representatives. Many of the youth and antiwar leaders of the later 1960s and earlier 1970s are now in politics, and doing better than anyone could have predicted.

This strain is perhaps most clearly visible when we consider the second great theme of American history, the search for equality, around which serious conflicts have developed in recent years, with little chance that they will die away in the years to come. The young individualists fighting for the environment and safety and against big business were also fighting for equality, and much of the legislative revolution of the later 1960s and early 1970s dealt directly with equality, for racial minorities, for women, for linguistic minorities, for the handicapped, for the backward student of whatever kind, for the poor and the beneficiaries of government aid.

There was first important legislation—in 1964, 1965, 1968, and 1972—against discrimination on grounds of race, color, religion, or national origin in voting, employment, education, housing, public facilities, or any program receiving federal aid. Great changes took place on the basis of this legislation: segregation of students by race was finally wiped out in the South; employment practices began to change radically under the impact of the law; blacks began to vote in large numbers in the South in areas where they had been deprived of the vote, and began to elect state legislators, mayors, and other public officials.

Second, there was equally important action, independent of legislation, by the executive department of the federal government, the president, establishing affirmative action requirements for all federal contractors. A "federal contractor" was any business or other institution receiving federal funds—and that meant almost every business or institution. "Affirmative action" meant statistically based programs to hire certain specified groups—blacks, Hispanic Americans, Asian Americans, American Indians, and women. These programs became powerful tools pressuring businesses and universities to hire and promote the specified minorities and women.

Third, the federal and state courts mandated, on the basis of legislation and executive action, and also independently on the basis of Constitutional clauses whose interpretation was broadened, quotas in hiring in many businesses, and in many local and state governments; more radical desegregation of the schools ("bussing"); better treatment for welfare recipients, patients in mental hospitals, prisoners, handicapped people, and children who required special attention in schools.

All of this had substantial impact on daily life. In some cities, one third or more of the schoolchildren are now transported out of their neighborhoods so that each school might have a better mix of races. In some states, mental hospital and jail administration is now in the hands of federal judges, who may require heavy expenditures to improve facilities. Almost everywhere, judges require expensive education for children with learning difficulties so that they might have a better chance of attaining education similar to that normal children attain. This has contributed to the financial crises of states and cities. "Due process" now protects the poor and recipients of government funds in many respects; thus, families and individuals cannot be cut off from welfare, or tenants evicted from public housing projects, or children expelled from school without some degree of due process.

From one point of view, of course, we have seen a vast expansion of equal, or more than equal, treatment, owing to "due process" and "equal protection of the laws," but this development has not received universal applause. It makes more difficult the expulsion from welfare of those who lie to get it, from housing projects of disruptive and criminal tenants, from school of undisciplined children who prevent other children from learning. It greatly increases the cost of government, as courts mandate new expenses. And it raises troublesome questions as to whether the basic Constitutional division between executive, legislative, and judicial powers has not been transgressed when judges, in pursuit of "due process" and "equal protection," impose heavy charges on local, state, and federal governments.

I give this background to the equality revolution in the United States in order to raise a grave question: whether the equality revolution has now progressed so far that certain aspects of individualism are now in danger. One may ask, how can the expansion of equality threaten individual rights? Of course, observers of democracy have long understood—and once again we can refer to Tocqueville—that there are inherent conflicts between equality and individualism, or, if one will, liberty. Tocqueville was so sharply aware of them because the French Revolution, which swept away the inequalities in law that separated Frenchmen from each other, finally led to Napoleon's despotism. And Napoleon was able to present himself as fulfilling the aims of the French Revolution because, indeed, in the course of his progress through Europe he swept away the distinctions of the old regime and brought legal equality to all men—but an equality in which they were equal under despotic power. And subsequent revolutions have told the same story.

But whatever the long-range threats that equality holds for individualism, the problem in the United States is not that the drive to greater equality is laying the groundwork for the destruction of liberty. The situation that has developed in the conflict between equality and individualism is one that has not been clearly foreshadowed by political philosophers, one that is unique to the United States. The steady push toward equality begins to threaten individualism not because opinion is limited—it has never been freer in the United States; not because access to politics is limited—access has never been easier, as the party structure breaks down; not because access to the mass media to express unpopular opinions is limited—every opinion, even the most outlandish, finds access easy, and indeed the more outlandish the opinion, it often appears, the easier for it to find expression. The egalitarian drive threatens individualism specifically because it is directed toward the great American problem, the race issue, and in doing so it is erecting official racial and ethnic categories, on the basis of which rights, privileges, and duties are distributed by government, and by private employers and institutions under governmental pressure. This is a totally unexpected development, and one that has created the uneasy feeling that in the United States today the individual is no longer evaluated for purposes of employment or access to education as an individual, without regard for his or her race or ethnic group, but is regarded precisely as a representative of or member of some specific group, to get one kind of treatment if the individual falls in one category, and another if the individual falls into another category.

Of course, this has happened in other democratic societies, too. In India, for example, reservations for employment and study and political representation are made for groups that have been subject to deep and severe discrimination. In other countries, one finds the same reservations, not because one group has particularly suffered discrimination, but because a stable political balance in a deeply divided country seems to require it. Such "reservations"—in the United States, "goals" and "quotas"—are not necessarily incompatible with a democratic and just social order. Indeed, they may be necessary to achieve it. But much depends on the nature of the society in which they are introduced. In a society in which two or more groups are clearly defined and are expected to maintain their integrity indefinitely—let us say language groups in such countries as Canada or Belgium, or national groups as in Yugoslavia—justice may require equal representation for each group in many spheres, and this kind of arrangement may be most conducive to internal peace in a society.

But the United States has not defined itself as such a society. It has been a federation of states, not of peoples. Whatever the discrimination to which races and ethnic groups were subjected—and in some cases, in particular for blacks, Japanese, and Chinese, this discrimination found expression in public law—it was always the hope of the central body of American public opinion that all Americans would eventually be integrated into a common society without distinction of race, color, or religion. These categories, it was hoped, would become purely private matters, and government would not need to take cognizance of them. This hope was realized in the federal legislation of 1964 and later, according to which these distinctions could not be taken account of by any public body, and indeed could not even regulate private behavior when it came to such key areas of life as education, employment, housing, and access to public facilities.

It was the hope of the civil rights movement of the earlier 1960s that we would erect in the United States a color-blind society. But quite rapidly after 1964 that hope was reshaped, and public action increasingly took place on the basis of specific racial and ethnic categories. It is true that this public action was taken to undo the discrimination of the past, but it became very difficult to draw a line between the "quotas" that undid the effects of discrimination in the past and the "goals" that demanded employment on the basis of race and ethnic group in the future. Similarly, it became difficult to see the distinction between actions to break up segregated schools—something widely applauded—and actions to create a fixed racial proportion in each school, "bussing," which was strongly opposed. The achievement of employment goals and fixed racial proportions in the schools meant that government must once again number people by race and ethnic group, this time, it was explained, not for purposes of discrimination, but for purposes of making good the effects of discrimination.

But of course it is very difficult to draw a distinction between discrimination against and discrimination for. Indeed, all discrimination for must be against someone. Today it is sadly taken for granted by most white males, regardless of training and talent, that their chances of getting jobs in universities, against the competition of governmentally favored minority group members and women, are slim. Undoubtedly there are two sides to this question, and both are really on the side of the angels: those who call for goals and quotas want to see groups that have had modest or little representation in certain fields of professional work and in certain areas of employment better represented; those who argue against these measures want to see individual effort rewarded. And so we have the conflict between the goals of equality and the age-old individualist thrust in American life, one that has given it so much of its distinctive quality.

The two goals are now in deep conflict. A young man, Marco

DeFunis, white and Jewish, was denied admission to the University of Washington Law School, while others with lower scores, whom he felt deserved admission less, were accepted because of their minority membership. He could, of course, have argued that he was a member of a minority, too, but his minority, whatever the degree of discrimination against it in the past, was very well represented in the law schools and legal profession. Blacks, Mexican Americans, and other groups were poorly represented. But that was not his argument. He did not demand to be numbered among the favored minorities, but said that no one should be favored on grounds of race and ethnic origin. His case went up to the Supreme Court—which decided to take no action on it. But it could not escape so easily. Another case, that of Allan Bakke, who tried to enter the medical school of the University of California at Davis, has been settled by the Supreme Court, but not in a way that settles the issue, for while the judgment of the Court was that Bakke should be admitted to medical school, it also ruled that race could be taken into account in making decisions on admission.

DeFunis and Bakke wanted to be treated as individuals, and argued that their race or ethnic group should play no role in whether or not they were granted admission to highly sought places in law and medical school. The schools in question asserted they had a right, an obligation, to ensure equality of treatment, not of individuals, but of groups, so that groups that were poorly represented would be better represented. That, they asserted, was what the achievement of equality demanded. And so such questions were raised as the following. Is it not the individual who has the right to fair and nondiscriminatory treatment, and if the individual gets that, must it not follow that the group—simply an aggregation of individuals—is getting fair and non discriminatory treatment, too? If groups are to be equally represented, in medical schools, law schools, university employment, among business executives, in the civil service, must it not follow that individuals will get less than equal treatment? But if we concentrate on individuals alone, and some groups as a result are sparsely represented among important elites, will not the group suffer and therefore be deprived of equal treatment? Does not each group need its own doctors, lawyers, professors, government officials, business executives? How are we to ensure that they get their fair share unless we divide sought-for positions on the basis of population? But if we do that, do we not then give up the hope of an integrated and color-blind America in favor of one in which persons bear the marks of race and ethnicity, and are treated on that basis? Will this equal treatment by groups be only temporary, until each group reaches an approved percentage? And even if we are assured this is temporary, what happens when we turn color-blind—and a group begins to fall below its percentage, as a result of the fact that our efforts to recruit, train, and place members of that group have been given up? One can add to the questions— they are endless, but they are the questions we must live with in the later 1970s, and the 1980s, and perhaps beyond.

Let me make the problem more concrete. In 1965 American immigration laws were revised, and all reference to race and ethnic background was eliminated. There was no longer any limitation—as there had been for many decades—on the immigration of Asians, or any other group, for that matter. In response to this change in law, the number of Indian immigrants to the United States rose rapidly. From under three thousand a year in the early 1960s, the number of Indian immigrants rose to about fifteen thousand a year between 1971 and 1975. Many of these immigrants were professional workers—doctors, engineers, and the like. Now, under affirmative action procedures, employers who are government contractors—and just about every hospital and engineering and scientific research firm is a government contractor—must have an affirmative action plan. They must set "goals" —numbers for each group—and try to reach those goals. One of the four ethnic categories for which they must set goals is "Asian Americans." But who are Asian Americans? When the affirmative action procedures were set up in the mid-1960s, there were very few Indians in the United States, and what government agencies had in mind were Chinese and Japanese, who had been discriminated against in various ways in the United States. I believe that by the mid-1960s most people would have said that this discrimination was a thing of the past, and statistics showed that by that time Chinese and Japanese were better educated, had jobs of higher status, and earned higher incomes than the average American. Nevertheless, governments operate in strange ways, and they were included as one of the four groups, along with blacks, Hispanics, and American Indians, on whom employers had to report, and whom employers had to include in their affirmative action plans.

But what about Indians from India, who were very often in the same occupations, and competing for the same jobs, as Chinese and Japanese? The affirmative action guidelines were silent on Indians.

They, it seems, were to be considered "Caucasian/White," and therefore not one of the groups favored for employment under affirmative action. An employer could gain a credit for getting closer to his affirmative action goal by hiring a Chinese or Japanese, but not an Indian.

Indian immigrants were thus placed in a dilemma. I am sure Indians immigrate into the United States for the same reasons other people do: they are engaged in an individual search for education, or jobs, or income, or a way of life they prefer. They may expect to maintain their culture, religion, and language, but through their own efforts, and they hope to be treated as individuals by government, employers, and schools, on the basis of their merits. But it turned out that they were not being so treated. Should they petition for what we might call "minority" status? Should they demand that government agencies in charge of the key forms that employers fill out be instructed to include Indians among "Asians"? Should they demand that the Census Bureau set up a special category for Indians—for if it did not, no one would officially know the number of Indians in the United States, and an affirmative action plan would not be possible, because the plan can require only that employers reach goals set on the basis of an official count of the group. Some Indians resisted this approach; after all, they said, we have come as individuals, we want to be treated as individuals. But others argued that Indians were being treated less than equally simply because other groups were the special object of governmental solicitude. At a meeting called to consider what action should be taken, one Indian asserted: "Indians should make it a point to be judged on merit alone, wherever they are." Another answered: "I endorse your views, but the tragedy is that the slate is not clean. The distinctions have been made, and we have to face it." In the end, the decision was to request that Indians be listed under "Asians" for purposes of affirmative action, and that the Census Bureau set up a special category for Asian Indians.

This is a minor eddy in the swirling conflict between the individualistic and the egalitarian trends in American society, but it is one that reflects larger and deeply troubling issues. We are far past any simple stage in the struggle for equality in the United States. As Tocqueville foresaw, equality was to become *the* great goal of society. But equality is no simple matter. One can pass the right laws, eliminate acts of overt discrimination, open entry to schools and employment and government and public places. But at each stage new questions are raised, questions never dreamed of at the stage before. Those who in the early

1960s thought equality demanded that no person be required to give his race or ethnic group in applications for admission to schools and employment now think that it is essential, in order to achieve equality, that every person be required to do so. Troubling and difficult questions have been raised as government, to achieve a greater equality, begins itself to impose limits on the dreams and aspirations of individuals on the basis of their race or ethnic group. There is only one comfort to be taken from the present situation: we deal with these more complex questions of reconciling individual rights and equality only because, happily, we have already dealt with the simpler ones.

NOTES

1. Alexis de Tocqueville, *Democracy in America* (New York: Knopf, 1946), 2: 98, 99.
2. Ibid., p. 100.

7

AN UNEMPLOYED FAMILY

THOMAS J. COTTLE

It goes without saying that unemployment has the most profound economic implications for an individual and his or her family. One repeatedly hears of unemployed people desperately selling belongings or being caught up in the bureaucratic mazes of welfare and insurance offices. Yet there are other significant implications to unemployment. A person's sense of worth is called into question; political and religious attitudes, as well as feelings about one's country, are re-evaluated. Unemployment makes one redefine one's sense of masculinity and femininity. It turns people against their spouses, parents, and children. In the most perplexing ways, it demands that people devise new philosophies of living and dying, philosophies that either justify their struggle to survive, or end their lives. It is not melodramatic to say that the effect on many people of being out of work is so severe that they are forced to find not merely alternative sources of income, but alternative philosophies and styles of living.

Long-term unemployment may well be likened to an illness. It assaults people, affecting their physical and mental health, as well as their spirit. Unemployment has been shown to be related to increased rates of depression, infertility, tooth decay, impotence, backache, infant mortality, child- and wife-beating, theft, homicide, and suicide. It can destroy individuals as well as families. Research performed by Dr. Harvey Brenner of Johns Hopkins University showed that in New York State, over the last 127 years, admissions of psychiatric patients to hospitals increased markedly with each significant national economic decline.[1] Brenner's finding of the relationship between psychiatric illness and economic problems was confirmed in studies done in New Jersey and California.

Presently, we are in possession of a great deal of data on unemployed people. We know the rates of unemployment in the major census tracts of the United States; we know, too, how politically charged these rates become during periods of national elections. While these figures are familiar to many people, it is worthwhile to review some of them, even though they shift daily, as a function of myriad economic and market factors.

As of January 1977, the *Monthly Labor Report* indicated that 7.7 percent of America's labor force, or approximately 8 million people, were out of work.[2] Generally, unemployment is highest among people aged 16 to 19 (19 percent), and specifically among blacks of this age group (37.1 percent). Black men of 20 years and older show a 10 percent unemployment rate. In addition, 10 percent of women who head families are out of work, as are 8.1 percent of full-time workers and 7.9 percent of married women whose spouses live in the house. In terms of occupation, blue-collar workers (9.4 percent), operatives (10.8 percent), nonfarm laborers (15.6 percent), construction workers (15.6 percent), and agricultural wage and salary workers (11.7 percent) reveal the highest unemployment rates. Not so incidentally, veterans of the Vietnam War also show high unemployment rates. Over 500,000 veterans are out of work, with the highest rates occurring among veterans aged 20 to 24 (11.3 percent) and 30 to 34 (5.1 percent). Unemployment, moreover, runs higher among black veterans (30.5 percent in September 1977) than white veterans.

In general, the average duration of unemployment is 15.8 weeks.[3] Normally, unemployment lasting 15 or more weeks is called "long-term unemployment," while that lasting 27 or more weeks is called "very long-term unemployment."

In contrast to the typical picture of unemployment affecting poor and working-class people is the surprisingly high rate of unemployment in middle- and upper-middle-class communities. As Keniston recently observed, all families in the United States, and especially the poor ones, are experiencing extreme pressures of one sort or another.[4] But the fate of poor families must not obscure the destructive quality of unemployment among more affluent families. The data on unemployment rates among affluent families are far from precise. Leventman reported that in 1971, 20 percent of America's technical professionals—scientists, engineers, data analysts, and so forth—were out of work.[5] According to Leventman, many of these professionals never got "hooked back" into jobs after their initial layoffs. Indeed, of the approximately one hundred unemployed men she interviewed in 1971, 80 percent still had not settled securely into new jobs when she interviewed them again in 1975. Many had found work on contract jobs ranging in duration from several months to a year, but contracts afford neither job security nor fringe benefits.

In an article published in the *New York Times*, A. H. Raskin, a specialist in labor affairs, pointed to perhaps the most telling of the statistics regarding the unemployed, and more specifically, the long-term unemployed. He wrote that unemployment insurance, the major source of income for the unemployed man or woman, will soon be exhausted for more than two million workers. Furthermore, in many states the period of unemployment insurance is gradually being shortened, just as the amount paid is being reduced. Obviously, these facts hurt the very long-term unemployed person, the person who has not worked in more than twenty-seven weeks the most, although ironically, it is the long-term unemployed worker about whom we know the least. Typically, these are people who have lost their jobs rather than voluntarily moved out of the labor market. They amount to about one million people. Two and a half million heads of families, male and female, have been out of work for more than fifteen weeks, according to Raskin.

What do the long-term unemployed do? Even with Raskin's figures, the work done by Professor Eli Ginzberg, the chairman of the National Commission for Manpower Policy, and government studies, the answer is not entirely clear. One study, for example, indicated that about 25 percent of long-term unemployed people simply gave up looking for jobs within a year or so after their unemployment insurance ran out. Contrary to popular belief, fewer than 10 percent of the long-term unemployed had turned to welfare by this time. Fewer than 25 percent had applied for food stamps. Many borrowed money, although here whites had a distinct advantage over blacks, and many more white families than black families showed a spouse with some job.

As a final statistical note on a subject where the statistics can at best be considered imprecise and tentative, the government lists some 815,000 men and women as "discouraged workers," people who have given up the hope of finding employment. They are not physically or psychologically handicapped people, or people who drift in and out of the labor market and who in their work-nonwork patterns cause minor fluctuations in labor statistics. They are people perfectly willing and able to work who have quit looking for re-employment.

For the last ten years, my research has been devoted to studying how life is led by people in poor and working-class American communities. The actual research consists of nothing more than conversing with people over long periods of time and then, when the moment seems propitious, writing about these people so that others may know of them and the conditions in which they live. It is a form of research enlightened by the work of social scientists and writers, clinicians and journalists. One is constantly tracking down stories, listening as a clinician might to the special problems and despair people are able to share, seeking relationships between individual lives and significant political, economic, and religious issues. And then there is the final writing, the form and style of which in great measure reflect one's attitudes toward the people with whom one has been speaking. For better or for worse, one's own personal experiences make their way into these conversations, and one's reactions to them. Not to be confused with a clinical or medical case study—for the people I have spoken with are not patients—the life study finds its origin in the act of bearing witness or testimony. It is an elaborate profile in which one relies heavily on reporting the words of one's informants. Emphasizing the subjective analysis of materials, the technique depends in great measure on selecting and ordering materials so that a coherent and, ideally, artistic product is achieved.

Unemployment statistics, however essential they may be to our understanding of the problem, cannot tell the complete story of the effect of long-term unemployment on people. To know this effect, and equally importantly, to *feel* it vicariously, one must listen to the words of the unemployed and their spouses, children, parents, friends. And one must honor these accounts of the *experience* of long-term unemployment in the same way that one honors hard-earned statistics. For at times it seems that we prefer to think of the unemployed as statistics. Or perhaps we would rather read fictional accounts of unemployed men and women, for while they may touch us deeply, we may "protect" ourselves with the notion that, after all, it is still fiction.

Among the more than sixty-five families I have studied in which one or more family members were unemployed, many workers have been hospitalized for organic and psychological reasons, some have committed suicide, several have murdered their wives or children, some are in jail, many have children presently serving jail sentences. The families live in rural as well as urban areas. Some were once quite rich, others have known nothing in their lives but poverty, while still others would be called representatives of the working and middle classes. They are as young as fourteen, and as old as seventy-seven. Some were born in the United States; others are immigrants. They live in the North, South and Midwest. Some are formally educated, having earned college and advanced degrees; some have completed no more than six years of grade school. They represent the major religions, the major trades, and seemingly every point on the political spectrum.

My conversations with unemployed people and their families are often tape-recorded. More often, however, they are reproduced and then shown to the people, who are asked to point out errors of content and tone. In all cases, the final manuscripts are approved by the families, who grant permission for publication.

Clearly, a study of long-term unemployed men and women is addressed not only to a major social and political issue, but to the meaning of work as well. It is addressed to topics like physical and intellectual competence, the recognition and utilization of one's talents and capacities, the union of education or training and career. Only some of us will attempt to improve the conditions of the unemployed, and indeed find satisfactory employment for them. But all of us must learn from these people, as well as learn how to feel about them and their circumstances, for their experiences and accounts enlighten our own understanding of ourselves, our work, and the culture in which individuals and forms of work evolve. All people have their work stories; millions in the United States now have out-of-work stories. Each of these stories is different, but many of them, while clearly unique to the individuals involved, speak to issues and feelings that great numbers of families know only too well. What follows is but one of these stories, one of these life-histories.

When Davey Sindon was small, Victoria, his mother, used to put him on her lap and sing, "Davey Sindon's gone to sea, leaving his father and his sister and me." No matter how often she did it, the little boy laughed and bounced up and down, giving all the signals he could conjure up to get her to repeat it. By the time he was five, he could not remember his mother's ever singing to him. As for the verse, "Davey Sindon's gone to sea," he was not even certain what it meant. "Is daddy a sailor?" he would ask his mother earnestly, not sure what exactly a sailor did.

Like his older sister, Effie, Davey gave his mother great pleasure. Indeed, the two children were Victoria Sindon's only source of pleasure. She could be tough with them, though never mean, but she never did anything that would make her children question her love for them. The rule for Victoria was constraint. She never left the children unattended, never surprised them with changes of mood or deviations in the pattern of their lives. People wondered how she did it, in light of the ferocious world in which she lived, married to Ollie Sindon, but Victoria always said, "It's easy to be a gentle boat when the sea is roaring. If the sea roars, boat doesn't have to do nothing but hold on to its course." Her friends would smile. Victoria had a way with words. She had a way with people, too, that rare ability to make the hard times seem easy, to make human survival during its most precarious moments seem effortless. She also had that special talent for keeping people from asking her pressing questions when they knew she was ducking away from personal turmoil. All one had to do was walk past the Sindon house when Ollie was going through what Victoria called his "complaining lessons," and one knew her life was difficult to the point of disaster.

The problem was not Ollie Sindon's mercurial temperament, his fiery responses to everything from politics to changes in the weather. Rather, the problem was his being out of work. The problem was his moroseness and anger and sickness over being turned down by employers, being lied to, having his few hopes shattered. "They're bombing me out," he would roar, if he was not weak from drinking. "Bombing me out with their promises and their bullshitting. I had it with those folks, all them folks, long, long time ago. They hate us Niggers till it just about kills them to have to look at us. Give us a job, shit, they'd just as soon give what little they got to an animal 'fore they'd give us a look. Go in there with them white faces looking at me. Oh-oh, here comes another Nigger wanting to be lazy on another job. Close the door on him 'fore he gets in too far so's we can't throw him out. You got a family, man? Holy shit, here's another family man out on the street. Hey, but what the hell, Niggers don't give no shit for their families. His old lady's probably doing it with some son of a bitch right now, so what's this guy care. He don't care. Do you care? You goddamn right I care, Mister White face or black face. You goddamn right I care. 'Cause I ain't working. You hear me? I ain't working, and if I ain't working, I ain't living, 'cause I don't live if I don't work. You hear me, man? I'm not living no more till you give me a job. You got to give it to me."

Victoria would stare at him as hard as she could, and without raising her voice she would warn him: "You don't talk that way with me or I take those children and I leave. I am just as nervous and upset about your not working as you are, but I will not have everybody's life being spoiled by your problems. We live on what we have, what we'll get. But don't you go on playing those plays of yours. I will not be your audience any more." Then she would leave him before he had a chance to speak, and by his own admission, he would be happy that she had silenced him, for his complaining hurt him almost as much as his not working. And there was hope. Jobs had turned up in the past; they would turn up in the future. "Just let the future come quick," he would whisper, following Victoria into the back room, the single bedroom in the apartment, where the children slept. What a feeling to look down at the two of them, so little, asleep, breathing so slowly and regularly, the two of them so wondrously unaware of his problems and the miserable times they might be facing.

Ollie Sindon knew perfectly well that he wanted to share his agony at being unemployed with his children, despite the fact that they were too young to understand what it meant. He wanted them to say, Dad, you got the rawest deal any man on this earth ever got. But you'll see, if things don't turn out better, we're going to make it better for you. We're going to stay by you no matter what, even if it means we'll never get married or move away. You did the best you could for us, and we're going to do the same for you. But no matter what happens, we'll never see you as a failure. It's the country, the world, the society that's at fault, not you! You did the best you could. Ollie Sindon wanted so much to be happy. He saw his life as complicated, but he never gave up the idea that he could be satisfied. He was willing, he told himself, to settle for very little, but one requirement was steady work until he was sixty-five and ready to retire. He dreamed of the day he would be too old to work and he would say to his son, Well sir, Davey, the load's all yours. From now on, you look after this family. And Davey would say, You worked steady all your life, dad, now it's my turn. The daydreams were plentiful, all of them realistic, all of them with happy endings, but each one based on the idea of a man working his forty good hours a week and bringing home a paycheck for his wife, his children, and himself.

Victoria Sindon was the only one who knew about Ollie's fantasies. She used to tease him about them, at least when she was certain his mood was strong enough to take her chiding. She would say, "You know, my husband, for someone who spends so much time dreaming all the time, your dreams aren't too rich, are they?"

"What do you mean rich?" he would ask her, obviously insulted.

"Well, if I was dreaming, I'd put us in a big house somewhere, but all you see is working steady forty hours a week."

"That's all I see," he'd answer quietly.

"Maybe that's all any of us have the right to see. Well, maybe someday you should think big, dream about working steady forty-five hours a week. Then we'd have that little bit of extra."

"Listen, chum," he would say, both of them starting to laugh, "if I start dreaming really big, I'm going to dream about working steady twenty hours a week and still end up better than what I got right now."

"Bet you would, too."

"You know I would. Then I'd add a little more. I'd add that I could see my boy working even less and getting even more. No. Let him work just as long as I did, only let him come out of it a whole *helluva* lot better than I did. I wouldn't want no one to repeat what I went through."

Ollie Sindon's wishes never came true. His career was at best spotty; his periods of unemployment were frequent. He was never a skilled laborer, but no one could work harder. He rarely looked at his watch. He quit when the job was done, even if it meant coming home a few hours late. Victoria never liked to add to his burdens, or shake his luck, but when he was working and the job looked as if it might last, she would not hesitate to ask about his long hours. "No one's asking you to work more than eight hours a day," she would say when he came home, exhausted and dripping with sweat. "You aren't that young that you can go on like a boy."

Ollie loved to hear her talk this way. He loved the feeling of being exhausted from a hard day of work and knowing that no one in the world could tell him he had not put in one amazing day. "I got pride," he would tell his wife. "I may not love what I'm doing, but I'm working, and working is the great act, the act we're put on the earth to do."

"Glad you told me," she would wink at him, " 'cause a person like myself's always happy to know why we were put on the earth. Now that I know it's because we get a chance to dig ditches for some rich white man, all of us can sleep better tonight."

"Don't you fool yourself, Victoria. Everyone gets the most gratification out of his work he can. Doctor gets his kind of gratification, butcher gets his kind, even an old women like you gets her kind. You work 'cause that's what we're meant to do. Some folks use their heads, some folks use their hands, but it don't make no difference, 'cause the society needs all of us to be doing our work, even if the work's so terrible we can barely get ourselves out of bed in the morning to do it. There is no world without people working. I'm digging holes for telephone poles. Wouldn't exactly call it the greatest job in the world, but it's important. If I don't do it, I don't stay alive."

Victoria Sindon was happy when her husband worked. Her children, too, she imagined, seemed healthier when he was working. They ate better, and it was good knowing there was a little money left over to buy those special treats the family liked. There was not a man in the world who liked steak like Ollie Sindon, steak followed by strawberry ice cream. It was there when he worked; it was never talked about when he did not.

By the time he was eleven years old, Davey Sindon knew all about his father's difficulties in finding jobs. He knew it was bad luck to say anything about a job his father held or might get, for even breathing a word of it might mean the end of the job. He knew not to speak to his father about where his father had gone on a particular day. Ollie arrived home around six o'clock. Maybe he had worked, maybe he had not, but one waited to see what he would say. His children did not ask questions, nor did his wife. Most days no one had to ask; it was clear he had not worked. His eyes and posture told everything. Maybe he would ask Davey if he wanted to throw a ball around. Davey would grab their mitts and a ball and be downstairs on the street in seconds. His father would follow minutes later, walking slowly, wearing his suit jacket, and they would throw the ball back and forth, his father's mind clearly on something a million miles away. It was better, naturally, when Ollie was in a good mood, when he was working. Then there was real excitement in the game. They pretended to be professional ball players, and Ollie would do a play-by-play description of their game.

"There's a ground ball in into the hole," he would shout, rolling the beaten-up old ball down the sidewalk. "Sindon over to his right, makes a great pick-up and throws him out. What a play, what a play!" Then Ollie would tell his son, "Put your foot behind your hand on grounders. It's added protection." Davey would lean down and try it. "The other hand, the one with the mitt."

"Do it again," his son would order.

"Ground ball to Sindon. He hasn't much time, Morgan can really fly, but he throws him out. Get down lower, David. Lower to the ground." Davey tried to follow his father's instructions. "Lower still, that's it. What, you afraid the ball's going to hit you in the face?" Davey had to admit he worried about the ball skipping off the concrete and hitting him squarely in the mouth. "Hey, listen," his father would shout at him, his hands on his hips, "you want to be a major leaguer, you got to take the chances. It's just a job, with its own kind of chances. Man digs holes, there's the danger he could fall in one of them. Man digs for coal, there's a chance he can get caught in the collapse. Man flies a plane, there's a chance he falls right out of the sky. You go for a grounder, someone leaves a little bitty stone out there, that ball's going to pop up right over your head. Got to have fast hands, fast hands."

"You play ball, Ollie, when you were a kid?" Davey would ask, for when they played together he pretended they were teammates rather than father and son.

"Did I play ball when I was a kid?" Ollie would shout back in disbelief. Victoria would be watching them from the window, barely able to hear them, and making certain Effie did not fall off the ledge. Effie always cried because Davey would never let her play when he was playing with his father. "Did I ever play ball when I was a kid?" Ollie's deep voice would rush in through the window like thick smoke. "Who do you think taught Billy George Blatter everything he knows about baseball?"

"Billy George *who?*" would come Davey's little voice. No matter how many times Ollie pulled the routine, Davey went for it.

"You don't know Billy George Blatter?" Ollie would say with exaggerated incredulity.

"No. Who's Billy George whatever his name is?"

"Victoria," Ollie would shout up to his wife. "This boy of yours doesn't know who Billy George Blatter is."

"Suppose you just tell my son then who he is."

"Tell him yourself," he would shout, laughing until his mitt would fall off and he would drop the ball, which only irritated Davey that much more.

"How the hell should I know? Anyway, hurry up because the steak's almost ready."

"Steak!" Davey would scream, forgetting all about Mr. Blatter, and off he would dash, leaving Ollie to carry the mitts and ball upstairs. At dinner he would tell Davey that Billy George Blatter was a little boy who went to the same church as he when he was a little boy. Truthfully, he could not figure out why that name had come into his mind, but one thing he did remember about little Billy Blatter was that he was the worst athlete in the neighborhood, maybe the worst in the state. Ollie even remembered hearing the boy's father say that Billy George was so bad at sports, he must have had white blood in him. He was going to speak to his wife about that. The thought made Ollie Sindon laugh out loud. "I think even Effie could have taught that boy a thing or two about playing baseball."

Davey would have lost interest in the story by this point. His father's enjoyment at such a foolish story irritated him. "We ought to have steak every night," he would say.

The remark would quiet Ollie. For a few minutes the family would eat in silence.

In the beginning, no one knew exactly what had happened to Ollie Sindon. Merely remembering the event was difficult enough. It was a Wednesday morning, *that* Victoria knew for certain. A Wednesday morning when he was out of work. He awoke and found he could not get out of bed. Victoria told him to quit joking, but he insisted he could not move his left leg. Soon he realized that he had lost all sensation in the leg. Victoria was terrified. Fortunately the children were at school. A police ambulance arrived, and two attendants carried Ollie down the stairs. In time he recovered most of the feeling in the leg, although no amount of therapy healed his limp. The leg was never as strong as before, and while he tried to hide his slight handicap from potential employers, his chances of finding a job grew even thinner.

Ollie Sindon suffered his minor stroke when Davey was thirteen and a half. Victoria took on odd jobs—sewing, house cleaning, laundering—when she could find them. She disliked being away from her husband, who had grown depressed after his illness. The energy he had always been able to draw upon during the long weeks and months of unemployment had vanished. He would threaten suicide, go several days without speaking to anyone, demand to be fed when he knew there was no food in the house. When Victoria offered to go shopping for bread and the kind of cheese he liked, he would yell at her for leaving him alone in the house. What if he needed her suddenly. What if he fell, or suffered another stroke.

"Get someone else to go shopping for you and arrange your life better to shop when Effie's here. And how come Davey isn't home at night? Why don't you talk to him about why he's never home when he's supposed to be? Just 'cause I'm not working don't mean he's supposed to be playing around all the time. What do you tell him? His father's a cripple? That his father's a bum? That why he's not here? What is it with all these kids, anyway, that they get so damn disrespectful? Girls, too. Who they think they are, anyway, acting like they're superior to everyone, wanting only this kind of food or wearing only that kind of clothes? I'd like to tell them about what *real* hard living's all about. I'd like to see them do a whole lot better what with the conditions I had facing me. Big time, that's all they want, the big time. Hell, I'll bet they sit around talking about me. 'My father don't work no more 'cause he's got a bum leg that keeps him home. 'Course, even if he didn't have it he wouldn't work anyway 'cause he always had trouble. Probably didn't want to work, neither. That's the real story behind it. Never saw an old man so lazy. Hell, he didn't even have time to play with me when he wasn't working. Told my mother, you're not supposed to work, then he didn't work himself. So what'd he expect, us to work, me and my sister? Laziest Nigger in the city, my father. Wasn't even a good ball player.'

"VICTORIA! Where the hell are you?"

"I'm here," Victoria would scream right back at him. "I am god-damn sick myself with all your complaining. You've complained about one thing or another from practically the day we got married. Now what the hell is it? You want to eat, I told you I'd go to the store. You want to talk, we'll sit here and talk. But if it's the feel-sorry-for-the-poor-old-man bit, I have had it up to here. You want to complain about how you're the only person in the world who's got problems, you go right ahead, but I ain't listening to it, and I'll be damned if I'm ready to tell my son he has to sit here at night with his father and listen to all the garbage that flies out of your mouth. It's just garbage, and I don't want to hear it no more!"

Ollie Sindon listened to his wife when she spoke to him. He felt increasingly sorry for himself and would not let her gain an inch of advantage over him. He fought her, defended his position, but he listened to her because, like her, he blamed himself for his troubles. Still, he fought her.

"You don't want to hear me talking, that's fine. Why don't you just pack your little bag and take all your junk and get out of here. Take the children, empty out the kitchen, take all your friends for all I care. I'd be better off without them floating in here all the time asking me about this job or that job, or saying it don't look to me like you got any problem with your leg. Take 'em all. Or maybe you'd like me to leave. That's it. I'll leave. I'll run out of here. Why don't you go down to the five and dime and buy me a track suit and I'll run out of here. Give all of you the big laugh you want out of me. What the hell, you laugh at me behind my back, might as well do it in front of me. I sure would love to know one of these days just what it is you tell that boy about me."

"What the hell are you talking about?" Victoria would come into the living room and stare at him, but Ollie would pretend he did not know she was there.

"Well, son," Ollie would begin, "it's like this. Your father's a big bust. Just another one of those dumb Niggers that didn't spend enough time in school, so here he is, a big failure, not that anyone ever thought he'd come to much more than what he is. He tried. Even thought he'd be able to make it, but it didn't work out. He's just a two-bit bum! Tell you, son, there's only one thing a man's supposed to do, and that's work. If he don't work, well, he just ain't a man. So you see, son, your old man ain't a man at all. He's just a dumb old NIGGER!"

"Shut up," Victoria would cry out. "Just shut up or I *will* leave."

"Go on. Who the hell needs you around here, anyway—all you do is mother people. Hell, you been mothering me like I was the boy's brother instead of his father."

"You act like you were his *baby* brother 'stead of his father. That's the first true thing you said all day. 'Bout time you started acting like his father."

" 'Bout time you shut your face up."

"I don't see where just because you ain't working don't mean you can't take a little fatherly interest in him."

"A little fatherly interest in him," he would mock her.

"That's exactly what I mean. A little fatherly interest."

"You know something, Victoria, you're beginning to sound like some of those high-class white folks you been working for. Maybe that's what you want, too, since you are the man of the family. Ain't that it?"

"What you want to eat?"

"You didn't hear me?"

"What do you want to eat?"

"I'm asking you a question," he would scream at her.

"What do you want me to say?" She could not have sounded more bored.

"I want you to say that because I don't work and never worked regular like a man should, I'm only his father by title. That's all. I carry the title, just like I carry a card that says I got a right to work. Neither of them does no good. I'm a shit ass father, man, and you know it. World's number one worst father, to both of 'em. But I ain't got no excuses. I ain't making excuses to nobody. I don't care what happens to either of them, 'cause I came first, man. I'm the one. You get it? I don't have a job, there ain't no work in this country, bad leg or not, then I don't mess around with no children. That's your job. Ain't my job. Don't give a damn about them. Don't need to see them, don't need to talk to them, don't need them for the slightest goddamn thing. Boy wants to talk with some man, let him find somebody at his school. Better yet, let him go find one of those bullshit Nigger ministers. You want real men with real jobs, hard-working men, men working their asses off for the community and just for the love of God, then that's who he can go talk to. That's your real man. Go in the church, man, with all those guys running around in there. 'Hey man, what you do?' 'I work for God, man.' 'Oh, yeah? What you do for God, man?' 'I light candles and keep people from sinning.' 'Yeah, that right, man?' 'Sure is, man. Get money for it too, telling all the little children with fathers who don't work what to do.' 'Yeah, what you tell 'em to do?' 'I tell 'em how they got to have compassion for their poor old stumbling fathers. Got to have all kinds of compassion. Poor old dudes just sitting up there in their ridiculous little houses watching the walls and waiting to die. Got to advise all those little children so's they see the light of God.' 'Hey, man, that's one helluva job you got there working for the church. I talk to those children myself, man.' 'Yeah? Ones with the unemployed fathers?' 'Sure, man. I talk to 'em just like you do.' 'Yeah? That a fact? And what do you tell 'em?' 'Me? I tell 'em if you're old enough to see your old man ain't working and you're old enough to understand that if he don't work it means he ain't bringing home a fuckin' dime, then you're old enough to get away from that man as soon as you can, 'cause he ain't no man. He ain't your father. He's nothing, man, absolutely nothing. And the sooner you forget the sight of him, the better off you're going to be. Don't hang around him if he ain't working. He'll just bring you down with him.' "

Victoria would close the door to the apartment and start down the stairs quietly. She would be weeping. Then Ollie's big voice would bellow from the living room. "Victoria, Victoria," he would be yelling. "You get back in here at once. You come back in this house in one minute or I won't be here when you get back. You can just say good-bye right now. You come back here!"

Victoria would leave and buy strawberry ice cream for him, even though the doctor said Ollie would do better without too many starchy foods.

No matter how hard she tried, Victoria Sindon could never convince her husband that being out of work did not reflect on him as a man. He was a good man, a good father, she tried to assure him. But there was no convincing him. A job possibility would arise through some friend, and his spirits lifted, but Victoria could see that he was scared now because of the uncertainty and the months of inactivity. There were days when the little bit of hope she wanted to hold on to seemed real enough, but no jobs ever lasted, and Ollie was not getting any younger. Indeed, he seemed to be aging more quickly than anyone she knew, with the exception of her son.

At fourteen, Davey Sindon was an extremely strong young man, quiet, polite, but filled with anger. Several close friends spoke with him, but he let very few others know what he was thinking and feeling. Surely his father had lost touch with him, and while his mother believed she knew what he was doing, Davey insisted she had not the slightest notion of who he was. A deeply complex person with many talents and a rich intelligence, he dreamed of becoming all sorts of things, and was blessed with a miraculous memory. But in most conversations that focused on his life, the matter of his father's unemployment played a significant role. It was like a fire in him that never went out, a haunting demon. He himself could not define what it was, exactly, that infuriated him: the conditions that made for widespread unemployment, or the mere fact that his father spent so much time out of work. He might start a tirade against America, its racism, the fact that the country allowed so many people to be poor, but soon he was haranguing against his father, calling him weak, a quitter, a man who rolled over and played dead with his own kind. He labeled his father "the nice little Nigger man" in the company of white folks. Davey Sindon believed that since the odds were so stacked against him and his family, the only way to lead his life was to let nobody see he was afraid of anything and to take the attitude that he had everything to win and nothing to lose, except the respect of a few people, like perhaps his own father.

Davey Sindon had grown up to be a tough boy. His manner troubled his mother, infuriated his father. "They're all fancy big shots," Ollie Sindon would growl at Victoria when Davey strutted out on a Friday night, dressed in clothes that Ollie disapproved of and believed to be stolen. "Phoney big shots. Son of a bitch child looks down his nose at me, and there he is strutting around as if he were the goddamn tax collector. If he disapproves of me so much, let him get his own goddamn home. He can do so much better without me, then let's see him try. They can both go, far as I'm concerned. Let him show this great big world he thinks he's discovering and all these people he finds to hang with to his sister. Then *she* can be a phoney big shot, too. Where's he get those clothes?"

Victoria would not answer. She held the same fears as her husband about where her son went and what he did. Victoria's problem was to get Ollie to turn his attention from his own concerns to those of his son. No one needed to tell Ollie that he was a failure, that with each passing day his chances of resurrecting his life grew slimmer. No one needed to tell him, as he himself said, that his salvation lay in making certain that his children would not share the fate he had known. But something always kept him from putting his own problems aside long enough to attend to his children, and especially his son. No matter how intensely he resolved to devote himself to Davey, his bitterness at being sickly and out of work never allowed him to carry out his wishes. He would try, but then Davey would say something, and he would give up all ideas of befriending his son.

"You know where that boy's going to end up, Victoria?" Ollie would mutter when Davey had left.

"I know exactly where he's going to end up," would come the voice from another room, for Victoria made it her business to overhear the conversations between her husband and son. "He's going to end up in jail. Won't be long now."

"Way you say it, makes it sound like that's what you want."

Victoria would not bother to respond.

The thought that he might end up in jail had crossed Davey Sindon's mind as well: "Could happen, man," he would say, beginning to smile his smile of toughness and defiance. "Could happen all right. Steady work though, in jail, ain't it. I mean, you don't even have to go looking for it, or have some Mr. Nobody with a big stomach interview you or nothing. You walk in there and the cat says, your job's working in the carpentry shop. You got a job, man. They even pay you to work. That's true, ain't it? Pay you a little money, ain't much, but what the hell, working for peanuts is better than not working for no peanuts. You don't believe me, you just ask my old man. He'll tell you all about working. Man, has this country screwed *that* guy up. Sent him this way, sent him that way, scratching for jobs. Down on his knees, I'll bet, more times than he'd ever admit, begging for people to give him a job. So what the hell if I am in jail. They give me the work, I'll blow out my time there.

" 'Course, my old man, he'd be so angry 'bout me being in the slammer. Love to see that man's face when the cat comes and tells him, We got your little boy locked up for ripping off a bank. Son of a bitch kid, he'd be yelling at my mother. Told you he was no good. Told you he was the biggest bust this side of Africa. Yeah, but tell me, copper, how much the boy rip that bank off for? Couple thousand maybe. Couple thousand, man? Shit. I may go into some prison somewhere, if they catch me. But if I go I ain't going for no two thousand dollars, baby. I go in for the kill. Six figures right up front, man, or I don't even talk about the job. You see my old man starting to smile, laugh out loud. Hey, is that a fact? Old Davey boy ripped 'em off for six figures. Son of a bitch kid didn't do so bad at that, even if he is in prison. Hell, time will come when they got to let him out. Hey, tell me, copper, they find out maybe he left a little money for his poor old mom and dad. Ain't worked in twenty years, man. Bet he left something outside for me. Hell he did, old man. Told me to tell you you played the good little Nigger part too long, man, way too long. You could have been in on anything you wanted to. Yellow shit bastard that you were. Sitting in that chair of his, bitching all the time 'bout this and that to my mother, my *mother*, man, like she was the governor or something.

"You get a load of that guy, man, begging in the streets so's he got the whole community laughing at him, and he's putting it to my mother? What the hell he think she's ever going to do for *him*. That son of a bitch walked, she walked blocks, man, more streets than you could count, looking for the food he told her he wanted. You imagine that, man, sending that woman 'round the city shopping in just the stores *he* wants, buying him just the certain kind of ice cream he wants, 'cause you can't get the brand in stores 'round here? Son of a bitch worked, hell, no more than a few years all together since he was married, and he's pushing her 'round like some big king. Should have seen him too when he got sick, you know with that leg of his. Doctor told my mother he was fine. He went around acting like they took the leg off him or something. He's an actor, my old man. Makes everybody treat him special like he was somebody famous. Who the hell are you, man, Martin Luther King or someone, that you're acting so high and mighty all the time? He's nothing, man. He can't stand to face it, but he's nothing. The more a man is nothing, the harder it is for him to let on that he is. You want to bullshit the guys at the poolhall, let 'em think you ain't drawing welfare? That's okay, man. Nobody wants to be seen as a bum. Nobody says you got to advertise your losses, you know what I mean. But that man was acting like he was doing all right in his own home, in his own home, man. Front of me and my mother and my sister. Who's he think he's kidding?

"And that's another thing. All this time he ain't working, all he's thinking about is me, his famous son. Half the time I think he's try- ing to figure out ways I won't end up being like him. But the other half, man, I really think the son of a bitch was plotting how to have me end up in the same shit pile as him. Swear to God, man. I think it'd kill him to see me successful when he failed so bad. There ain't no one talked so bad as he did. But don't think once he's paid any attention to my sister. I can't even remember him asking her what's she doing, like at school. And that kid is smart, man, she can read, man, like a son of a bitch. She reads out loud to my mother some- times at night. I tell her to shut up, you know, 'cause I'm trying to sleep, but I'm only pretending, 'cause I love to hear her read. Kid's out of sight, man. Adult books. My mother gets her all these adult books and she goes through them, zip zap zip, and she's finished. She remembers 'em, too. I do too when I hear her reading them out loud. She's terrific. But you think my old man has once said, hey, you know what, Effie, you're the best reader in this city. I'm proud of you, Effie. Good Effie. Fuck you, Effie. Don't say a word to her, man. Man's got two things on his mind. He ain't got no job so he thinks he's got the right to order us around. Nobody's told him you got to earn your place in the house. You don't just get it for free.

"Other thing he thinks about is how soon it's going to be 'fore I end up in the slammer. Shit, I got a mind to walk in on him one day, you know, and say, Hey Pop, I'm going to take a big load off your mind, listen here. I'm going to be in jail in less than a year, so now all you got to worry about is feeling sorry for yourself. But don't trouble yourself none, 'cause it wouldn't look right, somehow, your getting off your sweet ass trying to find a job somewhere so's your old lady might have a couple of nice days on the earth before she croaks. And while I'm in jail, pop, why the hell don't you introduce yourself to the little skinny girl who lives in the same apartment as you. You named her after your own mother, so you must have been interested in her once. Instead of sitting there trying to convince everybody you can't walk and that's why you don't go looking for a job, have her read out loud to you. You'll be surprised. Shit, man, I'm not so sure my old man even knows how to read himself. I guess he must, I see him with the newspaper every day. Don't do him a helluva lot of good, though, does it? Maybe he don't know they print jobs available in it. Probably all he's doing is choking himself to death on the comics.

"I don't know, sometimes I feel sorry for the guy. Tell myself, hey, the world is tough, 'specially if you're black. Lots of folks out of work. Lot of white folks out of work. Nobody cares all that much about how many folks don't have jobs when it's just black folks out of those jobs. Going around mumbling, can't get good help these days. Ain't like the old days. Uppity Niggers won't work for twenty cents an hour no more. Terrible times. Then all of a sudden, like, all these white dudes, they start losing their jobs too, high-paying guys, vice presidents, lots of 'em are out of work. Then all of a sudden that's all you hear about, unemployment, unemployment. Ten years ago nobody said a word. Now everybody's bitching and moaning. Who was looking out for my old man ten years ago? Nobody, man. They were just out there on the streets looking for the cheapest labor they could find. Hell, those bastards, they knew they could buy men like my father cheap, and man did they ever give 'em the shittiest jobs in this city. Holy Jesus, man. They had my father standing waist-high in shit, honest to God. They had him up to his ass in shit, digging, and the son of a bitch came home proud of his work, telling my mother he did a good day's work. They paid him shit, man, for working in shit. And the man felt proud. He felt proud like he just done something fantastic. I can't believe it, man. I know it's what happened, but I can't believe it. He used to come home—I remember 'cause most of the time when I came home he was already home, which meant he didn't work that day—he'd be smelly like you couldn't imagine. Me and my sister couldn't stand how much he smelled. We had to get out of the house, man. I mean, we got out of there. My father, he and my mother pretended to be angry with us for walking out like that, but you could see they were only pretending. Everybody was happy then, 'cause the man had work. When he was working, we were happy, 'specially my mother, no matter how much he smelled. I was happy, too. I was only little, so I didn't know. I mean, I wasn't old enough to be ashamed of what he did for a living. What's your old man do? My old man's a lawyer. What's your old man do, David? My old man stands ass-high in shit and shovels it around, but he's happy 'cause he's got a steady job. Little kids ain't ashamed of their fathers. They don't know what being out of work is all about. They don't even know where the old man goes, or what he does or doesn't do.

"But all that's different now, man. He never works. We never have enough money, so I ain't got a single reason in the world why I should stay around that house. I might have thought he was pretty cute when I was small, but I don't see nothing cute about him now. It's my job to make sure my mother and Effie are going to be all right, 'cause he sure gave up on that job a long, long time ago. Man doesn't take responsibility for no one. He'll push my mother around, man, about the slightest thing that bothers him. Hey, Victoria, there's a fly buzzin' 'round my chair. Hey, Victoria, how come my shirts ain't clean? Hey, Victoria, how come your son's always getting into trouble? He's tough on her, man, like you couldn't believe. But she takes it. Maybe there's something wrong with her, too, I don't know, in her head I mean, to take all his pushing her around like that. Hell, if I was her I'd tell him, Hey, lookit here, man. You work for a living, get up off your ass one second of the day, and I'll *think* about obeying some of your orders. But if you just sit there looking so goddamn mad at the world all the time, I wouldn't go across this room to open the goddamn window for you. She don't tell him nothing, though, man. She just takes it. Almost like he's got some special right to be out of work. It's like he's always telling her, all these cats are out of work, so he ain't special. Ain't his fault. Lots of guys like him out of work. You can't argue with the man. Black folks are getting killed without jobs. They're getting murdered, man. They'll take a black man's job from him ten times faster than a white man's job. You got a bunch of cats working, say, on some big construction job downtown and the word comes down to cut off some men, who you think they're going to cut first? They're going to cut every black man off that job, unless the dude is so well trained, like he's in some specialized job, they can't get along without him. But there ain't a lot of specialized cats, 'cause they don't train 'em until they've trained all the white guys they can find. Then, if they got some good jobs left over and they can't find no white guy, they'll go train some black guy. Shit, jobs being what they are, you can be damn sure that cat's going to turn his back on his own brothers if he can save his job.

"So who's my father got helping *him* out in the world, man? He ain't got nobody, man. They're ain't nobody out there, unless it's somebody watching him, figuring out how he's going to take my old man's job, if he ever gets one. Guy don't stand a chance. He's got a one in a million chance, man, just to earn a living. You imagine how that makes him feel? Man has to pull his body out of the bed every morning knowing he's got a one in maybe ten million chance to make his goddamn living. I ain't talking, man, of making a lot of money, not even the money he *needs*. I'm just talking about the man's chances of making *any* living. It's no wonder he got sick like he did. This thing breaks your spirit, your body, there's nothing left of the guy. When I was small, you know, and he was working, not all the time but a helluva lot more than he does now, that man was fun to have around. Man used to play ball with me, cat was a stitch. He'd clown it up, make it fun for me, 'cause it sure couldn't have been too much fun for him. Hell, I couldn't catch the damn thing, and half the time I had him running in the street or down some cellar stairs. But he was a jive, man. He had everybody laughing. Folks used to stand around and watch him. He knew everybody, man. After work, all the men would come down to watch my old man play ball, and all these little kids wanted to play with us. I didn't want 'em to, you know, but I didn't say nothing 'cause my father would probably say, you gotta share, you gotta share. But he knew I didn't want to play with 'em. He knew what I was thinking even without me saying a word. He'd tell 'em, Hey, this scene's just with me and my son. This here's our special after-work baseball game. Man, I felt fantastic. I'd think, son of a bitch, man has to be the greatest father alive.

"Hey, but you grow up, you learn what's really happening in the world. Hurts you to learn, but that's what it's all about. You see your father sitting home all the time, bitching 'bout that, moaning 'bout that, and no matter what he says about how black folks got it tough, and the world don't want no part of us, I see him not working. You know what I mean? Words are one thing, but what he does or doesn't do, that's a whole other thing. And the dude ain't working. Never. Just picking on my old lady, every day when I'm around, which means he's probably knocking hell out of her when me and Effie ain't there. But she don't say much. When he screams, she screams back, and the rest of the time she don't say nothing at all, man. I used to think to myself, why's she take it like that. I used to think, too, I'm going out to make money. I'll give 'em both all my money. You see me, ten years old, looking for a job in this city? I think I'll be a president of some big company. Why not. Get me fifty, sixty thou a year and give it to my folks. Little kids and all their dreams, huh?

"I'll tell you, man, I really didn't know what to do with either one of my folks when it got so bad. I said to myself, I'm either going to run away or I swear to God I'm going to kill 'em both, 'cause they're both crazy. I'm watching my mother, this is, like, two years ago, and she's not well. Effie doesn't know what's happening, but she don't look good to me at all. But I don't say nothing. What am I going to do about it anyway? I was waiting for my old man to do something, or say something, but he don't move up off his ass far as I could tell. This is when he maybe didn't work, like, one week out of fifteen, man. So he's bad off like always, but my mother's getting to be bad off, too.

"So one day I come home from school, and I got to take a piss something terrible, man. So I run up the stairs, thinking for sure I'm going to do it in my pants and I, like, fly into the toilet, and there's my mother sitting there crying, you know. She's surprised to see me, but the tears are all over her face. All of a sudden I didn't have to piss no more. I mean, you see your mother and she's all by herself and she's crying, that scares the piss out of you, right? So I ask her over and over again, 'What's wrong, what's wrong?' and she keeps saying, 'Nothing's wrong, nothing's wrong.' 'But you're crying,' I tell her. 'That ain't nothing,' she says. 'I don't know why I was crying. Something in my eye.' Yeah, sure, you got something in your eye, you ain't sitting in the bathroom looking like she looked. My father, he was sitting in the living room like he always did, he didn't even know she was in there, 'cause I went in there and asked him and he was surprised. He even called her, you know, 'You crying, Victoria?' and she comes out and says 'No.' She don't have to tell me not to tell him no more. I can see plain as hell she don't want him to know nothing about nothing. So I don't say nothing.

"Then nothing happens for a while. My mother's going 'round acting like everything's fine and like what I saw in the bathroom never happened. Then about a month later I heard my aunt talking to my mother's best friend. They're outside on the sidewalk, but I could hear 'em 'cause I hid behind the door. I could see 'em, too. My aunt is talking and she's telling Morane, that's my mother's friend, how my mother's sick and what she has to do, which is to go, like, once a week to this place, where she gets an x-ray. I can't figure out what they're talking about, 'cause this was a couple of years ago and I thought x-ray was like when you broke something. But this was something different. Like, they were trying to make her well with it 'stead of taking pictures of her with it. Anyway, I figured some of it out and Morane told me the rest later. You know my mother had cancer, maybe she still has it, and she was afraid to say nothing about it to my father, 'cause she said she didn't want to bother him about it 'cause he was too upset about his own life to hear any more bad news. You believe that woman acting like that? Shit, man, I get cancer and wonder if I'm going to die any minute, I'd go crying to anybody I could find, and the first person I'd cry to is my husband. He tell me not to moan 'cause he's got worse problems, I tell him to get the fuck out of this house and don't ever come back. Ever!

"That woman hid that she was sick from him. He didn't know till after she was done going for those treatments. Then she had to keep going back to see if she was well. They can burn you up but good and it still grows back. I learned all this from one of my teachers. She said, you worried by all this, David? I said, 'No, what's to be worried about. She's only got it in one part of her body.' I didn't even know where she had it. Teacher asked me, but I didn't even know, man. When I found out where it happened I almost threw up. I mean, I never thought too much about how women are put together, and then this teacher tells me how they do it, and I imagined my mother lying there on this table and them putting this machine over her, man, and it doing whatever it does, and all I could think about was her sitting in that bathroom and not telling my father what was happening, 'cause she was worried about *him* all the time. About *him*, 'cause he was always so down about not working. Still is down. He's always down. But with her, it was always my father who was the bad-off one. Shit, I'd have killed the man for acting like that with her being sick. Never got her flowers or nothing, or bought her a present or helped her in the house. The both of them were just walking around pretending nothing was wrong with her. I couldn't believe it, man, and the worst thing was, like, Effie didn't know nothing about none of it. Didn't even know my mother was sick, and I didn't know if she was better from all the treatment. I had to ask Morane, who had to ask my aunt. Even my mother didn't know for sure. Morane knew about everything that was going on, and she for sure didn't know what I knew. I had to tell my teacher, be sure you don't tell either my mother or father what you been telling me. You want to hear something? When I told my teacher, you know, not to say nothing to my folks, she goes, 'I didn't even know your father was alive. You never say nothing about him.' It was true, too, 'cause most of the time at school I was always so ashamed about him never working, I pretended like he was dead, 'cause I never wanted no one asking me about him.

"But the thing was, my dad was upset by everything going on. He got scared about my mother same as I did. Then he got feeling really sorry and bad 'cause he'd been such a bad husband to her. That's all he could say for months. 'I been bad, Victoria. I been bad.' He was like a little kid. I didn't know whether to feel sorry for the guy 'cause he had no job and his wife might be dying, or angry with him 'cause he was acting like a baby. He never made it easy for any of us to know how to feel about him. You could love him or hate him practically in the same minute. Hell, I got so frustrated from seeing him acting like he did, I decided I'm getting out of that house as much as I can, all the time if I have to. I know my father real well, and I know what he was thinking. He was thinking, Dear Lord, let me find a job with my wife sick. Anything. I'll do *anything*, but I need a job *now*. But he couldn't get nothing, man, not a dime's worth of work anywhere. So between him not working and my mother lying on that table once a week with that x-ray machine burning her insides out, where a woman has her baby, you know, shit, you can imagine how we were doing.

"Effie, though, she was doing fine, which sort of made me happy. She'd come home and read and read and help my mother, or whatever she'd do. You couldn't tell by looking at her she knew anything different from before. Fact is, I was certain she didn't know nothing. So one day I took her with me outside, you know, and I said to her,

'Effie, you got any idea what's going on in our house?' 'You mean dad not working?' she goes. 'I say, that ain't new.' 'You mean about mom and the x-ray treatments?' 'Yeah. You know where she's getting them?' 'At the hospital, I suppose. Never asked.' That's what she said. 'Not in the hospital. Where in her body, you know, where they're working on her?' 'Yeah.' She knew. I tell you, man, the kid's out of sight. 'They're working on her uterus,' she said. 'On her what? What they call it?' 'They call it a uterus,' she goes. Then she says, 'Don't worry about it none, you ain't got one, so you ain't going to get sick there.' And all that time I was walking 'round trying to make sure my kid sister doesn't know what's happening. So I asked her, 'How come you know so much?' So she says, ' 'Cause I talked to the same teacher you did. She even gave me a book to read.' Effie's going to be all right. Someday she's going to be successful, even though she is the daughter of a sick old mother and a father who's just barely staying alive.

"Then there's me. I got the same parents, and look at me. David Sindon the nothing. Kind of sad, I'd say, way I'm turning out. I'm sure it makes my old man sad, my old lady, too. I don't know what Effie thinks. Can't think much of me, I'd say. Can't see how any-body'd think too much of me by this time. Most of the time now I don't know whether to blame people for what's happening or just forget them or what. Talking with my old man doesn't help, 'cause no matter how good he sounds when he's talking, I just can't get up the respect for the guy. Like, when he talks to me about being a man, it makes sense, but it'd be a whole lot better if someone else was talking, 'cause he ain't much of a man himself. I mean, I'm sitting there, man, and the man's telling me about working and getting jobs and making steady money and having a nice wife and kids, and maybe taking vacations, which is something we never did once in our life. I don't blame him for not having vacations, but what's he talking about all this stuff about living in the middle-class scene, man, when he ain't worked, like, for years, man. There ain't nothing he's done that makes him so much of a man that he can talk like that to me. Just 'cause he's my father? Hell, it ain't nothing to be a father. It's the woman does all the work, not the man. In my family my old man could have done a lot more than he did, too, 'cause he didn't have nothing else to do with himself. Just like me now. We both got all the time in the world on our hands. Neither one of us no better than the other."

David Sindon was fifteen years old when he knifed Jared Alexander in a street fight. Both boys had been drinking. Indeed, the young men who witnessed the fight reported that the two combatants did most of their fighting kneeling and lying down because they were so drunk. Nobody knew what started the fight. David had cajoled a woman into buying liquor for a group of boys. Suddenly David and Jared were fighting. Jared produced a long knife, and David broke a bottle and foolishly threw it at Jared, leaving himself without a weapon. But Peter Mixley threw him his knife, and the boys wrestled around and crawled and fell over one another. Finally, a gurgling, painful sob came from one of the boys, and there was Jared Alexander lying doubled up in the street, David's knife stuck in his abdomen. Blood was everywhere, and the boys were terrified. At first, David thought of leaving Jared there, but Peter insisted they had to call the police. David argued with him, but their discussion was superfluous, since another boy had already run off to get help. Three men appeared, and in a matter of minutes the police were present.

David Sindon was charged with manslaughter and put in jail to await trial. His parents were sickened by the news. They visited him every day, worrying about him, and confused by the long wait before his trial. Because of their financial situation they were obliged to accept a court-appointed lawyer, who met with David three times in five months.

Victoria Sindon had not responded well to the x-ray treatment and underwent surgery. The cancer had spread to her bowel, a section of which had to be removed. Her son cried when he heard the news of the operation. Effie came to the prison and talked with her brother, but David preferred that she stay away. She was too good and too smart to get messed up by his troubles, he told her. She offered to come and read to him but he refused this, too, even though he loved listening to her. Ignoring his request, she visited him every week and brought him magazines. She had landed a job with a neighborhood store and spent her money on little gifts for her brother in prison and her mother, who was recuperating at home. Amazingly, Effie Sindon's schoolwork remained steady. Her aunt and her mother's friend, Morane, helped out at home, for everyone wanted to make certain that not all of the family's burdens fell on her shoulders. "Effie's going to make it," her father said. "With her brother and her mother and me and every other problem in the world she has to face, the girl's still going to make it."

Friends rallied around the Sindons. Every day one could find some-one in their apartment, preparing food, cleaning up. A woman would leave her child in the care of another woman at the Sindon's so that Victoria would not be alone and Effie would have time to do her schoolwork. David's friends, too, wanted to help. They washed win-dows and floors and ran errands for the Sindons. In time, Victoria seemed to be recovering. Much of her strength returned, although she would never be the woman she was. Ollie Sindon became extremely quiet and depressed. No one could lift his spirits, no one could con-vince him that what he called his collapse as a man had not brought down his entire family. He made arrangements to visit his son every day. Even when David rejected him, he sat alone in the waiting room of the jail. He never read or spoke to anyone; he merely sat, his eyes fixed on the door leading to the cells, hoping his son might change his mind. When visiting hours ended, he rose and walked to the bus stop, waited for the bus, and began the one and a half hour journey to his home.

In the year following David's trouble, Ollie Sindon lost fifty-five pounds. While he had always been somewhat overweight, no one could say he was fat. Whereas once he had an enormous appetite, now he missed meals. Even at dinner, he just picked at his food. He ate better on the evenings when his son had met with him in the visiting room, but even these occasions did not raise his spirit. He blamed himself for everything; this was his punishment.

"Going to starve myself," he said, "till I find out about my son. It ain't going to be good with him no matter how it comes out, but it don't make no difference to the way I feel about myself. You take any human tragedy, and you'll find right off the one person who's to take the blame for it. You may not be able to put your finger on him, but he's there somewhere. Got to be that way. You take an airplane crash, someone's to blame. Don't matter if it's bad weather or what, someone messed up, and he's to blame. It's the same with me. I can go the rest of my life saying bad economic times, that's why there weren't jobs. I can say racism, black folks always have it the worst. That's just like the bad weather in an airplane crash. Some pilots got through the weather; they all didn't come through. Some black men found work. Even if they have twenty percent unemployed now, they still have eighty percent employed, don't they, and a lot of that eighty percent is black, ain't they? So lots of men living right in this com-munity may be in the same boat I am, but most of 'em ain't. I *know* they ain't. So there *is* someone to blame, and you don't need the police to find him.

"My God, my life has been wasted, and wasteful. Never was much as a kid, still ain't nothing much as a man. I have a wife who wouldn't be as bad if I was working. I got a kid in jail who for sure wouldn't be there if I was working. I got Effie, God bless her. Maybe I go on just for her, or maybe for all of 'em, I don't know anymore. Maybe I never did know. I could quit. You got lots of folks in this country quitting where I'm going on, you know. Guys blowing their brains out when they lose their jobs. Holding on for a while, then sticking the old shotgun down their throats. Rich ones, too, folks used to having everything they want and suddenly they got a whole new life. They see where it's at. You got a lot of reason to call it quits, I can tell you. Saddest thing to me is I don't even know how to go about thinking about all this. I never did much at school, quit going to church a long time ago. When I do go I don't learn anything from it. I don't even know what I'm supposed to know or not supposed to know about living and dying. Way it looks to me now is the whole point of living is dying. That's the way *I'm* living, at any rate. 'Cept I know there's one hulluva lot more to living than that. I never thought that way when I was working. I didn't think much of dying when I was working regular. Just took what come each day and let it go at that. Time's got tough, things would just work themselves out, I'd say. Work themselves out. I didn't think about dying. Now I ain't got anything else *to* think about.

"This whole thing's a goddamn war. I'm fighting a goddamn war, and I'm losing, I can tell you. That enemy out there is coming in on top of me, beating the shit out of me, man, and I'm not up to taking it much longer, which is probably a lie 'cause I been taking it this long, I suppose, I might just go on and on taking it. Man like me wants to yell out it's somebody else's fault, not my fault, don't look at me like that. But it's my fault. Like I say, I could go on about doing it all so different it makes me sick. Could have done so it would have come out much better, believe me. Just like I said, man, I'm running out of words. I don't know how to go about even thinking this thing through. My boy don't always talk to me, my wife's been sick, my daughter could go at any time, and I'm walking around wishing my own mother was still on the earth so she could fix everything. Now, is that the way a man goes through his life, wishing his mamma were still here to take care of him? That's a beaten man talking. That's a man getting his teeth kicked down his throat talking. That's no winner coming at you, no winner at all. Holy Jesus, I got so much pain now; pain inside pain inside pain. There's not a doctor in the world could fix me now. Take one pain away, and I'd come up with a hundred more to take its place.

"Holy Jesus, give me a break, will you. Ain't it been long enough? You want to punish me, punish me, but get it the hell over with already. What I need to take more pain for? I'll tell you why He gives me all that pain, too. Because He knows I can take it. He knows I ain't about to jump out of no window or stick no gun down my throat. He's got an easy victim with me. Yessir. Tells all His angels, lookit down there at old man Sindon. Got a boy going to jail, got a wife going to go back to the hospital one of these days, that's the guy you want to give your pain to. Man hasn't worked all this time, so he's got nothing to do with his time but take all your pain. So give it to him. Give it to him hard as you can. I know that man down there, he's going to take it, has no choice but to take it. There's nothing he's going back to or forward to. We're going to give him the job he's been looking for all these years. We're going to give him the job of taking all this pain we're going to give him. You hear us, Ollie, we got a job for you, full-time job. You're going to be working now day and night, seven days a week, three hundred and sixty-five days every year. You're going to be a pain hauler. Don't make much money hauling pain, but it'll keep you out of trouble. Keep you from getting bored, keep you from eating like you should and sleeping like you should. You just relax now, man, 'cause we got mountains of the stuff for you to haul, and the rest of your life to do it. What the hell, man, you ought to be in good shape for it, too. You ain't been doing nothing to tire yourself out for the last ten years. You deserve this, man. This job is marked just for you. You're the only man who can do it, you pain hauler, you!"

NOTES

1. See M. Harvey Brenner, "Personality, Stability and Economic Security," *Social Policy* 8 (1977): 2–4.

2. On a monthly average, 3,000,000 people lose their last job. Some 900,000 leave their last job, while 900,000 seek their first job. Also on a monthly average, 2,000,000 people re-enter the work force. But let us be reminded that each month the work force increases, so even if unemployment percentages remain the same or dip slightly, actual rates of unemployment may be increasing.

3. On a monthly average, one finds an almost equal number of people (some 2,500) unemployed for less than 5 weeks, 5–14 weeks, and more than 15 weeks.

4. See Kenneth Keniston, *All Our Children* (New York: Harcourt Brace Jovanovich, 1977). See also Joseph Becker, ed., *In Aid of the Unemployed* (Baltimore: Johns Hopkins Press, 1965).

5. See Paula Leventman, *Professionals Out of Work* (New York: Free Press, in press). See also her "Nonrational Foundations of Professional Rationality: Employment Instability Among Scientists and Technologists," *Sociological Symposium* 16 (1976): 83–112.

8

DEVELOPMENT NINETEENTH-CENTURY STYLE: SOME HISTORICAL PARALLELS BETWEEN THE UNITED STATES AND JAPAN

HIDETOSHI KATO

FRONTIERS

The greatest tourist attraction of the city of Sapporo, the prefectural capital of Hokkaido, the northernmost island of Japan, is the campus of Hokkaido University with its statue of Dr. William Smith Clark. The famous words he addressed to his students—"Boys, be ambitious"—are inscribed on many souvenir items. Indeed, the name of Dr. Clark has become so famous that more than 80 percent of Japanese high school and university students today can identify who he was and what he did in Hokkaido. It is doubtful if 10 percent of American intellectuals, or the students of Amherst College, where Clark was president in the 1870s, know his name. Clark is one of the few Americans whose reputation is uncontestably more widespread among Japanese people than among his countrymen.

Clark came to Japan in 1876 at the invitation of the Japanese government to help inaugurate a new agricultural college in Sapporo, and he was appointed schoolmaster. He persuaded Kiyotaka Kuroda, the commissioner of the island, to establish a completely new school system based on his own philosophy. He lived in the dormitory with the students and took them on field expeditions into the wild woodland—Clark was a botanist—opening their intellectual curiosity while instilling spiritual aspirations. Hokkaido at that time was inhabited by a small population of aboriginal Ainu and was not agriculturally developed.

The enrollment of the new college was extremely small, only twenty-four students altogether, but their backgrounds and qualities were extraordinary. They were boys who had already been enrolled as the students of the Tokyo English school (which later became the preparatory school for Tokyo University) but had decided to quit it in order to join Clark's new school. It was as if in the middle of the nineteenth century a group of students from a prestigious East Coast school had suddenly left it and moved to an unknown new school in Minnesota or Nebraska. The twenty-four boys dared to take the chance, partly because the government had promised a generous stipend, but mostly because the whole setting—a vast wasteland, a new school, a new educational philosophy—was attractive and challenging.

Clark stayed in Hokkaido for only eight months and then went back to Amherst, so his encounter with the students was extremely brief. At the farewell party held for him, Clark left those three famous words, that was all. But he made an incredible impact. The boys stayed to be "ambitious." Moreover, the words were inscribed in the minds not only of those twenty-four students but of millions of young men who heard about the episode. The challenge "Boys, be ambitious" has been inherited from generation to generation, and even today the sentence is one of the most popular English sayings in Japan.

Among the students who studied with Clark were such eminent figures as Shosuke Sato, Kanzo Uchimura, and Inazo Nitobe, who later became leaders of Japanese education. The agricultural college grew into Hokkaido University, one of the seven major national universities in Japan. It is hard to think of any other American who left so extraordinary an impact on a foreign country.

Why was there such an impact? Why did twenty-four boys decide to come to Hokkaido without hesitation? Why did Clark come? The answer to these questions is found in the sociopolitical significance of Hokkaido in the middle of the nineteenth century. Hokkaido had been the land of the native Ainu, covered by heavy woods with millions of deer, bear, and wolves. The sea and inland rivers were rich with salmon, herring, and seaweed, and as early as the fourteenth century small settlements by Japanese were established in the southern part of the island, mainly for trading with the Ainu. Migration from Japan continued, and in the seventeenth century the Matsumae clan occupied the southern peninsula and established it as a part of Japan. From 1799 through 1807, the Tokugawa government sent explorers to the island and declared sovereignty to check the Russians, who were trying to migrate to it from Siberia. A certain ambiguity combined with power politics prevailed in regard to the sovereignty of Hokkaido, but somehow the Tokugawa succeeded in including the island as a part of the Japanese nation.

The political and military importance of Hokkaido was recognized by the officials of the Meiji government. They were deeply concerned with international relations, and believed that Hokkaido was the most urgent problem that the new Japan had to deal with. For Hokkaido to become part of Japan under international law, it had to be legally annexed to the nation, and Japan's sovereignty had to be approved by the international powers. In order to strengthen their de facto sovereignty over the island, it was necessary to have Hokkaido inhabited by a large Japanese population. The government encouraged migration to the wilderness. There were, fortunately for the government's policy, people who were willing to migrate. They were former samurai, loyal to the old regime, who had belonged to the army defeated in the civil war (1864–68) and had thus lost their status and position under the new government, which was dominated exclusively by anti-Tokugawa elements. They needed new jobs and assignments, just as the officers of the Confederate Army did after the American Civil War, and their former status, pride, and discipline seemed to be ideally suited to the new venture in Hokkaido. Kuroda, the newly appointed special commissioner of Hokkaido, encouraged them to go to the island as "special military police," to protect the island from attack, presumably from Russia. They were given individual houses with huge lots of land for cultivation. The heads of households were armed with guns so that in case of emergency they could form an organized militia. In peacetime, they were independent farmers. The first group was recruited from Tohoku (the northern part of Honshu) in 1875, and 208 households migrated to Hokkaido in 1876, the year Clark came to establish the new school. One of these pioneering ex-samurai, Tomohiko Abiko, wrote in his diary, "I came here with the pride of serving for the nation and the aspiration to cultivate the virgin land." Recruitment continued until 1899. By that time the number of households that had migrated to Hokkaido was 7,337, with a total population of more than 40,000 scattered in thirty-seven new village communities; 40 percent of the heads of households were ex-samurai. Other than those selected by the government, there were many civilians who lookd to Hokkaido as the land of promise. In 1897 the total population of Hokkaido reached 700,000, mostly farmers. The native Ainu were suppressed, and many of them died. Deer, whose meat was one of their major foods, almost disappeared because of hunting by the immigrants and merchants.

This picture suggests a parallel with American social history of the same period: the ambiguity of territorial sovereignty, the unexplored wilderness, rich natural resources, the encouragement given by the government, the fate of ex-officers of a defeated army (even the timing of the two civil wars coincided, though the scale was quite different), the suppression of native tribal people, the crude exploitation of resources by profit-seeking merchants, the disappearance of the deer paralleling the disappearance of the buffalo, and above all the existence of "frontiers," even though the Japanese frontier was much more modest in size than that of the United States. Genius and wisdom, combined with intuitive judgment, led Commissioner Kuroda to follow the American frontier model. First, he invited Horace Caplon, the U.S. commissioner of agriculture, to be a consultant for the reclamation and development of Hokkaido. Caplon came with a team of experts and proposed a major development plan that called for the investment of some 12,500,000 Yen, or $12,700,000, for a period of ten years, from 1872 through 1881. Kuroda not only invited experts from the United States, but also sent young people to study in America. In 1873 alone, the office of the commissioner sent twenty-three students to the United States with a budget of $22,400.

Kuroda and his officials were adventurous enough to follow much of the advice given by the Americans. For example, in planning the city of Sapporo, they followed American city-planning practice exactly, using a geometrical grid with numerical street numbers, so that the American natural historian Edward Morse, visiting Sapporo in 1878, wrote in his diary, "The streets of Sapporo are wide and cross one another at right angles. The whole town suggests a new but thriving village in our Western States."[1] Even today, Sapporo is an exceptional and exotic city in Japan because of its completely American style of city layout. For obvious traditional reasons, the commissioner's office had hoped to develop the island by growing rice, but the technical advisors insisted on converting the land into pasture to feed cattle. The commissioner's office followed the suggestion. Hokkaido thus became cattle country, and it still is famous for its dairy products. In short, the island of Hokkaido was turned into a small-scale frontier society on American lines.

Other American items were brought to the virgin island. For example, Caplon found that the Japanese were not equipped for the extremely cold weather in Hokkaido, except for their small hibachis, and introduced the Franklin stove. The device was so efficient that manufacturers in Tokyo started producing it, not only for the people of Hokkaido, but for the Japanese market at large. Caplon wrote that the stove was a small souvenir to the people of Japan from America.

It was in this historical context that Clark came to Sapporo. It was quite probable that he saw, perhaps to his surprise, the same social and spiritual atmosphere he might have found in the western territories of North America. Like their counterparts on the American frontier, the new immigrants to Hokkaido looked on the island as a dreamland where infinite possibilities might be realized. On the main islands, new, tight administrative organizations were being established, but Hokkaido seemed to have more freedom and elbowroom. That was why twenty-four ambitious young men did not hesitate to go to study with Clark in the wilderness.

Tocqueville refers in a famous passage to the difference in the patterns of colonization of North and South America, saying that the colonizers of the former conformed to a pretentious morality and legality, while those of the latter occupied the territory with violence. Japanese policy toward the Ainu was somewhere between the two, and the government headed by Kuroda must be condemned for handling the Ainu tribes as their counterparts in the "wild West" handled the Indians. (As a matter of fact, inspired by the recent activism of Native Americans, a social movement on behalf of the Ainu population has arisen in Japan in the 1970s.)

Because the island was so underpopulated, and because there were so many people who wanted to make the move, immigrants from widely different social classes, localities, and backgrounds crossed Tsugaru Strait, the fifty kilometers that separated the island from the mainland of Japan. The immigration pattern was extraordinary in that, for the first time in Japanese history, people from various parts of the nation mixed on the frontier. A man from a small southern island might meet and work with a man who came from a mountain village of central Japan. In that respect, Hokkaido became a melting pot on a tiny scale, an exceptionally "cosmopolitan" territory compared with the local, even chauvinistic, territories of mainland Japan. Here again, it can be argued that there was a certain resemblance between the frontier cultures of the American West and Hokkaido.

Even today there is no distinctive dialect in Hokkaido, for people picked up their vocabulary from the various dialects of Japan. Traditions of many areas of mainland Japan were mixed and more or less integrated. A traditional New Year's card game was transformed into something unique with which mainlanders are quite unfamiliar. Though the context is very different, the process of assimilation of many immigrant cultures in America found a miniature counterpart in Hokkaido, ten thousand miles west across the Pacific. In other words, the historical and cultural situation and conditions of Hokkaido in the early Meiji era prepared it, by a historical coincidence, to respond to the "frontier spirit" represented by Caplon, Clark, and other American advisors.

EQUALITY AND MOBILITY

Hokkaido provided a geographical frontier, but more important for Japan generally was the social and psychological mobility that characterized Japan after the Meiji revolution. As a matter of fact, the leaders of the new government themselves demonstrated the possibilities of upward mobility. As E. H. Norman has pointed out, the new leaders who overthrew the old establishment, that is, the traditional Tokugawa elites, came from the lower-ranking samurai classes, and some were unknown common men. Though there were strong factions inside the new government, the new leaders shared one thing in common: they had been at the bottom of the Tokugawa social structure and had never dreamed of coming to the top. Saigo, the first modern Japanese army general, was from a lower-ranking samurai family of Satsuma. Iwakura was the son of a noble family in Kyoto, but his family's position in the court was peripheral, and it never had any significant power. In spite of his noble title, he lived poorly until the revolution took place. Ito, one of Japan's most famous politicians and the prime minister who was responsible for the construction of the Imperial Constitution, came from a poor samurai family of Choshu. Indeed, the new elites came to power by chance. The life of Kawaji, the first superintendent general of the metropolitan police, was an extreme example of success by chance. He had been another young, unknown, poor samurai of Satsuma. On the day that Saigo left the port of Satsuma to lead a troop of his army against the Tokugawa, Kawaji happened to be at the pier. Noticing him, Saigo shouted from the deck, "Hey, why don't you come with me," and Kawaji suddenly decided to join. Two years later, Kawaji was sent to France to study the police system, and upon his return, he was appointed head of the police. Appointments to key positions were often arbitrary. When the new leaders found intelligent young men, they thrust them into high-ranking positions in the government. The leaders could say to a young man, "I think you should come to the Department of Justice," and the next day he would appear in the office as the chief of a section. The leaders themselves were young, too. In the 1860s many of them were in their mid-thirties, and some were in their late twenties.

The government needed bright people, regardless of their birth or family status, though the Satsuma-Choshu factions were dominant, and boys from these territories had far better chances than others of getting good government appointments. Thus the Meiji revolution stirred up the stagnant Tokugawa system, and the society became extraordinarily mobile. What Daniel Lerner labeled "psychic mobility" was released with incredible velocity and on a huge scale. Everybody, especially young men, looked for success, and *Risshin Shusse*, meaning "raise yourself and make your way in the world," became their motto. Dore has remarked that "the prevalence of this belief that courage, energy, and initiative could carry a man anywhere, however humble his origin, is clear enough in the biographies of those who were young at the time."[2]

The theme of "success" was dominant in the literature of the Meiji period, especially in the 1870s. The translation of Smile's *Self-Help* was very widely read, and many people looked forward to making a bright personal future. As in the America of the 1870s, optimism prevailed in the minds of the younger generation. It is true that there was misery in the Japan of the 1870s, but one should not ignore the fact that the society as a whole was mobile, or at least many people thought it was. David McClelland was right when he inferred that between 1800 and 1920, "obviously a number of countries experienced the 'take-off' into rapid economic growth—e.g., Germany, France, the United States, Japan," and that in these countries "a wave of achievement motivation should have preceded the economic 'take-off.' "[3] He exemplified this hypothesis by a case study of America, where the peak of achievement motivation was observed sometime around the 1870s. Probably the same trend could be observed in Japan almost simultaneously, although no systematic survey has yet been made.

Indeed, "success stories" were one of the most popular kinds of

literature in Japan as well as in the United States, and these two countries were, and still are, rather exceptional in the degree to which
success stories have become established as a genre of popular literature. It is difficult, for instance, to find success stories in the British
or French literary tradition, except for certain works of Dickens and
Stendhal. But "success" was the great objective for the younger generation in the early Meiji period. One good example is an autobio-
graphical novel of Kenjiro Tokutomi (1868–1927), *Notes of Reminiscence* (*Omoide no ki*). Born at the time of the Meiji revolution,
the hero was an ambitious boy, like many of his contemporaries. With
a small amount of money he received from his mother, he went to a
prestigious university, studying hard while working as a newspaper
delivery boy. Finally he became a successful and famous author, with
a happy family and a comfortable life. The competition with his class-
mates and friends was extremely severe, and the hero's attitude toward
competitive situations is crude and arrogant. For him the world is a
place where only the hard-working can win the battle for success and
fame.

It is interesting to note in this connection that the tradition of
severe competition has continued and even been strengthened in contemporary Japan. It may be seen in the severe entrance examinations
for prestigious schools from kindergarten to the graduate level: in the
entrance examination to a school like Tokyo University, fewer than
one in ten can succeed. Although there is much less chance of success
today than there was in the early Meiji era, many people still believe
in "success," like their counterparts in the United States. A cynic
might say that "success" is a myth in an organized, or even overorgan-
ized, society like contemporary Japan. But surprisingly large numbers
of people in the Japanese upper-middle class—business executives,
lawyers, doctors, and other professionals—today come from rather
poor families. Many of these people are "self-made" men and women,
and there are indications that Japan is still a very mobile country
where one can grasp one's chance and become a success. For instance,
according to Dore's comparative study of social mobility, the percentage of "farmers' and agricultural workers' sons entering non-
manual occupations" in Japan is 22 percent (in the United States,
24 percent; in France, 16 percent), and the percentage of "farmers'
and agricultural workers' sons entering professional and managerial
occupations" is 7 percent (in the United States, 8 percent; in France,
3 percent; and in Great Britain, 2 percent).[4] The prototype of success

made in the 1870s is still functioning in Japan a hundred years later. Indeed, as Bellah suggested in his scheme of social organization, Japan is a country where "achievement" orientation was dominant rather than "ascription."[5]

A survey reveals that the contemporary author most widely read among business people is Ryotaro Shiba. A study of the contents of his works shows that his themes are more or less "success" oriented. Shiba likes to write about heroes who live in a mobile world, where a peasant's son, by a strange quirk of fate and by effort, becomes a famous general or an influential political figure. His touch is always realistic and semidocumentary. Readers of Shiba's novels may well identify themselves with his heroes, based on men who helped to make Meiji Japan, who usually demonstrate extraordinarily high aspiration and effectiveness in decision making. The fact that his biographical novels are popular with millions of readers suggests that, for modern Japanese, the late nineteenth century was the time when people enjoyed change and mobility, both social and psychological. Many biographies and autobiographies of successful businessmen, politicians, and professional people of the Meiji era (as well as many who were born after the Meiji revolution) boast of the poverty of their families and the misery of their early lives. Indeed, the heroes of success stories in modern Japan *must* come from poor family backgrounds. Here again, one is impressed by the parallelism between the United States and Japan—the nineteenth century was the time when the log cabin mythology of the Midwest became dominant, and self-made men replaced the East Coast quasi-aristocracy. And like presidents of the United States from Jackson to Hoover, Japanese prime ministers found it an advantage to come from poor agrarian backgrounds.

The basic question, then, is why Japan, which had been so stagnant and hierarchically organized, transformed itself rapidly into such a mobile society? Several factors that encouraged mobility and the philosophy of mobility must be carefully examined here. In the first place, it should be noted that at the time of the establishment of the new government, the principle of "equality of four peoples" (*Shimin Byodo*) was propagated—meaning that the four social classes (samurai, farmers, craftsmen, and merchants), rigidly defined during the feudal era, had to be abolished. In the new era created by the rebellions against the Tokugawa regime, an individual could choose, at least theoretically, his or her own occupation and career. A farmer's son was no longer constrained to stay in the village. He could go to a big city and look for a job or study at any school to which he was admitted. The "equality" principle officially declared by the government meant the total disorganization of the feudal hierarchy. It is in this context that Fukuzawa asserted, at the beginning of his enormously influential book, *An Encouragement of Learning*, "It is said that heaven does not create one man above or below another man. This means that when men are born from heaven they are all equal. There is no innate distinction between high and low."[6]

Scholars agree this passage may have been a modified translation of the American Declaration of Independence, but the important thing is that Fukuzawa not only advocated equality, but also tried to practice the principle in his everyday life. For example, in his autobiography he describes a visit by a friend in the government who wanted him to accept a position of honor for his contribution to the nation. Fukuzawa refuses the offer, saying, "What is remarkable about a man's carrying out his own work? The cartman pulls his cart; the bean-curd makers produces bean-curd; the student reads his books. Each one follows what is his obligation. If the government wants to recognize the ordinary work of its subjects, let it begin with my neighbor, the bean-curd maker. Give up any such ideas about my special work."[7] Many of his contemporaries approved this radical equalitarian attitude.

Another source of equalitarian thinking was the teaching of American missionaries. Dr. Clark himself was a devout Protestant, and taught the Gospel of Christ along with the new agricultural technology. At the end of his stay in Hokkaido, his twenty-four students assembled and signed a pledge as believers of Jesus Christ. For those young people, every individual, regardless of origin, was equal in the light of Christian universalism. As a result, Sapporo Agricultural College produced such devout Christians as Kanzo Uchimura, who went to Amherst and became an extremely puritanical Christian. However, in his case there seemed to be elements inherited from Japanese culture that were attuned to the missionary spirit of nineteenth-century America. In *A Diary of a Japanese Convert*, published in 1895, he describes his grandfather, who lived in the late Tokugawa period, as a crystalization of honesty and his grandmother as a diligent woman for whom "vivere est laborare." The asceticism of the samurai spirit that Uchimura inherited found a real kinship with the individualistic Protestant ethic of nineteenth-century New England. He idealistically admired American Puritanism and criticized simple-minded American missionaries in Asia. Upon his return to Japan, he argued the essentials of true Christianity against eleven American missionaries in Niigata, basing his defense of Buddhism on his belief in a law of the universe, rather than in the narrow interpretation of biblical documents. He quit his appointment at a Christian college after serving only three months.

Not only the samurai tradition, based on Confucian philosophy, but also certain sects of Buddhism, could be connected with nineteenth-century American Puritanism. For example, a group of young Buddhists belonging to the Shinshu sect, in which Bellah found certain parallels with Protestantism, began publishing in 1887 a magazine called *Temperance* (*Hanseikai Zasshi*), whose main purpose was to propagate abstinence from alcohol. They gathered news from abroad, especially from America, and saw in temperance a social issue that they could share with Protestant asceticism. In short, the government's declaration of "equality of four peoples" remobilized latent individualistic, achievement- and mobility-oriented traditions, which were stimulated and encouraged by the intellectual and spiritual atmosphere of mid-nineteenth-century America.

EDUCATION

In this world in which everyone believed that success was possible, education was emphasized as the means to take advantage of opportunity and rise in the world, in Japan even more than in the United States. One indication of the extraordinary appeal of education was Fukuzawa's *An Encouragement of Learning*. According to Fukuzawa's own records, this book, first published in 1872, with continuous editions through 1876, sold 220,000 copies. The population of Japan at that time was approximately thirty-five million, and a simple calculation tells us that one out of every 160 Japanese purchased the book. Presumably younger people between the ages of fifteen and twenty-five were the most attracted, and one may estimate, taking account of the book reading and borrowing habits of the day, that Fukuzawa reached more than 50 percent of the youth of the 1870s. Fukuzawa presents his argument simply. After emphasizing the theme of the equality of man, in a passage we have already quoted, he stresses the vital importance of education as the way to get ahead: "There are no innate status distinctions separating the noble and base, the rich and the poor. It is only the person who has studied diligently, so that he has a mastery over things and events, who becomes noble and rich, while his opposite becomes base and poor." Differences in status and wealth "are entirely the result of whether one has or does not have the powers which learning brings."

He was well aware of the revolutionary possibilities for social change in the principle of "equality of four peoples," and wrote, "Looking back upon the developments of recent times, we see that the peasants, artisans, and merchants have risen in dignity a hundred times over their former statuses, and have gradually reached the point of standing on equal terms with the former Samurai families. So today, employment in government service is open to men of character and talent among the formerly non-Samurai groups." Under these new circumstances, he wrote, ". . . the state is now grounded on the principle that all men are socially equal. Therefore, from the present day forward, there will be no such thing as hereditary class rank among the Japanese people. A man will have rank only on the ground of his talents, virtues, and accomplishments."

Undoubtedly these words encouraged and motivated ambitious young people, and many of them, like the hero of *Notes of Reminiscence*, tried to enter competitive academic institutions and test themselves against their age-mates. Thus, Yorozu Oda, a well-known professor of law and a practitioner in international law, recalls in his autobiography the competitive entrance examination for the government law school: "There were more than 15,000 applicants who took the examination. Many of them came from various local prefectures, and the first screening test continued for several days. Those 150 who passed the test had to take a second test, and finally 50 students were selected." The chances of success were one in 300, but once accepted, a student was provided with free tuition and a stipend by the government, so that he could concentrate on learning. The examination was open to all applicants without bias. The sole purpose of selection was to recruit bright young people who could take key positions in the government.

Those who failed were able to try again the next year, or to try other schools, though in private schools the tuition fees came to be burdensome. But students were proud of their status, for they knew that good job opportunities awaited them. A student's song of the day ran, "Don't laugh at poor students, all the ministers were once poor students, too."

Emperor Meiji himself was very much concerned with higher education, and in 1872, the year when Fukuzawa published his book, the emperor visited Tokyo Kaisei Gakko (later Tokyo University), where he inspected each department and gave his greetings: "His Majesty celebrates the progress of knowledge. The schools of professional knowledge are the places where talents grow. His Majesty expects the expansion of higher education of various branches. You should be reminded of His Majesty's deep concern." The "encouragement of learning" was thus everywhere, not only in the title of Fukuzawa's book. A Chinese poem written by a Japanese Confucian scholar of the eighteenth century was revived. It may be translated: "With ambition, I, a man, leave my home country. If I cannot fulfill my aim to study, I will not come back, not even to die. The place of my tombstone is not destined to be my home country. For me, green mountains are everywhere." All possible sources, old and new, from east and west, that could ignite the desire for achievement of a new generation, were mobilized and propagated.

As a result, in the 1870s Tokyo became a vibrant city to which thousands of young people came from every corner of the country, mostly on foot. High aspirations for learning prevailed; as Daikichi Irokawa aptly said, Clark's slogan, "Boys, be ambitious," was "strong gunpowder thrown into a fire."[8] According to one study, several hundred compositions written by school children and appearing in a children's magazine of the 1870s and 1880s were dominated by the themes of "study," "diligence," "fighting handicaps," "hard work," and other achievement-oriented motives. The "encouragement of learning" was a fever that attacked the new generation of the early Meiji period.

The recognition of the importance of education was, however, not the result of the Meiji revolution only. Rather, it was a continuation from the late Tokugawa period, as Passin has suggested in his intensive study of modern Japanese education.[9] Elementary schools called "terakoya" had been established in many communities since the beginning of the eighteenth century, and by the time of the Meiji revolution, it is estimated, almost 100 percent of samurai, 70 to 80 percent of merchants, and 50 to 65 percent of artisans in the big cities were literate. In rural villages, the heads of communities were

100 percent literate, and even among small tenants 20 percent were able to read and write. Respect for intellectual achievement was part of the Japanese tradition. Indeed, as early as the 1780s, Chikuzan Nakai advocated a compulsory education system on a national scale, and many people were aware that education was the basis for national development. It was no wonder, therefore, that the elites of the Meiji government felt mass education was their most urgent task.

The zeal for education was thus the product of the acceleration of the aspirations that had been latent in the pre-Meiji period. In 1871 the Ministry of Education was founded, and in 1872 four years of compulsory education were instituted. The legislation asserts in its preface that "learning is the basis for a person to be independent, and every individual person is obliged to learn." The purpose of compulsory education was clearly stated as "to let no household in a community remain unlearned and to let no individual in a household remain unlearned." The tone of the legislation was quite similar to that of Fukuzawa's book, though the latter was more radical and had greater impact. There was little disagreement among government policy, liberal thinkers like Fukuzawa, and, above all, the general public. Everyone welcomed the new era as far as the diffusion of education was concerned.

It is worthwhile to observe an almost parallel development in the United States at approximately the same historical point. Preceded by pioneering movements such as the Pennsylvania Society for the Promotion of Public Schools (established in 1827), Horace Mann succeeded in 1852 in getting legislation passed establishing compulsory education in Massachusetts, though the actual enforcement of the law had to wait until the late 1860s. In 1871, New Hampshire, Michigan, and Washington decided to enforce compulsary education; in 1872, Connecticut and New Mexico; in 1873, Nevada; and in 1874, New York, Kansas, and California adopted similar legislation. This movement fulfilled the hopes of Jefferson's "Bill for the More General Diffusion of Knowledge" (1779), in which he stated that "those persons whom nature has endowed with genius and virtue should be rendered by liberal education worthy to receive, and able to guard the sacred deposit of rights and liberties of their fellow citizens, and that they should be called to that charge without regard to wealth, birth or other accidental condition or circumstances." Indeed, what Fukuzawa emphasized in 1872 almost coincides with Jefferson's statement, though the sociohistorical context was rather different.

As suggested before, the 1870s were the age of the frontier in America, when mobility, both geographical and social, was accelerated, and ambition and success came to be basic American values. A close observation of the American scene of the 1870s amazes a historian of Japan, because developments in education and popular aspiration are so similar. One suspects that if Fukuzawa had ever had a chance to meet Jefferson, they would have been surprised at how much they had in common. Furthermore, the United States and Japan seem to have shared a common orientation toward "practical" education. Fukuzawa was extremely insistent on this point. He was critical of the nonpractical, philological approach to knowledge, which had been dominant in Japanese higher education in the pre-Meiji period, and emphasized the need for "practical" knowledge. He wrote, for instance, "Letters are the instruments of learning. They are like hammers and saws to build a house. Although hammers and saws are indispensable tools for building a house, a person who only knows their names but not how to build a house cannot be called a carpenter. For this reason, a person who only knows how to read letters but does not know how to discern the principles of things cannot be called a true scholar." In another passage he wrote: "The object of one's primary efforts should be practical learning that is closer to ordinary human needs. For example, a person should learn the forty-seven letter *Kana* syllabary, methods of letter writing and accounting, the practice of the abacus, the way to handle weights and measures, and the like." Fukuzawa was undoubtedly a "pragmatist," one who preceded John Dewey.

Another parallel in education was the positive acceptance of Social Darwinism, especially the work of Herbert Spencer. It is well known that Darwinism was not immediately accepted in Europe, but found much less resistance in the United States and Japan, and Spencer's Social Darwinism became a dominant theme in the social sciences in both countries in the late nineteenth century. The Japanese people were rather happy to learn that the ancestors of mankind were primates, because it fitted so well into the scheme of the Buddhist cycle of reincarnation. Japan was a paradise for Darwin, and his theory as well as Spencer's, simplified and misinterpreted, was used to justify the competitive new world, where the "survival of the fittest" was the rule. Shoichi Toyama, who is regarded as the founder of sociology in Japan, was a student of Spencer's, and the first book of sociology translated into Japanese was Lester Ward's *Dynamic Sociology. The Prin-*

ciples of Sociology, by Franklin Henry Giddings, was translated into Japanese in 1899, only three years after its original publication.

PATTERNS OF DEVELOPMENT

Both the United States and Japan were "developing countries" in the mid-nineteenth century. By historical coincidence, the 1860s were a period of civil war in both countries, and the effect of the civil wars was to strengthen both countries as independent nation-states. A dominant theme in both was the exploration and exploitation of the frontier, and its incorporation into the central society. Though the United States was far ahead of Japan industrially, the hegemony of industry was in the hands of European nations, especially Great Britain, and thus both countries may be seen as "trying harder" because of their number 2 position. Both countries were optimistic about their future, and their peoples responded to opportunities and hoped for individual success. The Protestant ethic, whether Christian or Buddhist, worked as a driving force. Social mobility was encouraged, and radical equalitarian philosophies were advocated and practiced. "Progress," with all its infinite possibilities, was believed in by many, and catching up with the "developed" world—Great Britain and other European nations—became a major national goal in both countries. Indeed, Commodore Perry's aggressive descent on Japan in 1853 was for dual purpose of investigating the possibility of direct American trade with China, which until then had been monopolized by the British, and exploring the sea route across the Pacific so that American trade with the Far East might compete with the European trade via the Indian Ocean. It was an adventure appropriate to a number 2 nation competing with a number 1 nation.

Japan at that time was unaware of the international pecking order among nations. Her concern was rather to avoid becoming another China, which was being exploited by the West. But as soon as the new course was established by the Meiji government, Japan aspired to compete with the industrial nations of the world, and as suggested at the outset of this paper, some government officials, including Kuroda, intuitively looked to America for a "model" of development. As the experience of the American frontier seemed to be applicable to the Japanese frontier, Japan thought that America, as a "developing" nation, could give her more insights than a "developed" country like Great Britain could, though missions were sent to Europe, too.

In order to achieve the national goal of industrialization, Japan emphasized the role of education. Though there was no such term as "social investment in education," what Japan did in the nineteenth century was what twentieth-century development experts would call adopting a "manpower strategy." In a lesser degree, American also was aware of the importance of education for social development.

Though there were, and are, many obvious historical and cultural differences between the two countries, the United States and Japan had, and have, one significant similarity as "developing" countries of the nineteenth century. Their patterns of development were fundamentally different from those of the eighteenth century, which may be represented by Great Britain, in which colonial exploitation was the basic mode. The two developing nations of the nineteenth century concentrated their efforts on education and technology, based on pragmatism.

One hundred years later, the United States and Japan appeared on the international economic scene as giants. The "developing" countries of the nineteenth century found themselves ahead of the former "developed" nations, having become a second generation of "developed" countries. It is interesting and important to note, however, that a number 2 consciousness still persists in the two countries. It is my impression that there is a strong belief that the present is "imperfect" and that "perfection" can never be achieved, or that it may be achieved someday, but not now. Therefore, something "new" is always being tried. The sense of "imperfection" is one of the basic themes in both American and Japanese culture. From the number 2 point of view, number 1 is a model; in city planning, for instance, Victorian London or Napoleonic Paris. Unlike London and Paris, the big cities of number 2 are imperfect. They need modification, rezoning, redevelopment, and new planning constantly: Tokyo and New York are always "under construction." There must be something better, something newer. In this sense, the two cultures are metabolic, or at least quasi-metabolic, and the cult of sociocultural metabolism is the basis of the "American dream," and, in a lesser degree, of the "Japanese dream."

Are these dreams and beliefs disappearing or declining? With the arrival of a radical left, an ecology movement, consumerism, and the women's liberation movement, in both societies, one must ask this question, but no definite answer seems to be presented yet. It should be noted that we may see another style of development, which may be called "development twentieth-century style," in the "developing countries" or the "Third World," different from both the eighteenth-century and the nineteenth-century styles. A fundamental historical question—one which we will have to leave of the future—is whether the twentieth-century style, perhaps represented by China, is going to succeed the nineteenth-century-style countries, as they have succeeded the eighteenth-century-style countries.

NOTES

1. Edward Morse, *Japan Day by Day* (Boston: Houghton, 1917), p. 9.
2. Ronald Dore, ed., *Aspects of Social Change in Modern Japan* (Princeton: Princeton University Press, 1967).
3. David McClelland, *The Achieving Society* (Princeton: Van Nostrand, 1961), pp. 149–50.
4. Dore, *Aspects of Social Change.*
5. Robert Bellah, *Tokugawa Religion* (Glencoe, Ill.: Free Press, 1957).
6. Yukichi Fukuzawa, *An Encouragement of Learning* (Tokyo: Sophia University, 1969).
7. Yukichi Fukuzawa, *Autobiography* (Tokyo: Hokuseido, 1953).
8. Daikichi Irokawa, *Kindai Kokka no shuppatsu: Nihon no rekishi* [The Beginning of a Modern Nation: History of Japan], vol. 21 (Tokyo, 1966).
9. Herbert Passin, *Society and Education in Japan* (New York: Bureau of Publications, Teachers College, Columbia University, 1965), p. 57.

Part II

AMERICAN INSTITUTIONS AND
SUBCULTURES–STILL CHANGING

9

SYMBOLIC ETHNICITY: THE FUTURE OF ETHNIC GROUPS AND CULTURES IN AMERICA

HERBERT J. GANS

INTRODUCTION

One of the more notable recent changes in America has been the renewed interest in ethnicity, which some observers of the American scene have described as an ethnic revival. This paper argues that there has been no revival, and that acculturation and assimilation continue to take place. Among third- and fourth-generation "ethnics" (the grandchildren and great-grandchildren of Europeans who came to America during the "new immigration"), a new kind of ethnic involvement may be occurring, which emphasizes concern with identity, with the feeling of being Jewish or Italian, etc. Since ethnic identity needs are neither intense nor frequent in this generation, however, ethnics do not need either ethnic cultures or organizations; instead, they resort to the use of ethnic symbols. As a result, ethnicity may be turning into symbolic ethnicity, an ethnicity of last resort, which could, nevertheless, persist for generations.

Identity cannot exist apart from a group, and symbols are themselves a part of culture, but ethnic identity and symbolic ethnicity require very different ethnic organizations and cultures than existed among earlier generations. Moreover, the symbols third-generation ethnics use to express their identity are more visible than the ethnic cultures and organizations of the first- and second-generation ethnics. What appears to be an ethnic revival may therefore be only a more visible form of long-standing phenomena, or of a new stage of accul-

193

turation and assimilation. Symbolic ethnicity may also have wider ramifications, however, for David Riesman has suggested that "being American has some of the same episodic qualities as being ethnic."[1] In effect, both kinds of being are also new ways of striving for individualism.

ACCULTURATION AND ASSIMILATION[2]

The dominant sociological approach to ethnicity has long taken the form of what Neil Sandberg aptly calls "straight-line theory," in which acculturation and assimilation are viewed as secular trends that culminate in the eventual absorption of the ethnic group into the larger culture and generation population.[3] Straight-line theory in turn is based on melting pot theory, which implies the disappearance of the ethnic groups into a single host society. Even so, it does not accept the values of the melting pot theorists, since its conceptualizers could have used terms like cultural and social liberation from immigrant ways of life, but did not.

In recent years, straight-line theory has been questioned on many grounds. For one thing, many observers have properly noted that even if America might have been a melting pot early in the twentieth century, the massive immigration from Europe and elsewhere has since then influenced the dominant groups, summarily labeled "WASP," and has also decimated their cultural, if not their political and financial, power, so that today America is a mosaic, as Andrew Greeley has put it, of subgroups and subcultures.[4] Still, this criticism does not necessarily deny the validity of straight-line theory, since ethnics can also be absorbed into a pluralistic set of subcultures and subgroups, differentiated by age, income, education, occupation, religion, region, and the like.

A second criticism of straight-line theory has centered on its treatment of all ethnic groups as essentially similar, and its failure, specifically, to distinguish between religious groups, like the Jews, and nationality groups, like the Italians, Poles, etc. Jews, for example, are a "peoplehood" with a religious and cultural tradition of thousands of years, but without an "old country" to which they owe allegiance or nostalgia, while Italians, Poles, and other participants in the "new immigration" came from parts of Europe that in some cases did not even become nations until after the immigrants had arrived in America.

That there are differences between the Jews and the other "new" immigrants cannot be questioned, but at the same time, the empirical evidence also suggests that acculturation and assimilation affected them quite similarly. (Indeed, one major difference may have been that Jews were already urbanized and thus entered the American social structure at a somewhat higher level than the other new immigrants, who were mostly landless laborers and poor peasants.) Nonetheless, straight-line theory can be faulted for virtually ignoring the fact that immigrants arrived here with two kinds of ethnic cultures, sacred and secular; that they were Jews from Eastern—and Western—Europe, and Catholics from Italy, Poland, and elsewhere. (Sacred cultures are, however, themselves affected by national and regional considerations; for example, Italian Catholicism differed in some respects from German or Polish, as did Eastern European Judaism from Western.)

While acculturation and assimilation have affected both sacred and secular cultures, they have affected the latter more than the former, for acculturation has particularly eroded the secular cultures that Jews and Catholics brought from Europe. Their religions have also changed in America, and religious observance has decreased, more so among Jews than among Catholics, although Catholic observance has begun to fall off greatly in recent years. Consequently, the similar American experience of Catholic and Jewish ethnics suggests that the comparative analysis of straight-line theory is justified, as long as the analysis compares both sacred and secular cultures.

Two further critiques virtually reject straight-line theory altogether. In an insightful recent paper, William Yancey and his colleagues have argued that contemporary ethnicity bears little relation to the ancestral European heritage, but exists because it is functional for meeting present "exigencies of survival," particularly for working-class Americans.[5] Their argument does not invalidate straight-line theory but corrects it by suggesting that acculturation and assimilation, current ethnic organizations and cultures, as well as new forms of ethnicity, must be understood as responses to current needs rather than departures from past traditions.

The other critique takes the opposite position; it points to the persistence of the European heritage, argues that the extent of acculturation and assimilation have been overestimated, and questions the rapid decline and eventual extinction of ethnicity posited by some straight-line theorists. These critics call attention to studies indicating that ethnic cultures and organizations are still functioning, that exogamous marriage remains a practice of numerical minorities, that ethnic differences in various behavior patterns and attitudes can be identified, that ethnic groups continue to act as political interest groups, and that ethnic pride remains strong.[6]

The social phenomena that these defenders of ethnicity identify exist; the only question is how they are to be interpreted. Straight-line theory postulates a process, and cross-sectional studies do not pre-empt the possibility of a continuing trend. Also, like Yancey and his co-authors, some of the critics are looking primarily at poorer ethnics, who have been less touched by acculturation and assimilation than middle-class ethnics, and who have in some cases used ethnicity and ethnic organization as a psychological and political defense against the injustices that they suffer in an unequal society.[7] In fact, much of the contemporary behavior described as "ethnic" strikes me as working-class behavior, which differs only slightly among various ethnic groups, and then largely because of variations in the structure of opportunities open to people in America, and in the peasant traditions their ancestors brought over from the old country, which were themselves responses to European opportunity structures. In other words, ethnicity is largely a working-class style.[8]

Much the same observation applies to ethnic political activity. Urban political life, particularly among working-class people, has always been structured by and through ethnicity, and while ethnic political activity may have increased in the last decade, it has taken place around working-class issues rather than ethnic ones. During the 1960s, urban working-class Catholic ethnics began to politicize themselves in response to black militancy, the expansion of black ghettoes, and government integration policies that they perceived as publicly legitimated black invasions of ethnic neighborhoods, but which threatened them as working-class homeowners who could not afford to move to the suburbs. Similarly, working- and lower-middle-class Catholic ethnics banded together in the suburbs to fight against higher public school taxes, since they could not afford to pay them while they also had to pay for parochial schools. Even so, these political activities have been *pan-ethnic*, rather than ethnic, since they often involved coalitions of ethnic groups that once considered each other enemies but were now united by common economic and other interests. The extent to which these pan-ethnic coalitions reflect class rather than ethnic interests is illustrated by the 1968 election campaign of New York City's Mario Proccaccino against John Lindsay. Although an Italian, he ran as a "candidate of the little people" against what he called the "limousine liberals."

The fact that pan-ethnic coalitions have developed most readily in conflicts over racial issues also suggests that in politics, ethnicity can sometimes serve as a convenient mask for antiblack endeavors, or for political activities that have negative consequences for blacks. While attitude polls indicate that ethnics are often more tolerant racially than other Americans, working-class urban ethnics are also more likely to be threatened, as homeowners and jobholders, by black demands, and may favor specific antiblack policies, not because they are "racists," but because their own class interests force them to oppose black demands.

In addition, part of what appears as an increase in ethnic political activity is actually an increase in the visibility of ethnic politics. When the pan-ethnic coalitions began to copy the political methods of the civil rights and antiwar movements, their protests became newsworthy and were disseminated all over the country by the mass media. At about the same time, the economic and geographic mobility of Catholic ethnic groups enabled non-Irish Catholic politicians to win important state and national electoral posts for the first time, and their victories were defined as ethnic triumphs, even though they did not rely on ethnic constituents alone and were not elected on the basis of ethnic issues.

The final, equally direct, criticism of straight-line theory has questioned the continued relevance of the theory, either because of the phenomenon of third generation return, or because of the emergence of ethnic revivals. Thus, Marcus Hansen argued that acculturation and assimilation were temporary processes, because the third generation could afford to remember an ancestral culture that the traumatic Americanization process forced the immigrant and second generations to forget.[9] Hansen's hypothesis can be questioned on several grounds, however. His data, the founding of Swedish and other historical associations in the Midwest, provided slender evidence of a widespread third-generation return, particularly among nonacademic ethnics; in addition, his theory was static, for Hansen never indicated what would happen in the fourth generation, or what processes were involved in the return that would enable it to survive into the future.[10]

The notion of an ethnic revival has so far been propounded mostly by journalists and essayists, who have supplied impressionistic accounts or case studies of the emergence of new ethnic organizations and the revitalization of old ones.[11] Since the third- and fourth-generation ethnics who are presumably participating in this revival are scattered all over suburbia, there has so far been little systematic research among this population, so that the validity of the revival notion has not yet been properly tested.

The evidence I have seen does not convince me that a revival is taking place. Instead, recent changes can be explained in two ways, neither of which conflicts with straight-line theory: (1) today's ethnics have become more visible as a result of upward mobility; and (2) they are adopting the new form of ethnic behavior and affiliation I call "symbolic ethnicity."

THE VISIBILITY OF ETHNICITY

The recent upward social, and centrifugal geographic, mobility of ethnics, particularly Catholics, has finally enabled them to enter the middle and upper-middle classes, where they have been noticed by the national mass media, which monitor primarily these strata. In the process they have also become more noticeable to other Americans. The newly visible may not participate more in ethnic groups and cultures than before, but their new visibility makes it appear as if ethnicity had been revived.

I noted earlier the arrival of non-Irish Catholic politicians on the national scene. An equally visible phenomenon has been the entry of Catholic ethnic intellectuals into the academy and its flourishing print culture. To be sure, the scholars are publishing more energetically than their predecessors, who had to rely on small and poverty-stricken ethnic publishing houses, but they are essentially doing what ethnic scholars have always done, only more visibly. Perhaps their energy has also been spurred in part by the need, as academics, to publish so that they do not perish, as well as by their desire to counteract the anti-ethnic prejudices and the entrenched vestiges of the melting pot ideal that still prevail in the more prestigious universities. In some cases, they are also fighting a political battle, because their writings often defend conservative political positions against what they perceive—I think wrongly—as the powerful liberal or radical academic majority.

Paradoxically, a good deal of their writing has been nostalgic, celebrating the immigrant culture and its Gemeinschaft at the same time that young Catholic ethnics are going to college partly in order to escape the restrictive pressures of that Gemeinschaft. (Incidentally, an interesting study could be made of the extent to which writers from different ethnic groups, of both fiction and nonfiction, are pursuing nostalgic, contemporary, or future-oriented approaches to ethnicity, comparing different ethnic groups, by time of arrival and position in the society today, on this basis.)

What has happened in the academy has also happened in literature and show business. For example, although popular comedy has long been a predominantly Eastern European Jewish occupation, the first generations of Jewish comic stars had to suppress their ethnicity and even had to change their names, much as did the first generation of academic stars in the prestigious universities. Unlike Jack Benny, Eddie Cantor, George Burns, George Jessel, and others, the comics of today do not need to hide their origins, and beginning perhaps with Lenny Bruce and Sam Levinson, comics like Buddy Hackett, Robert Klein, Don Rickles, and Joan Rivers have used explicitly Jewish material in entertaining the predominantly non-Jewish mass media audience.[12]

Undoubtedly, some of these academics, writers, and entertainers have undergone a kind of third-generation return in this process. Some have re-embraced their ethnicity solely to spur their careers, but others have experienced a personal conversion. Even so, an empirical study would probably show that in most cases their ethnic attitudes have not changed; either they have acted more publicly and thus visibly than they did in the past, or in responding to a hospitable cultural climate, they have openly followed ethnic impulses that they had previously suppressed.

A similar analysis may explain the resurgence of traditionalism among some Jews and Protestants. In both instances largely middle-class young people are perceived as having become newly orthodox (or fundamentalist), and in some cases this is undoubtedly true. Religious conversions may have increased in the last decade, partly because of the ideological and other turbulence of the 1960s, but also because the postwar affluence spawned a cohort of parents who were so upwardly mobile that they were too busy to pay attention to their children. These children developed a strong need for substitute parental guidance, which later manifested itself by their joining the theocratic Gemeinschafts that can be found among virtually all of the recent neotraditional movements. Converts are, however, also the most visible, since they tend to be leaders and are thus most often monitored by the mass media. At the same time, they have been joined by less visible young people who were already orthodox, but perhaps quiescently so, either because orthodoxy was in disrepute among their peers while they were growing up, or because they were uncomfortable in orthodox groups dominated by old people.[13] Only empirical research can indicate the proportions of third-generation returnees and already orthodox people in these groups, but in any case, it seems wrong on the part of enthusiastic observers of a religious revival to group the neotraditionalists with earlier traditional groups, such as the Chassidim, the non-Chassidic Orthodox Jews living in such enclaves as New York City's Boro Park, and rural groups like the Amish.[14] These groups have survived by insulating themselves from the larger society, rarely take in converts, and thus have also insulated themselves from the neotraditionalists.

ETHNICITY IN THE THIRD GENERATION

The second explanation for the changes that have been taking place among third-generation ethnics will take up most of the rest of this paper; it deals with what is happening among the less visible population, the large mass of predominantly middle-class third- and fourth-generation ethnics, who have not been studied enough either by journalists or by social scientists.[15]

In the absence of systematic research, it is difficult even to discern what has actually been happening, but several observers have described the same ethnic behavior in different words. Michael Novak has coined the phrase "voluntary ethnicity"; Samuel Eisenstadt has talked about "Jewish diversity"; Allan Silver about "individualism as a valid mode of Jewishness"; and Geoffrey Bock about "public Jewishness."[16] What these observers agree on is that today's young ethnics are finding new ways of being ethnics, which I shall later label "symbolic ethnicity."

I start my analysis with the assumption, taken from straight-line theory, that acculturation and assimilation are continuing among the third and fourth generations.[17] If these concepts were quantified, one might find that upwardly mobile working-class groups are moving out of ethnic cultures and groups faster than other ethnics as they try to enter the middle class, whereas those already in the middle class are now acculturating and assimilating at a slower rate, partly because they have already moved out of ethnic cultures and groups to a considerable extent, but also because they are finding that middle-class life is sufficiently pluralistic and their ethnicity sufficiently cost-free that they do not have to give it up deliberately.

In any case, for the third generation, the secular ethnic cultures that the immigrants brought with them are now only an ancestral memory, or an exotic tradition to be savored once in a while in a museum or at an ethnic festival. The same is true of the "Americanization cultures," the immigrant experience and adjustment in America, which William Kornblum suggests may have been more important in the lives of the first two generations than the ethnic cultures themselves. The old ethnic cultures serve no useful function for third-generation ethnics who lack direct and indirect ties to the old country, and neither need nor have much knowledge about it. Similarly, the Americanization cultures have little meaning for people who grew up without the familial conflict over European and American ways that beset their fathers and mothers: the second generation that fought with and was often ashamed of immigrant parents.

Assimilation is still continuing, for it has always progressed more slowly than acculturation. If one distinguishes between primary and secondary assimilation, that is, movement out of ethnic primary and secondary groups, the third generation is now beginning to move into nonethnic primary groups.[18] Although researchers are still debating just how much intermarriage is taking place, it is rising in the third generation for both Catholic ethnic groups and Jews, and friendship choices appear to follow the same pattern.[19]

The departure out of secondary groups has already proceeded much further. Most third-generation ethnics have little reason, or occasion, to depend on, or even interact with, other ethnics in important secondary-group activities. Ethnic occupational specialization, segregation, and self-segregation are fast disappearing, with some notable exceptions in the large cities. Since the third generation probably works, like other Americans, largely for corporate employers, past occupational ties between ethnics are no longer relevant. Insofar as they live largely in the suburbs, third-generation ethnics get together with their fellow homeowners for political and civic activities, and are not likely to encounter ethnic political organizations, balanced tickets, or even politicians who pursue ethnic constituencies.

Except in suburbs where old discrimination and segregation patterns still survive, social life takes place without ethnic clustering, and Catholics are not likely to find ethnic subgroups in the Church. Third-generation Jews, on the other hand, particularly those who live in older upper-middle-class suburbs where segregation continues, if politely, probably still continue to restrict much of their social life to other Jews, although they have long ago forgotten the secular divisions between German (and other Western) and Eastern European Jews, and among the latter, between "Litwaks" and "Galizianer." The religious distinction between German Reform Judaism and Eastern European Conservatism has also virtually disappeared, for the second generation that moved to the suburbs after World War II already chose its denomination on the basis of status rather than national origin.[20] In fact, the Kennedy-Herberg prediction that eventually American religious life would take the form of a triple melting pot has not come to pass, if only because people, especially in the suburbs, use denominations within the major religions for status differentiation.

Nevertheless, while ethnic ties continue to wane for the third generation, people of this generation continue to perceive themselvs as ethnics, whether they define ethnicity in sacred or secular terms. Jews continue to remain Jews because the sacred and secular elements of their culture are strongly intertwined, but the Catholic ethnics also retain their secular or national identity, even though it is separate from their religion.

My hypothesis is that in this generation, people are less and less interested in their ethnic cultures and organizations—both sacred and secular—and are instead more concerned with maintaining their ethnic identity, with the feeling of being Jewish or Italian or Polish, and with finding ways of feeling and expressing that identity in suitable ways. By identity, I mean here simply the sociopsychological elements that accompany role behavior, and the ethnic role is today less of an ascriptive than a voluntary role that people assume alongside other roles. To be sure, ethnics are still identified as such by others, particularly on the basis of name, but the behavioral expectations that once went with identification by others have declined sharply, so that ethnics have some choice about when and how to play ethnic roles. Moreover, as ethnic cultures and organizations decline further, fewer ethnic roles are prescribed, thus increasing the degree to which people have freedom of role definition.

Ethnic identity can be expressed in either action or feeling, or combinations of these, and the kinds of situations in which it is expressed are nearly limitless. Third-generation ethnics can join an ethnic organization or take part in formal or informal organizations composed largely of fellow ethnics, but they can also find their identity by "affiliating" with an abstract collectivity that does not exist as an interacting group. That collectivity, moreover, can be mythic or real, contemporary or historical. On the one hand, Jews can express their identity as synagogue members, or as participants in a consciousness-raising group consisting mostly of Jewish women. On the other hand, they can also identify with the Jewish people as a long-suffering collectivity that has been credited with inventing monotheism. If they are not religious, they can identify with Jewish liberal or socialist political cultures, or with a population that has produced many prominent intellectuals and artists in the last hundred years. Similar choices are open to Catholic ethnics. In the third generation, Italians can identify through membership in Italian groups, or by strong feelings for various themes in Italian or Neapolitan or Sicilian culture, and much the same possibilities exist for Catholics whose ancestors came over from other countries.

Needless to say, ethnic identity is not a new or a third-generation phenomenon, for ethnics have always had an ethnic identity, but in the past it was largely taken for granted, since it was anchored to groups and roles, and was rarely a matter of choice. When people lived in an ethnic neighborhood, worked with fellow ethnics, and voted for ethnic politicians, there was little need to be concerned with identity except during conflict with other ethnic groups. Furthermore, the everyday roles people played were often defined for them by others as ethnic. Being a drygoods merchant was often a Jewish role; restaurant owners were assumed to be Greek, and bartenders, Irish.

The third generation has grown up without assigned roles or groups that anchor ethnicity, so that identity can no longer be taken for granted. People can of course give up their identity, but if they continue to feel it, they must make it more explicit than it was in the past, and must even look for ways of expressing it. This has two important consequences for ethnic behavior. First, given the degree to which the third generation has acculturated and assimilated, most people look for easy and intermittent ways of expressing their identity, for ways that do not conflict with other ways of life. As a result, they refrain from ethnic behavior that requires an arduous or time-consuming commitment, either to a culture that must be practiced constantly, or to organizations that demand active membership. Second, because people's concern is with identity, rather than with cultural practices or group relationships, they are free to look for ways of expressing that identity which suits them best, thus opening up the possibility of voluntary, diverse, or individualistic ethnicity. Any mode of expressing ethnic identity is valid as long it enhances the feeling of being ethnic, and any cultural pattern or organization that nourishes that feeling is therefore relevant, providing only that enough people make the same choices when identity expression is a group enterprise.

In other words, as the functions of ethnic cultures and groups diminish and identity becomes the primary way of being ethnic, ethnicity takes on an expressive rather than instrumental function in people's lives, becoming more of a leisure-time activity and losing its relevance, say, to earning a living or regulating family life. Expressive behavior can take many forms, but it often involves the use of symbols —and symbols as signs rather than as myths.[21] Ethnic symbols are frequently individual cultural practices that are taken from the older ethnic culture; they are "abstracted" from that culture and pulled out of its original moorings, so to speak, to become stand-ins for it. And if a label is useful to describe the third generation's pursuit of identity, I propose the term "symbolic ethnicity."

SYMBOLIC ETHNICITY

Symbolic ethnicity can be expressed in a myriad of ways, but above all, I suspect, it is characterized by a nostalgic allegiance to the culture of the immigrant generation, or that of the old country; a love for and a pride in a tradition that can be felt without having to be incorporated into everyday behavior. The feelings can be directed at a generalized tradition, or at specific ones: a desire for the cohesive extended immigrant family, or the obedience of children to parental authority, or the unambiguous orthodoxy of immigrant religion, or the old-fashioned despotic benevolence of the machine politician. People may even sincerely desire to "return" to these imagined pasts, which are conveniently cleansed of the complexities that accompanied them in the real past, but while they may soon realize that they cannot go back, they may not surrender the wish. Or else they displace that wish on churches, schools, and the mass media, asking them to recreate a tradition, or rather, to create a symbolic tradition, even while their familial, occupational, religious, and political lives are pragmatic responses to the imperatives of their roles and positions in local and national hierarchical social structures.

All of the cultural patterns that are transformed into symbols are themselves guided by a common pragmatic imperative: they must be visible and clear in meaning to large numbers of third-generation ethnics, and they must be easily expressed and felt, without requiring undue interference in other aspects of life. For example, Jews have abstracted *rites de passage* and individual holidays out of the traditional religion and given them greater importance, such as the *bar mitzvah* and *bas mitzvah* (the parallel ceremony for thirteen-year-old girls that was actually invented in America). Similarly, Chanukah, a minor holiday in the religious calendar, has become a major one in popular practice, partly since it lends itself to impressing Jewish identity on the children. *Rites de passage* and holidays are ceremonial, and thus symbolic to begin with; equally importantly, they do not take much time, do not upset the everyday routine, and also become an occasion for reassembling on a regular basis family members who are rarely seen. Catholic ethnics pay special attention to the feast days of saints affiliated with their ethnic group, or attend ethnic festivals that take place in the area of first settlement or in ethnic churches.

Consumer goods, notably foods, are another ready source for ethnic symbols, and in the last decades the food industry has developed a large variety of easily cooked ethnic foods, as well as other edibles that need no cooking—for example, chocolate matzohs that are sold as gifts at Passover. The response to symbolic ethnicity may even be spreading into the mass media, for films and television programs with ethnic characters are on the increase. The characters are not very ethnic in their behavior, and may only have ethnic names—for example, Lieutenant Colombo, Fonzi, or Rhoda Goldstein—but in that respect they are not very different from the ethnic audiences who watch them.

Symbolic ethnicity also takes political forms, through identification or involvement with national politicians and international issues that are sufficiently remote to become symbols. As politicians from non-Irish ethnic backgrounds achieve high national or state office, they become identity symbols for members of their group, supplying feelings of pride over their success. For example, Michael Dukakis, ex-governor of Massachusetts, and John Brademas, congressman from

Indiana, may currently serve this function for Greeks, being the first members of the ethnic group to be elected to high office—other than Spiro Agnew, who, however, changed both his name and his religion before entering politics. That such politicians do not represent ethnic constituencies, and thus do not become involved in ethnic political disputes, only enhances their symbolic function, unlike local ethnic politicians, who are still elected for instrumental bread-and-butter reasons and thus become embroiled in conflicts that detract from their being symbols of ethnic pride. Thus, there was little pride in New York's Jewish community when Abe Beame was elected the first Jewish mayor of the city in 1973; in fact, some New York Jews opposed his election on the ground that any new difficulties facing the city during his administration would be blamed on the Jews. As it happened, the city's financial crisis turned disastrous while Beame was in office, and although he was widely criticized for his role in it, he was not attacked as a Jew, and was in fact succeeded by another Jewish mayor, Ed Koch.

Symbolic ethnicity can be practiced as well through politically and geographically even more distant phenomena, such as nationalist movements in the old country. Jews are not interested in their old countries, except to struggle against the maltreatment of Jews in Eastern Europe, but they have sent large amounts of money to Israel, and political pressure to Washington, since the establishment of the state. While their major concern has undoubtedly been to stave off Israel's destruction, they might also have felt that their own identity would be affected by such a disaster. Even if the survival of Israel is guaranteed in the future, however, it is possible that as allegiances toward organized local Jewish communities in America weaken, Israel becomes a substitute community to satisfy identity needs. Similar mechanisms may be at work among other ethnic groups who have recently taken an interest in their ancestral countries—for example, the Welsh and the Armenians—and among those groups whose old countries are involved in internal conflict—for example, the Irish, and Greeks and Turks since the Cyprus war of 1973.

Old countries are particularly useful as identity symbols because they are far away and cannot make arduous demands on American ethnics; even sending large amounts of money is ultimately an easy way to help, unless the donors are making major economic sacrifices. Moreover, American ethnics can identify with their perception of the old country or homeland, transforming it into a symbol, which leaves out those domestic or foreign problems that could become sources of conflict for Americans. For example, most American Jews who support Israel pay little attention to its purely domestic policies; they are concerned with its preservation as a state and a Jewish homeland, and see the country mainly as a Zionist symbol.

The symbolic functions of old countries are facilitated further when interest in them is historical, when ethnics develop an interest in their old countries as they were during or before the time of the ancestral departure. Marcus Hansen's notion of third-generation return was actually based on the emergence of interest in Swedish history, which suggests that the third-generation return may itself be only another variety of symbolic ethnicity. The third generation can obviously attend to the past with less emotional risk than first- and second generation people, who are still trying to escape it, but even so, an interest in ethnic history is a return only chronologically.

Conversely, a new symbol may be appearing among Jews: the Holocaust, which has become a historic example of ethnic-group destruction that can now serve as a warning sign for possible future threats. The interest of American Jews in the Holocaust has increased considerably since the end of World War II; when I studied the Jews of Park Forest in 1949–1950, it was almost never mentioned, and its memory played no part whatsoever in the creation of a Jewish community there. The lack of attention to the Holocaust at that time may, as Nathan Glazer suggests, reflect the fact that American Jews were busy with creating new Jewish communities in the suburbs.[22] It is also possible that people ignored the Holocaust then because the literature detailing its horrors had not yet been written, although since many second-generation American Jews had relatives who died in the Nazi camps, it seems more likely that people repressed thinking about it until it had become a more historical, and therefore a less immediately traumatic, event. As a result, the Holocaust may now be serving as a new symbol for the threat of group destruction, a symbol required, on the one hand, by the fact that rising intermarriage rates and the continued decline of interest and participation in Jewish religion are producing real fears about the disappearance of American Jewry altogether; and on the other hand, by the concurrent fact that American anti-Semitism is no longer the serious threat to group survival that it was for first- and second-generation Jews. Somewhat the same process appears to be taking place among some young Armenians who are now reviving the history of the Turkish massacre of Armenians some sixty years later, at a time when acculturation and assimilation are beginning to make inroads into the Armenian community in America. Still, good empirical data about the extent of the concern both with the Holocaust and the Turkish massacre are lacking, and neither may be as widespread among third-generation Jews and Armenians as among their professional and voluntary organizational leaders. Conversely, the 1978 NBC miniseries "The Holocaust" may be both an effect of rising interest in the tragedy and a cause of further interest, even if NBC commissioned the series in the hope of duplicating the earlier success of "Roots."

Most of the symbols used by third-generation ethnics are, however, more prosaic. Jews who take vacations in Israel and Catholic ethnics who go back to their ancestral countries may make these visits in part to satisfy identity needs. Some agnostic Jewish college students appear to have transformed Yom Kippur into a symbol of their Jewishness and stay away from classes even though they do not go to synagogue. It is even possible that the recent public emergence of Polish and other ethnic jokes serves some symbolic functions. Sandberg found that his Polish respondents were not particularly upset by Polish jokes, and perhaps third-generation Poles tell them to each other as negative symbols, which indicate to them what Polishness is not, and concurrently enable them to express their distaste for the butts of these jokes: Poles of an earlier generation or lower socioeconomic status.[23]

I suggested previously that ethnicity per se had become more visible, but many of the symbols used by the third generation are also visible to the rest of America, not only because the middle-class people who use them are more visible than their poorer ancestors; but because the national media are more adept at communicating symbols than the ethnic cultures and organizations of earlier generations. The visibility of symbolic ethnicity provides further support for the existence of an ethnic revival, but what appears to be a revival is probably the emergence of a new form of acculturation and assimilation that is taking place under the gaze of the rest of society.

Incidentally, even though the mass media play a major role in enhancing the visibility of ethnicity and communicating ethnic symbols, they do not play this role because they are themselves ethnic institutions. True, the mass media, like other entertainment industries, continue to be dominated by Jews (although less so than in the past), but for reasons connected with anti-Semitism, or the fear of it, they have generally leaned over backwards to keep Jewish characters and Jewish fare out of their offerings, at least until recently. Even now, a quantitative analysis of major ethnic characters in comedy, drama, and other entertainment genres would surely show that Catholic ethnics outnumber Jewish ones. Perhaps the Jews who write or produce so much of the media fare are especially sensitive to ethnic themes and symbols; my own hypothesis, however, is that they are, in this case as in others, simply responding to new cultural tendencies, if only because they must continually innovate. In fact, the arrival of ethnic characters followed the emergence and heightened visibility of ethnic politics in the late 1960s, and the men and women who write the entertainment fare probably took inspiration from news stories they saw on television or read in the papers.

I have suggested that symbolic ethnicity must be relatively effortless, but while this is probably true for the majority of third-generation ethnics, it is possible that more intense identity needs may produce a more intense form of symbolic ethnicity. Thus, Paul Ritterband has suggested that some aspects of the contemporary neotraditional movement among Jews may be in part symbolic, in that the movement is more concerned with strengthening feelings of Jewish identity and a sense of historic continuity than with perpetuating an Orthodox culture. Drawing on the distinction between *Halachah* (law) and *Aggadah* (myth), he suggests that such leading figures of the movement as Martin Buber and Abraham Heschel developed what he calls a new mythic culture, which manifests little relationship with an allegiance to the existing law-centered Orthodox Judaism. Consequently, it would be useful to study the members of this movement to discover to what extent they are pursuing new ways of being good Jews, and to what extent they want to perpetuate the laws and other dictates of Orthodoxy.

I noted earlier that identity cannot exist apart from a group and that symbols are themselves part of a culture, and in that sense, symbolic ethnicity can be viewed as an indicator of the persistence of ethnic groups and cultures. Symbolic ethnicity, however, does not require functioning groups or networks; feelings of identity can be developed by allegiances to symbolic groups that never meet, or to collectivities that meet only occasionally and exist as groups only for the handful of officers that keep them going. By the same token, symbolic ethnicity does not need a practiced culture, even if the symbols are borrowed from it. To be sure, symbolic culture is as much culture as practiced culture, but the latter persists only to supply symbols to the former.

Indeed, practiced culture may need to persist, for some, because people do not borrow their symbols from extinct cultures that survive only in museums. And insofar as the borrowed materials come from the practiced culture of the immigrant generation, they make it appear as if an ethnic revival were taking place.

Then, too, it should be noted that even symbolic ethnicity may be relevant for only some of the descendants of the immigrants. As intermarriage continues, the number of people with parents from the same secular ethnic group will continue to decline, and by the time the fourth generation of the old immigration reaches adulthood, such people may be a minority. Most Catholic ethnics will be hybrid, and will have difficulty developing an ethnic identity. For example, how would the son of an Italian mother and Irish father who has married a woman of Polish-German ancestry determine his ethnicity, and what would he and his wife tell their children? Even if they were willing, would they be able to decide on their, and their children's, ethnicity; and in that case, how would they rank or synthesize their diverse backgrounds? These questions are empirical, and urgently need to be studied, but I would suggest that there are only three possibilities. Either the parents choose the single ethnic identity they find most satisfying, or they encourage the children to become what I earlier called pan-ethnics, or they cope with diversity by ignoring it, and raise their children as non-ethnics.

THE EMERGENCE OF SYMBOLIC ETHNICITY

The preceding observations have suggested that symbolic ethnicity is a new phenomenon that comes into being in the third generation, but it is probably of earlier vintage and may have already begun to emerge among the immigrants themselves. After all, many of the participants in the new immigration were oppressed economically, politically, and culturally in their old countries, and could not have had much affection even for the villages and regions they were leaving. Consequently, it is entirely possible that they began to jettison the old culture and to stay away from ethnic organizations other than churches and unions the moment they came to America, saving only their primary groups, their ties to relatives still left in Europe, and their identity. In small-town America, where immigrants were a nu-

merically unimportant minority, the pressure for immediate acculturation and assimilation was much greater than in the cities, but even
in the latter, the seeds for symbolic ethnicity may have been sown
earlier than previously thought.

Conversely, despite all the pressures toward Americanization and
the prejudice and discrimination experienced by the immigrants, they
were never faced with conditions that required or encouraged them
to give up their ethnicity entirely. Of course, some of the earliest
Jewish arrivals to America had become Quakers and Episcopalians before the end of the nineteenth century, but the economic conditions
that persuaded the Jamaican Chinese in Kingston to become Creole,
and the social isolation that forced Italians in Sydney, Australia, to
abolish the traditional familial male-female role segregation shortly
after arriving, have never been part of the American experience.[24]

Some conditions for the emergence of symbolic ethnicity were present from the beginning, for American ethnics have always been characterized by freedom of ethnic expression, which stimulated both the
ethnic diversity and the right to find one's own way of being ethnic
that are crucial to symbolic ethnicity. Although sacred and secular
ethnic organizations that insisted that only one mode of being ethnic
was legitimate have always existed in America, they have not been
able to enforce their norms, in part because they have always had to
compete with other ethnic organizations. Even in ethnic neighborhoods where conformity was expected and social control was pervasive, people had some freedom of choice about ethnic cultural
practices. For example, the second-generation Boston Italians I studied had to conform to many family and peer-group norms, but they
were free to ignore ethnic secondary groups, and to drop or alter
Italian cultural practices according to their own preference.

Ethnic diversity within the group was probably encouraged by the
absence of a state religion and national and local heads of ethnic
communities. For example, American Jewry never had a chief rabbi,
or even chief Orthodox, Conservative, and Reform rabbis, and the
European practice of local Jewish communities electing or appointing
local laymen as presidents was not carried across the ocean.[25] Catholic
ethnics had to obey the cardinal or bishop heading their diocese, of
course, but in those communities where the diocese insisted on an
Irish church, the other ethnic groups, notably the Italians, kept their
distance from the church, and only in the parochial schools was there
any attempt to root out secular ethnic patterns. The absence of

strong unifying institutions thus created the opportunity for diversity and freedom from the beginning, and undoubtedly facilitated the departure from ethnic cultures and organizations.

Among the Jews, symbolic ethnicity may have been fostered early by self-selection among Jewish emigrants. As Liebman points out, the massive Eastern European immigration to America did not include the rabbis and scholars who practiced what he calls an elite religion in the old countries; as a result, the immigrants established what he calls a folk religion in America instead, with indigenous rabbis who were elected or appointed by individual congregations and were more permissive in allowing, or too weak to prevent, deviations from religious orthodoxy, even of the milder folk variety.[26] Indeed, the development of a folk religion may have encouraged religious and secular diversity among Jews from the very beginning.

Still, perhaps the most important factor in the development of symbolic ethnicity was probably the awareness, which I think many second-generation people had already reached, that neither the practice of ethnic culture nor participation in ethnic organizations was essential to being and feeling ethnic. For Jews, living in a Jewish neighborhood or working with Jews every day was enough to maintain Jewish identity. When younger second-generation Jews moved to suburbia in large numbers after World War II, many wound up in communities in which they were a small numerical minority, but they quickly established an informal Jewish community of neighborly relations, and then built synagogues and community centers to formalize and supplement the informal community. At the time, many observers interpreted the feverish building as a religious revival, but for most Jews the synagogue was a symbol that could serve as a means of expressing identity without requiring more than occasional participation in its activities.[27] Thus, my observations among the second-generation Jews of Park Forest and other suburbs led me to think, as far back as the mid-1950s, that among Jews, at least, the shift to symbolic ethnicity was already under way.[28]

Suburban Jews also built synagogues and centers to help them implant a Jewish identity among their children, and to hold back primary assimilation, particularly intermarriage. Jewish parents sent their teenagers into Jewish organizations so that they would date other Jews, and then to colleges where they would be most likely to find Jewish spouses. Rising intermarriage rates suggest, however, that their efforts were not always successful, but also that their fears of the consequences of intermarriage were exaggerated. By now, many Jewish parents realize that intermarriage need not inevitably lead to surrender of Jewish identity. Non-Jewish spouses of third-generation Jews sometimes convert to Judaism, more frequently adopt some trappings of Jewish culture and pay homage to Jewish symbols, and even raise their children as Jews, thus suggesting that even with third-generation intermarriage, the next generation will still consider itself to be Jewish.[29]

Actually, if being Jewish need only mean feeling Jewish and attending to Jewish symbols, the transmission of Jewish identity to the next generation is fairly easily achieved, even by non-Jewish parents. Although little is known about socialization for Jewish identity, it may require only a minimum of parental action, no cultural or organizational affiliation, and perhaps not even a Jewish education for the children. Some evidence suggests that at about age five, children begin to ask themselves, their peers, and their parents what they are, and being told that they are Jewish may be sufficient to plant the seeds of Jewish identity.[30]

Needless to say, a person's ethnic identity is not firmly established at five and can weaken or disappear in later years. Even when this does not happen, adolescents and adults often develop doubts about their ethnic identity, and particularly about their ability to pass it on to their children.[31] I have the impression that ambivalence about one's identity is weaker among third-generation Jews than it was among their parents, if only because ethnic identity is now not burdensome or beset with major social and economic costs. Still, unless strong incentives or pressures develop to encourage Jews to give up their identity, it seems likely that they will retain it in the fourth generation, especially since the demands of symbolic ethnicity are light enough not to cause conflict with other, more highly valued, identities and activities.

Some of these observations apply equally well to third-generation Catholic ethnics, especially those who live in the suburbs. They still attend church more frequently than Jews attend synagogue, generally marry Catholics, and are unlikely to give up their Catholic identity. They do not, however, feel a strong need to perpetuate their secular ethnicity, so that, for example, Italian parents do not press their adolescent children to date other Italians. Even so, it is possible that identity may also be transmitted to children by others besides parents, for example, grandparents and peers. In any case, Sandberg has shown that fourth-generation Poles still retain their Polish identity, and Crispino has found the same among Italians.[32]

As intermarriage increases, however, it will be important to discover which ethnic identity, if any, is transmitted to children by intermarried Catholic ethnics; whether mothers and fathers play different roles in identity transmission; and how grandparents and close friends act in this connection. Similar questions could be asked of hybrid ethnics, although it seems unlikely that they could even decide which of their many ancestries they should pass on to their children.

THE FUTURE OF ETHNICITY

The emergence of symbolic ethnicity naturally raises the question of its persistence into the fifth and sixth generations. Although the Catholic and Jewish religions are certain to endure, it appears that as religion becomes less important to people, they, too, will be eroded by acculturation and assimilation. Even now synagogues see most of their worshippers no more than once or twice a year, and presumably the same trend will appear, perhaps more slowly, among Catholics and Protestants as well.

Whether the secular forms of ethnicity can survive beyond the fourth generation is somewhat less certain. One possibility is that symbolic ethnicity will itself decline as acculturation and assimilation continue, and then disappear as erstwhile ethnics forget their secular ethnic identity to blend into one or another subcultural melting pot. The other possibility is that symbolic ethnicity is a steady-state phenomenon that can persist into the fifth and sixth generations.

Obviously this question can only be guessed at, but my hypothesis is that symbolic ethnicity may persist. The continued existence of Germans, Scandinavians, and Irish after five or more generations in America suggests that in the larger cities and suburbs, at least, they have remained ethnic because they have long practiced symbolic ethnicity.[33] Consequently, there is good reason to believe that the same process will also take place among ethnics of the new immigration.

Ethnic behavior, attitudes, and even identity are, however, determined not only by what goes on among the ethnics, but also by developments in the larger society, and especially by how that society will treat ethnics in the future: what costs it will levy and what benefits it will award to them as ethnics. At present, the costs of being and feeling ethnic are slight. The changes that the immigrants and their descendants wrought in America now make it unnecessary for ethnics to surrender their ethnicity to gain upward mobility, and today ethnics are admitted virtually everywhere, provided they meet economic and status requirements, except at the very highest levels of the economic, political, and cultural hierarchies. Moreover, since World War II, the ethnics have been able to shoulder blacks and other racial minorities with the deviant and scapegoat functions they performed in an earlier America, so that ethnic prejudice and "institutional ethnism" are no longer significant, except, again, at the very top of the societal hierarchies.

To be sure, some ethnic scapegoating persists at other levels of these hierarchies; American Catholics are still blamed for the policies of the Vatican, Italo-Americans are criticized for the Mafia, and urban ethnics generally have been portrayed as racists by a sometime coalition of white and black Protestant, Jewish, and other upper-middle-class cosmopolitans. But none of these phenomena, however repugnant, strike me as serious enough to persuade anyone to hide his or her ethnicity. White working-class men, and perhaps others, still use ethnic stereotypes to trade insults, but this practice serves functions other than the maintenance of prejudice or inequality.

At the same time, the larger society also seems to offer some benefits for being ethnic. Americans increasingly perceive themselves as undergoing cultural homogenization, and whether or not this perception is justified, they are constantly looking for new ways to establish their differences from each other. Meanwhile, the social, cultural, and political turbulence of the last decade and the concurrent delegitimation of many American institutions have also cast doubt on some of the other ways by which people identify themselves and differentiate themselves from each other. Ethnicity, now that it is respectable and no longer a major cause of conflict, seems therefore to be ideally suited to serve as a distinguishing characteristic. Moreover, in a mobile society, people who often find themselves living in communities of strangers tend to look for commonalities that make strangers into neighbors, and shared ethnicity may provide mobile people with at least an initial excuse to get together. Finally, as long as the European immigration into America continues, people will still be perceived, classified, and ranked at least in part by ethnic origin. Consequently, external forces exist to complement internal identity needs, and unless there is a drastic change in the allocation of costs and benefits with respect to ethnicity, it seems likely that the larger society will also encourage the persistence of symbolic ethnicity.

Needless to say, it is always possible that future economic and political conditions in American society will create a demand for new scapegoats, and if ethnics are forced into this role, so that ethnicity once more levies costs, present tendencies will be interrupted. Under such conditions, some ethnics will try to assimilate faster and pass out of all ethnic roles, while others will revitalize the ethnic group socially and culturally, if only for self-protection. Still, the chance that Catholic ethnics will be scapegoated more than today seems very slight. A serious economic crisis could, however, result in a resurgence of anti-Semitism, in part because of the affluence of many American Jews, in part because of their visibly influential role in some occupations, notably mass communications.

If present societal trends continue, however, symbolic ethnicity should become the dominant way of being ethnic by the time the fourth generation of the new immigration matures into adulthood, and this in turn will have consequences for the structure of American ethnic groups. For one thing, as secondary and primary assimilation continue, and ethnic networks weaken and unravel, it may be more accurate to speak of ethnic aggregates rather than groups. More importantly, since symbolic ethnicity does not depend on ethnic cultures and organizations, their future decline and disappearance must be expected, particularly those cultural patterns that interfere with other aspects of life and those organizations that require active membership.

Few such patterns and organizations are left in any case, and leaders of the remaining organizations have long been complaining bitterly over what they perceive as the cultural and organizational apathy of ethnics. They also criticize the resort to symbolic ethnicity, identifying it as an effortless way of being ethnic that further threatens their own persistence. Even so, attacking people as apathetic or lazy and calling on them to revive the practices and loyalties of the past have never been effective for engendering support, and reflect instead the desperation of organizations that cannot offer new incentives that would enable them to recruit members.

Some cultural patterns and organizations will survive. Patterns that lend themselves to transformation into symbols and easy practice, such as annual holidays, should persist. So will organizations that create and distribute symbols, or "ethnic goods" such as foodstuffs or written materials, but need few or no members and can function with small staffs and low overhead. In all likelihood, most ethnic organizations will eventually realize that in order to survive, they must deal mainly in symbols, using them to generate enough support to fund other activities as well.

Symbols do not arise in a vacuum, however, but are grounded in larger cultures. Moreover, insofar as ethnicity involves the notion of a heritage and an actual or imagined gloried past, contemporary symbols depend on older cultures. What kinds of symbols future generations of ethnics will want can hardly be predicted now, but undoubtedly some will want nostalgia, while others will use ethnicity as a substitute or indicator for other goals or purposes. Even now, ethnicity has served as an intentional or unintentional cover for racism, conservative political and economic ideologies, and the defense of familial and local structures and values against national forces and tendencies that drive American society further from Gemeinschaft and closer to a nationally homogeneous Gesellschaft.[34]

The demand for current ethnic symbols may require the maintenance of at least some old cultural practices, possibly as hobbies, and through the work of ethnic scholars who keep old practices alive by studying them. It is even possible that the organizations that attempt to maintain the old cultures will support themselves in part by supplying ethnic nostalgia, and some ethnics may aid such organizations if only to assuage their guilt at having given up ancestral practices.

Still, the history of religion and nationalism, as well as events of recent years, should remind us that the social process sometimes moves in dialectical ways, and that acculturative and assimilative actions by a majority occasionally generate revivalistic reactions by a minority. As a result, even ethnic aggregates in which the vast majority maintains its identity in symbolic ways will probably always bring forth small pockets of neotraditionalism—of rebel converts to sacred and secular ways of the past. They may not influence the behavior of the majority, but they are almost always highly visible, and will thus continue to play a role in the ethnicity of the future.

SYMBOLIC ETHNICITY AND STRAIGHT-LINE THEORY

The third and fourth generations' concern with ethnic identity and its expression through symbols seems to me to fit straight-line theory, for symbolic ethnicity cannot be considered as evidence either of a third-generation return or of a revival. Instead, it constitutes only another point in the secular trend that is drawn, implicitly, in straight-line theory, although it could also be a point at which the declining secular trend begins to level off and perhaps to straighten out.

In reality, of course, the straight line has never been quite straight, for even if it accurately graphs the dominant ethnic experience, it ignores the ethnic groups who still continue to make small bumps and waves in the line. Among these are various urban and rural ethnic enclaves, notably among the poor; the new European immigrants who help to keep these enclaves from disappearing; the groups that successfully segregate themselves from the rest of American society in deliberately enclosed enclaves; and the rebel converts to sacred and secular ways of the past who will presumably continue to appear.

Finally, even if I am right to predict that symbolic ethnicity can persist into the fifth and sixth generations, I would be foolish to suggest that it is a permanent phenomenon. Although all Americans, save the Indians, came here as immigrants and are thus in one sense ethnics, people who arrived in the seventeenth and eighteenth centuries, and before the mid-nineteenth-century old immigration, are, except in some rural enclaves, no longer ethnics even if they know where their emigrant ancestors came from. Admittedly, in recent years some upper-class WASPs have begun to consider themselves to be ethnics, but they have done so as a reaction to their loss of cultural power, and the feeling of being a minority that has accompanied this loss, and they have not identified themselves by their European origins.

The history of groups whose ancestors arrived here seven or more generations ago suggests that, eventually, the ethnics of the new immigration will be like them; they may retain American forms of the religions that their ancestors brought to America, but their secular cultures will be only a dim memory, and their identity will bear only the minutest trace, if that, of their national origins. Ultimately, then, the secular trend of straight-line theory will hit very close to zero, and the basic postulates of the theory will turn out to have been accurate—unless, of course, by then America, and the ways it makes Americans, have altered drastically in some now unpredictable manner.

NOTES

This paper was stimulated by S. H. Eisenstadt's talk at Columbia University in November 1975 on "Unity and Diversity in Contemporary Jewish Society." I am grateful to many people for helpful comments on an earlier draft of the paper, notably Harold Abramson, Richard Alba, James Crispino, Nathan Glazer, Milton Gordon, Andrew Greeley, William Kornblum, Peter Marris, Michael Novak, David Riesman, Paul Ritterband, Allan Silver, and John Slawson.

1. Personal communication. Incidentally, David Riesman is now credited with having invented the term "ethnicity" as it is currently used. (Hereafter, I shall omit personal communication notes, but most of the individuals mentioned in the text supplied ideas or data through personal communication.)

2. For the sake of brevity, I employ these terms rather than Gordon's more detailed concepts. Milton Gordon, *Assimilation in American Life* (New York: Oxford University Press, 1964), chap. 3.

3. Neil C. Sandberg, *Ethnic Identity and Assimilation: The Polish-American Community* (New York: Praeger, 1974). The primary empirical application of straight-line theory is probably still W. Lloyd Warner and Leo Srole, *The Social Systems of American Ethnic Groups* (New Haven: Yale University Press, 1945).

4. See, for example, Andrew Greeley, *Ethnicity in the United States* (New York: Wiley, 1974), chap. 1.

5. W. Yancey, E. Ericksen, and R. Juliani, "Emergent Ethnicity: A Review and Reformulation," *American Sociological Review* 41 (1976): 391–403; words quoted at p. 400.

6. The major works include Greeley, *Ethnicity in the United States*; Harold J. Abramson, *Ethnic Diversity in Catholic America* (New York: Wiley, 1973); and Nathan Glazer and Daniel P. Moynihan, *Beyond the Melting Pot*, 2nd ed. (Cambridge: MIT Press, 1970).

7. Class differences in the degree of acculturation and assimilation were first noted by Warner and Srole, *Social Systems*; for some recent data among Poles, see Sandberg, *Ethnic Identity*.

8. Herbert J. Gans, *The Urban Villagers* (New York: Free Press, 1962), chap. 11. See also Dennis Wrong, "How Important is Social Class," in Irving Howe, ed., *The World of the Blue Collar Worker* (New York: Quadrangle, 1972), pp. 297–309; William Kornblum, *Blue Collar Community* (Chicago: University of Chicago Press, 1974); and Stephen Steinberg, *The Academic Melting Pot* (New Brunswick: Transaction Books, 1977).

9. Marcus L. Hansen, *The Problem of the Third Generation Immigrant* (Rock Island, Ill.: Augustana Historical Society, 1938); and "The Third Generation in America," *Commentary* 14 (1952): 492–500.

10. See also Harold J. Abramson, "The Religioethnic Factor and American Experience: Another Look at the Three-Generations Hypothesis," *Ethnicity* 2 (1975): 163–77

11. One of the most influential works has been Michael Novak, *The Rise of the Unmeltable Ethnics* (New York: Macmillan, 1971).

12. See Phil Berger, *The Last Laugh* (New York: Morrow, 1975).

13. Similarly, studies of the radical movements of the 1960s have shown that they included many people who themselves grew up in radical families.

14. See, for example, Egon Mayer, "Modern Jewish Orthodoxy in Post-Modern America: A Case Study of the Jewish Community in Boro Park" (Ph.D. diss., Rutgers University, 1974).

15. Perhaps the first, and now not sufficiently remembered, study of third-generation Jews was Judith Kramer and Seymour Leventman, *The Children of the Gilded Ghetto* (New Haven: Yale University Press, 1961).

16. Geoffrey Bock, "The Jewish Schooling of American Jews" (Ph.D. diss., Harvard University, 1976).

17. I also make the assumption that generation is an important determinant of ethnic behavior, but I am aware that it is less important than I sometimes imply; that there are large differences in the experience of a generation within and between ethnic groups; and that the immigrants' age of arrival in the United States affected both their acculturation and that of their descendants.

18. The notion of primary assimilation extends Gordon's concept of marital assimilation to include movement out of the extended family, friendship circles,

and other peer groups. In describing marital assimilation, Gordon did, however, mention the primary group as well. Gordon, *Assimilation in American Life*, p. 80.

19. The major debate at present is between Abramson and Alba, the former viewing the amount of intermarriage among Catholic ethnics as low; and the latter, as high. See Abramson, *Ethnic Diversity in Catholic America*; and Richard Alba, "Social Assimilation of American Catholic National-Origin Groups," *American Sociological Review* 41 (1976): 1030–46.

20. See, for example, Marshall Sklare and Joseph Greenblum, *Jewish Identity on the Suburban Frontier* (New York: Basic Books, 1967); Herbert J. Gans, "The Origin and Growth of a Jewish Community in the Suburbs: A Study of the Jews of Park Forest," in Marshall Sklare, ed., *The Jews: Social Pattern of an American Group* (New York: Free Press, 1958), pp. 205–48; and Herbert J. Gans, *The Levittowners* (New York: Pantheon, 1967), pp. 73–80. These findings may not apply to communities with significant numbers of German Jews with Reform leanings. There are few Orthodox Jews in the suburbs, except in those surrounding New York City.

21. My use of the word "symbol" here follows Lloyd Warner's concept of symbolic behavior. See W. Lloyd Warner, *American Life: Dream and Reality* (Chicago: University of Chicago Press, 1953), chap. 1.

22. See Nathan Glazer, *American Judaism*, 2d. ed. (Chicago: University of Chicago Press, 1972), pp. 114–15.

23. Sandberg, *Ethnic Identity*, Table 5-20. Understandably enough, working-class Poles felt more offended by these jokes. Table 5-19.

24. On the Jamaica Chinese, see Orlando Patterson, *Ethnic Chauvinism* (New York: Stein and Day, 1977), chap. 5; on the Sydney Italians, see Rina Huber, *From Pasta to Pavlova* (St. Lucia: University of Queensland Press, 1977), part 3.

25. For a study of one unsuccessful attempt to establish a community presidency, see Arthur A. Goren, *New York Jews and the Quest for Community* (New York: Columbia University Press, 1970).

26. Charles S. Liebman, *The Ambivalent American Jew* (Philadelphia: Jewish Publication Society of America, 1973), chap. 3. Liebman notes that the few elite rabbis who did come to America quickly sensed they were in alien territory and returned to Eastern Europe. The survivors of the Holocaust who came to America after World War II were too few and too late to do more than influence the remaining Jewish Orthodox organizations.

27. Gans, "The Origin of a Jewish Community in the Suburbs."

28. See Herbert J. Gans, "American Jewry: Present and Future," *Commentary* 21 (1956): 422–30, which includes a discussion of "symbolic Judaism."

29. Fred S. Sherrow, "Patterns of Religious Intermarriage among American College Graduates" (Ph.D. diss., Columbia University, 1971).

30. See, for example, Mary E. Goodman, *Race Awareness in Young Children* (Cambridge: Addison-Wesley, 1952).

31. Sklare and Greenblum, *Jewish Identity on the Suburban Frontier*, p. 331.

32. Sandberg, *Ethnic Identity*; and James Crispino, *The Assimilation of Ethnic Groups: The Italian Case* (New York: Center for Migration Studies, 1979).

33. Unfortunately, too little attention has been devoted by sociologists to ethnicity among descendants of the old immigration.

34. The Ethnic Millions Political Action Committee (EMPAC), founded by Michael Novak, described itself as a "national civil rights committee, dedicated to a politics of family and neighborhood, to equality and fairness, to a new America." Conversely, Patterson sees ethnicity as a major obstacle to the achievement of a universalist, and socialist, humanism. Patterson, *Ethnic Chauvinism*.

10

A NEW MARITAL FORM: THE
MARRIAGE OF UNCERTAIN DURATION

ROBERT S. WEISS

The most striking characteristic of American family life today is the very great frequency with which it is disrupted by divorce. The number of divorces is now very nearly half the number of marriages: in the twelve months preceding November 1977, about 2,200,000 marriages took place and about 1,100,000 divorces.[1] Earlier estimates that between 35 and 40 percent of new marriages would eventually end in divorce now appear to be too conservative.[2] It should be kept in mind, too, that these figures deal only with formal divorce and so understate the degree of serious familial disruption. If we consider not just divorce but any voluntary separation in which partners move to different households without intent of future rejoining, it appears that well over half the marriages now being formed will experience a significant break.[3]

The rate of divorce in the United States has been increasing in a rather uneven fashion for as long as we have records. But after a postwar peak in 1945, it was temporarily stable through the decade of the fifties. In 1960 it resumed its increase, at first slowly, then quite rapidly. In 1975 the rate of increase suddenly slowed, and since 1976 the divorce rate has again been stable. Despite its present stability, the divorce rate now appears high enough to justify the assertion that we have developed a new marital form, a marriage that is about as likely to end in divorce as not: a marriage of uncertain duration.

Accompanying the higher rate of divorce is a greater ease in obtaining one. Twenty-five years ago, divorce was extremely difficult to obtain in most states. Divorce would be granted only to a husband or wife who could demonstrate that the other party to the marriage had been seriously at fault in a manner designated by the legislators of that particular state as grounds for divorce. If the husband and wife decided together, before going to court, that they would cooperate in obtaining the divorce, the judge might deny their petition on grounds of collusion. And even more of a barrier to divorce than legal restrictions, twenty-five years ago, was the scandal divorce would bring to one's family. Those who had been divorced were seen as odd and somewhat shady by respectable members of the community. A widely shared belief that marriage was to be endured, no matter what, prevented the unhappily married from even contemplating a visit to a lawyer.

Now all this has changed. Although marriages may be entered as hopefully as ever, separation and divorce are accepted as events that may happen to anyone. Most states have changed the statutes governing divorce to make it possible for divorce to be granted without demonstration of fault, so long as a judge can be satisfied that the marriage has suffered irretrievable breakdown. No longer is it necessary for a couple bent on divorce to concoct a story of mental or physical cruelty or to relate in court mistreatments that unhappily actually occurred. Nor do legislators find it desirable that couples with adequate income can obtain a migratory divorce by the wife's establishing token residence in Nevada or Alabama or Mexico, while other couples, who cannot afford the trip, must stay married. And even more important than change in statute law has been change in judicial treatment of divorce. It would be astonishing, now, to hear a judge express outrage on discovering that there had been pretrial agreement between husband and wife regarding the complaint to be made. Judges no longer recognize any mandate to protect marriages from the men and women within them.

The separated and divorced no longer are a pariah folk with whom the respectable feel uncomfortable. Separation may still be faintly discrediting, but it is now more often seen as a variety of misfortune than as a consequence of delinquency. We now accept that individuals who choose to end their marriages need not by so doing be demonstrating a character flaw.

A number of changes in our social life have contributed to this changed definition of the nature of marriage. Keniston finds an explanation for the increase in the divorce rate in a decreased interdependence of husband, wife, and children. When father worked long hours on the farm or in the factory and mother stayed home to care for the many children, neither father nor mother could function without the other. The marriage might be unhappy, but it would not end.[4] Yet this appraisal, though it may explain the steady rise in the American divorce rate since the country's earliest days, cannot explain the dramatic rise that began about 1960.

Something happened in the early sixties to the American understanding of familial responsibilities. One possibility is that the early sixties witnessed a very general movement to celebrate the rights of the individual in opposition to the rights of institutions. Certainly, there was at this time an upsurge in attacks on the legitimacy of institutions. Politicians had always been held suspect, but only in the early sixties did large numbers of Americans begin to question government itself.[5] It was in the sixties, too, that university students learned to criticize not only specific administrators but also administration itself, and to organize "free universities" as an alternative and a protest. Big business began to be portrayed as dehumanizing, and executive positions as traps rather than opportunities.

At a time when any corporate group might be seen as blocking the desires of its members rather than channeling, expressing, or responding to them, it would be surprising if marriage were not also subjected to the same criticism. The idea developed through the sixties that what really mattered in life was making the most of one's own potential. Service to others was performed by combatting repressive institutions and ensuring that opportunity would be available everywhere. This ethic of self-realization was not necessarily hedonistic in character. Indeed, it might lead to choice of a life that was stressful and ungratifying. But to refuse to be one's self, to choose security rather than self-expression and growth, to accept a good job one did not really want, to stay in a marriage that, while not actively unhappy, was stultifying, would be to fail in one's duty to one's self. It would be more than simply compromise; it would be cowardice.

The Women's Movement adopted this theme of self-realization. Saying that the housewife's role was self-abnegation, the Women's Movement insisted that women, too, ought to be able to grow, to become whatever they could. Strengthened by this viewpoint, and aided by antidiscrimination laws, women have achieved increased opportunity within the labor force. We still have far to go before we can claim sexual equality within the labor force, but the distance we have already come has greatly increased the practicality of a woman's going it alone. While it remains true that many long-married women are totally unprepared when overtaken by marital separation, it is much easier than it once was for a woman to get training and a job. In response to new definitions of the rights of the self when in contest with the demands of marriage, together with greater opportunities in the labor force, some women have reconsidered earlier decisions to devote themselves to family life and have embarked on new careers, on occasion interrupting or ending a marriage in the process.

The increased rate of separation and divorce has become self-reinforcing. It is much more difficult to stigmatize as pathological or irresponsible those seeking divorce when they become a sizable proportion of the population. The Catholic Church has recently modified its attitude toward its separated and divorced members; no longer are they required to consider themselves still married in the eyes of the Church. Twenty-five years ago, in a book titled *Divorce Won't Help*, Edmund Bergler could write that separation and divorce were consequences of neurotic conflict. While vestiges of this view are still expressed, the increased frequency of separation and divorce makes it evident that marital breakdown occurs to many different kinds of people and not only to the unusually unstable.

It is my impression, on the basis of crisis-focused work with a small number of divorcing individuals, and interviews with a more extensive number of single parents, that the increased acceptability of separation and divorce has had an effect on the way couples manage marital conflict. Husbands and wives appear now to be less tolerant of discomfort, and less willing to compromise their interests or to relinquish their hopes, in order to adapt to their marriages. An older respondent, now divorced, told us that early in her marriage, some twenty years ago, she discovered that her husband had fathered a child by another woman. Her reaction at that time was that marriage was for better or worse, and although hers was, regrettably, proving to be for worse, there was little she could do but continue to accept it. Today marriage appears to be for worse only up to a point—a point well within reach.

Twenty-five years ago the presence of children was a strong deterrent to voluntary dissolution of a marriage. For a given length of marriage, the divorce rate among parents was about 60 percent of the divorce rate among the childless. At that time, unhappily married parents told themselves and others that no matter how bad their marriages had become, they would stay together for the sake of the children. Their position was supported by a widespread belief that a broken home was a catastrophe for a child: a certain cause of distress and a likely cause of delinquency. No longer is this the dominant view.

Since the beginning of the sixties, the increase in the divorce rate among parents has been even more rapid than the increase in the overall divorce rate.[6] Parents seem to believe that children do better if they divorce than if they continue an unhappy marriage.[7] Although the issue is complex, many parents now accept the simplistic dictum "Better a happy home with one parent than an unhappy home with two." Indeed, couples on the brink of separation now sometimes decide to separate for the sake of the children. They believe that the children must suffer unremitting unhappiness in the embattled home and that they will later blame themselves for having kept the parents together. There are occasions, of course, when one parent believes a marriage must end because the children require protection from the other parent; but now it also happens that parents decide that even though they are both good parents, the children need protection from the unhappy marriage.

Evidence regarding the comparative well-being of children of divorced parents is, in fact, equivocal. A recent national survey conducted by the Foundation for Child Development suggests that children whose parents have separated or divorced are about as likely to be troubled as are children whose parents describe their marriages as unhappy.[8] The question of whether children are better off if their unhappily married parents separate may depend largely on whether the parents would have been able to provide a supportive setting for the children despite the parents' difficulties. Some unhappily married parents seem able to do so. If the result of their separation is a disruption of one or both parent-child relationships, the children may well be losers on balance.

There is still another factor that should be noted in connection with our high divorce rate, and that is the importance to us of marriage. It is extremely difficult for us in America, given the way we organize our lives, to tolerate an unsatisfactory marriage. The University of Michigan's Survey of the Quality of American Life found satisfaction with family life and satisfaction with marriage to be the most important determinants of overall satisfaction with life.[9] Individuals whose marriages have failed are peculiarly vulnerable to depression and self-doubt.[10]

We Americans tend to be distant from our kin in space if not in feeling, and the considerateness we display towards our friends includes an unwillingness to burden them with our troubles. Our primary sources of sympathy and support are our spouses. We are consequently both bruised and bereft when our spouses turn from allies to critics. In addition, because our feelings about ourselves are so accessible to influence from our immediate environments, we take to heart the negative appraisals we hear in our marital quarrels. We are deeply affected by the reflections of ourselves we see in the way we are talked to and treated by our spouses. Our marriages have much to do not only with our moods, but also with our notions of who we are.

With marital support so important, a spouse's slight can easily be felt to be a grievous injury, and what might appear to an outsider to be an unimportant misunderstanding can give rise to feelings of intolerable misuse. Often enough we counterattack: a reaction that may, perhaps, be especially marked among Americans. We Americans seem to earn self-respect by refusing to accept undeserved injury from another. We believe in standing up for ourselves whatever the cost. And so American marital quarrels easily lead to threats of separation, for neither husband nor wife is willing to sustain the narcissistic damage that would stem from apology.

Survey data suggests that marriages that encounter unusual stress are more likely to experience internal disharmony and so are more likely to move along the pathway to separation and divorce. The stress can be of any sort, but often it is economic. An unemployed husband and a depleted bank account have both been shown to be causally related to marital separation.[11] So might be a chonically ill child, unsatisfactory housing conditions, and shift work.

It is tempting, when reviewing the reasons for our high level of separation and divorce, to see ourselves as commenting on a social ill. Yet not so long ago the difficulty of obtaining a divorce might well have been viewed as the more significant problem. Not quite fifty years ago, several distinguished European and American writers contributed to a volume in which, with impressive uniformity, they held that liberalizing the restrictive divorce laws of that day was necessary to a better society.[12] We should not forget that divorce furnishes a remedy for those unhappy situations that might in an earlier time have permanently blighted the lives of trapped husbands or wives. Women are no longer condemned to life with a brutal husband. A loveless marriage is no longer required to continue.

But if our current situation is a solution to one set of problems, there is no gainsaying that it is a source of another. Marital separation is regularly a traumatic event.[13] Individuals discover that even though they may be relieved of an oppressive marriage, they are bereft of a relationship that, despite its discomforts, had provided them with an anchor for identity and a defense against loneliness. The parent who had, during the marriage, a normal level of parental investment in the children, and loses custody of them with the divorce, is apt to be severely depressed. Yet the parent who retains custody of the children may be distressed in a different fashion by the discovery that parenting alone is isolating and exhausting. And the childless as well as those with children are apt to discover that separation and divorce disrupt their linkages with others, that the friendships they made when married lose their validity, and that for a time they are socially marginal.

The increased frequency of marital separation does not reduce its traumatic impact. Increased frequency does lessen the sense of stigmatization that once accompanied marital separation, and has resulted in improved treatment of the separated and divorced by institutions: for example, it is now much easier for a divorced woman to obtain credit than it was only five or ten years ago. But the increased frequency of marital separation has not reduced the emotional and social upset it produces. In this respect marital separation resembles an auto accident: that it has happened to others does not make it hurt any less.

If this is the case for the couple themselves, it is even more the case for the children. For while husband and wife ordinarily can anticipate eventually entering a new marriage whose felicity may compensate for the pain of ending the earlier one, the children must live with the mutual distancing, and often the mutual animosity, of the only parents they will ever have. Adolescent children of divorced parents regularly complain of the difficulties of maintaining relationships with contesting parents, and of attempts by parents to make them allies, or to use them as messengers or spies. These adolescents have had to learn to recognize that their parent's lives are distinct from their own and that their parents are, perhaps more than other adults, troubled by ambivalences, moods, and irrational angers; and while all this may have provided the adolescents with early wisdom, it has also cost them energy they might otherwise have devoted to their own development. Again and again these adolescents say that they will not take their parents as models for their own lives.

It is not only those children whose own parents' marriages have ended who are affected by the high rate of separation and divorce. Many schools, especially those in apartment districts, have classrooms in which from a quarter to a half of the children are from single-parent households. The other children must give thought to their own situation: will their parents' marriages continue? They, too, must wonder about the reliability of marital commitments.

By the time children reach college age, they are wary of marriage. Often they want love and serious commitment, but they are afraid that marriage may be the first step to divorce. Many young people at our best colleges have implemented Margaret Mead's idea of a two-tier marriage system. Mead's proposal, described by her in a *Redbook* article and on national television, was that we should have two different kinds of marriage. One would be easy to enter and easy to leave. Individuals in it would be prohibited from having children. The other would be difficult to enter and even more difficult to leave, but couples would be permitted to have children. Young people seem to have adopted this system, except that they enter the first form of marriage, which they call "living together," without any ceremony. Then they have the usual ceremony when they enter the second form of marriage, "real marriage."

This system has as one consequence that individuals' first divorces are not registered, because their first marriages are not. And so the system, if it became widespread, would effectively reduce the divorce rate. But it is not evident how much of a solution the system offers to other problems. The distress attendant on the ending of a committed nonmarriage is nearly the same as that which accompanies the ending of a marriage. There may not be the same degree of social dislocation, but feelings of loss are as intense, and there is likely to be less support from friends and kin. One woman said that at about the time she ended a six-year relationship with the man with whom she lived, her sister ended a two-year marriage. Her parents shrugged off the ending of her relationship with the comment "How good it was that you did not marry!" Her sister received her parents' sympathy.

Nor does there seem much reason to believe that postponing "real marriage" to more or less coincide with parenthood would provide greater assurance that the children of the marriage would not eventually have to cope with the separation of their parents. It may even be that putting "real marriage" off until parenthood costs young people a chance to get used to marriage at a time when they do not yet have to respond to the additional demands of parenthood. Marriage is quite different from living together. In marriage, but not in unmarried cohabitation, people have to learn to function in the social roles of husband and wife; have to become accustomed to auxiliary membership in the family of the other spouse; have to accept the social understandings (regarding, for example, inheritance) implied by the phrase "next of kin"; and, perhaps more important than anything else, have to come to terms with the evocation of their own and their spouse's parental relationships produced by recognition that their marriages constitute a permanent connection to someone whose needs impose limits on their freedom. Living together only partially prepares people for marriage. If a couple are certain of their commitment to each other, they might do better to marry and learn to live as a married couple before they have children.

If one response among young people to their recognition that marriage today is of uncertain duration is to postpone it, perhaps until they are ready for parenthood, another is to accept marriage, hope for the best, and nevertheless be prepared for the dissolution of the relationship. Not only has increased employment opportunity for women contributed to the development of our new marital form, but recognition of this form has made it almost imperative that women develop skills that will enable them to support themselves if need be. At one time it was an unquestioned assumption in American society that women throughout their lives were dependent on a male relative for financial support and moral direction. The phases of a woman's life were marked by the male relative upon whom she depended: the father gave the woman away to her husband at the woman's marriage, and on the husband's death, the woman became dependent upon a mature son or, failing this, a husband's brother. Now, increasingly, it is understood that women go off on their own before marriage, and that even in marriage they retain the capacity to manage on their own. Young women who do not describe themselves as bent on careers nevertheless are likely to want to develop marketable skills so that if they have to support themselves, they can.

Another response to the recognition that marriage today is of uncertain duration is the drafting of premarital contracts that specify not only the rights and obligations of each partner, but also how property will be divided in the event of divorce and what then will be the husband's and the wife's rights and obligations in relation to the children. Such premarital contracts are as yet unusual, and so long as each new marriage is made in the spirit of "this time for keeps," they may continue to be so. Yet they are occasionally discussed in the popular press and may yet become a recognized, if infrequently adopted, practice.

Young people recognize that marriages today are of uncertain duration. That their marriages may end in divorce is a threat they must live with, in some ways like the possibility of cancer: something that happens to lots of people, but that one hopes will not happen to oneself. No one finds attractive the idea that a marriage may be less than lifelong.

We cannot, as a society, return to our former understanding of marriage. But we may be able to reduce the damage produced by our present system. What may be the most pressing need is protection of the well-being of the children. Recent research has convincingly demonstrated that children are intensely upset by parental separation.[14] Most children seem able in time to resume their developmental progress, but only after a difficult period.

We are beginning to be able to identify which children are at special risk when parents separate. Particularly likely to be upset by parental separation are children unprepared for the separation (some because they thought their parents happily married), children who were already doing badly with friends or at school, children whose parents after the separation are totally preoccupied with their own concerns, or, because of their own upset, keep the children's lives in a state of turmoil, and children who, because of the parents' separation, lose contact with a parent to whom they had been very much attached.

Parents can, to an extent, reduce their children's risk of continuing distress. They can provide their children with adequate preparation for a forthcoming separation, seek counseling themselves to help minimize their quarrels within the home, resolve not to display their anger with each other, and apportion some part of their time and energies to helping their children deal with the separation. An educational program for separating parents might be a useful service for their children.

We might consider modification of our present custody and visitation arrangements to make them more responsive to the emotional needs of children. The usual arrangement of custody to the mother and reasonable visitation to the father fails to work for many mothers and fathers and for most children. For the mother it implies the assumption of sole responsibility for the children, with the father relegated to the role of intermittent disrupter of her routine. It makes her the parent in charge of daily chores, the parent ultimately answerable for the children's care, while the father becomes the parent in charge of outings and happenings. For the father, however, the arrangement means that at weekly or biweekly intervals he must struggle to re-establish communication with his children and, shortly after achieving this, must relinquish it until the next time. It gives rise to repetitive loss and pain. And so the system sponsors resentment in the mother and frustration and anger in the father. Tension between parents exacerbates the children's conflicts of loyalty. In addition, the arrangement forces the children to see their father as distant, inaccessible except for his visits. He becomes a figure of diminished authority, perhaps a romantic figure, perhaps a sad one, but no longer much of a parent.

Certainly we can devise a better system than this for structuring the postmarital relationship of parents and children. One possibility is that responsibility for the children's care and control should remain in the hands of both parents, as would have been the case had the parents not separated. Both parents would continue to share responsibility for decisions regarding the children's schooling and summer camp and orthodontia and church attendance. In addition, the parents together would decide how the children's time would be divided and whose home would provide their bedrooms. It could be objected that divorced parents never agree, but all divorced parents somehow managed to arrive at decisions while their marriages were deteriorating; it should not be more difficult to arrive at decisions in the ordinarily more stable postmarital situation. The provision of mediation, perhaps through a social agency, might be necessary to back up this sort of shared custody. And should either parent act in a way that was destructive to the children, the other parent could then seek sole custody on grounds of neglect or abuse. Such a system, in which both parents are presumed to retain normal parental responsibilities for their children, should help to relieve mothers of a sense of unshared responsibility, encourage fathers to continue to invest time and energy in their children, and reassure the children that both their parents continue to function as parents.

Both parents should be aware of the importance of remaining accessible to the children. In the usual case, where both parents have been emotionally essential to their children, and especially if the children are small, parents should live as near to each other as they can and should keep both their homes open to their children at all times. When parents have participated equally in the children's upbringing, and have encouraged the children to accept both as providers of nurturance and security, then each is under severe obligation to remain accessible to the children after separation. A marriage in which parenting has been shared implies a separation and divorce in which children continue to have full access to both parents.

In an influential book, Goldstein, Freud, and Solnit responded to some of the problems of "custody to the mother and reasonable visitation to the father" by recommending that custody should not be limited by the requirement that the noncustodial parent be permitted to visit the children.[15] Rather, they said, the custodial parent should be able to decide whether there would be visitation. Their aim in this recommendation was to strengthen the position of the custodial parent. In opposition to the proposal, it may be argued that it is neither wise nor just to deny the right of noncustodial parents to keep in touch with their children. But apart from what might be the rights of noncustodial parents, the recommendation is mistaken in view of the children's stake in continuing relationships with both parents. Insofar as it would encourage the custodial parent to limit the children's access to the noncustodial parent, and discourage continued investment in the children by the noncustodial parent, the recommendation goes exactly counter to the children's interests.

The recognition that both parents remain important to their children implies that marital separation does not free the parents to begin a new life as though their marriage had never occurred. Marital separation may release husbands and wives from obligations to each other, but not from obligations to their children. It is as yet an unmet task for our society to work out how separated parents can best discharge these obligations.

NOTES

1. See *The Monthly Vital Statistics Report*, vol. 26, no. 11, "Births, marriages, divorces, and deaths for November, 1977," National Center for Health Statistics, 1978.

2. See Hugh Carter and Paul Glick, *Marriage and Divorce*, 2d. ed. (Cambridge: Harvard University Press, 1976). Carter and Glick assumed a continuation of 1975 rates. Current rates are about 5 percent higher. Even taking current rates into account, the Carter and Glick estimate appears conservative.

3. See Robert S. Weiss, *Marital Separation* (New York: Basic Books, 1975), chap. 2.

4. Kenneth Keniston and the Carnegie Council on Children, *All Our Children: The American Family Under Pressure* (New York: Harcourt Brace Jovanovich, 1977), pp. 20–21.

5. "Trend data available from the Center for Political Studies have shown a dramatic deterioration of public trust in the rectitude, competence, and responsiveness of the national government which was underway as early as 1964 and has continued downward through the recent writing (1973)." Angus Campbell, Philip E. Converse, and Willard L. Rodgers, *The Quality of American Life: Perceptions, Evaluations, and Satisfactions* (New York: Russell Sage Foundation, 1976), p. 30. Other surveys have reported decreasing confidence in organized medicine, the police, business, and, with few exceptions, all other organized bodies.

6. See Alexander Plateris, *Children of Divorced Couples*, Public Health Service Publication, series 21, no. 18 (Washington, D.C.: National Center for Health Statistics, 1970), p. 2.

7. See Judson T. Landis, "A comparison of children from divorced and non-divorced unhappy marriages," *Family Life Coordinator* 2 (1962): 61–65.

8. Nicholas Zill, "Divorce, marital happiness and the mental health of children: findings from the Foundation for Child Development National Survey of Children," a working paper prepared for the National Institute of Mental Health Workshop on Divorce and Children, Bethesda, Maryland, 7–8 February 1978 (New York: Foundation for Child Development, 1978).

9. Angus Campbell et al., *The Quality of American Life*, p. 85.

10. See Myrna M. Weissman and Eugene S. Paykel, *The Depressed Woman: A Study in Social Relationships* (Chicago: University of Chicago Press, 1974), chap. 7, pp. 87–102.

11. See Andrew Cherlin, "Economics, social roles, and marital separation" (Paper presented at the Meetings of the American Sociological Association, 1976).

12. Bertrand Russell, Fanny Hurst, H. G. Wells, Theodore Dreiser, Warwick Deeping, Rebecca West, Andre Maurois, and Lion Fuchtwanger *Divorce as I See It* (London: Noel Douglas, 1930).

13. For further material on this point, see my *Marital Separation*.

14. See Judith Wallerstein and Joan B. Kelly, "Children and Divorce," in *Basic Handbook of Child Psychiatry* (New York: Basic Books, 1976).

15. Joseph Goldstein, Anna Freud, and Albert Solnit, *Beyond the Best Interests of the Child* (New York: Free Press, 1973).

11

AMERICAN PASTORALISM, SUBURBIA AND THE COMMUNE MOVEMENT: AN EXERCISE IN THE MICROSOCIOLOGY OF KNOWLEDGE

BENNETT M. BERGER

Although my work on suburbia was the occasion of my first personal contact with David Riesman—who was then also writing on suburbs—I am no longer a student of suburbs.[1] When I was invited to contribute to this volume, I was working on a book about communes, and as it turns out, the rural commune movement contains some of the same themes that characterized the migration to suburbia a generation earlier.[2]

Instead of seeing the commune movement as a "revolt" by the children of the affluent against the "suburban values" of their parents (which, of course, to some extent it is, as just about every sympathetically partisan commentator on the movement has pointed out), I want to suggest that it can be understood in part as an extension of some of those values—as an attempt to set them in contexts more promising for their realization.

I had no sooner thought this, and said it, than it occurred to me that one of the typical forms that interpretive controversy takes is for one party to argue that a pattern of recent events constitutes a "revolt against" or a "reaction to" the established past, whereas an opposing party argues that these events are but the most recent expression of a long tradition continuously extending itself into the future. Although each of these arguments can be made in a spirit of ideological approval or disapproval (indeed, they lend themselves nicely to four-fold-table analysis), the latter argument often functions as a legitimation of the events at issue—and I made this kind of argument myself

235

some years ago in an article connecting some features of "hippie" culture to the 200-year-old bohemian tradition.[3]

Another recent example of this type of controversy (and most relevant to the topic at hand) was over the meaning of the political activism of New Left students in the 1960s. Lewis Feuer and other opponents of the movement derogated the motives of radical students by arguing that they were acting out unresolved Oedipal problems through hostility in the public forum rather than in the privacy of the family room.[4] However, survey data showed that student militants came disproportionately from families that tended to be well educated and liberal to left-liberal in political sentiment. These data were used by scholars like Richard Flacks and Kenneth Keniston (and others sympathetic to the movement) to defend the authenticity of its political dimensions by asserting that radical students were not rebelling against, but extending and realizing, the political persuasions of their parents.[5]

Neither view tells the whole story.[6] I tell part of it in order to suggest that for the rural communards I studied, the pastoral tradition in American history is the cultural analogue of the political liberalism connecting the parents of New Left activists to their children. Pastoral myth—the vision of a simple rural life in harmony with nature— connects the rural communards of today with the suburbanites of the 1950s and with the more distant American past.

In The Machine in the Garden, Leo Marx says that "American writers seldom, if ever, have designed satisfactory resolutions of their pastoral fables." The power of the fable rests, he says, in the gradual domination of nature by technology (symbolized by the roar of the locomotive violating the quiet of the Thoreauvian glade), revealing that "our inherited symbols of order and beauty have been divested of meaning," so that in the end, as he puts it, "the American hero is either dead or alienated from society."[7] If the heroes of American literature end up dead or alienated from society, it bodes ill for the rest of us, less heroic, who must live in that world divested of meaning in which, as Fitzgerald's narrator in The Great Gatsby (himself a great pastoral nostalgist) says, ". . . we beat on, boats against the current, borne back ceaselessly into the past." If American heroes just don't make it, if the best and the brightest wind up betrayed and betraying, and if Mick Jagger himself can't get no satisfaction, what will the rest of us do?

I remember the late Laurence Harvey in The Manchurian Candidate chanting over and over to himself, "I am not lovable," wistfully repeating it as if the only comfort to be drawn from the fact was his ability to reflect upon it, to recognize it, and perhaps to make himself a little more lovable by virtue of his acceptance of what he was—unlovable—and maybe neutralizing his potential critics by confessing a vice before others had a chance to discover it and point it out.

Can a whole society be unlovable? There is a sense in which the collective analogue of a person's self-image is the myth or myths that a culture invents about itself. When a myth is living or vital, it enriches the daily lives of individuals by justifying their actions, dignifying their motives, rendering their lives (and their deaths) "meaningful." In my more generous moods, for example, I like to think that the people who decorate their vehicles with "America, love it or leave it," or "I'm proud to be an American," are, in fact, in possession of such a myth. But I don't believe it (which is not to say that I don't believe that they believe they believe it), for it is no longer exactly a secret that the old myths (in whatever incarnation: Leo Marx's "pastoral," Henry Nash Smith's idea of America as "the garden," Fitzgerald's image of "the fresh green breast of America," rural values, "the Protestant ethic," or Frederick Jackson Turner's idea of free land beyond the frontier as the source of virtue and prosperity) no longer dignify the motives, justify the actions, or otherwise inform the daily lives of over two hundred million "postindustrial" people, most of them crowded into dense metropolitan areas in a culture that has little good to say about Megalopolis, struggling to get ahead in a culture that disdains status-seekers, working in enormous bureaucracies while taught contempt for Organization Men, pencil-pushers, and paper-shufflers, or shoulder to shoulder in a thousand football stadiums on autumnal weekends, apparently preferring vicarious experience to what they have been taught to believe is the real thing.

Well, what of it? Myths don't lay down and die just because the facts are at odds with them or because social and economic changes weaken their viability or because they are no longer "relevant" (they may be a little like college curricula in that respect); and if American culture has somehow failed to create an industrial or technological equivalent of the myth of rural virtue and self-sufficiency, and if the available stock of institutionalized fantasy does not enrich one's daily life, isn't an irrelevant fantasy life better than none at all? Isn't a "false consciousness" better than an empty or barren or cynical one?

In the age of television, the answer seems to be yes for a considerable majority of the American population.

Still, some people more than others can afford to attempt a life enriched by pastoralism. In an essay written around the time of my own dissertation, David Riesman pointed to some of the pastoral elements from America's first suburban migration (at the turn of the century) still visible when he was writing late in the 1950s. The desire for that little place in the country with its own piece of green was for him a re-evocation of the image of Jeffersonian independence and British gentry patterns. Riesman also saw in the suburban migration of the 1950s the desire of the new suburbanites to protect their children against the possibility of downward social mobility, symbolized by the increasingly dark ethnicities of the urban cores, in the same way that the earlier generation of wealthy suburbanites fled the central cities, corrupted in their view by the crowds of immigrant Irish, Italians, Jews, and Poles pouring into them. In the suburbanites of the fifties, Riesman saw, in addition, a desire to recreate the sense of community through primary-group ties and face-to-face relatedness in a domestic establishment spacious enough to permit the family to grow together, and in a suburb demographically homogeneous enough to permit the possibility of friendship developing into a kind of quasi kinship. The re-creation of community had a more practical meaning as well because most new suburbs had been mass produced, usually without much attention to the need for local services and institutions like schools, churches, community centers, hospitals, newspapers, public transportation, recreation, and the like, leaving to the new residents the work of creating these features of community from scratch. Finally, the antiurban and antitechnological animus of much of this migration encouraged Riesman to say that "Sometimes it seems to me that what people are seeking in the suburbs is a kind of pre-industrial incompetence and inefficiency."[8]

On an economic level higher than that of the average middle-class suburbs Riesman was talking about, the pastoral ideal is still more visible in the desire for a country house on land sufficient to sustain gardens, a stable and a few horses, and maybe some live-in retainers. It is now visible in a new wave with the boom in vacation and retirement homes at the beach, in the country, on a mountain—as the cities get more polluted and less safe. Advertising for such developments almost always emphasizes pastoral themes. A recent promotion for "La Costa" (an expensive San Diego suburb and retirement-vacation community) refers to polluted and problem-ridden cities and the "respite and refuge" provided by their community, "where life is healthier and less pressurized."

These survivals of the pastoral ideal are, of course, "corrupted"; they are mixed, that is, with dependence on industrial civilization— Leo Marx calls it "complex pastoralism." La Costa is perhaps an especially good and ironic symbol because it is rumored to have been built with Mafia money channeled through the Teamsters' union. Suburbia, of course, depends upon the automobile and the freeway; its very success sowed the seeds of its downfall as a pastoral ideal. Riesman's house in the country became millions of little houses in what is no longer the country. The quiet piece of green was invaded by a thousand power mowers, that other machine in the garden. The image of Jeffersonian independence became bondage to the long commute and the crushing enervation of fingers-drumming-on-the-wheel, bumper-to-bumper, rush hour traffic. The fresh air got smoggy, and the image of re-creating community yielded to "suburban" images of harried husbands, bored and harried wives, and teenage children who would almost always prefer to be somewhere other than at home, where the action wasn't. The reportedly high rates of transience in middle-class suburbs did not help the image of stable community, either. The suburban idyll of the little community restored, in short, became increasingly urban and increasingly privatized.

This "complex pastoralism," this corrupted ideal, eventually defeated by its dependence on the economic forces of industrial civilization outside it, evokes Frederick Jackson Turner's own ambivalence between "nature" and "civilization." Although Turner affirmed the myth of the garden with his frontier hypothesis, he also persisted in his belief that "civilization" was a higher stage of development. Turner's ambivalence on this point should be no surprise, because the power of pastoral myth has always been limited by political and economic constraints, as Leo Marx's book shows and as the experience of suburbia illustrates. But the myth has eluded simple political formulation or characterization because of the complex, even contradictory, ideological sources from which it has drawn. Modern pastoralism, for example, cannot be easily pigeonholed as "reactionary" or "progressive" or in terms of other simple political categories, because it has drawn not only (as Riesman suggested) from the anti-industrialism of the nineteenth-century British aristocracy (one of whose major contemporary survivals is the Sierra Club mentality), but also partly from the socialist critique of the wretched squalor created in the early stages of English industrialism, which, despite Karl Marx's remark about the idiocy of rural life, might well have made the community life of peasants seem in retrospect idyllic; partly, too, from German conservatism, even Fascism, with its emphases on ties of blood, soil, and Volk; and partly from the bohemian tradition, mostly French, which, although urban, strongly emphasized Rousseau's primitivism, wilderness, exoticism—and even mind-expanding drugs. A mixed ideological bag indeed.

The 1970s, when the ubiquity of words like "ecology" and "environment" and "pollution" suggests an intensification of the ill repute of uncontrolled technological development, seem a likely time for a renaissance of pastoralism, and this has been an increasingly evident theme in many of the "alternative life styles" much discussed in recent years. This brings me, finally, to rural hippie communes, and the extent to which they have used this mixed bag of available ideology from the pastoral tradition to confer honor on their style of life.

There are obvious continuities with the still-honored rural past of America. Rural communards look like down-home country folks, and they would not dress and adorn themselves differently if they could. There is a country tavern in northern California that, on Saturday nights during the period of my research, was usually jammed with family (commune) groups, children included, from Chicago and Brooklyn and Los Angeles and the Haight, in gingham and denim (not the twenty-dollar kind from chic stores, but the fifty-cent kind from garage sales), with an adult modal educational level of sixteen or seventeen years, mixed with local loggers and farm hands, drinking, dancing, singing, to country and western music played on instruments they brought and played (and in some cases made) themselves—in a scene that might have been out of rural Tennessee or West Virginia. During a screening of the movie McCabe and Mrs. Miller, ostensibly about life in a frontier community in the state of Washington around the turn of the century, I remember saying to myself, "This is a hippie movie!" not fully understanding what I meant, until I met someone involved in the production of the film who told me that they had used local communards in their everyday costume for some of the minor roles.

There are ideological continuities as well. Frederick Jackson Turner saw the availability of free land beyond the frontier as a safety valve, sparing the centers of civilization some of the potential ravages of urban poverty and discontent. Although prosperous suburban parents have been unable to prevent the downward mobility of some of their children, rural communal life provides an alternative to conventional downward social mobility for the children of the middle classes who have been unable or unwilling to meet the certification requirements imposed by institutions of higher education for high-prestige occupations. (Or, having met these requirements, they may have rejected the putative benefits as ultimately unrewarding.) These people may be poor and without salable skills, and their rejection of higher education (or their rejection by it) may have cut them off irrevocably from the prospect of middle-class affluence. But their involvement in groups committed to experimental living and other visionary ideals (often with a religious character) cushions the impact of those facts.

Moreover, Turner's safety-valve hypothesis is given added credence by the fact that despite widespread hostility to hippies and "counter-culture" phenomena, the rural communes studied by my research group have not been hassled by public officials nearly as much as one might expect, given this hostility and their vulnerability to harassment over issues such as drugs, sex, building and health codes, child welfare, and, formerly, draft evasion. Legal harassment of this population, according to safety-valve thinking, might well turn out to be more trouble than it is worth.

There may be an irony in the phrase "alternative life styles" to the extent that they are opted for by people without real alternatives, but the availability of pastoral myth as ideological currency constitutes a negotiable resource with which to clothe Necessity in the fine garments of moral choice. Nevertheless, philosophers of the New Left (for example, Herbert Marcuse) regard such communes with dismay because they drain off a lot of the energy that might have been devoted to urban radical movements (Rosabeth Kanter calls them "retreatist" communes).[9] The downward mobility is also ambiguous because it presents to social analysts the prospect of something unprecedented in this country, whose consequences are difficult to imagine: a small but strategic stratum of rural, poor people who have nevertheless been exposed to higher education and the sophistication of urban culture and middle-class heritage.

Finally, I want to turn to some of the specific ways in which rural hippie communards have selectively used ideological elements from the pastoral tradition, which were present in the myth of suburbia, to enrich the daily realities of communal living in a way that proved to be not viable for suburban living. Although I am less interested in the history of ideas than in the sociology of ideas, even here there are continuities: Greek philosophers defended slavery as a necessary condition without which the high achievements of Greek culture would have been impossible; eighteenth-century spokesmen for capitalism invoked Social Darwinism (before Darwin) in order to rationalize indifference to poverty in a competitive economy; Hell's Angels disdain bourgeois reliance on the police to do their dirty work, and in its place offer an eye-for-an-eye sense of the dignity of *personal* justice under conditions where they cannot rely on law enforcement authorities to do their "police" work; white convicts in San Quentin invoke an "Aryan" ideology to justify racial aggrandizement in the prison. From ancient Greece to contemporary San Quentin, the business of myth has always been *legitimation*, the attempt to create moral capital out of available ideological resources (meager or abundant) to justify action, dignify motive, and transform interest and power into right and authority.

I want to illustrate this relationship by reference to three important ideas of rural communards. The first of these is the idea of survival: their emphasis upon and their pride in the development of simple survival skills: putting in a healthy vegetable garden, the construction of a dwelling with a roof that doesn't leak, disposing of their shit in useful or otherwise benign ways, skill at scavenging the county dump, keeping their ancient vehicles in running order, keeping the moss off the apple trees, making cheese and yogurt and sturdy fences, becoming good farmers, woodsmen, resourceful rural folk. *Like the suburbanite twenty-five years ago*, freshly installed in a new tract house, the communards are very much into doing-it-themselves, proud of every step in their progress toward self-sufficiency.[10]

But unlike the suburbanites, who depended upon the central city, the pride communards take in surviving by doing it themselves is usually invoked in connection with a belief in the imminent collapse of industrial civilization. Now, urban industrial civilization may or may not sink into oblivion under the weight of its garbage, its pollution, its racial conflicts, its imperialist wars, and its individual loneliness; I do not know. But it is clearly more viable and self-serving to believe in the prospect of urban apocalypse if one is in possession (and committed to the future possession) of the necessities for surviving it; more viable, that is, than if one is incompetent to fix the plumbing or change a light bulb.

Indeed, it is reasonable to suggest that the hip communards' possession of these survival skills gives them *vested interests* in believing in the imminent doom of industrial civilization; after it happens, they will be more highly valued than they are now. But the major point to emphasize is the empirical relationship between ideas and social conditions: the communards' belief in the prospect of apocalypse dignifies their daily life; the myth of apocalypse lends dignity to the humble work of survival and self-sufficiency "on the land" (reverently uttered), as it could not for the suburbanite forever bound to his career in the city, and transforms that work from something absurd and reactionary (is *that* what the revolution was about—reversion to nineteenth-century conditions?) into something "meaningful" for the children of industrial affluence.

Take next the communards' ideological emphasis on intimacy, on living in groups that they define as "family," on the widespread use of kinship terms to refer to each other, on the elevation of "outfrontness" into a major human virtue. Aggressive assertion of honesty, candor, and bluntness as major virtues in human relations (as opposed to tact, discretion, or circumlocution) are likely to thrive where social circumstances make it difficult to hide or disguise or euphemize things. Intimacy was also affirmed in the suburban myth of middle-class family life ("togetherness"), but its larger context was a society in which mobility was stressed, bureaucratic impersonality was ascendant (and aparently necessary), and intimacy as a value was therefore subject to a great deal of strain because of its variable relevance from context to context. In rural communes, family *is* community; the closeness of living quarters makes it objectively difficult to dissemble; people's lives are more or less fully exposed to their "brothers" and "sisters"; and any attempt to disguise feeling is likely to be vain and therefore disapproved. Under these conditions, encounter-style "openness 'n honesty" is a self- and group-serving idea; in circumstances where emotional compatibility is a major aspect of what holds a group together, it constrains members to pay attention to their subtlest feelings; it enhances and deepens their mutual dependence, instead of evoking guilt and anxicty (as it may in contexts where there are strong bureaucratic counterpressures), or betrayal and manipulation (as it may in casually organized "groups" without much real solidarity).

Moreover, unlike William Whyte's transient suburbanites of the 50s, the areas of communal concentration we studied show good evidence of growing community cooperation and solidarity. Serious (stable) communards seem increasingly reserved toward transient hippies looking for a place to crash. And even old locals, initially hostile to the counterculture invasion, have more than begun to accommodate to the prospect of the continued presence of their landholding, taxpaying neighbors by distinguishing between "our hippies" (that is, good, hard-working ones) and the dirty filthies out hitchhiking on the highway.

Finally, I want to take up the equalitarian ethos in rural hip communes, as it bears upon the conceptualization and treatment of children, who tend to be regarded not primarily as a distinct subspecies of human being called "children," but as "small persons"—*members* of the intentional family, just like anyone else, perhaps less skilled, not necessarily less wise, recognized, in any case, as Bruce Hackett put it, primarily by lowering one's line of vision rather than one's level of discourse.[11] In these communes, children tend not to be protected or shielded from any dimension of group life in which the *interest* of children suggests some minimum competence of theirs to participate. This is true, for example, with respect to their "rights" to sexual behavior, drug use, autonomy in the settlement of their disputes (adults do not typically interfere), useful work, and a political voice in family/commune affairs.

There is a sense, then, in which the "permissive" character of liberal suburban child rearing has been extended just about as far as it can go toward "children's liberation" by the children of these suburbanites who are parents now themselves—another continuity. But unlike the by-the-book permissiveness of liberal suburban child rearing, which designated mothers as full-time socializers and which was unable to control the negative consequences of permissive child rearing when they became evident in the schools and other public places that valued "discipline" more, permissiveness in rural communes lets adults off the hook of heavy parenting, and frees them for the other necessary work of survival. Moreover, the relative isolation of many rural communes insulates them from negative feedback from the community, and the conditions of rural life in any case encourage bringing the communal young away from childish innocence toward the experience of equality as early as possible.

Communal parents tend to believe that a close connection exists between a child's expressed interest in, and his or her probable competence to use, the rights they have given their children—far more so, at least, than among middle-class parents I have observed, who may say that competence is a legitimate criterion for admission to adult activities, but who are also likely to minimize the probable competence they are willing to impute to "small persons"—not because they are "middle class," but because parents who are committed to roles as socializers of children develop vested interests in believing that those to whose care they are devoted "need" that care.

But just as the modern middle-class conceptions of what children are (not merely small adults) and what they need (a great deal of socializing input) reveal as much about the commitments of middle-class adults as they do about the nature and character and needs of children, much the same things are true of the hippie conception of children. Communards or not, hippies have rejected most of the prevailing models of middle-class adulthood or "maturity" as repressive and unrewarding, a bad bargain with life in which one gives up more than one gets in return. They also reject an image of children as utterly dependent for their proper growth on close parental supervision for a long time, and an image of parenting as a system of obligations that renders the adult "responsible" for how a child turns out —in spite of the fact that most parents most of the time are ignorant of the relationship bewteen what they do to their children and the developmental consequences of the doing. (Despite an abundance of theories, we are all pretty much in the dark here.) But the hippie conception of children as essentially healthy plants, needing only a little sun and water and space to grow up straight and tall, surely reinforces their Rousseauian naturalism, and rationalizes the preoccupations of commune men and women with things other than child rearing.

This analysis of the relationships between some of the beliefs of hip communards and the social situations in which they live constitutes in my mind a kind of microsociology of knowledge. In the past, sociology of knowledge, if it was at all empirical—as it usually was not— was concerned with the relationships of large or major ideas (political, aesthetic, or religious doctrines) to large or macrosocial structures (feudalism, capitalism, socialism). Regardless of the magnitude of the variables, however, there are common problems arising from doing sociology of knowledge that researchers too rarely confront directly. Should one, for example, be cynical about the self- and group-serving functions revealed by the sociological analysis of ideas?

If the idea of urban apocalypse serves the interests of survival-equipped communards, isn't that sufficient reason for being skeptical of it? If the idea of equal rights for children serves the purposes of those who have neither the time nor the inclination for middle-class parenting, isn't that reason for suspecting their motives? If the affirmation of authenticity in interpersonal relations serves the interests of people so situated that their dense interactional textures make them ill able to afford emotional disguises, isn't that reason to regard "openness 'n honesty" as simply another self-serving element of ideology (like belief in free speech by intellectuals or low taxes by the propertied)?

The answer provided by the major tradition of the sociology of knowledge would seem to be a resounding yes. More often than not, the sociological treatment of ideas has the consequence of "unmasking" or "demystifying" them. By such demystification, that is, by revealing the "real" interests or functions that ideas serve, sociologists of knowledge often weaken (and sometimes aim to weaken) the convictions of those who adhere to these ideas (and to strengthen the antipathy of those who oppose them).

There is a powerful irony here, because lurking behind this "unmasking" impulse is a sort of Protestant ethic, usually unrecognized: the notion that the harder it is to sustain one's moral beliefs, the more profound one's moral achievement—as if in order to be warranted, a claim to moral status had to be founded on the suffering or inconvenience it caused to the claimant. Bernard Shaw put it well: "The English think they are being moral when they are only being uncomfortable." The irony is that in regarding ideas as epiphenomenal or as instrumental to material interests, sociologists of knowledge (of all people) might be expected to respect ideas that enable people to get on with their lives more successfully, rather than to regard these ideas as mere or otherwise unworthy because they are self-serving. What, after all (asks the historical relativist), are moral ideas for? To suffer in the name of? Or are they tools, instruments, like shovels, rakes, and chain saws to help people get through their days, and in helping them through, to provide some comfort, pride, even ennoblement for having got through safely?

If the ruling ideas of an age are the ideas of the ruling class, then the revolutionary ideas or the "alternative" ideas of an age might be expected to come from revolutionary or otherwise dissatisfied classes. Most Marxist sociologists of knowledge do, of course, respect the ideas that serve the revolutionary interests of the working class (as distinguished from the ideas that the working class, at least in the United States, actually believe they believe). But then they usually do not apply the method and spirit of the sociology of knowledge to these ideas—perhaps precisely because this tradition of analysis has created a spirit of contempt for ideas that may be so understood.

That a sort of Protestant ethic lurks triumphant here is indicated by the fact that when the self- and group-serving functions of apparently elevated and disinterested moral ideas are pointed out, the pointing is likely to be done cynically, as if the revelation of their functionality somehow dishonored them. Do professional intellectuals regard the First Amendment as the cornerstone of our democracy? Well, of course, they have vested interests in free speech and social criticism, which more ordinary citizens rarely, if ever, have occasion to use. Do university professors believe that higher education enriches the human spirit? How convenient for them! But in an era of tightened university budgets, if too many potential students agree with them, work loads may be increased, speedups may occur, and an idea is now gaining currency among educators and other taxpayers that college may be a waste of time for many young people, and that there are other, alternative, and more efficient ways of becoming qualified to lead a productive and satisfying life.

"As if the revelation of their functionality somehow dishonored them." But surely sociologists of knowledge do not believe that moral claims must generally be rooted in self-denial. Moral values, we have learned, are "relative"; circumstances generate them, changed circumstances may change them, and this can be a painful process. I emphasize "process" because I described the relations between the ideas of communards and their social circumstances as if they were structurally fixed, when, of course, they are not. If, for example, the rhetoric of universal hip brotherhood among communards opens communes to everyone, and some of these individuals turn out to be rip-off artists or energy drains on the resources of the group, it may lead (and has, in fact, led) to a policy of more selective recruitment (or even a "closed" policy), and then to a modification of the group's belief in brotherhood—or, more precisely, a *redefinition* of brotherhood that excludes undesirables. But should this change be understood cynically, as a "selling out" of one's original faith, or as the adaptive modification of an ideal whose pursuit had, under existing circumstances, destructive consequences for the group? Similarly, if a commune's ideological commitment to "consensual decision making" leads to political paralysis (no decisions) or a drift toward authoritarianism (usurpation of power by *ad hoc* leaders), a "reversion" toward majority rule and parliamentary procedure may occur. Or a solution may be found in another direction by invoking "encounter" or other critical and self-critical techniques to overcome the resistance of dissidents. In either case, appropriate moral justifications are at hand.

In the past (and in some of my work), I myself adopted a skeptical and sometimes cynical attitude toward ideas whose self- and group-serving functions I could see through. But then I began to understand, partly through my commune research experience, that that cynical attitude was itself an expression of a severe and disappointing ethic, Judeo-Christian asceticism: that the test of your beliefs was whether you suffered for them, that if you felt guilty and tight, you must be doing something right—a view that sees virtue as resistance to temptation (in this case resistance to the practical comfort ideas can provide) instead of (its original sense) as *competence* or excellence at accommodating ideals to circumstances.

In *Darkness at Noon*, Arthur Koestler's Rubashov was finally persuaded by his Inquisitor that it was correct for him to confess to crimes against the state that he had not actually committed: "correct" because it would further the interests of the revolution, and that was more important than mere fidelity to fact. Thirty-eight years ago, Koestler intended that as a monstrous idea; today, somehow, it seems less monstrous, if still not exactly noble. That change, I think, is partly a result of the diffusion of sociological perspectives on ideas. Like the law, which is said not to respect persons, a sociology of ideas should have some difficulty respecting beliefs, for out of the almost limitless number of ideas that people somewhere, sometime have believed are self-evidently true, beautiful, good, reasonable, or useful, surely it must seem astonishing that any given group or individual should have hit upon the specific set of convictions that they have. But because I am a sociologist, my own conviction is that I do not *understand* any of these ideas unless I can find their relevance to the circumstances (historical and contemporary) in which they are espoused, and to the material interests of the social groups that carry them through time and preside over such lives and careers as ideas may be said to have. It is in this spirit that I have tried to understand the pastoral sources of some of the ideas of communards and the relationship of these ideas to the daily lives communards face.

However deep or shallow that understanding is, I try not to delude myself that it has much relevance to my *feelings* about ideas, which, like anyone else's, are conditioned by factors of which I am, at best, only partly aware. Powerful ideas—for example, myths—are usually potent enough to survive analysis, to survive even a preponderance of evidence against them. In the preface to the 1968 edition of *Working-Class Suburb,* I said that "despite everything reasonable I have said about suburbs, I *know* that the fact that I unreasonably dislike them has been conditioned beyond the possibility of redemption by mere research." In 1978, despite everything analytic I have said about communes, I know that the fact that I unanalytically like at least some of them is an expression of the utterly wholesome and captivating (to me) myth of what they are about: friends as family always gathered round; working, playing, singing, dancing, rapping, hanging out together.[12] One is reminded of Huckleberry Finn and the raft, lighting out for the Territory ahead (even if it seems behind). That image is respectable, and I respect it; far more so, anyway, than the available alternatives offered by the CBS evening news.

NOTES

The research on which this paper is based was supported by Grant #MH 16579–01 from the National Institute of Mental Health.

1. There is a sense in which I never was a student of the suburbs. The research that eventuated in *Working Class Suburb* (Berkeley: University of California Press, 1960) began as a study not of suburbia, but of automobile workers. That a lot of these workers happened to be living in new suburbs was what Robert Merton once called "serendipitous," and that a lot of unanchored ideas about suburbia were adrift in the culture and ripe for critical analysis from primary data was one of those lucky-for-me junctures of history and biography.

2. For another version of this idea see Keith Melville, *Communes in the Counter Culture* (New York: William Morrow, 1972), chap. 4.

3. Bennett M. Berger, "Hippie Morality/1967," in *Looking for America* (Englewood Cliffs, N.J.: Prentice-Hall, 1971).

4. See Lewis Feuer, *The Conflict of Generations* (New York: Basic Books, 1969).

5. See Kenneth Keniston, *Young Radicals* (New York: Harcourt, Brace and World, 1968), and Richard Flacks, "The Liberated Generation: An Exploration of the Roots of Student Protest," *Journal of Social Issues* 23 (1967): 52–75.

6. For more of it see Bennett M. Berger, "Alternative Life Styles and the Quality of Life," in Ronald O. Clarke and Peter C. List, eds., *Environmental Spectrum* (New York: Van Nostrand, 1974).

7. Leo Marx, *The Machine in the Garden* (New York: Oxford University Press, 1964).

8. David Riesman, "The Suburban Dislocation," *Annals of the American Academy of Political and Social Science* 314 (November 1957): 123–46.

9. Herbert Marcuse, *Counter-Revolution and Revolt* (Boston: Beacon Press, 1973); Rosabeth Kanter, *Commitment and Community* (Cambridge: Harvard University Press, 1972).

10. The self-sufficiency does not come easily. Indeed, most communes still depend for cash income on some form of welfare, although this is less true now than, say, in 1970. In any case, self-sufficiency remains a goal toward which they work.

11. For a fuller treatment of this theme, see Bennett M. Berger and Bruce M. Hackett, "The Decline of Age-Grading in Rural Hippie Communes," *Journal of Social Issues* 30 (1974): 163–83.

12. I emphasize the *image* of what they are about. The reality, unfortunately, is often quite different. Rural communal life is not easy; there are many crises, many defeats. Poverty, the fragility of nuclear couples, tendencies toward authoritarianism or anarchy sometimes involve heavy costs. The number of communal "failures" is high—although proportionately probably no higher than other forms of small enterprise (which is, I believe, the right comparison).

12

FEAST OF STRANGERS: VARIETIES OF SOCIABLE EXPERIENCE IN AMERICA

REUEL DENNEY

More and more, our observations have led us to conclude that sociability remains inadequate without the guidance of leaders sensitive not only to a group's mood but to things and values outside the group, to the possibility of participating vicariously in experiences not directly accessible. An overegalitarian ethos has the same effect on sociability as on the schools: by denying differences of skill and motivation, it compresses all into a limited range of possibility.[1]

1

Most of us who have puzzled ourselves about the variety of American experiences have heard the following questions. Have the convivial gatherings of Americans changed in their nature over the past 350 years? If they have indeed changed markedly, has this also resulted in the evolution of forms that are by now distinct from those of our European cousins? Can we observe changes over time in the scale, institutional bases, moods, and expressive styles of American sociability? If so, what are the reasons for these changes? An egalitarian ethos? Greatly increasing wealth since the early seventeenth century? New conveniences in transportation and communication? Changes in the family and in religion? The great overlapping waves of immigration that once filled American boarding houses with that rough sociability that could well be described as a feast for strangers, by strangers, and of strangers?

These are some of the often-repeated questions that must be taken as starting points for the study of sociability in America.

The main purpose of this paper is to sketch one particular approach that might prove helpful in sorting out the evidences about sociability contained in American memoirs, records, travelers' accounts, and other such sources. The suggestions for it developed out of my participation in a 1954 seminar on play and leisure at the University of Chicago, organized by David Riesman and Nelson Foote, and in the subsequent Sociability Project, directed by Riesman, Foote, and Jeanne Watson.[2]

For the purposes of this paper the definition of "sociable" activities is that of George Simmel.[3] Within the whole range of social relations, he suggests there is a subset, the sociable, which is marked by a particular motivation on the part of its enactors. Unlike more forced and formal situations, such as those concerned with work, sociability brings us together to enjoy each other's company for its own sake. Our enjoyment of such sociable meetings is sometimes frustrated by the intrusion of other structures and pressures: social class, aspirations toward higher status, even by the tendency for people to pollute sociability by using other persons as objects in a play for power. Nevertheless, by contrast, while a banding together for sheer survival in economic activity or in war may display some sociable elements, it is clear that conviviality is not the main goal of a company of fishermen at sea or a regiment in combat. But it is the main goal of a sociable occasion.

Simmel's definition is the heir of an idealistic and formalistic approach in German sociology. But perhaps it can be allowed to stand, for the purposes of this paper, if it is complemented by the following references to some common patterns affecting our use of the word "sociability."

The word can mean a style of hospitable interaction, as in: "The sociability of the Politano family was firmly based on good homemade red wine." Or it can mean a collective pattern of companionable relationships, as in: "The sociability of our beach resort centered that summer on the tennis club." Or it can be used in still another way, which conveys a tone of approving judgment: "Their family life was marked by warm hospitality and sociability." What is more, the word manages to express a wide band of reference to social tonalities ranging from the more intimate realms of family and friendship to the more public realms of the party or the festival or club life.

After the Sociability Project, I pondered about what it was that I wanted to do with the "historical" aspects of sociability. As a collaborator on *The Lonely Crowd,* one who acquired most of his knowledge of changes in American culture and character by working with Riesman on that book, I thought it logical to try to think in terms of the rise and fall—or better, *successions*—of certain sociable forms in America. In this way it might be possible to relate themes of sociability to themes of family formation, socialization, education, and career in America. But what "succession"? Of what "forms"?

The best I could do at first was to note that I was interested in defining successive locales and institutional bases of sociability, with the idea of seeing more clearly:

- Periods of transition when an earlier-emphasized sociable center —for example, the family—was forced to yield some of its influence to a later-emphasized social center—for example, the club.
- Periods when the socialization of the young was transformed, as when adolescent peers, "working at" their school life and their sociability, shifted their allegiance in that direction, and away from parents.
- Periods when there was said to be a crisis for one sociable form or another, as in the 1840s when lodge life was the storm center of conflict over Freemasonry; or in the earlier twentieth century, when the club was the center of conflict over ethnic and religious exclusion; or in the later twentieth century, when the club was the center of conflict over black and oriental exclusion policies.
- Periods when anxiety about one of the forms stimulated debate about its nature, as when local and neighborhood sociability were thought to be threatened in one way or another. In the early part of the twentieth century, it was the urban ghetto that was often accused of corrupting true sociable bonds. After World War II, anomie was blamed on suburban sprawl and suburban self-isolation.

2

From the beginning of my researches on the historical aspects of sociability, I knew that my main problem would be to find certain sociological, anthropological, and psychological guides to classification. I felt that my best help here would probably come out of the findings of the Project itself. Robert Potter had done much to organize and clarify certain "types" of sociability out of the range of taxonomies that bubbled up in Project discussions. However, it seemed necessary to consider the possible usefulness of approaching the subject through the following sources:

- Studies of voluntary associations—especially clubs and lodges. This is the field of investigation so well summarized, up to 1963, by David Sills in his article in *The Encyclopedia of The Social Sciences*.[4]

- Studies in which stratification and mobility are explored as part of the context of sociable interactions. This is the field in which Digby Baltzell, William F. Whyte, and Cleveland Amory, for example, are very helpful.[5]

- Studies emphasizing the spatial conditions of sociability—neighborhoods, regions, "territories," ghettos, convenanted residential areas, and such like. This is the field in which the work of Herbert J. Gans, Jane Jacobs, and Vance Packard is useful.[6]

- Studies of the leisured, as in Thorstein Veblen and Thomas Wolfe, for example.[7]

- Studies emphasizing temporal aspects—especially seasonal, calendrical, holiday, and ritual elements, as in John Huizinga, and in Lloyd Warner's study of Memorial Day in *Yankee City*.[8]

- Studies emphasizing the terms of social and symbolic action, as in Simmel, Riesman, and Erving Goffman—the latter's "dramatistic" model draws on, among others, George Herbert Meade.[9]

- Studies that throw new light on racial, ethnic, and sex-role channels (and constrictions) of sociability.

It should be apparent that recognizing the importance of such approaches is easier than applying them in some fashion to records and traces of sociability preserved from the American past. What was needed was an array that would provide, perhaps for the first time, "sorting boxes" for the historical materials. It took much too long to realize that the problem had already been half-solved by Robert Potter.[10] In his work with Riesman and Watson, Potter gradually focused on five types of "acquaintanceship" that he thought especially salient in sociability: "casual," "expanding," "friendly," "institutional," and "familiar." The uses that Potter made of these "axes" of acquaintanceship and sociability are not the point here. Rather, it is the fact that around 1974 it finally occurred to me, following along Potter's lines, that I could sort out my historical materials by placing them on a scale whose parts were determined by different "institutional" settings. The result of attempting to do that is the array seen below.

There are nine persistent forms of sociability whose definitions might help us to review and classify the American experience. Each form is characterized by the social situation of two individuals who are connected by the sociable "axis" in point. It is possible that these nine forms could be applied to any society in any time or place, but that is not the intention here.

1. Familial sociability—a relation of kinsman with kinsman—which is most often a relation between persons of the same ethnic, linguistic, and religious stock. The forms of sociability that go with courtship and the forms of sociability—some of them racist—that separate the ethnic groups are still strongly influenced by the family.

2. Local sociability—a relation of neighbor with neighbor, often of a church parishioner with another parishioner.

3. Amicable sociability—a relation of friend with friend, quite often of schoolmate with schoolmate.

4. Affable sociability—a relation of host with guest.

5. Incorporational sociability—(a) congregational, based on a relation of churchmember with churchmember; (b) fraternal-sororal, a relation of clubmate with clubmate.

6. Collaboral sociability—a relation of worker with worker, unionist with unionist, colleague with colleague; sometimes of manager with employee or of athletic teammate with teammate, often of university graduate students with each other.

7. Political sociability—a relation of political partisan with copartisan.

8. Cross-cultural sociability—a relation of two persons from different cultures.

9. Casual sociability—a relation of stranger with stranger.

The array suggested here obviously lacks the integrity and flexibility of a scale. It does not construct a continuum in which a single variable is seen to be moving from one state to another, and the categories are not mutually exclusive. But the array does in its own approximate way have some of the characteristics of such ways of arranging things. With respect to the individual in his life cycle, the movement is from earlier in life to later; from the primary associations to the secondary; from the more intimate to the less intimate;

from the realm of stronger affect to the weaker; and from the less monetized forms of social interaction to the more monetized. It is clear enough that the sequence suggested does not, for any individual in any time or place, follow its arithmetical ordering in either the stages of development or their relative importance.

The array also has another, albeit looser, reading. It bears some resemblance to successive phases of American social development in general. Despite our recent and now corrected overemphasis on the family and the neighborhood in seventeenth- and eighteenth century America, there is no doubt that in those times they provided more important bases and niches, relative to other settings for sociability, than they do today. Again, while transactions of a cross-cultural nature were not absent in the days of contact between whites and Indians, British and French, British and Spanish, they were not, by and large, sociable contacts. They were matters of national, ethnic, religious, and martial rivalry. Forms of sociability capacious enough to tolerate and be enriched by ethnic and cultural differences developed slowly in the United States and they are still a patchwork of the open and the closed styles of interaction. Nevertheless, a sequence can be observed, a sequence that says more about the successes of democracy than its failures.

It is true, of course, that some of the most important changes in American sociability did *not* occur as a matter of the movement of emphasis from a locus earlier on the array to a later one. What has been called "affable" sociability is an example of this. This form of sociability has had its own natural history in the United States. The early host was one who entertained his guests within his own household and domain. It was only later, for various reasons too complex for analysis here, that the middle class increasingly entertained itself in the resort, the restaurant, the hotel, and the club. But even this movement within a given form of sociability exhibits some chronological harmony with the rest of the array—it definitely points to a relative decline of entertaining at home, and vaguely points to the modern elaboration of the more public scenes of club life and the "casual" sociability of tours, cruises, resorts, and night life.

3

Any one of these types of sociability could perhaps be illuminated by finding familiar popular, graphic, or literary images associated with it.

1. *Familial.* The images of domestic sociability to which we are treated by the mass media today are very strongly influenced not only by Anglo-Saxon, but also by German and Dutch traditions in the United States. In the graphic inheritance, the paintings of Norman Rockwell on Thanksgiving and Christmas themes are the descendants of Netherlandic family portraiture and anecdotal realism. In the emblematic tradition, the Christmas tree is a Teutonic gift. In the verbal tradition, a great, fairly well-known American hero of domestic sociability, Clement Moore, happened to be of Anglo-Irish stock, but he could not have written "The Night Before Christmas" except by drawing deeply on the Dutch folklore of Manhattan. He is honored by American journalism as the figure of "The Good Father," who can be identified with the Saint Nick he wrote about in his celebrated verses. A later and also idealized picture of domestic sociability is found in the often underestimated romantic poem "Snowbound" by John Greenleaf Whittier.

2. *Local.* The history, folklore, and literature of the United States are not rich in profiles of celebrated "good neighbors," possibly because, as H. L. Mencken might have phrased it, the "good" ones do not make the news. On the other hand, regional fiction is full of good neighbors—the ones who come to help raise the barn, for example; and one of our historical heroes can make the largest social claims in this respect. Roger Williams was the first American to declare, in settling and dominating a region, that it would observe tolerance in religion. He succeeded in making the townships of Rhode Island a haven for a variety of believers. On this ground alone he should perhaps be declared one of the great American heroes of local, neighborly sociability. Not a little of the credit due to him is associated with his grants of asylum to dissidents. He was the founder of a great sociable tradition in the United States.

The force of local bonds was troubled in the seventeenth century by the conflict between a great sociable "antihero," Thomas Morton of Merrymount, and John Bradford, magnate of the Massachusetts Bay Colony.[11] Morton's idea was to fraternize with the Indians on his own exploitative terms, as a trader of liquor and guns for furs, without regard to the safety or policies of the Colony. He was outspoken in his liking for the aborigines and in his scorn for the conventional hatred and misuse of them. He lost his battle with the Colony and took his revenge by writing *The New English Canaan*. As a "bad" neighbor to his settler compatriots, Morton was a kind of "Lord of

Misrule," and he established a sociable profile that was later emulated by a variety of frontier and gangster kingpins who ran little kingdoms of their own all the way from the Pecos or Sacramento to Surinam. His image turns up in many movies as the Early Settler who will not give up his bad old ways when the later settlers try to establish their farms along with their requirements of civility, cooperation, restraint, and community-mindedness.

The relation of "local" with "local," or neighbor with neighbor, is, of course, a main theme of many works of regional writing in America, including the urban as well as the rural regions. The theme emerges strongly in a book concerned with the uprooting of neighbors, John Steinbeck's *The Grapes of Wrath*—a work in which we see people who were originally regional neighbors to each other in Oklahoma driven to seek a new life in the Pacific West.

3. *Amicable*. Popular and literary and mass media images of friends in America are extraordinarily various and rich. Whitman's creed of comradeship is both cosmic and narcissistic. The portrait of friendship in *Huckleberry Finn* is worked out with great literacy virtuosity and spiritual insight—if not in the Huck-Tom relationship, certainly in the Huck-Jim relationship. The modern nonfiction literature of making and breaking friendships is prolific, even if it is not marked by much philosophic or moral merit. The three-sided friendship of Henry Adams, Clarence King, and John Hay probably has perennial interest.[12] We can say, at least, that their correspondence with each other, and the historical record of their concern for each other, stand as witness to the warm comradeship of three Americans who shared a concern for the qualities of life in the United States.

4. *Affable*. Particularly in boom times, the United States has produced many famous hosts and hostesses, whose styles were later emulated by others acting on a smaller stage. They left few reports on their own lives; their motives and achievements are largely known through journalistic accounts. But there is at least one American who looms alive and large in this category—mostly because he recorded his own activities. William Byrd II of Virginia, the lusty squire of Westover, is, with "King Carter," the archetype of many who came after him as a "Master of Revels." His *Diary* gives us a candid view of the pleasures and vexations of being a frontier leader of sociability and jollification.[13] Part of his role was inherited in the late nineteenth

century by commercial *maîtres-d'* or Bonifaces like Delmonico, and by rising female leaders of sociability.

The relation of host with guest plays its subtle part in the background of many works of American writing from Irving's *Knickerbocker's History of New York* to nineteenth- and twentieth-century novels on the sociable ambits of Washington. Perhaps the most telling modern exploitation of the vacuities and ironies in the host-guest relationship is to be found in the scenes of the parties on the Long Island estate in *The Great Gatsby* and in Broadway musicals such as *Call Me Madame* and *Mame.*

In many ways, the most fascinating chapter of this evolution occurred in the late nineteenth century, when assertive women of wealth put themselves at the head of leisure-class sociable circles. This led, in the twentieth century, to significant feminine leadership (by "Mrs. Jack" Gardner and Mabel Dodge Luhan, for example) of unconventional, even Bohemian, salons.[14]

5. *Incorporational.* a. Congregational. The sociability of churchmember with churchmember is generally thought to have peaked very early in American experience, when parishes were small and supposedly tightly knit. Yet recent reinterpretations suggest that the United States began to become a "churched nation" only in the mid-nineteenth century; and it appears that sociable events became a well-acknowledged part of church processes only after about 1830. Perhaps the most important thing to notice under this heading is the variety of sociable styles introduced by the large Catholic immigrations, including the Latin elements, which did much to enrich the urban sociable calendar. The Catholic sociable heroes in this case, perhaps, were the saints who inspired parish confessors to celebrate them. The Protestant heroes were the pious, evangelical men who extended sociable aspects of the evangelical tradition into the great networks of religious clubs and colleges and the YMCA and YWCA.

The sociability of believer and believer finds one of its most exquisite American expressions in the journals of the Quaker John Woolman.[15] In his writing we can feel the denominational spirit so deeply informed by a regard not only for the other "Friend" but for all men that it quietly glorifies the hope of fraternity in all human relationships.

b. Fraternal-Sororal. As Washington was the father of his country, Franklin was the father of his country's clubs. He founded more

voluntary associations than anyone up to his time in American life—
some of them, like the Junto, for partly sociable purposes. He was the
ancestor of the Rotarian and of Dale Carnegie, author of *How To
Win Friends and Influence People*. In his youthful, perhaps fool-
hardy, experiments with bladder "wings" for swimming, he was a
distant Nestor of modern clubs devoted to self-improvement and
self-destruction in sports. He was the primordial "Club President"
or "Fraternity Brother."

Club life in the United States does not appear to have enjoyed such
high-level fictional treatment as that in Great Britain. *Pickwick* is
inimitable, and the club passages in "Saki," Wodehouse, Burgess,
and others are often masterpieces in miniature. However, Robert
Benchley's essay, "The Treasurer's Report" still has its readers, and
the references to Boston club life in John Marquand (*The Late
George Apley* and other fiction) are both insightful and amusing.[16]
Both these writers inherit a bit, it appears, from Richard Harding
Davis, who portrayed the turn-of-the-century clubman in his "Van
Bibber" stories.[17] The period after World War II does not seem to
have been a rich period in club literature.

A subsidiary purpose of this paper is to suggest that, for Americans,
the middle term in this sociability scheme—that dealing with the
relation of clubmate to clubmate—is the *pivotal position*. It marks the
point, both in the history of social groups and in the individual life
cycle from birth to maturity, at which the more personal relations of
the earlier part of the scale are augmented and paralleled, and sometimes even displaced, by the more impersonal relations toward the
end of the scale. It is also the location on the scale that displays sociability in one of its purest forms—association that implicitly asserts
itself to be free from dominance by kinsmen, comrades, or hosts,
while at the same time it is not necessarily commandeered, as it is
later in the scale, by work teams or politics or cultural hierarchies.

6. *Collaboral.* The sociability of worker with worker, and indeed of
workers and their bosses in smaller enterprises, has not developed a
hero figure in American history or mythology. True, John Smith of
Virginia established some fame as a *macho* who led his settlers in play
as well as work.[18] Perhaps some cattleman and cowboy founders of
rodeo events were also leaders of this sort. But big industrialism increasingly separated the work and leisure lives of the laborforce from
those of the owner-managers.

Pictures of a sociability that is almost entirely dominated by team-work are provided in Chapter 53 of Melville's *Moby Dick*, dealing with the sociability of the crews of two whaling ships that happen to meet at sea. It is also present, in a very different way, in the "university novel," with its portrayal of the witch's brew that results when the ingredients of the academic bureaucracy and the cocktail party or pot party are mixed together.

7. *Political.* The sociability of political partisan with partisan is a subtopic of Madison's paper "Federalist Number 10." In that discussion, Madison is concerned with the effects of "faction" on the proposed government. The idea of "faction" includes not only the notion of a group with a common interest (such as creditors vis-à-vis debtors, or merchants vis-à-vis farmers), but also that of a group whose social and sociable bonds act to reinforce its identity and its goals. Since the time of this primal reference by Madison, legislation and journalism and fiction have shown concern with the sociable activities of men with political aims. We need only to remind ourselves of the "guilt by association" themes of the early 1950s.

The hobnobbing of politician with politician, political partisan with partisan, brings immediately to mind the chicken-and-peas dinner circuit of the election campaign. But as many reports and novels tell us, this is only the surface of many relations that range from the entertainments provided by lobbyists to the hunting-lodge meetings of people of political power with common interests. History and folklore relate the careers of Burr and Hamilton to their social trajectories, and the popularity of Jackson to his common-man sociable style. Perhaps the creation of Tammany Hall, with its combination of male sociable gatherings and electioneering punch, is the stellar contribution here.

8. *Cross-cultural.* The sociability of natives with strangers is perhaps more a myth of the travel posters than a social fact. It might be better to describe most of us in our role as tourists in a strange culture as travel-customers, sealed in a through-delivery package, round-trip. Yet every culture seems to have its experts in receiving and training the stranger, whether it be the hotel man, guide, cicerone, pimp, concierge, or foreign-language teacher.

In some times and places individuals have achieved this role on a rather glamorous scale. Duke Kahanamoku, the Olympic athlete who

became a kind of "greeter" for Hawaii, was one of that sort.[19] There
is no doubt that he and his indigenous culture were commercially
exploited, both consciously and unconsciously, by his promotion in
this role. But the duke, great gentleman that he was, had a magical
genius for transcending this, leaving his promoters, rather than himself, soiled by the process.

9. *Casual.* The sociability of stranger with stranger is both modeled
and purveyed by the entertainers of the culture, those whose per-
formances bring large audiences of strangers together and whose en-
actments suggest a stance that can be shared by those who witness
their performance. In our time, the range and potency of these celeb-
rities has been multiplied by the mass media in a way that is all too
well known. Its stars include athletes and sportsmen as entertainers
and as setters of a leisure style of interaction. The American Josephine
Baker in France and Louis Armstrong in the USSR have been modern
pacesetters of this kind.

The foregoing review illustrates by impressionistic detail and profiles of "sociable types" that convivial habits, schedules, and roles are
deeply interwoven with the family lives, the socialization, the educational institutions, and the career lines of Americans. Not only does
the family observe sociable forms, but sociable forms such as friendship and courtship are among the very conditions for its continuance.
In educational institutions, the relation between student and student
and between students and teacher is affected by many received forms
of sociability of a collaboral nature; but over and beyond this the life
of students in voluntary associations and clubs—especially fraternities
—has been a subject of both praise and blame for 150 years. Finally,
the movement of the individual into occupation and career is recognized as having sociable preconditions and sociable commitments.
One of the everyday recognitions of this is the common belief—not
too oversimplified—that to be a companionable golfer is as much of a
prerequisite for selling insurance successfully as training in financial
counsellorship.

4

For a long time now, sociologists and social historians have not paid
much heed to clubs in the United States. Perhaps the 1930s depression was a primary cause of this. It focused attention on serious social

ills and turned it away from an institution that can create uneasiness by its association with themes of privilege and snobbery. The fact that fraternal connections of some sort are open to almost everyone in the United States, including even the men and women behind the bars, seems to have been lost sight of. Urban dislocations and ethnic struggles after World War II reinforced sociological disinterest in social clubs. The 1960s interest in the commune, with its countercultural overtones, could be interpreted as a reaction against conventional clubs of almost any sort.

A major exception to this was the appearance in 1963 of *Clan, Caste and Club*, by H. F. Hsu, whose *Americans and Chinese* (1953) established him as the greatest foreign-born observer of American life since Tocqueville.[20] In *Clan, Caste and Club* he outlined his reasons for thinking that the American voluntary association (including the club that mixes sociable with other functions) is for the United States the key institution that caste is for India, and the clan for China. Hsu, with his modest yet magisterial sense of historical imperatives, was prophetic in part of his title. It was not so long after his book's appearance that inquisitiveness about clubs and the way they served American life began to be expressed by the law and the tax collectors. The question of ethnic discrimination in clubs and lodges was brought to the attention of judges, themselves barely tainted, to be sure, in the 1960s. In a major case, the Supreme Court found that it was unlawful for a certain club to prevent the entrance of Negro guests, in view of the fact that the club was quasi-public in one of its privileges—the privilege, under a state liquor law, of operating a bar on the premises. During the same period, in the absence of legal pressure, and as the result of changing attitudes, many clubs relaxed their ancient racist rules of membership and extended more and more rights to women. But no sooner had these affable revolutions in conviviality occurred than clubs found themselves challenged from another, higher direction.

Even before President Carter's 1977 expression of dislike for the tax-deductible "three-martini lunch" enjoyed by businessmen, there were distant rumblings of criticism along these lines from various sources. Now, in 1978, when more fundamental changes in laws affecting the tax-deductibility of business "entertaining" are being considered, clubs are justifiably worried. They protest that a sizable, and certainly pivotal, portion of the revenues that support them are the fruit of tax-deductibility accounting by their members. Like certain restaurants favored by the sociability of the business world, they warn that stricter new laws may lead them straightway into red ink and possible extinction.

I should now observe here that this paper would never have reached its present form without encouragement from David Riesman. Neither of us was particularly magnetized by American club life, since our sole purpose for meeting at a club, over a long period, was to get away from our offices for as outrageously long as possible to play tennis or squash. Riesman has been known, however, to dazzle lecture rooms and seminars with an instructive analysis of the differences in club life manifested by the older Harvard and Yale. At Harvard, the hereditary principle of membership was a firm, nose-up adherence to the idea of status by ascription. If it got under the skin of outsiders, they could at least say that their failure to enter a club was not a matter of their own lack of merit, but the mere absence of the requisite grandfather. At Yale, the order of the day was the idea of status acquired by achievement. Almost anyone with the appropriate color and ethnicity could set his heart on proving himself worthy of membership. The only trouble with such relatively open lodge-doors was that if one did not ultimately join the happy few, one had no one but oneself to blame.)

The pivotal place claimed for the club in this paper is not of course, a new idea. In its more general form, it occurs in Tocqueville's brilliant observations on the voluntary association in America. The importance of this form in American development is eloquently restated by Robert Nisbet in The Twilight of Authority: "It is in the context of such association, in short, that most stages in social progress have taken place. To compare our bureaucratised, politicised age with some age in the past when individuals were obliged to look out for themselves, singly or in small households, is mere fantasy. Once we look carefully into the matter we are surprised to see how many social groups, associations, and communities there actually were through which the fragility and precariousness of individual and family life were moderated."[21]

Nisbet, to be sure, is one of those who believe that the impulse to form such associations has declined in modern times. While he may be correct that the rich flowering of church congregations, unions, credit associations, and corporations is behind us, this is not necessarily true of the club, which is associated chiefly with leisure and the uses of sociability. Indeed, a withdrawal of interest and affect from the types of association that were closely connected with the necessities of production and survival may have made it possible to shift that interest and affect to the socially oriented club.

We ourselves live in a time when the sociability of the club has attained its greatest attractiveness for the American consumer of sociability in any period in American history. The evidence for this is to be found in the Gale *Book of Associations* over the recent years, with its array of country clubs, sports clubs, special-interest clubs, all alongside built-up (deep) layers of social clubs originating as far in the past as the mid-eighteenth century.

It seems probable that for the American male, the club as an institution acquired something like as much weight and interest as kin-centered, neighborly, and collaboral sociability only after the American Revolution. To put it another way, the more generalized democratic opportunities for fraternal association seem not to have occurred much before 1825. Around this time, the system of "lodges" began to grow rapidly, and the male college fraternity system had lately been instituted. However, it appears that the greater flowering of such associations did not occur until after the Civil War, achieving by the 1890s the general class-stratified and ethnically divided club pattern that was thereafter retained until well into the middle of the twentieth century.

The club in its American form was created by Benjamin Franklin. Before him there existed White's and Boodle's in London, the Athenaeum in Boston, and Freemasonry. But after him came the great growth of the male middle-class clubs and lodges that held a dominant place in the American nineteenth and early twentieth centuries —the age of Babbitt. It was not that Britain had fewer such clubs than America. It was rather that Americans enjoyed them on an economic scale that, for most British middle- and working-class males, was unheard of, mostly because it was beyond their purse.

Moreover, the later nineteenth-century attempts to create a club life to be eternally closed to all but a few newcomers (as in London) failed in the United States by about 1930. For a long time, exclusive clubs in the United States (on the model of the New York Yacht Club) maintained their privacy, though at the expense of their political power. But most clubs became more and more open after 1930.[22]

The various voluntary associations founded by Benjamin Franklin and his followers were based largely on the sociability of the English-speaking middle and upper classes of the Middle Atlantic states and were not necessarily designed or intended to perform the task of helping to incorporate the debarking immigrants into colonial and national life. Nevertheless, it seems clear that the voluntary association directed toward partly sociable purposes actually did have that effect in at least three ways.

For one thing, the growth of voluntary associations after the founding of the nation had the effect of making it possible for many of the English-speaking males who came as greenhorns into the country to find at least one voluntary association in which they could meet the earlier arrivals and learn the customs of the country. Second, the habit of tolerating and encouraging social clubs and lodges made it possible for new immigrants from non-English-language groups (especially the club-oriented Germans and Scandinavians) to establish their own sociable circles without the suspicious hindrance of homeland monarchical police looking for subversives. Third, the existence of a great range of sociable clubs and lodges made it possible for the non-English-speaking males to enter gradually, in the second and third generations, into associations that had been founded and led by Anglo-Saxons. Some of the most visible exceptions to this are to be noted in the sociable careers of the poorest Catholic Southern Europeans, the Eastern European Jews—and the Western European Jews after the 1870s, when anti-Semitism made its first full-scale showing in the United States.

5

Enough has been said to suggest that no observant modern European traveler in the United States would find American sociable habits entirely strange and mysterious. He would recognize, by reference to their European ancestors, the profiles of the Lords of Misrule, Masters of Revels, Club Presidents, Bonifaces, Maîtres d', Tutors in Sociability, Mistresses of Salons, and Tour Guides or Cicerones. However, if he were French, he might feel that our passion for club-like sociability has turned the domestic dwelling into a clubhouse, as compared with his own foyer; the teenage sociable traffic in the home is an example of this. If he were British, he might think that despite obvious elements of social class in our sociable arrangements, the tonalities of American seclusiveness and exclusiveness are qualitatively different from what they are on his own turf.

Much discussion of American sociability seems to be based on the assumption that it somehow *ought* to be a stage setting for the accommodation of individuals who are engaged in upward social mobility, and that it has either been beneficent in this regard or has acted badly —as a rearguard action against the fulfillment of this ideal. But the idea of frictionless upward mobility seems as unreal in most senses as the idea of a perfectly free economic market. What has been said in this paper can be read to suggest that sociable drives toward seclusiveness are not regarded by Americans as an affront to an egalitarian ideal, but are logically independent of whether one values that ideal highly or not. Thus, a belief that higher status can be attained by achievement does not mean to Americans that such achievement should be automatically rewarded by an invitation to join a club. (In fact, the club that expresses interest in someone may turn out to be a real-estate scheme to sell him a condominium in golf-land.) Nor does it mean that the sociable habits of clubmembers who have inherited wealth and status by ascription are so enviable and interesting that one should want or should be able to buy or talk his way into their ambit. To put it another way: a gang in the South Bronx is as determinedly exclusive as Bohemian Grove, and for some of the same lively reasons of association and territoriality and self-regard.

The question of whether American sociable habits have contributed, if not to equality, to freedom, may be the most important and demanding question. Tocqueville seems to have been right in guessing that they did so in his time and that they would continue to do so in the future. But he was one who believed that the appearance of the new society could be interpreted as part of a divine agenda for man—a view he avouches in his remarks on "Providence" in the preface to his famous work.

The fact is that most of the creative critics of sociability and civility from whom our major insights have been inherited, such as, for example, Erasmus and Castiglione, have expressed a suspicion that, considering its role as an institution that serves both to join and to separate the private and the public, sociability—and especially club-life sociability—is shadowy and elusive.[23] Perhaps this should be no surprise. The self-concealing capacities of voluntary associations, at any rate, are not by any means limited to "secret" societies; they play a part in the functioning of all of them. An extreme development of this occurs, perhaps, when even the clubmembers themselves are required, as in Mycroft Holmes' London club, "The Diogenes," not to speak to each other on pain of expulsion.[24]

NOTES

Feast of Strangers is the title of a book in progress. Dr. Margaret King made many helpful suggestions about the content and organization of this paper.

1. David Riesman, with Robert J. Potter and Jeanne Watson, "Sociability, Permissiveness and Equality: A Preliminary Formulation," in David Riesman, *Abundance for What?* (Garden City, N.Y.: Doubleday, 1964), pp. 196–225, passage quoted at p. 225.

2. David Riesman and Jeanne Watson, "The Sociability Project: A Chronicle of Frustration and Achievement," in Phillip E. Hammond, ed., *Sociologists at Work* (New York: Basic Books, 1964), pp. 235–321.

3. George Simmel, *The Sociology of George Simmel*, ed. and trans. Kurt Wolff (Glencoe, Ill.: Free Press, 1964).

4. David L. Sills, "Voluntary Associations," part II: Sociological Aspects, in David L. Sills, ed., *International Encyclopedia of the Social Sciences* (New York: Macmillan and Free Press, 1968), 16: 362–79.

5. Edward Digby Baltzell, *The Protestant Establishment: Aristocracy and Caste in America* (New York: Random House, 1964); William Foote Whyte, *Street Corner Society: The Social Structures of an Italian Slum* (Chicago: University of Chicago Press, 1943); Cleveland Amory, *The Last Resorts* (Westport, Conn.: Greenwood Press, 1973).

6. Herbert Gans, *The Urban Villagers: Group and Class in the Life of Italian-Americans* (N.Y.: Free Press, 1962); Jane Jacobs, *The Death and Life of Great American Cities* (New York: Random House, 1961); Vance Packard, *A Nation of Strangers* (New York: McKey, 1972).

7. Thorstein Veblen, *Theory of the Leisure Class* (New York: Modern Library, 1934); Tom Wolfe, *Radical Chic and Mau Mauing the Flag Catchers* (New York: Farrar, Straus & Giroux, 1970).

8. John Huizinga, *The Waning of the Middle Ages* (London: E. Arnold, 1927); William Lloyd Warner, *Yankee City*, abridged ed., selected and edited by W. Lloyd Warner (New Haven: Yale University Press, 1963).

9. Erving Goffman, *The Presentation of Self in Everyday Life* (Garden City, N.Y.: Doubleday, 1959; George Herbert Mead, *Mind, Self, and Society from the Standpoint of a Social Behaviorist* (Chicago: University of Chicago Press, 1934).

10. Robert Potter, "Interpersonal Ties and Interaction" (Ph.D. diss., University of Chicago, 1965).

11. Thomas Morton, *New English Canaan*, Introduction and Notes by Charles Francis Adams, Jr. (Boston: Prince Society, 1883): see also John Lothrop Motley, *Merry Mount: A Romance of the Massachusetts Colony* (Boston and Cambridge: J. Munroe, 1849).

12. Henry Adams, *The Education of Henry Adams: An Autobiography* (Boston and New York: Houghton Mifflin, 1918).

13. William Byrd, *The Secret Diary of William Byrd of Westover*, ed. Louis B. Wright and Marion Tinling (Richmond, Va.: Dietz Press, 1941).

14. Louise Hall Tharp, *Mrs. Jack* (Boston: Little, Brown, 1965); see also references to Mrs. John Lowell ("Jack") Gardner, Jr., in Cleveland Amory, *The Proper Bostonians* (New York: E. P. Dutton, 1947); Mabel Ganson Dodge Luhan, *Intimate Memories* (New York: Harcourt, Brace, 1933–1937).

15. John Woolman, *The Journals of John Woolman* (London: Headley Bros., 1903).

16. Robert Benchley, *The Treasurer's Report and Other Aspects of Community Singing* (New York and London: Harper & Bros., 1930); John Marquand, *H. M. Pulham Esquire* (Boston: Little, Brown, 1943).

17. Richard Harding Davis, *Van Bibber and Others* (N.Y. and London: Harper & Bros., 1892).

18. John Smith, *Travels and Works*, ed. Edward Arber; new ed., with a biographical and critical introduction by A. G. Bradley (Edinburgh: J. Grant, 1910).

19. Joseph Brennan, *Duke Kahanamoku: Hawaii's Golden Man* (Honolulu: Hogarth Press, 1974).

20. Francis L. K. Hsu, *Clan, Caste and Club* (Princeton: Van Nostrand, 1963); and *Americans and Chinese: Two Ways of Life* (New York: H. Schuman, 1953).

21. Robert Nisbet, *Twilight of Authority* (New York: Oxford University Press, 1975).

22. G. William Domhoff, the author of the amusing *The Bohemian Grove and Other Retreats* (New York: Harper and Row, 1974), might argue that "most clubs" are not the issue; the issue is the "cohesiveness" of a ruling class through its memberships in a few powerful clubs.

23. Erasmus wrote a guide to manners for young men and boys: *De Civilitate Morum Puerilium Libellus* (Antwerp, 1526); Baldassare Castiglione, *The Book of the Courtier*, trans. Sir Thomas Hoby; Introduction by W. H. D. Rouse (London: Dent, 1928).

24. A. Conan Doyle, "The Greek Interpreter," in *The Complete Sherlock Holmes* (Garden City, N.Y.: Doubleday, 1930).

13

ASPECTS OF DIVERSITY IN AMERICAN HIGHER EDUCATION

MARTIN TROW

HISTORICAL SOURCES OF DIVERSITY IN AMERICAN HIGHER EDUCATION[1]

The great, unique feature of American higher education is surely its size and diversity. It is this diversity—both resulting from and making possible the system's phenomenal growth—that has enabled our colleges and universities to appeal to so many, serve so many different functions, and insinuate themselves into so many parts of the national life. In a time of low growth and tight resources, however, diversity is being threatened by powerful forces tending toward the centralization and homogenization of our institutions. Yet it is through the preservation of diversity that our system will be best prepared to respond to changing demands and new challenges in the years ahead. To see why this is so, it may help first to review briefly the historical roots of diversity in American higher education and the benefits we derive from the way it works today.

Actually, this diversity was present from the very beginning. America had established 9 colleges by the time of the Revolution, when 2 —Oxford and Cambridge—were enough for the much larger and wealthier mother country. The United States entered the Civil War with about 250 colleges, of which over 180 still survive. Even more striking is the record of failure: between the American Revolution and the Civil War perhaps as many as 700 colleges were started and failed.[2] By 1880 England was doing very well with 4 universities for a

271

population of 23 million, while the single state of Ohio, with a population of 3 million, already boasted 37 institutions of higher learning.[3] (And a joke is told in England about the visitor from Ohio who claimed to be an alumnus of one of the ten leading universities in the state.) By 1910 we had nearly a thousand colleges and universities with a third of a million students—at a time when the 16 universities of France enrolled altogether about forty thousand students, a number nearly equaled by the faculty members of the American institutions. Today there are more than three thousand accredited colleges and universities in the United States, with a total enrollment of over eleven million students. Roughly half of all American youths pursue some form of higher education after high school, and in some states, such as California, about 80 percent of high school graduates go on to the postsecondary level.

The extraordinary phenomenon of high fertility and high mortality rates among institutions of higher learning is still with us. Between 1969 and 1975, some 800 new colleges (many of them community colleges) were created, while roughly 300 were closed or consolidated, leaving a net gain of nearly 500 in just six years. We are, of course, dealing with a phenomenon unique to the United States, one that resembles the birth and death of small businesses in modern economies, the patterns of success and failure of small capitalist entrepreneurs. This is in sharp contrast with the slow, deliberately planned creation of institutions of higher and further education in most other advanced industrial societies, or their even slower and rarer termination. And this points to the very strong link between higher education in the United States and the mechanisms of the market. This link to the market was and still is a major factor in the emergence and persistence of large numbers and diverse forms of colleges and universities in America.

The great diversity of American higher education arose in part from the multiplicity of forces and motives that lay behind the establishment of colleges and universities throughout our history. These included a variety of religious motives, a fear of relapse into barbarism at the frontier, a need for various kinds of professionals, local boosterism, philanthropy, and speculation in land, among others, and in all combinations. But diversity has developed also in the absence of any central force or authority that could restrain it, that could limit or control the proliferation of educational institutions. Especially important has been the absence of a federal ministry of education with the power to charter new institutions, or of a single pre-eminent university that could influence them in other ways.

The closest we have come as a nation to establishing such a central force was the attempt, first by George Washington, and then by the next five presidents, to found a University of the United States at the seat of government in Washington. The story of the effort to create a national university during the first decades of our national life is not well known, perhaps because historians are more inclined to write about the many things that did happen than about the infinite number of things that did not. Nevertheless, for the later development of American higher education, something that did not happen—that is, the creation of a national university early in our national life—may be quite as important as anything that did.

Benjamin Rush made the first detailed proposal for a national university in an essay published in 1787, the year of the Constitutional Convention. He urged that such a university be created to serve republican ideals, to indoctrinate its students with patriotic ideas, and to provide the practical education needed by the young republic: training men in government, science, and law. History, natural history, and languages were also to be taught. Conspicuous by its absence was theology, the most important subject in the majority of existing colleges in Amercia. Rush's plan for the curriculum would have made this institution a distinctly progressive one by the educational standards of the day. It would have accepted the graduates of existing colleges, offering them what we would now call postgraduate studies.

Rush's plan was briefly debated at the Constitutional Convention, where James Madison suggested that the power to establish a university be specifically mentioned as one of the powers of Congress. But Madison's proposal was defeated, the majority of the delegates apparently agreeing that such a specific reference to a university was superfluous, since Congress would have the necessary authority in any event.

The idea, in one form or another, was put forward and supported by each of our first six presidents, and by none with more personal interest and conviction than George Washington. Washington, in fact, made provision for such a university in his will, and mentioned it in his first and last messages to Congress. His strongest plea for it came in his last message, where he argued that it would promote national unity, a matter of deep concern at a time when the primary loyalties of many citizens were to their sovereign states rather than to the infant nation.

In addition, Washington saw the possibility of creating one first-class university by concentrating money and other resources in it: "Our country, much to its honor, contains many seminaries of learning highly respectable and useful; but the funds upon which they rest are too narrow to command the ablest professors in the different departments of liberal knowledge for the institution contemplated, though they would be excellent auxiliaries." Here, indeed, Washington was right in his diagnosis. The many institutions that sprang up between the Revolution and the Civil War all competed for very scarce resources, and all suffered to some degree from malnutrition.

The objections in Congress and the country were many. Some were concerned about the costs of such an enterprise; others saw little need for an institution devoted to postgraduate studies that would educate, perhaps beyond any practical need, only a tiny elite at public expense. Still others were opposed on constitutional grounds, seeing the national university as an infringement of states' rights.

The opposition on principle was reinforced by state and sectional jealousies. The presidents of the existing colleges, as well as the representatives of the several states, many of which were beginning to think about the establishment of state universities, may not have taken kindly to Washington's notion that existing or future provincial colleges "would be excellent auxiliaries." They may have had their suspicions, and with some reason, about the effect of a capstone postgraduate university at the seat of government. And Benjamin Rush may also have frightened congressmen by suggesting that "only graduates of the federal university were to be eligible for the administrative offices of the federal government."[4] Nevertheless, there was a moment during Washington's administration when a crucial step toward a national university failed by only one vote in Congress.

Defeat of the national university meant that American higher education would develop without a single capstone institution. Had we instead concentrated resources in a university of world standard early in our national life, it might have been the equal of the great and ancient universities of Europe or the distinguished new universities then being established in Germany and elsewhere. As it was, whatever the United States called its institutions of higher learning, the nation simply did not have a single genuine university—no institution of really first-class standing that could bring its students as far or as deep into the various branches of learning as could the institutions of the old world—until after the Civil War.

A national university would have profoundly affected American higher education. As the pre-eminent university—the proud young republic could hardly have let it starve—it would have had an enormous influence, direct and indirect, on every other college in the country, and through them, on the secondary schools as well. Its standards of entry, its curriculum, its educational philosophies, even its forms of instruction, would have been models for every institution that hoped to send some of its graduates to the university in Washington. It is likely that the graduates of the national university would have been in demand for chairs in both state and private colleges, and for headmasterships of secondary schools. Even without federal legislation giving the national university statutory power over other institutions, its influence in all areas of academic life would have been enormous. It would in fact have established national academic standards for the bachelor's degree, for the undergraduate curriculum, for the qualifications for college teachers, even for entrance to college, and thus for the secondary schools. Eventually it would have governed, shaped, and surely constrained the growth of graduate education and research universities in the United States.

However attractive all this may have appeared to its supporters, and may even seem to us, the price paid by higher education would have been great. The national university, for all it could have contributed to our intellectual and cultural life in the nineteenth century, would almost certainly have prevented the emergence of that big, sprawling, unregulated system of higher education that developed in its absence, a system that I believe, in the American context, to be infinitely preferable to the tidier system of smaller size and higher uniform standards that would have resulted from the creation of the University of the United States.

The University of the United States would have been prestigious, with its comparative wealth, its attractiveness to the finest scholars and students, and its links to power. It would have been successful; there was no possible competitor among state or private universities for a hundred years. But the very success of a national university would almost certainly have made it a profoundly conservative influence on American higher education. Starting as the most modern and advanced institution in 1800 or 1810, it would surely have institutionalized its curriculum, made it the basis for the organization of disciplines, of careers, of examinations, and of academic loyalties—and this institutionalized complex of forces would have resisted the enormous changes in the curriculum that came after the Civil War with the breakup of the classical curriculum, the emergence of the elective principle, and the impact of German ideas and models on the newly emerging research universities.

But even more serious than its eventual conservatism is the likelihood that it would have limited or constricted the growth of the system. A federal university of high standard would surely have inhibited the emergence of the hundreds of small, weak, half-starved state and denominational colleges that sprang up over the next 170 years. They simply could not have offered work to the standard that the University of the United States would have set for the baccalaureate degree, and demanded of applicants to its own postgraduate studies. The situation would have been familiar to Europeans, for whom the maintenance of high and, so far as possible, common academic standards throughout their systems of higher education has been a valued principle, almost unchallenged until recently. In the United States, after the defeat of the University of the United States, no one has challenged the principle of high academic standards across the whole system because no one has proposed it: there have been no common standards, high or otherwise. Indeed, if Europe's slogan for higher education has been "nothing if not the best," America's has been "something is better than nothing." And with that modest but oddly buoyant motto on our somewhat tattered ensigns, we have created a multitude of institutions of every sort, offering academic work of every description and at every level of seriousness and standard. And by so doing we have offered Europeans nearly two centuries of innocent amusement at our expense. The level of work done in many of our colleges, and even in some of what we are pleased to call universities, is derisory by the high standards of European universities. Nor, perhaps, has their work, in purely academic standards, come up to the level of the European selective gymnasiums, upper secondary schools, lycées, or grammar schools.

Our hundreds of modest colleges might never have been born if there had been a great federal university in Washington to establish and monitor academic standards. Or if those colleges had been created (for many of the forces behind them would still have existed), it is likely that they would have been relegated to a separate second class of institutions, offering post secondary training in vocational subjects for young men and women of modest social origins, but not the same curriculum, credits, or degrees offered by the small number of colleges and universities able to meet the standards established by the national university. Indeed, this two-class system in higher education exists today in many European countries.

The University of the United States failed: we did not go that way, and the ironic result is that without any central model, or governmental agency able to create one or more national systems, all of our three thousand institutions, public and private, modest and preeminent, religious and secular, are in some way part of a common system of higher education. What holds it together is difficult to describe; but perhaps more importantly, there is no central power to hold its members apart, to manage their life chances, and to assign them to separate sectors. In that freedom, the diversity of their forms of development has been characteristically American.

ELITE AND MASS EDUCATION

To talk about the role of diversity in contemporary American higher education—a diversity that I believe is our chief resource as we face an uncertain future—I have to use the terms "elite" and "mass" higher education.[5] "Elite" as applied to higher education has become part of the vocabulary of abuse, and yet we cannot just abandon it because it points to something for which no other term will quite serve. It has been used, almost always pejoratively, to refer to a kind of education available to children of wealthy and powerful families but not to those from families of lower status and less power, wealth, or income. It has also been used to refer to a traditional, humanistic education centering on the study of the classics, which included ancient history, philosophy, modern history, and mathematics. This curriculum has been extended in the course of centuries to take in modern languages and literatures, the sciences and social sciences, which together provide a broad cultural rather than a narrowly practical vocational training.

But there is another way of viewing "elite higher education": not in terms of the students' social origins or the substance of what is studied and taught, but instead by reference to the forms of education and the level of intensity and complexity at which subjects are pursued. In this last sense it stands in contrast with "mass higher education," which has been developing in the United States for the past hundred years, and which has emerged in every other advanced industrial society since World War II. It is in this sense that I will be using the term. For today there is really no agreement on what is the necessary, irreducible content of elite higher education, and we are obliged to characterize it more by its forms than by its subject matter.

I see three defining features of elite higher education:

1. It undertakes to socialize, and not merely to train or inform students; that is, it tries to shape qualities of mind and feeling, attitudes and social character. It may also try to transmit skills and knowledge, but that is not what makes it elite.

2. It is carried on through a relatively close and prolonged relationship between student and teacher, and depends on the creation and survival of milieux, of social and physical settings, within which that kind of relationship can exist.

3. Whatever the specific content of the curriculum—and that indeed varies very widely—elite forms of higher education convey, and intend to convey, to students that they can accomplish large and important things in the world, that they can make important discoveries, lead great institutions, influence their nation's laws and government, add substantially to knowledge, and so forth.

In this sense, institutions of elite higher education are machines for raising ambition and for providing social support and the personal and intellectual resources for the achievement of high ambitions. By contrast, mass higher education centers on the transmission of skills and knowledge through relations between teachers and students that are more fleeting and impersonal, and is designed to prepare those students for relatively modest roles in society, even in such high-status occupations as the professions, the civil service, and business management. I must place special stress on the encouragement of ambition as a central distinguishing characteristic of elite higher education. That is what, for example, differentiates it from the myriad small, often denominationally linked, liberal arts colleges that also seek to shape character through close personal relations.

Elite higher education makes large demands on students, not only in the severity of its curriculum, but also implicitly in its emphasis on socialization as against training. And that places it in sharp competition with other groups and institutions in society that also want to shape the student's mind and character—for example, the family, jobs and careers, peers, militant political movements. Elite higher education thus places its students in situations of psychological and role conflict in ways that mass higher education does not. It may also provide greater social and psychological support for students experiencing those strains. It is hard, for instance, to meet the demands on time and energy that elite higher education makes if a student is working part-time, or is married and has children. This is one reason why elite institutions have in the past not encouraged or admitted part-time or older students. Moreover, to increase its impact, elite higher education is more likely to be residential than is mass higher education.

Elite higher education is not confined to what we ordinarily think of as the elite private colleges and universities. For example, a great deal of graduate education in the big public universities is, in fact, a form of elite higher education. But on the whole, public authorities in the United States—federal, state, or local—have not been prepared to support undergraduate colleges that are sufficiently selective or richly staffed to sustain the necessary forms of elite higher education. Efforts have been made in the public sector to create small undergraduate units that resemble the best elite liberal arts colleges. Some have succeeded for a few years while they concentrated special resources around a small number of teachers and students in an experimental college within a large university or university system. But over time the enthusiasm that fuels such experiments and the special resources temporarily allocated to them run down, and they usually have been transformed or absorbed back into the mass institution.

There is another form of higher education growing in the United States, marked by its own forms and principles: "universal access" higher education. If the distinguishing feature of elite higher education is the shaping of character, mind, and sensibility through close and prolonged personal relationships, and that of mass higher education the transmission of skills and knowledge in the service of competence in life and work, then the distinguishing quality of post-secondary education committed to universal access is its concern with the idea of "value added." It asks of its students not whether any standard of achievement has been reached but whether any gains have been made, and it judges them and itself by that criterion. That idea is coming into institutions devoted primarily to mass higher education; and when it does, it sets up its own tensions within these institutions—again, tensions centering on academic standards, modes of instruction, and so forth. In our hundreds of junior and community colleges, the principles of mass and universal access education contend and coexist, centering respectively on the students preparing to transfer to four-year colleges, and the others for whom the junior college is a termination of their formal education. And there are an increasing number of institutions—for example, the City University of New York—in which all three principles are present and visible, often in different parts of the same institution, but nonetheless contending in a very complex way at the boundaries between them.

ON THE DIVISION OF LABOR WITHIN AMERICAN HIGHER EDUCATION

We may stress, as I have done, the role of diversity in American higher education in greatly extending the variety of students that it can serve, the variety of functions beyond teaching and research that it can perform. There is another aspect of diversity that is worth attending—that is, the effects of different kinds of institutions within our system on one another. The first emphasis sees diversity as the central strength of our system of higher education in its relation to a heterogeneous and rapidly changing society. The second perspective emphasizes the division of academic labor within the system, and the ways that different kinds (and parts) of institutions influence one another.

These influences are of very many kinds and have effects both good and ill. We know something, and sense even more, of the very great influence of the leading ten or twenty universities on all our three thousand institutions—on their conceptions of the role of students and of college teacher, of academic freedom and tenure, of administration and governance; indeed, every aspect of academic life everywhere in this country is shaped and formed by the realities and perceptions of what academic life is like at the leading public and private universities. That is not to say that every modest denominational or state college can, in fact, conduct itself as if it were Princeton or Yale. It does mean that these elite institutions, and in a somewhat different way the leading state universities, are seen as models for mass institutions—subject, of course, to their own special circumstances, the kinds of students and ambitions they serve and shape, and the variety of functions they perform. Their local constituencies, private bene-factors, state legislatures, and life itself remind them that they are not Princeton in the provinces, for poorer or less academic students. And yet, the impact of these great elite institutions on the rest of the system is continually refreshed, especially through faculty members and administrators who, if they did not do their graduate work at Princeton or Michigan or Berkeley, almost certainly studied with people who did.

These models of elite higher education, present and working in institutions whose circumstances and missions make them part of mass higher education, generate very strong tensions in those institu-tions. And to a considerable degree the story of any given college or university in this country is the story of how it manages these ten-sions. The unique character and identity of a non-elite institution is in a sense defined by the role of elite concepts in it—concepts of institutional autonomy, of modes of instruction, of the role of faculty in institutional governance. The existence and the strength of those concepts gives to a college president in a non-elite institution much of whatever freedom and discretion he has under what are often highly constrained circumstances.

The tensions between elite and mass models of higher education are often perceived and experienced as problems and frustrations. They are also the source of a very great strength in American higher education—they are, in fact, what makes our system a system within which we can meaningfully speak of an academic division of labor. Consider one point only: the movement of students and faculty be-tween institutions of elite higher education and of mass education would simply not be possible were it not for the active presence of elite concepts and values in the mass institutions (and conversely, if certain principles of mass higher education were not accepted by the predominantly elite institutions). Indeed, in other countries, where the systems of higher education are more neatly rationalized—where elite and mass institutions are more sharply distinguished from one another—there is almost no movement of students or faculty between those different systems.

Within our system, however, influence flows not only vertically—from the more distinguished to the more modest, from the elite to the mass institutions—but horizontally as well. In this regard, the exist-ence of the great private universities is, I believe, absolutely crucial to the leading state multiversities that Clark Kerr has described so well. For example, Stanford plays a variety of crucial roles for my own university at Berkeley, and for the University of California as a whole. I refer not merely to the many academic and scholarly links between us; more subtly, but at least as significantly, Stanford is a ghostly presence and informal participant in Berkeley's encounters with the state government, with the governor and the legislature. Pointing to Stanford, Cal Tech, and other leading private universities, we say to our state government: "That is what a world-class university looks like, that is how it behaves when it is not under the constraints of the governor's budget and the scrutiny of the State Department of Finance and the criticism of the Office of the Legislative Analyst. Do you want the leading publicly supported university in this state to be a comparable kind of institution? If so, then we too must be able to look and behave like that. And for that, we must have comparable freedom and resources."

Unfortunately, the question "Do you want the leading public university to be comparable in quality with the elite private universities?" is not a rhetorical one in California or elsewhere, and more than one state governor has been willing to let the private colleges and universities have a monopoly on elite higher education. But comparability with education of the highest standard continues to be a powerful argument for maintaining an elite component and elite principles in our leading state universities, especially if the argument is not used too often.

Moreover, and in part as a result of the effectiveness of that argument for comparability, the leading state universities also sustain a tension *within* themselves between the forms and concepts of elite and mass higher education—between models of excellence and the requirements of a democratic state and a populist society. Berkeley and Michigan resolve those tensions somewhat differently from public and private four-year colleges, but the elite private universities play an even larger role in that never-ending struggle within the state universities—a struggle sometimes over academic standards, sometimes over the internal allocation of funds, sometimes over the location of power and authority within the institution.

Though perhaps harder to demonstrate, the impact of public higher education on the elite private universities has been substantial. For one thing, the state universities have demonstrated what additional functions and activities might be compatible with excellence in teaching and research (and no less usefully, which ones are not). But their influence has been subtler and more varied than that. For example, it was member of the Board of Regents of the newly founded University of California who, in 1872, spoke to the relation of university and state in the following terms:

> The University is founded primarily on that essential principle of free republican government which affirms that the state is bound to furnish the citizen the means of discharging the duties it imposes on him: if the state imposes duties that require intelligence, it is the office of the state to furnish the means of intelligence.[6]

Among the "duties that require intelligence" are the duties of self-government through republican institutions; among the "means of intelligence" was the University of California.

That seems to me to define very well one facet of the right relation between the state and institutions of higher education. Insofar as that conception has been accepted by state and federal governments, it has provided an alternative basis on which private universities could legitimately claim and gain support from public funds—not merely as the contractual purveyor of specific goods and services, but as institutions of intrinsic worth, important to the survival of a free and self-governing society.

The influence of the leading public and private universities on one another I think has been an almost wholly unqualified good (though a financial officer in a private institution might take a different view). But somewhat more doubtful is the impact of the ideas and forms of mass higher education on the elite institutions. There is no question that American colleges and universities (considered as a system) must provide a wide range of functions and services beyond teaching and learning at the highest levels of excellence. What is very much in question is how many other such functions any specific elite university ought to provide—whether it ought to be a major instrument for extending educational opportunities, or for adult and continuing education, or for providing advice and service to other public and private institutions, or for supporting movements for social reform, and so forth. Which and how many, if any, of these ancillary functions it performs is, of course, a question that each elite university must answer for itself, insofar as it has any choice.

But just as the struggle between the balance of elite and mass functions animates the public colleges and the state universities, so a similar set of tensions is experienced by the great private institutions. It is experienced on one hand as a commitment to their own elite traditions, the shaping of mind and character through teaching and learning of the most demanding kinds, and on the other hand as a response to the demands of a democratic conscience and a need for the resources that flow from the provision of useful services to state and industry and other interested parties. Often the private universities resolve, or better, manage, these tensions through a kind of internal division of labor—for example, letting some schools and departments be guided chiefly by the logic of development internal to their disciplines, while others respond more to the cues and rewards of other institutions in a society that needs new ideas at least as much as new sources of energy. And the character of each private university lies in just how it resolves these tensions between the autonomous and the popular, the elite and the democratic, functions of higher education. Put slightly differently, this is a question of whether and to what extent any specific elite university chooses to encompass the division of academic labor (between mass and elite functions) within itself, among its own schools, departments, and institutes, or accepts a more specialized, or "pure," role, allowing the division of academic labor to be accomplished by the system of higher education as a whole.

Whatever the decision of a specific institution may be—which is to say, whatever character it chooses to sustain and defend—it seems to me clear that in the United States in the last decades of the twentieth century, the survival of elite higher education depends absolutely upon the existence of a comprehensive system of non-elite institutions. I think we see more clearly in the United States than is yet true in Europe that mass higher education, or institutions of universal access, or such forms as continuing education, are not the enemies of elite forms of higher education. On the contrary, in modern societies these democratic forms of postsecondary education must be broad and flourish if elite higher education is to survive. Our society must provide for the broadest access to institutions of higher education— for political, economic, and cultural reasons, as well as for greater social justice. But the bulk of that provision need not, and I believe cannot, be in elite forms of higher education. For one thing, elite higher education is too costly; for another, only a fraction of students and teachers have the interests, motivations, and ability to profit from the intense and demanding personal and intellectual relationships that mark it.

Modern systems of higher education must reflect a broad diversity of student interests and social functions. That supposes a parallel diversity in the forms of higher education. Elite forms of higher education are a part of that diversity: important and necessary, but only a part, and not even a dominant part. In the broad spectrum of post-secondary education, elite higher education must find its ecological niche, relatively modest in size and cost, though I believe of transcendent importance to the life of society and to those that experience it.

THE FUTURE OF DIVERSITY IN AMERICAN HIGHER EDUCATION

I have described briefly the historical roots of diversity in American higher education, and tried to suggest a few of the ways diversity shows itself in our contemporary system—as, for example, through the complex academic division of labor among different kinds of institutions, and through the vivifying tension that our system sustains between the forms and processes of elite and mass higher education. I would like now to look ahead a bit, and to consider some of the problems facing American higher education, and particularly its distinctive diversity, in the decades ahead.

I take a dim view of our capacity to see very far ahead with any degree of clarity or accuracy, whether in the field of higher education or any other. One could argue this in a variety of ways, but perhaps it is not necessary to do more than to ask ourselves how well we could have foreseen the world of 1978 in the year 1968—or 1958. And yet how casually we project and forecast two decades ahead. But I do not believe we are much wiser or more prescient today than we were ten or twenty years ago; perhaps, given the accelerated rate of change, we are even less so.

Nevertheless, whatever the future may hold for higher education, people who make decisions about it, from students to presidents, are anticipating a very much lower rate of growth in the next two decades than in the last two, and rather tighter resources. If these predictions prove true, both trends will work to strengthen the centralization of academic decision making. It is already occurring at every level: in the power of chairmen over their departments, of deans over their schools, of presidents over their colleges and universities, and, in the public sector, of chancellors over their multicampus systems, of state administrative agencies or legislative committees over the state systems. This is, of course, a reversal of the freewheeling dispersion of power and initiative we saw in the decades of rapid growth.

Centralization of academic authority has several sources: first, it appears to permit more efficient institutional management, of both funds and other resources such as personnel and space, than is possible through loosely coordinated, autonomous decisions of many smaller component units, whether individual faculty members, departments, or campuses. The efficiencies thus pursued may turn out to be artifacts of accounting systems, achieved at the expense of the effectiveness of academic programs. Much hinges on what outcomes of higher education are taken into account in the assessment of efficiency, and how these outcomes are measured. In any event, conventional wisdom, reinforced by new mechanisms of rationalized management such as program budgeting and benefit-cost analysis, tends to see central management as inherently more efficient than the dispersal of authority, which appears from the outside to be something near to organizational anarchy.

Second, more centralized control allows an institution to use whatever marginal discretionary resources it can gather or reclaim from ongoing operations for new and innovative programs, and this at a time when it is especially difficult to find funds for new ventures. Decentralized decision making, it is widely believed, tends to apply new funds to old activities, especially under conditions of budgetary stringency. Under the condition of level or declining budgets, most new programs can be created only at the expense of existing programs. Centralization of authority is seen as strengthening an institution's capacity to reallocate resources, and to make decisions that cannot be made by the component units involved, whether these be departments or campuses.

Third, the demands of external agencies for fuller and more detailed justification of the activities and expenditures of colleges and universities, a process under way everywhere, increase the size and importance of central administrations. Since these central bodies are held responsible for the activities of their component units, they respond quite naturally by claiming and exercising greater control over them. In short, stronger pressures for accountability strengthen central authority, both in the institutions and in the systems as a whole.

For these and other reasons, the tendency toward increased central authority under conditions of stable or declining budgets is both inevitable and seemingly desirable. But while the newly powerful central authorities celebrate these tendencies toward the concentration of authority in higher education, there is also a new appreciation of the importance of diversity in academic life, and especially so at a time of declining growth and high uncertainty about the future.

Higher education comprises an extraordinary range of studies, services, types of students, forms of institutional organization, modes of governance, sources of support. But while this diversity has increased with the growth of the system—diversity both resulted from and made possible that growth—it is also the central resource of the system as it faces a future of low growth and high uncertainty. Diversity allows the system and its component institutions to respond to unforeseeable demands and opportunities, and to shift resources among units and programs that already exist, rather than face the larger task of creating new ones.

If there is any single answer to the terribly difficult question of how to plan in the face of uncertainty, it surely is: sustain and expand institutional and systemic diversity, and thus strengthen the capacity to respond wisely and effectively to demands whose precise character and weight cannot be predicted. Our dilemma arises out of the fact that the initial response of American higher education to declining growth and support has been the centralization of academic authority, but that in turn poses a serious threat to academic diversity.

It is not that strong central authorities necessarily want to reduce diversity but that, for reasons which are perhaps inherent in the nature of central authority, this seems to be the usual outcome. For one thing, maintaining high levels of diversity involves an equally high measure of what economists call "slack"—that is, resources that cannot be specifically allocated or justified by current demand. Central authority, in part because it also centralizes responsibility in the service of narrow conceptions of efficiency, tends to trim programs to meet current rather than uncertain future needs. It tends to be more highly rationalized and bureaucratized than the smaller dispersed governing organizations of component units. And this means that central authority tends to develop systems involving the uniform, standardized application of administrative forms and principles, such as formulae linking support to enrollments; formulae governing building standards and the provision and allocation of space; formulae governing research support, and so forth. All of this can be seen as the bureaucratic strain toward uniformity in the service of orderly and efficient administration.

In addition, central authorities are governed by broad norms of equity that prescribe equal treatment for equivalent "units" under a single governing body. This is, in a sense, the same norm that says that to a parent all children are of equal worth and deserve equal treatment. But diversity rests very often on unequal treatment, unequal support, unequal forms of rules, and unequal application of rules. The application of norms of equitable treatment tends to have a marked leveling effect on component units and programs, reducing at least some dimensions of their genuine diversity. These norms of equity are especially strong when resources are constrained. It is one thing to administer inequalities when all budgets are rising; it is quite a different and more difficult matter when budgets are constant or falling.

The forces behind uniformity and equity come together in the increasing formalization of academic procedures. This is illustrated by, but not confined to, the great increase in appeals to due process in academic decision making. Academic decisions are often an exercise of judgment by one or more individuals in ways that reflect their wisdom and understanding, intelligence and character. These are all subjective qualities, and thus the decisions are heavily influenced, for better or worse, by the personal qualities of the people who make them. Due process, by contrast, is intended to curb arbitrary and personal power, to subordinate it to the rule of law and accepted procedures. Whether or not increased formalization makes decisions wiser or more just, it almost certainly will mean a greater uniformity of treatment of individuals and academic units, at the expense, I fear, of the diversity among them.

The United States is a society in which egalitarian values are very strong and apparently growing stronger, and where powerful groups and forces define all differences among institutions and programs as inequalities, and all inequalities as inequities. These strong populist forces reinforce the norms of equity that inhere in central authorities, and work directly parallel to the leveling and standardizing tendencies of bureaucratic organization mentioned above.

Increased central authority can be reconciled with academic diversity, at least rhetorically. A wise and able authority can include the maintenance of diversity as a central element in its forward planning. But for the reasons I have suggested, central authorities have strong inherent tendencies toward the reduction of diversity in the service of "efficiency," of orderly administration, of equity and equality and accountability. It will take more than rhetoric—it will take wisdom, high administrative skill, and political courage for academic leaders to preserve diversity in the face of all these pressures.

A commitment to diversity is no substitute for the exercise of judgment on the many occasions that call for difficult decisions in higher education. The principle of diversity does not indicate what priorities are to be placed on the diverse elements: whether, for example, to strengthen or to abolish a small, weak program, or to use discretionary funds for a proven program or an untried but innovative one. Indeed, the principle of diversity, taken uncritically, provides justification for a bit of everything. It can lead to the dilution of support for, and the consequent weakening of, all existing programs and activities in an institution, or to an overcommitment to new functions and activities when resources are inadequate to support existing ones.

But any principle can become a dogma, a substitute for judgment rather than a guide and touchstone for decision making. The principle of diversity can more properly enter academic decisions as a counterweight to short-term and narrow conceptions of academic efficiency. And it can remind administrators and planners of the irony of functional adaptation, an irony known to students of biological evolution, that short-run efficiency associated with highly successful adaptation to present circumstances may be maladaptive to the future. Conversely, a degree of organizational complexity and diversity that is "inefficient" in the short-run may prove more adaptive to unforeseen problems and opportunities, demands, and pressures that lie ahead. That lesson, implicit in the whole history of American higher education, has to be learned anew in every generation.

NOTES

1. This essay, like any on the theme of diversity in American higher education, is almost of necessity an extended footnote to the work of David Riesman, starting with his *Constraint and Variety in American Education* (Lincoln: University of Nebraska Press, 1956), and continuing on to his latest study (with Gerald Grant) of experiment and reform in higher education, *The Perpetual Dream* (Chicago: University of Chicago Press, 1978).

2. Frederick Rudolph, *The American College and University: A History* (New York: Knopf, 1962), p. 47. See also Donald G. Tewksbury, *The Founding of American Colleges and Universities before the Civil War* (New York: Teachers College, Columbia University, 1932); and John S. Whitehead, *The Separation of College and State: Columbia, Dartmouth, Harvard and Yale, 1776–1876* (New Haven: Yale University Press, 1973).

3. Rudolph, *The American College and University*, pp. 47–48.

4. David Madsen, *The National University* (Detroit: Wayne State University Press, 1966), pp. 19–20.

5. Martin Trow, "Elite Higher Education: An Endangered Species?" *Minerva* 14 (1976): 355–76.

6. Rudolph, *The American College and University*, p. 278.

14

JOURNALISM AND SOCIAL SCIENCE: CONTINUITIES AND DISCONTINUITIES

GERALD GRANT

Critics of the mass media seem obsessed of late with the performance of the journalist as an actor and thinker. There has been a rather extraordinary shift of attention away from questions of context, content, and control. An earlier generation of critics wrote about managers, advertisers, and owners who set the context of the news and determined what appeared in print. The reporter was something of a pawn in the process. In 1918 Max Weber warned of the rising influence of the "capitalist lord of the press," and later writers like A. J. Liebling took pains to show how the "pre-vertebrate reflexes" of publishers influenced the news. George Lundberg's 1936 biography of the Imperial Hearst was the first of many portraits of press barons, who were revealed as manipulating the news flow, later reflected in more academic studies such as Warren Breed's "Social Control in the Newsroom," which showed how media managers exercised indirect control without making explicit demands.[1] Much of the academic criticism of recent years has focused on the shortcomings of the journalist as a thinker and knower. Journalism has been portrayed as the "underdeveloped profession," staffed by ideologues who are untrained, uncritical, or lacking the methods to ascertain truth. The comparison, whether implied or explicit, has often been with the work of the social scientists who authored these critiques.[2]

Some of the "new journalists" have, by making large claims, invited a critical examination of their role. In an information-rich and increasingly complex world, there is a keener appreciation of the journalist's role in shaping the public agenda and interpreting events. Popular treatments of the journalist have also presented more glamorous and potent images. In contrast to the scheming dunderheads who sat around the press room in Ben Hecht and Charles MacArthur's *Front Page*, the Watergate investigative reporters Woodward and Bernstein are genuine media heroes. Paradoxically, the Nixon administration's harassment of some members of the press, through its attempts to intimidate and investigate specific journalists, probably served to give journalists higher standing in the public eye.

All of these factors partially explain the contemporary attention to the role of the journalist on the part of many critics, particularly social scientists. Yet one wonders why in this re-examination by academics one sees so little acknowledgment of an amelioration of the journalist's condition and an unusual improvement in the last fifteen years in the quality of journalistic intelligence. These improvements have not occurred uniformly across the journalistic landscape, but few serious readers doubt the transformation of a paper like the *Los Angeles Times*, or the rise to world-class journalism of the *Washington Post*, or the increased staffing of specialists on papers like the *Boston Globe*, the *Philadelphia Inquirer*, the *Chicago Sun-Times*, the *Louisville Courier-Journal*, and many others.

The criticism of the journalist comes after a decade of enormous inflation in the ranks of social scientists and at a time when the social sciences have fallen into basic disputes about what they teach and who is qualified to teach it. Not surprisingly, social scientists have become more sensitive to the distance between themselves and journalists at a time when it is more difficult to draw precise boundaries. As academic *arrivistes*, social scientists may be eager to separate themselves from their journalistic origins, and, like any newly arrived class, are likely to distort their origins and natural affinities and to act as if there were no commonalities, when of course there are. I say this with some authority, since I am writing about an earlier version of myself, when, after earning a doctorate, I was much too sensitive about references to my status as a "former journalist."

One of the aims of this essay is to show that recent critiques are misleading precisely because the discontinuities between the work of the social scientist and that of the journalist are overdrawn, and the continuities are scarcely recognized. Many critics fail to distinguish between types of journalists, treating a part for the whole, which is like basing an analysis of academics upon a sample drawn at Bob

Jones University. Nor do they take adequate account of significant improvements in resources devoted to more intelligent analysis of many issues, or of rising levels of expertise and knowledge on the part of many journalists.

1

The category "journalist" is not unitary and homogeneous, but as wide as the census category of "managers" that includes candy-store proprietors and managers of highly technical industrial enterprises. If we restrict the term "journalist" to daily print journalism, as is intended here, it includes reporters on small dailies who earn $7,500 a year and journalists on elite papers where minimum wages for journeymen now exceed $25,000.

In terms of their roles and cognitive styles, however, there are three types of journalists—if we set aside the literary journalist or novelist manqué who hopes to emulate Faulkner or Hemingway (once perhaps the principal career aim of many journalists, but a motive that has declined sharply, I suspect, in comparison with the rise of motivations that animate most social scientists).

Type 1 is the pressroom or police reporter, who is dependent upon official sources: this is the classic reporter who accepts the official version of events, or agrees to operate within the definitions of reality that officials provide, even if he or she is skeptical about what the official sources have said, as were many reporters who wrote stories on cue for Senator Joseph McCarthy. This view characterizes much reporting from the White House as well as from police headquarters. Such reporters seldom assume personal responsibility for what they write. If challenged as to the accuracy or truthfulness of what they have written, they will tend to point to the official who said it or failed to say it as the culpable party, not themselves. The reporter's world tends to be defined by the "sources" he is assigned to cover, and a collection of sources defines a "beat."[3] The subject matter of the "news" tends to be patterned on official activity: a campaign to snag scofflaws, a narcotics raid, an investigation of youth gangs. Much effort is expended in predicting the pattern of official activity, such as appointments of important persons, and scooping the opposition.

The story does not arise from an independent assessment of events or a question in the writer's head; the argument among reporters is not about what the "story" is but, given what has been said, or handed to them, what is the lead.[4] The reporter is thus a transmission belt; he or she writes reports about events as defined by others. The job is to convey this information clearly and quickly. It is an important function. Although some reporters spend a lifetime in such work, pure types are hard to find. Even the most hard-bitten police reporter will occasionally decide on his or her own that conditions in the local jail are intolerable and ought to be exposed, or that a police chief's new policy of "preventive detention" violates civil liberties. This may be written on the reporter's own authority, but usually an "official source," such as the local American Civil Liberties Union lawyer, will be found as a peg on which to hang such a story.

Veteran White House reporters convince themselves that they are not really passive receptors by telling about the telephone calls they made to lower-echelon officials, resulting in modifications of the story the press secretary wanted them to put out. But most of the time, they put it out; that is their function. They are to some degree propagandists for the party in power, or, more benignly, dissemination is a legitimate function of journalists who report on democratically elected officials. A few, of course, are more than conduits, these are usually journalists from papers large enough to double-staff the White House, thus leaving one person free to forage and to think. Although he wrote as though he were talking about all journalists, Murray Kempton (himself an excellent example of the analytical type) partly explained the resentment of pressroom reporters in the Nixon White House when he wrote, "The journalist is, by habit and necessity, increasingly dependent for his rations upon government officials who are more and more inclined to lie."[5]

Just such suspicions—and they occurred long before Watergate—gave rise to the Type II journalist, the inside dopester and investigative reporter who develops sources he or she can trust. The Type II journalist works by personal, confidential contacts. In the case of the investigative reporter, these are usually antiestablishment or undercover sources, but the inside dopester is characterized by having backdoor access to important informants who relay privileged information to the anointed. Social standing, the right address, and invitations to the right clubs and cocktail parties are essential passports to success for the inside dopester. Charles Bartlett, a little-known reporter on the *Chattanooga Times* who had been an old school friend of John F. Kennedy's, was suddenly offered a syndicated column when Kennedy moved to the White House. Elite journalists in Washington formed various insiders' clubs where leading political figures could furnish inside dope. In the 1960s, Godfrey Sperling of the *Christian Science Monitor* initiated a breakfast club, at first limited to a handful of leading political reporters, where Robert Kennedy, Spiro Agnew, Nelson Rockefeller, and others shared some of their first formulations of campaign strategies on an off-the-record or not-for-attribution basis. Jack Germond of the Gannet newspapers initiated a rival supper club limited to fourteen capital correspondents.

Investigative reporters also work essentially by establishing confidential sources and following up inside tips, but they are more likely to be mavericks and underdogs than members of a social elite. Jack Anderson and Les Whitten have their counterparts on every newspaper. These are reporters who are known as crusaders or have a reputation for ferreting out evidence of corruption or wrongdoing. Aggrieved parties, those with an axe to grind, or simply persons with a keen sense of justice will leak information to them on a confidential basis.

Good reporters of this type work for their salary, however, since after days of checking and cross-checking, a tip may prove to be malicious or unfounded. Some investigative journalists were themselves members of a deviant community or had special links to one: for instance a reporter with relatives in the Mafia. More often, however, an investigative reporter works by slowly establishing confidence with a source, in the way that Woodward and Bernstein describe repeated trips to the homes of secretaries who worked for the Committee to Re-Elect the President. In one case, they returned fifteen times. The secretary finally talked to them on the night they helped her clear the dishes after waiting for her party guests to leave.

Investigative journalists, operating without powers of subpoena and without the buffer of lapsed time that helps to open attics and locked drawers for historians, resemble private detectives more than either scholars or journalists of the first type.[6] Type I journalists are lap dogs, generally content with what they are fed, whereas journalists of the investigative type are hound dogs willing to bite the hand that feeds them. Yet while investigative reporters are more critical than pressroom types, their adversary styles and topics of investigation are predictable, and they are highly dependent on handouts, even if undercover. Although some investigative reporters rise to Holmesian heights of deductive reasoning, they are less often capable of systematic analysis of complex problems.

It is the capacity for such complex and creative intellectual activity that distinguishes Type III, the analytical journalist. Once quite rare, limited to an occasional columnist or editorial page writer, the analytical journalist now constitutes an emerging and significant type on the staffs of elite newspapers. And here we are talking not just about the *New York Times* and the *Washington Post*, but about more than a dozen serious papers in major cities (but by no means in all, for New Orleans, San Francisco, and Cincinnati, for example, have none).[7] These journalists are better paid (on the best papers, with salaries as high as those of professors at major universities) and better educated (often with graduate training and occasionally a Ph.D.) than their cohorts a generation ago.[8] Differences in educational levels between journalists on elite and nonelite media are particularly significant (with elite media defined here as those regarded as "the fairest and most reliable" news organizations by journalists themselves). About 80 percent of the elite journalists are college graduates (with proportionately more graduating from the most selective colleges), and 17 percent have graduate degrees. Among the nonelite, only half have college degrees and less than 5 percent have graduate degrees.[9]

The general increase in educational attainment throughout the society has undoubtedly had some effect in creating a demand for more intelligent journalism at the same time that it has provided higher levels of training for those entering the field. Newspapers have been influenced in their forms of coverage by the unexpectedly large audiences drawn to new mediating journals in the social sciences— such as *Psychology Today*—and by the advances demonstrated by educational television. New salary levels and the increased willingness on the part of elite media to offer more space and other resources to more serious forms of journalism have created new opportunity structures for those with advanced training in the social sciences.

For example, Michael T. Kaufman, a *New York Times* correspondent in Nairobi, focused on a debate over a proposed change in marriage laws that would give wives a veto over a husband's polygamous plans and permit them to share control of family property. The attention to such an issue is itself a significant indicator of the shift to more analytical journalism, and the quality of the analysis was penetrating. Here is the third paragraph of Kaufman's report:

> African tribal society is by no means monolithic. There are more cultural, linguistic and even physiological differences among black Africans than there are among white Europeans. But one component of African

cultures that is fairly universal is the extended family system, which through an intricate blend of rights and responsibilities assured the continuance of the family and security for its members. Sex roles were clearly defined. The system tended to be polygamous and was adapted to rural and agricultural settings where people lived in relative isolation.[10]

Kaufman's story went on to discuss the ways in which increasing social mobility, socialist regimes, and Western influences have eroded the cultural legacy of African traditions. His analysis was sociologically and anthropologically informed; he drew on scholarly sources and independently paid careful attention to changing images of marriage and the family as they were portrayed in the popular press and television in Nigeria. Other examples could be cited.[11] The hard-drinking foreign correspondent who slammed out copy on the basis of a few English-speaking contacts has been largely replaced today by journalists who have some academic preparation for their assignments, usually speak a foreign language, and, like Michael Kaufman, would regard the spot news and travelogue coverage of an earlier day as unworthy of their talents.

Evelyn Waugh described the trench-coat types of an earlier era in his novel *Scoop*, which Phillip Knightley argues was no fictional parody of the foreign correspondent but rather close to a factual account of the antics of reporters covering the Italian invasion of Addis Ababa in 1935. Waugh's protagonist, Corker of the *Universal News*, speaks for the art of journalism in that day:

> You know, when I first started in journalism I used to think that foreign correspondents spoke every language under the sun and spent their lives studying international conditions. Brother, look at us. On Monday afternoon I was in East Sheen breaking the news to a widow of her husband's death leap with a champion girl cyclist. Next day the chief has me in and says, "Corker, you're off to Ishmaelia." "Out of town job?" I asked. "East Africa," he said, just like that, "pack your traps." "What's the story?" I asked. "Well," he said, "a lot of niggers are having a war. I don't see anything in it myself, but the other agencies are sending feature men, so we've got to do something."

Knightley concludes his study of 120 years of war correspondence with the observation that not until the Vietnam War did the war correspondent begin to emerge as a "partisan for truth," and that it was in Vietnam that "correspondents began seriously to question the ethics of their business." It was one of the few instances where an American correspondent (Harrison Salisbury reporting from Hanoi for the *Times*) made an objective effort to assess civilian damage in enemy territory, forcing publicists in the Pentagon to reverse themselves.[12] I do not think that Henry Kissinger was merely trying to court favor with the press when he said that "the more sophisticated of the journalists often have a reservoir of knowledge and continuity that is better than that of many of the top officials [in the State Department]. I could name individuals who, on arms control, on Vietnam negotiations, could spot subtleties that many of the officials could not see." Of course Kissinger was talking only about some journalists when he made this comment midway in his term of office. In his farewell talk to the Washington press corps he concluded, "I will think of you with affection tinged with exasperation."[13]

2

If it is true, as I have argued thus far, that distinctions between journalists and social scientists are overdrawn rather than spurious, what distinctions are valid? It seems to me that the most useful way to examine these distinctions is to look at them not as sharp breaks, but as spectra. There are differences of orientation along several dimensions, with Type I journalists usually at one end of the spectrum and Type III journalists often approaching the boundaries of social science at the other. Four such dimensions will be examined here. These are qualities of time, voice, knowledge, and reference group.

Time. The Type I journalist is typically breathless, in pursuit of the ephemeral event. The social scientist may plan his observations to coincide with the natural cycle of human action or, when dealing with events that are either physically or historically remote, devote time to more leisurely and prolonged analysis and searches of relevant literatures and comparative frameworks.

Many social scientists defend their months or years in the field against "mere journalists who drop in for a day or two" and scribble hasty impressions. They overlook journalists like Joseph Lelyveld of the *Times*, who repeatedly visited a Harlem classroom over the course of a year and perceptively wrote about the struggles the teacher encountered. Similarly, Donald Bartlett and James B. Steele of the *Philadelphia Inquirer* spent the autumn of 1972 coding for computer analysis more than ten thousand criminal records. They examined

twenty thousand pages of courtroom testimony and hundreds of psychiatric and probation reports in order to analyze discriminatory patterns in the adjudication of 1034 cases in the Philadelphia courts.
Some reporters on the *Los Angeles Times*, *Wall Street Journal*, and
Washington Post are allowed months to work up major analyses.
Such generous leads have not become the norm, even among elite
newspapers, but these examples are no longer rare occurrences.

Voice. A sense of personal responsibility for what is written marks
the work of the Type III journalist. In this he or she lies close to the
social scientist, who is scrupulous about distinguishing his own analysis from that which is borrowed, and far from the Type I journalist,
who is generally a mouthpiece for others. The Type II journalist, or
investigative reporter, lies between the two in that he or she engages
in independent analysis and speculation, but most often relies on an
inside source. The *Philadelphia Inquirer's* Steele rejects the description "investigative reporter" on just such grounds: "The challenge is
to gather, marshal, and organize vast amounts of data already in the
public domain and see what it adds up to. Inside sources can't
always do that for you. They're too involved."[14] Steele exemplifies
the Type III journalist, who takes pride not in achieving a scoop, or
grooming a confidential source, but in the quality of his analysis.

Knowledge. The kind of knowledge the writer possesses is a critical
distinction. Compared with other journalists, the analytical or Type
III journalist possesses greater breadth of general knowledge and
often has depth in an area of specialization. Architectural writers today often have some training in architecture. Journalists with training
in law, economics, and the social sciences are no longer rarities. Institutes and training programs for science writers are increasingly
common. The *Times* has employed a medical doctor to write medical
news.

Yet when compared to social scientists, Type III journalists differ
on two critical dimensions of knowledge: theory and method. The
pure social scientist holds theoretical knowledge most dear. He or she
aims first at the development of theory, second at the development
of method. In the workaday world, however, most academics do not
expect to make major contributions to theory. Their claims lie in the
less exalted domain of method; they take pride in having mastered
methods for gathering and sifting evidence, for establishing standards

of reliability and validity. Even among social scientists who do not aspire to the mantle of the great man of theory, one can discern differences in theoretical awareness, or in the degree to which their investigations are theoretically informed. Good social scientists are conscious of the variety of theoretical lenses through which one may examine the social world. Three different theorists sitting in the same classroom would "see" three different worlds: a symbolic interactionist would be inclined to attend to the way meanings are socially constructed; a structural-functionalist would be more likely to focus on the way that schools serve the latent functions of preparing children for life in a complex industrial society; a neo-Marxist might examine the way that the class background of children influences their assignments to academic tracks; and examples could be furnished under every theoretical or conceptual label.

The theoretically informed person is at once conscious of how his or her own theoretical presuppositions influence what is observed, and of what aspects of that social world would appear in a different light if refracted through another theoretical lens. Analytical journalists differ sharply from social scientists in that their choice of vocation signifies that they have no aspirations of contributing to theory as theory. They differ less sharply, although still considerably, on the question of theoretical awareness. Hilton Kramer on art, Wolf Von Eckhardt on architecture, Leonard Silk on economics, and David Broder on politics are theoretically informed. The newspaper audience limits a writer's appetite for theory and abstraction; such readers are often in search of information or escape. Yet, as the quotation from Michael Kaufman's article and the accompanying notes illustrate, what editors regard as the tolerable limits of a more theoretically informed style have been broadened appreciably.

Of course, most Type I and Type II journalists remain random empiricists, focused on particular events, operating without any general framework of ideas or consciousness of their own theoretical orientations. They operate on the assumption that the facts are sufficient for understanding. It may be that reporters ignore the truth that all facts are "theory-laden" out of a subconscious wish to avoid ideological conflict or to reinforce commonly accepted notions of the status quo,[15] but I suspect it is less that than reinforcement of traditional notions of descriptive storytelling, where the emphasis is placed on colorful, readable accounts of events regarded as unique rather than as recurring as part of larger patterns. Young reporters with literary aspirations idealize their work as a defense of the concretely human against what the humanist feels as "the mostly violent and stupid formulations about the abstractly human." Social scientists, however, are inclined to view facts as mostly propaganda in the absence of any theoretical frameworks (that is, abstractions) for making sense of them.

The analytical journalist is to some degree theoretically informed, but is oriented more to the world and to action than to structures of knowledge. He or she is neither consciously testing theory nor primarily interested in the cumulative programs of the academic disciplines. But such journalists are beginning to be in some degree conscious—in the way just noted—of the different lenses through which one may view the occurrences of the social world. Similarly, their reading habits differ significantly from those of Type I and Type II journalists. They do not read the academic journals in the basic disciplines or, generally, works of pure theory. But they are likely to be critical consumers of midrange literature of the social and behavioral sciences and to read those journals edited for creative intellectuals and those concerned with critical analysis of public affairs: *Foreign Affairs, The Public Interest, Transaction and Society,* the *New York Review of Books,* and professionally oriented academic journals within their fields of interest. Analytically oriented education writers, for instance, read the *Harvard Educational Review, Teachers College Record, Phi Delta Kappan,* publications of the National Education Association, and a wide stream of government reports in the field of education. They are more likely to read serious contemporary books than classics in the field: say Martin Mayer or (somewhat fewer) Christopher Jencks, but not Durkheim or Willard Waller. Such journalists have a general framework of ideas, though not a precise theoretical scheme. The analytical journalist is an eclectic—a fox, not a hedgehog—who has begun to develop a larger view. They have partially realized Robert E. Park's hope that journalists might be capable of viewing daily events in "their more general bearings." Park, one of the founders of American sociology, had himself been a newspaperman before returning to the University of Chicago, and he believed that the newspaper could be a "powerful agency" for education and reform. Park said he had been influenced by John Dewey's notion "that thought and knowledge were to be regarded as incidents of and instruments of action, and I saw in the newspaper, responsible for its mission, an instrument by which this conception might be realized in action, and on a grand scale."[16]

Journalists who are theoretically informed are also attentive to data and are becoming more adept at generating data for analysis. The sophisticated social surveys by Philip Meyer of the Knight newspapers following the 1967 Detroit riots were a breakthrough. But modern survey techniques have now been adopted by a number of elite newspapers, and they are no longer restricted to election polls. For example, a recent story in the New York Times, drawing on technical assistance from a Princeton social scientist, analyzed a Times poll of 593 randomly selected residents of a Queens school district that had refused to supply the federal government with ethnic breakdowns of its staff members and students, thus jeopardizing programs to aid disadvantaged students. Prior to the poll, the Queens community school board had been portrayed as racist. The poll analysis, with accompanying charts, showed that 70 percent of the residents, 40 percent of whom were Jewish and 40 percent Catholic, backed the board. The analysis then turned to an examination of why this might be so and raised the possibility that it was not raw prejudice, since most of the residents were not opposed to integrated education, but evidence of increased middle-class resentment over social policy that excludes their children from federal programs their taxes support.[17] In recent years, the quality and frequency of such analysis has increased appreciably. Certainly one index of analytical journalism ought to be a decrease of anecdotal evidence and some increase in quantifiable data. As a very rough indicator, I totaled the space given to charts and graphs and other quantified data in the Times for the month of September in 1935, 1955, 1965, and 1975. Excluding weather charts, stock tables, the sports pages, and other repetitive material, I found that nearly twice as much space is now given to quantified material as in previous decades:

Year	Column Inches of Charts and Graphs
1935	128
1955	150
1965	122
1975	283

The complexity of treatment of the data and the quality of analysis in recent years, while impossible to quantify, have been impressive. For example, in the midst of the New York City teacher negotiations and with a strike threatened, Edward Fiske of the Times surveyed teacher benefits in ten large cities. His data—arrayed in matrix spread across four columns—compared teachers on thirteen complex variables, including class size, preparation periods allowed, sabbaticals, pensions, length of working day, and relative cost of living.[18] Election polls have moved far beyond the straw vote stage or mere predictions of who is ahead. The *Washington Post* has employed Louis Harris, and the *Times* has employed a variety of social scientists to assist its own staff, including Garry Orren of Harvard and Michael R. Kagay of Princeton. In the last presidential primary, the *Times's* new sophistication was illustrated by its poll of voters as they came out of the booth in order to analyze the results by ideology, religion, occupation, age, education, and race.[19]

The influence of analytical journalists on papers like the *Washington Post, Los Angeles Times,* and some other elite newspapers has increased in the last decade as these papers established news services serving hundreds of provincial papers. This reduces the reliance of the latter on the Associated Press and United Press International, which formerly dominated the field with what I have described here as Type I coverage. In an analysis of the press's handling of concern about the possibility of a swine flu "epidemic," David Rubin noted the contrast in reporting between a number of elite papers and the standard wire services. While science reporters on some elite papers provided coverage of "depth and sophistication," the routine wire service coverage was "exceedingly superficial," focusing on the "defenses of the public health establishment rather than on the underlying logic of the entire program." Rubin found that the science and medical background of the analytical reporters was the "single most important variable in the quality of coverage," whereas the wire service reporters "were not equipped to ask basic scientific questions about the vaccine, its administration, its composition, and the immunlation programs as a whole." Second, Rubin found a direct correlation between the quality of coverage and the number of sources cited in the coverage. The *New York Times* drew on twenty-two sources, The *Washington Post* seventeen, and the *Miami Herald* twelve, compared with the *Denver Post's* two and the *Caspar* (Wyoming) *Star Tribune's* one.[20]

Reference Group. The cooperation between reporters and social scientists on survey teams indicates a small but important shift in the character of the analytical journalists reference group—that loosely defined group of significant others whose expectations influence one's performance in a role. The significant others for the Type I reporter are sources on his beat whom he tries to please and editors who assign stories and (sometimes without even consulting him) rewrite his copy. The significant role models for the Type II reporter are the muckraker and prize-winning journalist stereotypes—the reporter whose exposé puts wrongdoers behind bars. The Type III or analytical journalists, by virtue of their educational background and their need to be critical consumers of a wide range of reports written by social scientists, are more inclined to compare their work to social science models. One salient model is provided by the social scientist who does not write primarily for his or her academic peers but for a more general intellectual audience of whom fellow social scientists are but one subset. Social scientists of this generalized type (although not only them)—persons like David Riesman, Daniel Bell, Nathan Glazer, and, in his later writings, James Coleman—are strong influences on analytically oriented journalists.[21]

Other models are also having an impact as the exchanges between journalists and social scientists have increased and new relationships have been created. Many of the forms of cooperation that I suggested in an essay nearly a decade ago—considered utopian by some at the time—have been tried in recent years.[22] Analyses written by academics appear more frequently in newsprint (as contrasted with the earlier practice of restricting such contributions to signed opinion pieces opposite the editorial page).[23] The Russell Sage Foundation has sponsored internships on newspapers for doctoral candidates, and academic sabbaticals for journalists are more plentiful. Newspapers have brought academics into the newsroom for short-term projects and have commissioned research.[24] Academics have been more hospitable to contributions from analytical journalists on some journals and have occasionally invited journalists to participate in research projects.[25] These new networks and affinities are creating new standards of comparison.

But reference groups have a normative as well as a comparative aspect; that is, they shape the values by which judgments are made as well as provide standards against which to measure oneself. One of the ways in which analytical journalism is growing closer to the norms of science is in its willingness to examine its own performance. The most striking evidence of a more reflexive attitude is found in the appointment of staff critics or ombudsmen who have the power to investigate complaints about the newspaper's performance and publish the results. The first such position was created by the *Louisville Courier-Journal and Times* in 1967. Within a decade, fifteen papers have followed suit. Corrections are now published more readily, and in a less aggrieved tone.[26]

The National News Council, with its broad oversight powers, had a slow birth, greeted skeptically by some leaders in journalism, welcomed by others, and opposed by a few (including the *New York Times*).[27] Since its establishment in 1973, it has won the endorsement of the American Society of Newspaper Editors. Now the Council's often witheringly critical reports of individual papers and journalists are regularly published in the *Columbia Journalism Review* in the manner of censures reported by the American Association of University Professors. The News Council has had some influence in elevating the discourse on ethical issues—a topic sorely in need of discussion when a major newspaper publishes a column defending its "journalistic enterprise" by arguing that "a newspaper should . . . stick to what it does best—which is to steal other people's books."[28]

The *Columbia Journalism Review* was itself a lone voice when established in 1961 "to assess the performance of journalism in all its forms, to call attention to its shortcomings and strengths, and to help define—or redefine—standards of honest, responsible service." But more than a dozen such reviews have come into existence since, most on a regional or local level.

All this is not to argue that journalism is a science or that analytical journalists are colleagues of social scientists in a formal sense. A reference group is not a peer group. The work of journalists is not refereed by colleagues in the way that manuscripts are passed upon by social scientists. And despite liberalizations in both the length of newspaper articles and the length of time given to prepare them, and improved educational levels of analytical journalists, the audience for which they write does not have the tolerance for ambiguity and complexity that social scientists may take for granted.

3

The qualities just discussed define a new class of journalists—as yet a tiny minority—whose emergence Robert Park and John Dewey would greet with joy. These journalists are educationally prepared to engage in analysis. They are not mere functionaries, but thoughtful social observers who have developed their own intellectual agendas. Although they vary greatly in the degree to which they are theoretically informed, they are oriented to social science methods, and their search for evidence is increasingly scrupulous, if not yet deserving the description "scientific." The acknowledgment of this new class has been obscured by increased attention to the real shortcomings of the press in other respects and a failure to distinguish among the multiple realities that go by the name of "journalism."[29] The analytical journalist is not yet fully institutionalized, and the role has created some dynamic tensions within journalism and in its relation to social science. Predictions are always risky, but several developments seem probable in the next decades.

The traditional rugged individualism of the reporter's trade will be in conflict with the need for teamwork and new forms of group journalism influenced by social science methods. Elite journalism is intensely competitive. After a year-long immersion in the newsroom, Chris Argyris concluded that life at the *New York Times* was characterized by high competition and low trust. He noted this typical comment by an editor about reporters: "They're competitive as the devil, they're competitive for a sandwich, they're jealous of each other...."[30] Journalists who are out to best the competition and each other concentrate more on winning than on cooperating, yet analytic journalism adopting social science methods requires cooperation in teams. The new italic prefaces delineating the various contributions of reporters on team-written stories are one indication of the rise of analytic journalism. The italic replaces the larger boldface bylines, reflecting in typesize the reduction of ego required in cooperative modes. This tension between individualism and cooperative enterprise will not be easily overcome. Even when it does not mean working in teams, analytic journalism means that a reporter's name does not appear in the paper as often, and that his or her articles will more likely appear inside than "out front" on page one.

As more persons with advanced training in the social sciences are drawn into journalism—as I believe more should be and will be in a time of "excess capacity" in the nation's graduate schools—tensions between generalists and experts will increase. The generalist philosophy that any staffer should be ready on demand to cover any assignment or chase any fire engine remains potent. The new experts of analytical journalism have won privileges and exemptions informally, on a case-by-case basis. But pressures will increase to define their statuses and privileges in more formal ways. In the future, analytical journalists will seek more clearcut protection against irrelevant assignments and unauthorized changes in their copy—if not some journalistic analogue to formal rights of academic freedom.[31]

These tensions will be played out in the executive suites in the next decade as new editors are selected. If they come from the ranks of generalists, analytical journalism may continue to be seen as important, but somewhat of a deadend. If analytical journalists rise to the top, its practice will be rewarded. The feelings will be not unlike those expressed by academics about the appointment of a dean or president —will he or she be one of us, nourishing the values we respect, or just another "manager"? The economics of modern journalism will play a critical role, with many profit-minded publishers seeking leadership that will increase circulation and advertising revenue. One of the strongest countervailing pressures to the advance of a more analytical journalism will come from such publishers, who will want gossipy features and splashy new sections devoted to hobbies or housewares rather than an increase in the allotment of serious journalism. Serious journalists of the type I have described are going to become more militant about trivialization of the news. But the powers of journalists and publishers are unequal. The outcomes are highly uncertain.

In addition to the foregoing, which are struggles within the journalistic profession, tensions between this emerging class of journalists and social scientists may also increase. In an earlier time, social scientists were wary of popularizations and oversimplifications of their work in the mass media. Journalists were viewed as the boobs who might hold them up to ridicule. Now the concern is that journalists will cream off their work without giving proper credit, a concern highlighted recently when a UCLA psychiatrist sued a journalist, Gail Sheehy, for plagiarizing his work.[32] Resolution of these tensions will draw journalists into consideration of more thoughtful codes of ethics and more careful attribution and acknowledgment of sources. The *New York Times* will never appear with footnotes, but the day may not be far off when some stories will end with a paragraph or two of agate type giving a more careful account of interviews and scholarly sources that cannot be easily acknowledged in the body of an article.

The kind of interaction that journalists and social scientists achieve will bear importantly on the development of the Type III journalist. This new form of journalism seems likely to develop in one of two ways: toward the analytical style sketched out here, heavily influenced by social science models, or toward free-standing social criticism. Although social criticism has a long and honorable tradition, it is also much more open to abuse.[33] The social critic gives dominance to personal expression. What matters is filtering a question through his or her sensibility and expressing an opinion about it. It can easily degenerate into the application of a fairly predictable ideological stance, as it sometimes does in the columns of William Safire or Anthony Lewis, for example. What is often missing in social criticism is a certain kneading of the dough, a submission to disciplined interaction with others. Analytical journalists who are oriented to social science models will give dominance to the quality of the data, tests for it, synthesis, reading into and around a topic, and exploration of the complexities. They will be distinguished by greater detachment and more careful acknowledgment of sources. In the writings of the social critic, voice dominates data, whereas the contrary is true for the analyst.[34]

Journalists are not fixed in typologies, but develop in dynamic relationship to opportunities and interactions with significant others, most of which still occur after entry rather than in formal training prior to launching a career. Social scientists can influence that dynamic process toward the analytical model in several ways. They can be more circumspect in using the word "journalism" as a pejorative and acknowledge the real achievements of many analytically oriented journalists as persons who, if they are not colleagues, are fellow members of a fraternity of scrupulous observers and interpreters of the social world.[35] Instead of putting up fences and drawing moats around an illusory world of pure social science, they can recognize the commonalities and the possibilities of cooperation. More sabbaticals for journalists are needed, and more social scientists should venture into newsrooms and television studios as members of survey teams or as advisers and subeditors. Serious journalists should be welcomed into professional academic associations as associate members.[36] Graduate students with a bent for journalism should be encouraged to experiment in that direction without feeling they have made an unalterable choice or turned their backs on "science." Social scientists should provide more responsible criticism of media performance, giving recognition to exemplary performance, perhaps by establishing awards that would rival the Pulitzers, and providing specific and detailed analyses of the shortcomings of the press along with suggested practicable remedies. In short, there has been too much condemnation of the press, some of it self-serving, and too little appreciation of the actualities and imaginative possibilities of more productive interactions between journalists and social scientists. What is at stake is nothing less than securing a basis for more intelligent human action in a democratic society.

NOTES

Work on this essay was supported by a Spencer Fellowship of the National Academy of Education.

1. Max Weber, "Politics as a Vocation," in H. H. Gerth and C. Wright Mills, eds., *From Max Weber: Essays in Sociology* (New York: Oxford University Press, 1958), p. 97; A. J. Liebling, *The Press* (New York: Ballantine Books, 1961); George Lundberg, *Imperial Hearst* (New York: Equinox Cooperative Press, 1936); and Warren Breed, "Social Control in the Newsroom," *Social Forces* 33 (1955): 326–35.

2. For a sampling of recent criticism in this vein, see Edward J. Epstein, "Journalism and Truth," *Commentary* 57 (April 1974); Daniel P. Moynihan, "The Presidency and the Press," *Commentary* 54 (1971); Paul H. Weaver, "The New Journalism and the Old—Thoughts After Watergate," *The Public Interest* 35 (1974): 67–88; and, in the humanistic tradition, brilliant and outraged, Leopold Tyrmand, "The Media Shangri-La," *American Scholar* (1975/76): 752–75. More theoretically oriented examinations of the journalist's role may be found in Joseph Bensman and Robert Lilienfeld, *Craft and Consciousness: Occupational Technique and the Development of World Images* (New York: John Wiley, 1973), and Barbara Phillips, "The Artists of Everyday Life: Journalists, Their Craft, and Their Consciousness (Ph.D. diss., Syracuse University, 1975).

3. The police reporter, like all ideal types, is a stereotype. To some degree these tendencies are shared by all reporters who staff pressrooms in the Pentagon, city hall, and other institutions, and are fed a steady diet of press releases, sometimes to distract them from other news less flattering to officials. Richard Goodwin once described to a group of Nieman fellows at Harvard the "snow jobs" or blizzards of paper generated in the Johnson White House for just such purposes. Not all reporters assigned to beats get lost in those storms or are simple transmitters, of course. Given the constraints of time and competitive pressures, and the need to shift rapidly from one story to another (particularly for so-called "general assignment" reporters), some do miraculously well in rising to more penetrating levels of reportage.

4. Timothy Crouse, in *The Boys on the Bus* (New York: Ballantine, 1974), vividly describes the reporters crowding around Walter Mears of the Associated Press after a debate in the 1972 presidential campaign and shouting, "Walter, Walter, what's our lead?" (p. 22). Some who deviated from the AP's norm had to answer call-backs from their home offices to explain why they did not have the same lead that Mears's wrote for the AP. Stewart Alsop also wrote about reporters traveling in a pack with the "anxious, preoccupied, self important air of beagles" on a hunt. "The beagle is a highly competitive dog, but he is always ready to follow uncritically any other beagle who claims to have smelled a rabbit."

5. Murray Kempton, *Harper's*, August 1974.

6. Leonard Downie, Jr., an editor on the *Washington Post* who has worked with many investigative reporters, notes that he had to work with them "in an adversary way, since an investigative reporter does not record an event in an objective fashion. He subjectively presents what amounts to his theory of the

evidence against someone he believes has done something wrong. He can be no more impartial about his inquiry than a good police detective or prosecutor, no matter how hard he tries. It is up to the editor to maintain the distance that the reporter has lost and bring to the story the skepticism that the reporter can no longer muster." Downie, *The New Muckrakers: An Inside Look at America's Investigative Reporters* (Washington: New Republic Book Co., 1976) p. 39.

7. The newspapers named "fairest and most reliable" in a recent survey of journalists would constitute a list of those employing many Type III journalists. In rank order, they were: the *New York Times, Washington Post, Wall Street Journal, Christian Science Monitor, Los Angeles Times, St. Louis Post-Dispatch, Chicago Tribune, Washington Star, Milwaukee Journal, Miami Herald, Louisville Courier-Journal, Boston Globe, Minneapolis Tribune,* and *Baltimore Sun.* I would add the *Chicago Sun-Times, Atlanta Constitution,* and *Providence Journal* as papers with the resources and ambitions to support at least a sprinkling of Type III journalists. The ranking is reported in John W. C. Johnstone, Edward J. Slawski, and William Bowman, *The Newspeople: A Sociological Portrait of American Journalists and Their Work* (Urbana: University of Illinois Press, 1976), p. 224.

8. Nearly 11 percent of all journalists earned more than $20,000 in 1970. Nearly a fourth of younger journalists now have some graduate training, 56 percent of them in fields other than journalism. Training in the social sciences (17 percent) is strong, and other fields include English (10 percent), history (8 percent), education (5 percent) and law (3 percent). The percentage with some graduate training drops from 23 percent of the journalists aged 25 to 34 to 14 percent of those over 55. Johnstone et al., *The Newspeople,* pp. 200–203.

9. Johnstone's data also support contemporary criticism about the liberal bias of the elite media, where 52 percent of the journalists and 63 percent of the news executives characterize themselves as left-leaning, compared to 40 percent of the reporters and 29 percent of the executives among the nonelite sector. Johnstone et al., *The Newspeople,* p. 226. Jews are also overrepresented on elite media, where 10 percent of the staffs are Jewish, compared with 4 percent among the nonelite.

10. Michael T. Kaufman, "Tradition a Big Barrier in Kenya's Marriage-Reform Drive," *New York Times,* 23 October 1976.

11. Steven V. Roberts's recent discussion of class identities in an analysis of a *Times* survey ("Social Mobility Found Key to U.S. Views on Class," 24 April 1978) is another example of what I describe later in this essay as a theoretically informed style: "The survey's purpose was to determine what the idea of class means to Americans today. . . . Three-quarters of those polled said that they did belong to a social class, and close to half said that the main factor determining class identity is income, but few demonstrated a strong class consciousness. Only 2 percent identified themselves as members of the upper class, and 8 percent put themselves in the lower class. The rest split evenly between the middle class and the working class, but few Americans mean working class in the classic Marxist sense of an oppressed proletariat. . . . The poll demonstrates that one reason few Americans seem to have developed a strong class consciousness is that they feel rapid mobility between classes is possible. . . ." Yet another is Kenneth A. Briggs, "Psychiatry and Religion: A Rapprochement," *New York Times,* 21 April 1978: "In separate, often conflicting ways, both religion and psychiatry attempt to cure the loss of purpose and meaning. But since the turn of the century, when Sigmund Freud proclaimed his atheism, the two fields have tended to see each other as threats and competitors. . . . Underlying much of the strain of the past was a battle for authority and status. The claims of religion were in the midst of staggering challenges from science when psychiatry began to emerge as a further alternative to explain human nature. Many believed psychology would replace religion. . . ."

12. Phillip Knightley, *The First Casualty: From the Crimea to Vietnam: The War Correspondent as Hero, Propagandist, and Myth Maker* (New York: Harcourt Brace Jovanovich, 1975), especially chaps. 8 and 16. However, Peter

Braestrup argues that his fellow correspondents in Vietnam went so far in their reactions to official half-truths that they erred on the side of chronic pessimism and were too ready to believe the worst about American conduct of the war while accepting inflated estimates of Communist successes. Braestrup, *Big Story: How the American Press and Television Reported and Interpreted the Crisis of Tet 1968 in Vietnam and Washington* (New York: Doubleday, 1978).

13. Transcript of an interview published in *Newsweek*, 30 December 1974, p. 32; and report of his farewell talk at the National Press Club, *New York Times*, 10 January 1977.

14. Steele adds that he does draw upon expert sources, but that comes after independent analysis: "After we've got all the information we can find and have come to some tentative conclusions, we try them out on expert sources . . . authorities on different subjects all over the country." This is analogous to the practice of social scientists, who circulate drafts of their work for comment prior to publication. Quoted in Downie, *The New Muckrakers*, pp. 99–100.

15. See Morris Janowitz, *The Community Press in an Urban Setting* (Chicago: University of Chicago Press, 1967); and Phillips, "The Artists of Everyday Life," particularly chap. 3, "The Journalist as a Bricoleur."

16. Robert E. Park, "Life History," *American Journal of Sociology* 79, (1973): 255. I am indebted to Barbara Phillips for drawing this to my attention.

17. Ari L. Goldman, "Poll Finds 70 Percent of Residents Back Ousted Queens Board," *New York Times*, 20 March 1978.

18. Edward B. Fiske, "City is Rated High in Teacher Pay," *New York Times*, 8 September 1975.

19. Maurice Carroll, "Jackson Won in New York by Narrowly Based Voting: Did Best in Queens with Jews and Moderates," *New York Times*, 8 April 1976. Another recent example would be the charts, covering nearly half a page, that compared students graduating from high school in 1973 and 1978, showing significant declines in the percentages who completed academic courses in English and math. Samuel Weiss and Edward B. Fiske, "Rigorous High School Courses Attract Fewer in New York City," *New York Times*, 23 March 1978.

20. David M. Rubin, "Remember Swine Flu?" *Columbia Journalism Review* 16 (July/August 1977): 42–46. Rubin surveyed coverage in nineteen papers, the United Press International, and the three major television newscasts for the week the swine flu inoculation program began. He cited four papers—the *New York Times*, *Washington Post*, *Los Angeles Times*, and *Miami Herald*—for their distinguished coverage, and noted that although coverage elsewhere was superficial, it was "with few exceptions, neither sensational nor inaccurate."

21. Talcott Parsons and Gerald Platt describe such persons as intellectuals as "generalists," those who provide "cultural definitions of the situation." See Parsons and Platt, *The American University* (Cambridge: Harvard University Press, 1973), p. 267.

22. In response to my essay "The 'New' Journalism We Need," *Columbia Journalism Review* 9 (Spring 1970), a Princeton historian wrote: "It's too bad that your fantasied collaboration between newspapermen and academics has never proved feasible. The two worlds don't get along well together at all, I've found."

23. Academic contributions have been particularly evident in the *Washington Post*'s "Outlook" section, and the *Times*'s business pages. Marilyn M. Machlowitz, a doctoral candidate in psychology at Yale, provides an example of the new marriage with her examination of the way psychologists and psychiatrists have influenced corporate management, "An Age of Industrial Psychiatry," *New York Times*, 3 April 1977.

24. Although Chris Argyris concluded that the *New York Times* (thinly disguised as "The Daily Planet" in his *Behind the Front Page* [San Francisco: Jossey-Bass, 1974]) was not willing to act on the implications of his analysis, anyone who knows anything about the internal dynamics of most newspapers can recognize what a dramatic step it was for the *Times* to invite Argyris into its inner sanctums, allowing him to interview all top news and editorial personnel, to observe and

tape record at will any meeting between two or more persons, and to work with teams of executives with the aim of creating "newspapers that are self-examining" (p. ix). An example of research of a more conventional sort was the action of both the New York Times and the Washington Post in commissioning the Metropolitan Studies Program at Syracuse University to do studies of the tax burdens in their respective cities.

25. Academic invitations to journalists to participate in research projects are rare, but they are one indication that some academics are paying more attention to serious-minded colleagues in journalistic fields. A group of the nation's leading geographers recently asked Theodore Shabad of the New York Times to join them in a two-year study of the impact of Soviet natural resources on the world economy.

26. "In-house Press Critics: A Selection of Recent Work by Newspaper Ombudsmen," Columbia Journalism Review 16 (July/August 1977): 48–52. The Washington Post, Boston Globe, Sacramento Bee, and Washington Star were among those sampled. The New York Times has not appointed an official critic, but it has made a point in recent years of examining the press's role in creating or distorting news events, and looked at other aspects of press performance, as, for example, in Joseph Lelyveld's examination of the presidential primary as a "media event": "Press, TV and Politics," 31 January 1976. Leopold Tyrmand's stinging critique of the press in the American Scholar fails to take account of these developments, although it remains true that some papers, when obliged to publish corrections, seem to feel wronged, as though they "were paying a brutally exacted tribute."

27. The Council grew out of a task force organized by the Twentieth Century Fund in 1971 and was established with two purposes: "To examine and to report on complaints concerning the accuracy and fairness of news reporting in the United States, as well as to initiate studies and report on issues involving the freedom of the press."

28. Richard Cohen, "Haldeman Book Creates a Journalistic Stir," Washington Post, 21 February 1978.

29. As noted earlier, this leads to criticisms that mistake a part for the whole. For example, Laurel R. Walum, discussing the "processes by which sociology is transformed into journalism," criticizes reporting of a paper she delivered at a meeting of the American Sociological Association. She lauds Israel Shenker of the Times for his "imaginative rendering and interpretation" of her work, but criticizes the widespread use of his story by reporters who cribbed from it and trivialized it. His imaginative interpretation became the "facts" for others. This is a classic instance of the style of Type I reporters, only in this case they are treating the story of a Type III journalist (Shenker) as the authoritative source or press release. But Walum writes as if, with the exception of Shenker, all journalists could be equated with Type I reporters. See Walum, "Sociology and the Mass Media: Some Major Problems and Modest Proposals," The American Sociologist 10 (1975): 28–32. Some of Edward Jay Epstein's criticism, as in his essay, "Did the Press Uncover Watergate?" Commentary 58 (July 1974): 21–24, sets up the Type II journalist as the straw man for all.

30. Argyris, Behind the Front Page, p. 10.

31. A small step in this direction occurred at the Washington Post in the mid-1960s when reporters insisted on inserting a clause in their contract prohibiting an editor from putting a reporter's byline on a story when the reporter objected, either because of the way it was edited, or for any other reason.

32. Sheehy's articles appeared originally in New York magazine, and later as a book, Passages: Predictable Crises of Adult Life (New York: E. P. Dutton, 1976). The psychiatrist, Roger Gould, won a settlement that included a payment of $10,000 and 10 percent of the royalties.

33. Paul Starr writes brilliantly of the different orientations of the social critic and social scientist in "The Edge of Social Science," Harvard Educational Review 44 (1974): 393–415.

34. Thus, a *New York Times* reporter who had been given advanced training in survey research moved away from it after a few years, telling a former colleague that writing articles based on surveys was "too limiting."

35. For a marvelous discussion of this topic by two editors of journals that bridge the worlds of social science and journalism, see Irving Louis Horowitz and Paul Barker, "Mediating Journals: Reaching Out to a Public Beyond the Scientific Community," *International Social Science Journal* 26 (1974): 393–403, and the discussion on pp. 403–10.

36. Perhaps a new association should be formed with the aim of furthering the convergence between journalism and social science, especially if it could be done in such a way as to attract leaders in both fields. More short-term institutes are also needed where journalists and academics could share perspectives on common fields of inquiry and concern: opinion polling, race and desegregation, economic issues (still a scandalously weak area on many newspapers), and ethics, to suggest a few. While some editors and publishers have adopted more enlightened attitudes about freeing reporters for such activity, many have not; such an association could help to prepare the ground for more liberal policies by educating the editors and setting new standards of continuing education.

EPILOGUE

EVERETT C. HUGHES

A *Festschrift* is written to honor a man at a certain point in his career. It is assumed that more of his career lies behind him than ahead of him. It is also assumed that it has been a very successful career. The people who write for the *Festschrift* have had some part in that career. Their own careers have been strongly affected by his. Usually they are younger than he.

It is out of order for me to write about Riesman. I am older than he, and past my prime. But I have played and occasionally worked with him for about thirty years. Many others have known him well and could write more accurately and sensitively about his life and his work. He has lighted the torches of many now distinguished persons. Many of them have written about him in widely circulated organs. His name and his work are known far beyond academic circles.

Karl Mannheim would limit use of the word "career" to the course of a man through a bureaucracy. In that course, he knows what duties, what deference, what emoluments are his due at each step. One starts at the bottom of the ladder, enters by the right gate, takes the right turns, weds the right spouse, learns the skills and appropriate conduct.

David Riesman's career does not fit Mannheim's definition. None of his positions has been the accepted bureaucratic sequel to the one he has just left. He has never, I believe, moved from one rank to another in a particular institution. He can never be found on an organization chart.

He graduated from Harvard College with high honors in chemistry. It is said that the bottles broke when he entered the laboratory. He then went on to law school and finished with honors there, also. After that he served a year's legal novitiate under the mastership of Supreme Court Justice Brandeis. The next step was a teaching post in the law school of the University of Buffalo. Then came the practice of law in a Boston firm: while there he learned to keep talking firmly and clearly when the judge listening to his brief fell asleep. Judges wakened from sleep by the silence of the lawyer decide for the other side.

At this point he began to teach social science in the College of the University of Chicago. He began to be spoken of as a "sociologist." He has a professional degree in law and a bagful of honorary degrees of one kind or another, but he does not have an earned degree in sociology.

The teaching of social science in the College at Chicago was done by a team. A team, one should add, of individualists. After some years he was appointed a University Professor at Harvard. His chair was in the Social Sciences, but he attached himself firmly to the sociologists at Harvard, first in the Department of Social Relations, and after it disintegrated into its former parts, in the Department of Sociology. He is as near to being officially a sociologist as he ever will be. But if he is a voting member of a department of sociology, he still seeks his colleagues by instinct. He finds them everywhere. He is an undepartmentalized man.

If Riesman has not had a career in Karl Mannheim's bureaucratic sense, he has stuck firmly to his course in another sense. Even as an undergraduate, long before he turned to sociology, he had become interested in how people function in societies, and how education can help them do so. While a college student at Harvard, David Riesman once went to Labrador, where he studied the world view people gained there, and what was being done to improve their knowledge and understanding of their condition. When he finally went into teaching, he pursued basically the same interests, although far more extensively and intensively.

For about the last twenty years, one of his primary interests has been undergraduate and graduate education. During much of that period, he has been deeply engaged in the work of the Carnegie Commission on Higher Education. In this capacity, he has traveled the country to study American colleges and universities, and has written books and parts of books about them. He has been awarded a large number of honorary degrees. In each case the institution gets more than it gives, for he steps up to the platform armed with more data about the history, present condition, and prospects of the granting institution than most of its faculty, administrators, and alumni have. He gives them something of an education then and there. He cooperates with the people who are in the "education" business, and he is at present holding a seminar at the Harvard School of Education. The students are themselves administrators in institutions of higher education. I would wager that while they have great stacks of facts about many institutions, they will find that Riesman has more basic knowledge about them and their problems than they have. His gift is that of seeing the deeper structure in masses of facts. However, the getting of the facts is not a gift. It is the result of unbelievably hard work.

When we both lived and taught at the University of Chicago, he at the undergraduate college and I in the Social Science Division, we both worked hard. He worked harder than I, but we had time for long walks, time to see *My Fair Lady* and other plays, time for dinners and parties. As the years went on he had less time for such things. His only leisure activity became work itself. That work consisted more and more of participating in the work, the thinking, the learning, and the teaching of others. He got into more and more studies of education. He got more and more people at work on each of his projects. I wish one could say that he delegated more and more of his work to others. There was no such calculus. The more he took on, the more he delegated to himself. More was done by everyone in his orbit: himself, his wife and constant companion, his collaborators, his students. And his orbit still increases. There is talk of *total* war, make it *total* work and you have David Riesman.

A BIBLIOGRAPHY OF
DAVID RIESMAN'S PUBLICATIONS

1939

"Possession and the Law of Finders." *Harvard Law Review* 52:
1105–34.
"Under Thirty." *Atlantic*, January, p. 96.

1940

"Government Service and the American Constitution." *University
of Chicago Law Review* 7:655–75.
"Legislative Restrictions on Foreign Enlistment and Travel." *Colum-
bia Law Review* 40:793–835.
Review of *Punishment and Social Structure*, by O. Kirchheimer and
G. Rusche. *Columbia Law Review* 40:1297–1301.

1941

"The American Constitution and International Labor Legislation."
International Labor Review 44:123–93.
"Government Education for Democracy." *Public Opinion Quarterly*
5:195–209.
"Law and Social Science: A Report on Michael and Wechsler's Class-
book on Criminal Law and Administration." *Yale Law Journal*
50:636–53.
Review of *Juvenile Delinquents Grown Up*, by Sheldon and Eleanor
Glueck. *Columbia Law Review* 41:358–62.

Review of *The Majority of the People,* by Edwin Mims, Jr. *Iowa Law Review* 27:355–58.

"What's Wrong with the Interventionists?" *Common Sense* 10: 327–30.

1942

"The Cash Customer." *Common Sense* 11:183–85.

"Civil Liberties in a Period of Transition." In Carl J. Friedrich and Edward Mason, eds., *Public Policy,* 3:33–96.

"Democracy and Defamation: Control of Group Libel." *Columbia Law Review* 42:727–80.

"Democracy and Defamation: Fair Game and Fair Comment I." *Columbia Law Review* 42:1085–1123.

"Democracy and Defamation: Fair Game and Fair Comment II." *Columbia Law Review* 42:1282–1318.

"Equality and Social Structure." *Journal of Legal and Political Sociology* 1:72–95.

"The Politics of Persecution." *Public Opinion Quarterly* 6:41–56.

1943

"An International Bill of Rights." *Proceedings of the American Law Institute* 20:198–204.

1944

"The Present State of Civil Liberty Theory." *Journal of Politics* 6:323–37.

1947

"The Ethics of 'We Happy Few.' " *University Observer* 1:19–28.
    Reprinted in *Individualism Reconsidered* (1954), pp. 39–54.

"Some Observations on Community Plans and Utopia." *Yale Law Journal* 57:173–20.
    Reprinted in *Individualism Reconsidered* (1954), pp. 70–98.

"Toward an Anthropological Science of Law and the Legal Profession." Lecture to the introductory graduate course in sociology and anthropology at the University of Chicago. December.
    Revised as "Some Observations on Law and Psychology," and delivered at the meeting of the Association of American Law Schools. December 1950.

Reprinted in *University of Chicago Law Review* 19(1951): 30–44.

Reprinted as "Toward an Anthropological Science of Law and the Legal Profession" in *Individualism Reconsidered* (1954), pp. 440–66.

Reprinted in *American Journal of Sociology* 57(1957):121–35.

1948

"Men, Women, and Marriage," a review of *Emotional Security*, by Milton R. Sapirstein, M.D. *Nation*.

"A Philosophy for 'Minority' Living." *Commentary* 6:413–22.

1949

"The Meaning of Opinion." With Nathan Glazer. *Public Opinion Quarterly* 12:633–48.

Reprinted, abridged, in *Individualism Reconsidered* (1954), pp. 492–507.

"Of Men and Women," a review of *Male and Female: a Study of the Sexes in a Changing World*, by Margaret Mead. *Nation*.

"The Saving Remnant." In John W. Chase, ed., *The Years of the Modern*. New York: Longmans, Green, & Co. Pp. 115–47.

Reprinted in *Individualism Reconsidered* (1954), pp. 99–120.

"Social Structure, Character Structure, and Opinion." With Nathan Glazer. *International Journal of Opinion and Attitude Research* 2:512–27.

1950

"Authority and Liberty in the Structure of Freud's Thought." *Psychiatry* 13:167–87.

Excerpts reprinted in the *University of Chicago Roundtable*, no. 638, 18 June 1950, pp. 20–32.

"Criteria for Political Apathy." With Nathan Glazer. In Alvin Gouldner, ed., *Studies in Leadership*. New York: Harper & Bros. Pp. 505–56.

"Do the Mass Media 'Escape' from Politics?" With Reuel Denney. In Bernard Berelson and Morris Janowitz, eds., *Reader in Public Opinion and Mass Communications*. Glencoe, Ill.: Free Press. Pp. 327–33.

"Freud, Religion, and Science." Lecture to the Channing Club of the University of Chicago. 9 January.

Published, abridged, as "Freud: Religion As Neurosis" in the University of Chicago *Roundtable*, no. 638, 18 June 1950, pp. 13–20.

Reprinted, abridged, as "Freud, Religion and Science" in *American Scholar* 20(1951):267–76.

Reprinted in full in *Chicago Review*, Winter/Spring 1954, pp. 18–45.

"From Morality to Morale." Lecture at the Washington School of Psychiatry.

In Alfred H. Stanton and Stewart E. Perry, eds., *Personality and Political Crisis: New Perspectives from Psychiatry and Social Science for the Study of War and Politics*. Glencoe, Ill.: Free Press, 1951. Pp. 81–120.

"Langdon Narbeth." In *Social Sciences 2, Syllabus and Selected Readings*. Staff enterprise. Chicago: University of Chicago Press. 2:121–35.

"Listening to Popular Music." *American Quarterly* 2:359–71.

The Lonely Crowd: A Study of the Changing American Character. With the collaboration of Reuel Denney and Nathan Glazer. New Haven, Conn.: Yale University Press.

Abridged paperback edition. Garden City, N.Y.: Doubleday, Anchor Books, 1953.

Yale paperback edition, with new Introduction. New Haven: Yale University Press, 1961.

Revised edition, with new Introduction. New Haven: Yale University Press, 1969.

Foreign editions: Czechoslovakian, Danish, Dutch, French, German, Hungarian, Indian, Italian, Japanese, Korean, Polish, Portuguese, Serbo-Croatian, Spanish, Swedish.

The Lonely Crowd [*From Morality to Morale: Changes in the Agents of Character Formation*]. Osamu Fukushima and Saikichi Nakashima, eds. Tokyo: Eyosha Ltd., 1973.

"The Neurotic Child," a review of *Love is Not Enough: The Treatment of Emotionally Disturbed Children*, by Bruno Bettelheim. *Nation*.

"One From the Gallery: An Experiment in the Interpretation of an Interview." With Nathan Glazer. Part 1. *International Journal of Opinion and Attitude Research* 4:515–50.

Part 2. *International Journal of Opinion and Attitude Research* 5(1951):53–78.

"Political Apathy in America." An NBC Radio Discussion by Herman Finer, Granville Hicks, and David Riesman. In the University of Chicago *Roundtable*, no. 657, 29 October, pp. 1–13.

Review of *The Open Self,* by Charles Morris. *American Journal of Sociology* 55:511–12.
Review of *The Human Group,* by George C. Homans. *New Republic.*
Review of *Men of Good Hope: A Story of American Progressives,* by Danial Aaron. *New Republic.*
"Tensions, Optimism, and the Social Scientist," an essay review of *Tensions That Cause Wars,* A UNESCO Conference Study, edited by Hadley Cantril. *Psychiatry* 13:518–22.
"The Themes of Heroism and Weakness in the Structure of Freud's Thought." *Psychiatry* 13:301–15.
"The Themes of Work and Play in the Structure of Freud's Thought." *Psychiatry* 13:1–16.

1951

"Bookworms and the Social Soil." *Saturday Review of Literature,* 5 May, pp. 31–32.
Reprinted in *Individualism Reconsidered* (1954), pp. 258–65.
"Comments on the Jewish Student." *Commentary* 11:524–25.
"Football in America: A Study in Culture Diffusion." With Reuel Denney. *American Quarterly* 3:309–25.
Reprinted in *Perspectives U.S.A.,* no. 13, pp. 108–29.
Reprinted in Leroy N. Rieselbach and George Balch, eds., *Psychology and Politics: An Introductory Reader.* New York: Holt, Rinehart & Winston, 1968.
"How Different May One Be?" *Child Study* 28:29–30.
Reprinted in *Individualism Reconsidered* (1954), pp. 266–70.
"Individualism Reconsidered." In A. William Loos, ed., *Religious Faith and World Culture.* New York: Prentice-Hall. Pp. 61–77.
Reprinted in *Individualism Reconsidered* (1954), pp. 26–38.
"Keeping Up With the Others." *Commonweal* 54:621–23.
"Leisure in Urbanized America." With Reuel Denney. In Paul K. Hatt and Albert J. Reiss, Jr., eds., *A Reader in Urban Sociology.* Glencoe, Ill.: Free Press. Pp. 469–80.
"The 'Militant' Fight Against Anti-Semitism." *Commentary* 11:11–19.
Reprinted in *Individualism Reconsidered* (1954), pp. 139–52.
"The Nylon War." *Common Cause* 4:279–85.
Reprinted in *Christian Century* 48(1951):554.
Reprinted in *Etc.* 8:163–70.
Reprinted in H. W. Sams and W. F. McNeir, eds., *New Problems in Reading and Writing.* New York: Prentice-Hall, 1953. Pp. 480–88.

Reprinted in *Individualism Reconsidered* (1954), pp. 426–34.

Reprinted, with introduction added, as "The Cold War" in Eugen Weber, ed., *The Western Tradition 1815–1984*. State University of Iowa, 1956. 2:307–17.

Reprinted in *Abundance for What?* (1964), pp. 67–79.

"The Path of Total Terror," an essay review of *The Origins of Totalitarianism*, by Hannah Arendt. *Commentary* 11:392–98.

Review of *The American as Reformer*, by Arthur M. Schlesinger. *American Journal of Sociology* 56:597–98.

Review of *The Effects of Mass Media: A Report on the Public Library Inquiry*, by Joseph T. Klapper. *Library Quarterly* 21:45–46.

Review of *Hollywood: The Dream Factory*, by Hortense Powdermaker. *American Journal of Sociology* 56:589–92.

"Some Observations Concerning Marginality." *Phylon: A Journal of Race and Culture* 12:113–27.

Reprinted in *Individualism Reconsidered* (1954), pp. 153–65.

"Some Observations on the Limits of Totalitarian Power." Address to the American Committee on Cultural Freedom. 28 November. *Antioch Review* 12(1952):155–68.

Reprinted in *Individualism Reconsidered* (1954), pp. 414–25.

Reprinted in *Abundance for What?* (1964), pp. 80–92.

"Some Observations on Social Science Research." With Nathan Glazer. *Antioch Review* 11:259–78.

Reprinted in *Individualism Reconsidered* (1954), pp. 467–83.

"Some Problems of a Course in 'Culture and Personality.'" *Journal of General Education* 5:122–36.

"Two Adolescents." *Psychiatry* 14:161–211.

1952

"Ambassadors to the Machine." *Griffin* 1:6–11.

Faces in the Crowd: Individual Studies in Character and Politics. With the collaboration of Nathan Glazer. New Haven: Yale University Press.

Paperback edition, abridged, with new Preface. New Haven: Yale University Press, 1965.

"The Fitness of the Social System," a review of *The Social System*, by Talcott Parsons. *Psychiatry* 15:478–81.

Introduction to *Commentary on the American Scene*, edited by Elliott Cohen. New York: Alfred A. Knopf.

"A Lecture on Veblen." *Journal of General Education* 6:214–23.

"Leisure in an Industrial Civilization." With Reuel Denney. In Eugene Staley, ed., *Creating an Industrial Civilization: A Report* on the Corning Conference. New York: Harper & Bros. Pp. 245–81.

"Modest Rationalization," a review of *Cultural Sciences: Their Origin and Development*, by Florian Znaniecki. *Progressive*, November, pp. 35–36.

"Movies and Audiences." With Evelyn T. Riesman. *American Quarterly* 4:195–202.

"Our Country and Our Culture." *Partisan Review* 19:310–15.
> Reprinted in *America and the Intellectuals, A Symposium*. Partisan Review Series, no. 4. New York, 1953. Pp. 95–99.

Review of *Dogma and Compulsion: Psychoanalytic Studies of Religion and Myths*, by Theodor Reik. *American Journal of Sociology* 58:118–19.

Review of *English Life and Leisure: A Social Study*, by B. Seebohm Rowntree and G. R. Lavers. *American Journal of Sociology* 57:600–602.

Review of *Men in Business: Essays in the History of Entrepreneurship*, edited by William Miller. *American Quarterly* 4:179–86.

Review of *They Went to College: The College Graduate in America Today*, by Ernest Havemann and Patricia Salter West. *New Republic*, 5 May, pp. 19–20.

Review of *The Uprooted*, by Oscar Handlin. *Progressive*, January, pp. 40–41.

Review of *White Collar*, by C. Wright Mills. *American Journal of Sociology* 57:513–15.
> Reprinted in *Scienza Nuova* (Oxford) (1954–55):62–65.

"Some Observations on Changes in Leisure Attitudes." *Antioch Review* 12:417–36.
> Reprinted in *The Antioch Review Anthology*, edited by Paul Bixler. New York: World Publishers, 1953.
> Reprinted in *Individualism Reconsidered* (1954), pp. 202–18.

"Some Observations on the Study of American Character." *Psychiatry* 15:333–38.

"Values in Context." *American Scholar* 22:29–39.
> Reprinted in *Individualism Reconsidered* (1954), pp. 17–25.

1953

"The American Scene in *Commentary*'s Mirror." *Commentary* 15:172–77.

"Arts, the Sciences, and Humanity." *New Republic*, 12 January, p. 18.

"Conspicuous Production." *Listener* 49:1009.

"Marginality, Conformity and Insight." Lecture delivered at Smith College. 12 March.

Reprinted in *Phylon* 14:241–57.

Reprinted in *Individualism Reconsidered* (1954), pp. 166–78.

"New Front." *Time*, 23 November, p. 97.

"New Standards for Old: From Conspicuous Consumption to Conspicuous Production." Lecture delivered in Barnard College series on "The Search for New Standards in Modern America." 10 March.

Reprinted in *Individualism Reconsidered* (1954), pp. 219–31.

"Psychological Types and National Character: An Informal Commentary." *American Quarterly* 5:325–43.

Reprinted in Hennig Cohen, ed., *The American Culture: Approaches to the Study of the United States*. Boston: Houghton Mifflin Co., 1968. Pp. 119–35.

"Quelques Remarques sur les Modifications à la Conception des Loisirs" ["Some Changes in Leisure Attitudes"]. *Profils* (France), October, pp. 104–22.

"Recreation and the Recreationist." Lecture delivered at the Chicago Conference on a Federal Department of Welfare. 27 February.

Reprinted in *Marriage and Family Living* 16:21–26.

"The Social and Psychological Setting of Veblen's Economic Theory." *Journal of Economic History* 13:449–61.

Delivered as a lecture to the Economic History Association, Bryn Mawr College. September 1953.

Reprinted in *Individualism Reconsidered* (1954), pp. 273–85.

Reprinted in *Abundance for What?* (1964), pp. 374–87.

"Some Observations on Intellectual Freedom." *American Scholar* 23:9–25.

Reprinted in *Individualism Reconsidered* (1954), pp. 123–38.

"Some Relationships between Technical Progress and Social Progress." Address to a Conference on Social and Technical Progress, Foreign Student Summer Project at MIT, Greenfield, New Hampshire. 28 August.

In *Explorations in Entrepreneurial History* 6(1954):131–46.

Reprinted in *Individualism Reconsidered* (1954), pp. 286–303.

"The Study of Kansas City: An Informal Overture." *University of Kansas City Review* 20:15–22.

Reprinted as "The Study of the City." *City Lights* (1953), no. 4 pp. 3–9.

Thorstein Veblen: A Critical Interpretation. New York: Scribner.

Paperback edition. New York: Scribner, 1960.

Reprint edition. New York: Seabury Press, 1975.

"Who Has the Power?" In Reinhard Bendix and S. M. Lipset, eds., *Class, Status and Power: A Reader in Social Stratification*. Glencoe, Ill.: Free Press. Pp. 154–162.

1954

"Freedom, New Style." *Time*, 27 September, pp. 22–25.

Individualism Reconsidered and Other Essays. Glencoe, Ill.: Free Press.

> Paperback edition, abridged. Garden City, N.Y.: Doubleday, Anchor Books, 1955.
>
> Paperback edition. Glencoe, Ill.: Free Press, 1964.
>
> Spanish edition. Buenos Aires: Editorial Paidos, 1974.

"Man and Machine in America." *Encounter*, September, pp. 32–37.

Review of *New Hopes for a Changing World*, by Bertrand Russell. *Scienza Nuova* (Oxford) 1(1954–55):56–60.

Review of *A Study of Power*, by Harold D. Lasswell, C. E. Merriam, and T. V. Smith. *Illinois Law Review*.

> Reprinted in *Scienza Nuova* (Oxford) 1(1954–55):60–61.

Review of *Symbolic Wounds: Puberty Rites and the Envious Male*, by Bruno Bettelheim. *Psychiatry* 17:300–303.

"Some Clinical and Cultural Aspects of Aging." *American Journal of Sociology* 59:379–83.

> Reprinted in *Individualism Reconsidered* (1954), pp. 484–91.

"Teachers Amid Changing Expectations." *Harvard Educational Review* 24:106–17.

> Further developed in "Thoughts on Teachers and Schools" in *Anchor Review* 1:27–60.
>
> Revised and expanded as "Secondary Education and 'Counter-Cyclical' Policy" in *Constraint and Variety in American Education* (1956), chapter 3, pp. 107–60.

"Veblen and the Higher Learning." *University of Chicago Magazine*, January, pp. 14–18

> Reprinted as Introduction to *The Higher Learning in America*, by Thorstein Veblen, Third printing. Stanford, Ca. Academic Reprints, 1954. Pp. ix–xx.

"Veblen's System of Social Science." *Explorations* 2:84–97.

1955

"A Career Drama in a Middle-Aged Farmer." *Bulletin of the Menninger Clinic* 19:1–8.

> Reprinted in *Abundance for What?* (1964), pp. 138–46.

"Careers and Consumer Behavior." With Howard Roseborough. In *Consumer Behavior*, edited by Lincoln Clark. New York: New York University Press. 2:1–18.

> Reprinted in *A Modern Introduction to the Family*, edited by

Norman W. Bell and Ezra F. Vogel. Glencoe, Ill.: Free Press, 1960. Pp. 143–62.

    Reprinted in *Abundance for What?* (1964), pp. 113–37.

"Comments on Dr. Kluckhohn's Paper." *Human Development Bulletin*, pp. 67–72, a response to a paper presented at the Sixth Annual Human Development Symposium, University of Chicago, in February 1955.

"Education Reconsidered." *Sarah Lawrence Alumnae Magazine*, May, pp. 3 and 17.

"Executive as Hero." With Eric Larrabee. *Fortune* 51:108.

    Expanded as "Company-Town Pastoral: The Role of Business in 'Executive Suite' " in Bernard Rosenberg and David Manning White, eds., *Mass Culture: The Popular Arts in America.* Glencoe, Ill.: Free Press, 1957. Pp. 325–37.

"The Intellectuals and the Discontented Classes." With Nathan Glazer. *Partisan Review* 22:47–72.

    Reprinted in Daniel Bell, ed., *The Radical Right: The New American Right.* Garden City, N.Y.: Doubleday, 1963. Pp. 87–114.

Introduction to *Automobile Workers and the American Dream*, by Ely Chinoy. Garden City, N.Y.: Doubleday. Pp. xi–xx.

"The Oral Tradition, the Written Word, and the Screen Image." Antioch College Founder's Day Lecture, no. 1. The Antioch College Press, Yellow Springs.

    Reprinted as "The Oral and Written Traditions." *Explorations: Studies in Culture and Communication* (Toronto) 6(1956): 22–30.

    Reprinted as "The Oral and Written Traditions" in E. S. Carpenter and M. McLuhan, eds., *Explorations in Communication.* Boston: Beacon Press, 1960. Pp. 109–16.

    Abridged and reprinted as "Books, Gunpowder of the Mind" in *Atlantic*, December 1957, pp. 123–64.

    Reprinted in Leo Hamalian and Edmond Volpe, eds., *Essays of Our Time.* New York: McGraw-Hill, 1960. 1:28–39.

"The Private School and Counter-Cyclical Education." *Exonian*, March, pp. 8–9.

"Self and Society: Reflections on Some Turks in Transition." With Daniel Lerner. *Explorations* 5:67–80.

    Reprinted in *Abundance for What?* (1964), pp. 402–417.

"Some Informal Notes on American Churches and Sects." *Confluence* 4:127–59.

    Reprinted with new Prologue in *Current: A Review of Catholicism in Contemporary Culture* 7(1966):17–35.

"Some Observations on the 'Older' and the 'Newer' Social Sciences." Address given on the occasion of celebrating the twenty-fifth anniversary of the Social Sciences Research Building at the University of Chicago. 11 November.

Reprinted in Leonard D. White, ed., *The State of the Social Sciences*. Chicago: University of Chicago Press, 1956. Pp. 319–39.

Further developed as "The Intellectual Veto Groups" in *Constraint and Variety* (1956), chapter 2, pp. 53–106.

1956

"Age and Sex in the Interview." With Mark Benney and Shirley A. Star. *American Journal of Sociology* 62:143–52.

"Asking and Answering." With Mark Benney. *Journal of Business of the University of Chicago* 29:225–36.

Constraint and Variety in American Education. Lincoln: University of Nebraska Press.

Paperback edition. Garden City, N.Y.: Doubleday, Anchor Books, 1958.

Paperback edition, with new Preface. Lincoln: University of Nebraska Press, 1965.

L'America Al Bivio Pedagogico. Florence: La Nuova Italia Editrice, 1974.

Landmark edition. Lincoln: University of Nebraska Press, 1977.

Introduction to *Crestwood Heights: A Study of the Culture of Suburban Life*, by John R. Seeley, R. Alexander Sim, and E. W. Loosley. New York: Basic Books. Pp v–xv.

Reprinted in *Abundance for What?* (1964), pp. 506–16.

"The Meandering Procession of American Academia." *Harvard Educational Review* 26:241–62.

Reprinted as "The Academic Procession" in *Constraint and Variety* (1956), pp. 15–52.

"Orbits of Tolerance, Interviewers, and Elites." *Public Opinion Quarterly* 20:49–73.

Reprinted in *Abundance For What?* (1964), pp. 540–67.

"The Sociology of the Interview." With Mark Benney. *Midwest Sociologist* 18:3–15.

Reprinted in *Abundance for What?* (1964), pp. 517–39.

"Some Continuities and Discontinuities in the Education of Women." Third John Dewey Memorial Lecture, Bennington College. June.

Reprinted in *Abundance for What?* (1964), pp. 324–48.

"Tocqueville and Associations: An Introduction." *Autonomous Groups* 12, no. 2, pp. 1–3.
"What They Think." *Newsweek*, 16 April, p. 105.

1957

"Autos in America." With Eric Larrabee. *Encounter*, May, pp. 26–36.
   Reprinted in *Der Monat* (Berlin), December 1957, pp. 14–24.
   Reprinted in Lincoln Clark, ed., *Consumer Behavior—Research on Consumer Reactions*. New York: Harper, 1958. Pp. 69–92.
   Reprinted in *Abundance for What?* (1964), pp. 270–99.
"Interviewers, Elites, and Academic Freedom." Paper presented for the twentieth anniversary of the Bureau of Applied Social Research at Columbia University. April.
   Published in *Social Problems* 6(1958):115–26.
   Reprinted in *Abundance for What?* (1964), pp. 568–83.
"Law and Sociology: Recruitment, Training, and Colleagueship." *Stanford Law Review* 9:643–73.
   Reprinted as "Law and Sociology." *Indian Journal of Social Research* 4(1963):102–4.
   Reprinted in *Abundance for What?* (1964), pp. 454–92.
"New Critics of the Court." *New Republic*, 29 July, pp. 9–13.
"The Suburban Dislocation." *Annals of the American Academy of Political and Social Science* 314(November):123–46.
   Reprinted in *Abundance for What?* (1964), pp. 226–57.
   Revised and reprinted as "The Suburban Sadness" in William Dobriner, ed., *The Suburban Community*. New York: G. P. Putnam's Sons, 1958. Pp. 375–408.
"Work and Leisure: Fusion or Polarity?" With Warner Bloomberg, Jr. In Conrad N. Arensberg et al., eds., *Research in Industrial Human Relations: A Clinical Appraisal*. New York: Harper & Bros. Pp. 669–85.
   Revised version, "Industrial Work and Leisure in America," in *Way Forum*, no. 26, December 1957, pp. 8–9 and 51–53.
   Reprinted in Sigmund Nosow and William H. Form, eds., *Man, Work, and Society*. New York: Basic Books, 1962. Pp. 35–40.
   Reprinted in *Abundance for What?* (1964), pp. 147–61.

1958

"Abundance for What?—How to Use the Rising Income that Economic Growth Makes Possible" in *Problems of United States Economic Development*. New York: The Committee for Economic Development 1:223–34.

Reprinted as "Abundance for What?" *Bulletin of the Atomic Scientists* 14(April 1958):135–39.

Reprinted in *Best Articles and Stories*, no. 6, June-July 1958, pp. 18–21.

Reprinted in *Abundance for What?* (1964), pp. 300–308.

"The College Student in an Age of Organization." *Chicago Review*, Autumn, pp. 50–68.

"Comments on Walt W. Rostow's Essay on 'The National Style.'" In Elting E. Morison, ed., *The American National Style: Essays in Value and Performance*. New York: Harper. Pp. 358–68.

"Four Professors and American Sociology." *Cambridge Opinion*, October, p. 25.

"Human Relations and National Boundaries." *Comprendre* (Venice) 19:1–12.

Introduction to *The Passing of Traditional Society: Modernizing the Middle East*, by Daniel Lerner. Glencoe, Ill.: Free Press. Pp. 1–15.

"Leisure and Work in Post-Industrial Society." In Eric Larrabee and Rolf Meyersohn, eds., *Mass Leisure*. Glencoe, Ill.: Free Press. Pp. 363–85.

Reprinted in *Abundance for What?* (1964), pp. 162–83.

"The Local Press and Academic Freedom." *Political Research: Organization and Design*, January, pp. 3–8.

Revised as "Academic Freedom and the Press" in *University of Houston Forum*, May 1958, pp. 31–34.

"Planning in Higher Education: Some Notes on Patterns and Programs." *Human Organization* 18:12–17.

"Private People and Public Policy." *Shenandoah* 10:17–67.

Reprinted in *Bulletin of the Atomic Scientists* 15(1959):203–8.

Reprinted in *Revista de Ciencias Sociales* 4(1960):541–60.

Review of the "Jacob Report." *American Sociological Review* 23: 732–39.

"Some Observations on the Interviewing in the Teacher Apprehension Study." A "Field Report" in Paul F. Lazarsfeld and Wagner Thielens, *The Academic Mind: Social Scientists in a Time of Crisis*. Glencoe, Ill.: Free Press. Pp. 266–370.

"Varieties of Excellence." *Journal of the National Association of Women Deans and Counselors*, March, pp. 99–114.

"Who Will and Who Should Pay for Higher Education?" an essay review of *Education As an Industry*, by Ernest van den Haag. *School Review* 66:218–31.

"Women: Their Orbits and Their Education." *Journal of the American Association of University Women*, January, pp. 77–81.

1959

"The Academic Career: Notes on Recruitment and Colleagueship."
Daedalus 88:147–69.
Reprinted as "The College Professor" in Brand Blanchard, ed.,
Education in the Age of Science. New York: Basic Books,
1959. Pp. 261–84.
Abridged and reprinted as "The Spread of 'Collegiate' Values"
in George B. de Huszar, ed., The Intellectuals. Glencoe, Ill.:
Free Press, 1960. Pp. 505–9.

"The American Crisis." With Michael Maccoby. Address to a group
of liberal Democratic congressmen. June.
Published in Commentary 29(1959):461–72.
Reprinted in James Roosevelt, ed., The Liberal Papers. Garden
City, N.Y.: Doubleday, Anchor Books, 1962. Pp. 13–47.
Reprinted in Abundance for What? (1964), pp. 28–51.

"Christmas in an Apartment Hotel." With Mark Benney, Robert S.
Weiss, and Rolf Meyersohn. American Journal of Sociology
65:233–40.

"Comments on 'American Intellectuals.'" Daedalus 88:491–93.

"Education and Exploitation." Convocation Address of the Rhode
Island College of Education. 24 April.
Published in School Review 68(1960):23–35.

"Flight and Search in the New Suburbs." International Review of
Community Development 4:123–26.
Reprinted in Abundance for What? (1964), pp. 258–69.

"The Influence of Student Culture and Faculty Values in the American College." The Yearbook of Education, 1959. London:
Evans Bros. Pp. 386–404.

Introduction to What It Means To Be a Politician, by Stimson
Bullitt. Garden City, N.Y.: Doubleday.
Paperback edition. Garden City, N.Y.: Doubleday, Anchor
Books, 1961.
Reprint edition. New Haven: Yale University Press, 1977. Pp.
ix–xxii.

"Permissiveness and Sex Roles." Marriage and Family Living 21:
211–17.

"The Problem of Assessing (and Improving) the Quality of a College." Stenographic report of a paper presented at the seventh
session of the Seminar on the Economics of Higher Education,
Endicott House, Dedham, Massachusetts. 21 April.

"The Search for Challenge." Kenyon Alumni Bulletin, January-
March.

Reprinted in *Merrill-Palmer Quarterly of Behavior and Develop-
ment* 6(1960):218–33.
Reprinted in *New University Thought* 1(1960):3–15.
Reprinted in *Abundance for What?* (1964), pp. 349–68.
"The Social Scientist's View." Symposium on "Modern Society's
Challenge to Education." *Rhode Island College Journal* 1:
15–16 and 32.
"Some Observations on Interviewing in a State Mental Hospital."
Bulletin of the Menninger Clinic 23:7–19.
"The State of Communications Research—Comments by David
Riesman." *Public Opinion Quarterly* 23:10–13.
"The Study of National Character: Some Observations on the Amer-
ican Case." *Harvard Library Bulletin* 13:520–24.
Reprinted in *Abundance for What?* (1964), pp. 584–603.

1960

Introduction to *The Vanishing Adolescent*, by Edgar Friedenberg.
Boston: Beacon Press.
"The Relevance of Thorstein Veblen." With Staughton Lynd. *Amer-
ican Scholar* 29:543–51.
Reprinted in *New Statesman* 59(1960):526–68.
Reprinted in *Abundance for What?* (1964), pp. 388–401.
"The Significance of 'Five Old Ladies and a Catalyst.'" Commen-
tary on an essay in the same volume by William S. Reed.
Intercollegian 77:7–8.
"Sociability, Permissiveness, and Equality: A Preliminary Formula-
tion." With Robert Potter and Jeanne Watson. *Psychiatry*
23:323–40.
Reprinted in *Abundance for What?* (1964), pp. 196–225.
"Their Tribes and Ours." *New Republic*, 22 February, pp. 15–16.
"The Vanishing Host." With Robert Potter and Jeanne Watson.
Human Organization 19:17–27.

1961

"Age and Authority in the Interview." With June Sachar Ehrlich.
Public Opinion Quarterly 25:39–56.
"Changing Colleges and Changing Students." *National Catholic Edu-
cational Association Bulletin* 58:104–15.
"Consumer Research for Collegiate Customers." *Collage*, December,
pp. 21–22. From the Preface to the paperback edition of
Constraint and Variety (1958).

"Dealing with the Russians over Berlin." *American Scholar* 31:13–39.

"Education for Women in America." Lecture delivered as the Seventh Takashi Saito Lecture, Tokyo Women's Christian College. 8 November.

Published in *Essays and Studies* 13:1–10.

"The Lonely Crowd: A Reconsideration in 1960." With Nathan Glazer. In S. M. Lipset and Leo Lowenthal, eds., *Culture and Social Character: The Work of David Riesman Reviewed.* Glencoe, Ill.: Free Press, 1961. Pp. 419–58.

"Social Problems and Disorganization in the World of Work." With Robert S. Weiss. In Robert K. Merton and Robert Nisbet, eds., *Contemporary Social Problems.* New York: Harcourt, Brace & World. Pp. 459–514.

Revised, updated, and rewritten as "Work and Automation: Problems and Prospects" in Merton and Nisbet, eds., *Contemporary Social Problems.* 2d. ed. New York: Harcourt, Brace & World, 1966. Pp. 553–618.

Revised, updated, and rewritten as "Work and Automation: Problems and Prospects." With Robert S. Weiss and Edwin Harwood. In Merton and Nisbet, eds., *Contemporary Social Problems.* 3d. ed. New York: Harcourt Brace Jovanovich, 1971. Pp. 545–600.

Revised, updated, and rewritten as "The World of Work." With Robert S. Weiss and Edwin Harwood. In Merton and Nisbet, eds., *Contemporary Social Problems.* 4th ed. New York: Harcourt Brace Jovanovich, 1976. Pp. 603–37.

"Some Issues in the Future of Leisure." With Robert S. Weiss. *Social Problems* 9:78–86.

Reprinted in *Abundance for What?* (1964), pp. 184–95.

Reprinted in Paul Hollander, ed., *American and Soviet Society: A Reader in Comparative Sociology and Perception.* Englewood Cliffs, N.J.: Prentice-Hall, 1969. Pp. 324–29.

"Styles of Response to Social Change." *Journal of Social Issues* 17: 78–92.

"Test Ban Needed for Peace." In *A Collection of Essays and Articles.* Tokyo: Hakumon Herald, Chuo University. Pp. 152–56.

"Thoughts on Returning from Japan." *International House of Japan Bulletin,* no. 9, pp. 24–29.

"Tocqueville as Ethnographer." *American Scholar* 30:174–87.

Reprinted in *Abundance for What?* (1964), pp. 493–505.

"The Uncertain Freshman." *Current* 2:117–25.

"Where is the College Generation Headed?" *Atlantic,* April, pp. 39–45.

Reprinted in Leo Hamalian and Edmond L. Volpe, eds., *Essays of Our Time II.* New York: McGraw-Hill, 1963. Pp. 52–64.

1962

"The American Model on the World Scene Today." Commencement
  Address delivered at Lincoln University, Pennsylvania. *Lincoln
  University Bulletin,* Summer, pp. 7–13.
"The Cold War and the West." *Partisan Review* 29:63–74.
  Reprinted in *Abundance for What?* (1964), pp. 93–102.
"Experiments in Higher Education." In Howard Mumford Jones,
  David Riesman, and Robert Ulich, eds., *The University and
  the New World.* Toronto: University of Toronto Press. Pp.
  33–72.
  Abridged in *Proceedings of the Symposium on Undergraduate
  Environment* at Bowdoin College, Brunswick, Maine. 1963.
  Pp. 28–35.
"The Intellectuals and the Discontented Classes: Some Further Re
  flections." With Nathan Glazer. *Partisan Review* 29:250–62.
  Reprinted in Daniel Bell, ed., *The Radical Right: The New
  American Right.* Garden City, N.Y.: Doubleday, 1963. Pp.
  115–34.
Lectures on Aspects of American Culture. Tokyo: Nan'un-do Con-
  temporary Library.
"The Organization Man Debate." In James M. Hund, ed., *Social
  Responsibility in Business.* Emory, Ga.: Emory University
  Press, 1962. Pp. 55–61.
"Patterns of Residential Education: A Case Study of Harvard." With
  Christopher Jencks. In Nevitt Sanford, ed., *The American
  College.* New York: John Wiley & Sons. Pp. 731–73.
"Reflections on Containment and Initiatives." Paper delivered at
  Symposium on "Studies of War and Peace," annual meeting
  of the American Sociological Association. September.
  Reprinted, abridged, as "Containing Ourselves" in *New Repub-
  lic,* 6 April 1963, pp 14–17.
  Reprinted in *Abundance for What?* (1964), pp. 52–66.
"The Sense of Despair." *New Republic,* 2 October, pp. 15–18.
"Some Observations on Lewis Mumford's 'The City in History.'" In
  the *Festschrift* issue for Lewis Mumford of *Washington Uni-
  versity Law Quarterly* 12:288–94.
"The U-2 Affair and After." *Commonweal* 76:273–76.
  Expanded and reprinted in *Council for Correspondence News-
  letter,* September 1962, pp. 4–12.
The University and the New World, edited by Howard Mumford
  Jones, David Riesman, and Robert Ulich. Toronto: University
  of Toronto Press.
"The Viability of the American College." With Christopher Jencks.

In Nevitt Sanford, ed., *The American College*. New York: John Wiley & Sons. Pp. 74–192.

1963

"Commentary." *Moderator* 2:17–18.
"The Impact of Examinations." In Leon Bramson, ed., *Examining in Harvard College: A Collection of Essays by Members of the Harvard Faculty*. Cambridge: Harvard University Faculty of Arts and Sciences. Pp. 71–87.
"Innovation and Reaction in Higher Education." Pamphlet issued by the YMCA. Pasadena: California Institute of Technology.
 Revised in Arthur A. Cohen, ed., *Humanistic Education and Western Civilization: Essays for Robert M. Hutchins*. New York: Holt, Rinehart & Winston, 1964. Pp. 182–205.
"A Problem of Reaction." *Correspondent*, no. 29, November-December, pp. 53–54.
Review of *Anti-Intellectualism in American Life*, by Richard Hofstadter. *American Sociological Review* 28:1038–40.
"Tootle: A Modern Cautionary Tale." *Wilson Library Bulletin*, October, pp. 160–61. From *The Lonely Crowd* (1950), pp. 104–8.

1964

Abundance for What? And Other Essays. Garden City, N.Y.: Doubleday.
 Paperback edition. Garden City, N.Y.: Doubleday, Anchor Books, 1964.
 London: Chatto & Windus.
 Foreign editions: Japanese, German, Italian.
"Alterations in Institutional Attitudes and Behavior." Address at the annual meeting of the American Council on Education, San Francisco, California. September.
 Published in Logan Wilson, ed., *Emerging Patterns in American Higher Education*. Washington, D.C.: American Council on Education, 1965. Pp. 66–73.
"Developments and Trends in Higher Education." Address given at the annual meeting of the Commission on Higher Education, National Council of Churches of Christ. 10 June.
"Faculty Culture and Academic Careers: Some Sources of Innovation in Higher Education." With Joseph Gusfield. *Sociology of Education* 37:281–305.

Foreword to "Change and Conflict in the Communist Bloc," by Sanford Gottlieb. In *Sane Report*. New York: National Committee for a Sane Nuclear Policy, April. Pp. 1–2.

Foreword to *The Reasonable Adventurer*, by Roy Heath. Pittsburgh: University of Pittsburgh Press. Pp. vii–xvii.

"Goldwater's People." *Correspondent*, no. 32, Autumn, pp. 3–12.

Introduction to *Academic Women*, by Jessie Bernard. University Park: Pennsylvania State University Press. Pp. xi–xxi.

Introduction to *The Astonished Muse*, by Reuel Denney. 2d ed. Chicago: University of Chicago Press.

> Reissued with new Foreword, 1974.

Introduction to *Return to Laughter*, by Elanor Smith Bowen [Laura Bohannon]. Garden City, N.Y.: Doubleday, in cooperation with the Natural History Press. Pp. ix–xviii.

"Japanese Intellectuals—and Americans." *American Scholar* 34:51–66.

"The New Education." In "The Environment of Change," report of a conference at Sterling Forest, Tuxedo, New York, 14–15 June. New York: Time, Inc. Pp. 99–104.

"The Price of Change." *Correspondent*, no. 31, March–April, pp. 60–63.

"Reflections on Self-Renewal," a review of *Self-Renewal: The Individual in the Innovative Society*, by John W. Gardner. *Virginia Quarterly Review* 40:302–6.

"The Sociability Project: A Chronicle of Frustration and Achievement." With Jeanne Watson. In Phillip E. Hammond, ed., *Sociologists at Work: The Craft of Social Research*. New York: Basic Books. Pp. 235–321.

"Two Generations." *Daedalus* 93:72–97.

> Reprinted in Robert Lifton, ed., *The Woman in America*. Boston: Houghton Mifflin, 1965. Pp. 72–97.

1965

Foreword to *The Free Man*, by John Ehle. New York: Harper & Row. Pp. vii–xi.

"Letter from England." *Correspondent*, no. 34, Spring-Summer (special U.N. issue), pp. 100–106.

"Notes on the Deprived Institution: Illustrations from a State Mental Hospital." With Donald Horton. *Sociological Quarterly* 6: 3–20.

"Some Dilemmas of Women's Education." *Educational Record* (American Council on Education) 46:424–34.

"Terrifying and Illuminating." Multilith from a letter for the Returned Volunteers Conference of March, and comments at a conference on the Peace Corps, July.

1966

"Academic Standards and 'The Two Cultures' in the Context of a New State College." With Joseph Gusfield. *School Review* 74:95–116.

"The Coming Victory of the Academic." *Windhover* (North Carolina State University) 3:22–35.

Comment. In Theodore M. Newcomb and Everett K. Wilson, eds., *College Peer Groups.* Chicago: Aldine Publishing. Pp. 270–82.

"Conversations With David Riesman." *University Review* (State University of New York) 1:19–26.

Freud Og Psykoanalysen. Copenhagen: Gyldendals Uglebøger. (Essays from *Individualism Reconsidered* [1954].)

"Notes on New Universities, British and American." *Universities Quarterly* 20:128–46.

"Shimer College." With Christopher Jencks. *Phi Delta Kappan* 47: 415–20.

"Styles of Teaching in Two New Public Colleges." With Joseph Gusfield. In Robert S. Morison, ed., *The Contemporary University: U.S.A.* Boston: Beacon Press. Pp. 242–65.

"The Urban University." Symposium at the installation of Chancellor Ryan, University of Massachusetts, Boston. 10 December.

Published in *Massachusetts Review* 8(1967):476–86.

1967

"The American Negro College." With Christopher Jencks. *Harvard Educational Review* 37:3–60.

Revised and reprinted in *The Academic Revolution* (1968), pp. 406–79.

"The Catholics and Their Colleges (I)." With Christopher Jencks. *Public Interest,* no. 7, Spring, pp. 79–101.

"The Catholics and Their Colleges (II)." With Christopher Jencks. *Public Interest,* no. 8, Summer, pp. 49–74.

Reprinted in *The Academic Revolution* (1968), pp. 334–405.

"Comentario por David Riesman." Chapter 8 in Orlando Albornoz, *Estudiantes Norte-Americanos: Perfiles Politicos.* Caracas: Instituto Societas. Pp. 197–212.

Conversations in Japan: Modernization, Politics, and Culture. With Evelyn Thompson Riesman. New York: Basic Books.

Reprinted. Chicago: University of Chicago Press, 1976.

"Notes on Meritocracy." *Daedalus* 96:897–908.
"Some Questions about the Study of American Character in the Twentieth Century." *Annals of the American Academy of Political and Social Science* 370:36–47.
> Reprinted in Saul D. Feldman and Gerald W. Thielbar, eds., *Life Styles: Diversity in American Society.* Boston: Little, Brown & Co., 1972. Pp. 32–44.

"Some Reservations about Black Power." *Transaction*, September, pp. 20–22.
"The War between the Generations." With Christopher Jencks. *Record—Teachers College* 69:1–21.
> Reprinted in *The Academic Revolution* (1968), pp. 28–60.

1968

The Academic Revolution. With Christopher Jencks. Garden City, N.Y.: Doubleday.
> Paperback edition with new Preface. Garden City, N.Y.: Doubleday, Anchor Books, 1969.
> Paperback edition with new Foreword by Martin Trow. Chicago: University of Chicago Press, 1977.

"America Moves to the Right." *New York Times Magazine*, 27 October, pp. 34ff.
"A Changing Campus and a Changing Society." Address at annual meeting of the American Association of State Colleges and Universities. November.
> Reprinted in *School and Society*, April 1969, pp. 215–22.

"A Conversation with David Riesman." *Evening Gazette* (Worcester, Mass.), 24 April, p. 7.
"David Riesman: An Exchange with Brazilian Students." *American Scholar* 37:275–91.
"Dilemmas of the Educated Woman." Commencement Address at Mount Holyoke College.
> Given as a Convocation Address at Chatham College as "Some Dilemmas of the Educated—Especially Women." 1969.
> Revised and published as "Dilemmas of the Educated: Especially Women" in *Pitzer Participant* 6(1972):4–10.

"In Memory of Harold W. Solomon: Comments on Southern California's Flyer in Legal Education." *Southern California Law Review* 41:506–13.
"Innovations in Higher Education: Notes on Student and Faculty Encounters in Three New Colleges." With Joseph Gusfield. In *Institutions and the Person* (1968), pp. 165–99.

Institutions and the Person: Essays in Honor of Everett C. Hughes. Edited with Blanche Geer, Howard Becker, and Robert Weiss. Chicago: Aldine.

"On Autonomy." In Chad Gordon and Kenneth J. Gergen, eds., *The Self in Social Interaction.* New York: John Wiley & Sons. 1: 445–61.

"On Class in America." With Christopher Jencks. *Public Interest,* no. 10, Winter, pp. 65–85.

> Expanded and reprinted as "Social Stratification and Mass Higher Education" in *The Academic Revolution* (1968), pp. 61–154.

"Professionalism and Its Consequences: The Graduate Schools of Arts and Sciences." With Christopher Jencks. *Triquarterly,* no. 11, Winter, pp. 197–218.

> Expanded and reprinted as "The Professional Schools" in *The Academic Revolution* (1968), pp. 199–256.

"Return to Hiroshima," a review of *Death in Life: Survivors of Hiroshima,* by Robert J. Lifton. *Dissent,* May-June, pp. 265–69.

Review of *Persistence and Change: Bennington College and Its Students after Twenty-five Years,* by Theodore Newcomb et al. *American Journal of Sociology* 73:628–30.

"Some Observations on Legal Education." *Wisconsin Law Review* 1:63–82.

"The Training of Scholars." With Christopher Jencks. *Dialogue* 1:57–65.

> Reprinted as "Where Graduate Schools Fail" in *Atlantic,* February 1968, pp. 49–55.

> Reprinted as "The Training of Scholars: Another Look" in *American Review* (New Delhi) 13(1968):79–86.

> Expanded and reprinted as "Reforming the Graduate Schools" in *The Academic Revolution* (1968), pp. 510–44.

"The Triumph of Academic Man." With Christopher Jencks. In Alvin C. Eurich, ed., *Campus 1980: The Shape of the Future in American Education.* New York: Dell Publishing Co. Pp. 92–115.

> Reprinted in Holger R. Stub, ed., *The Sociology of Education.* Homewood, Ill.: Dorsey Press, 1975.

"We are Slowly Growing Less Civilized." *New York Times Magazine,* 28 April, pp. 113–14.

1969

"Administrators Can Be Scapegoats for Unreachable Targets." *New York Times Magazine,* 4 May, pp. 137–38.

"The Collision Course of Higher Education." Address to the American College Personnel Association. March.

Published in *Journal of College Student Personnel* 10:363–69.

Reprinted in part as "Universities on a Collision Course" in *Transaction*, September, pp. 3–4.

Expanded and reprinted as "Inflation in Higher Education" in *McGill Journal of Education* 5(1970):3–12.

Commentary in *Colleges of the Forgotten Americans: A Profile of State Colleges and Regional Universities*, by Alden Dunham. Carnegie Commission Series. New York: McGraw-Hill. Pp. 167–77.

Commentary in *From Backwater to Mainstream: A Profile of Catholic Higher Education*, by Andrew Greeley. Carnegie Commission Series. New York: McGraw-Hill. Pp. 164–72.

Contribution to Symposium on "Universities and the Growth of Science in Germany and the United States." *Minerva* 7: 751–55.

The Lonely Crowd (excerpts). Tokyo: Taiyosha Press.

"The Lonely Crowd, 20 Years After." *Encounter*, October, pp. 1–5.

"The Search for Alternative Models in Education." *American Scholar* 38:377–88.

"Vicissitudes in the Career of the College President." Dedication of the O. Meredith Wilson Library at the University of Minnesota. 13 May. Brochure published by the University of Minnesota.

Reprinted and revised as "Predicaments in the Career of the College President" in Carlos E. Kruytbosch and Sheldon L. Messinger, eds., *The State of the University: Authority and Change*. Beverly Hills, Ca.: Sage Publications, 1970. Pp. 73–85.

"When If Ever Do You Call in the Cops?" *New York Times Magazine*, 4 May.

"The Young Are Captives of Each Other: A Conversation with David Riesman and T. George Harris." *Psychology Today*, October, pp. 28–67.

1970

Academic Values and Mass Education: The Early Years of Oakland and Monteith. With Joseph Gusfield and Zelda Gamson. Garden City, N.Y.: Doubleday.

Paperback edition. Garden City, N.Y.: Doubleday, Anchor Books, 1971.

Paperback edition. New York: McGraw-Hill, 1975.

Japanese edition. Tokyo: Misuzu Shobo.

"The Academy and the Polity." Panel discussion of the American Sociological Association. 31 August.

"Observations on Contemporary College Students—Especially Women." *Interchange*, no. 1, pp. 52–63.

Reprinted in *Radcliffe Quarterly*, December 1970, pp. 2–8.

"One-Eyed Views and the University." Commencement Address at the University of New Mexico. June.

Reprinted as "The Business of 'Business as Usual' " in *Change: The Magazine of Higher Learning*, September-October 1970, pp. 6–8.

Reprinted in *Inside Academe: Culture in Crisis*. New Rochelle: Change Magazine Books, 1972.

"Teaching Vs. Research." *Harvard Independent*, no. 11, 10-16 December, pp. 3–6.

1971

"Dialogue on a Possible Three-Year Baccalaureate Program for Harvard College." Multilithed interview of 8 July, by David Korzenik of the Committee on Undergraduate Education, Sociology Department, Harvard University.

"Erich Fromm and the Rebels." *Intellectual Digest*, no. 3, November, pp. 42–44.

Foreword to *Time's Children: Impressions of Youth*, by Thomas J. Cottle. Boston: Little, Brown. Pp. xii–xvii.

"The Great Academic Depression." Commencement Address at the University of Pennsylvania. 24 May.

Published in *Pennsylvania Gazette*, June, pp. 24–28.

Reprinted as "An Academic Great Depression?" in *Universities Quarterly* 26(1971):15–27.

Reprinted as "The Academic Depression" in *Worldview*, June 1972, pp. 17–22.

"Notes on Educational Reform." In Bernard Landis and Edward Tauber, eds., *In the Name of Life: Essays in Honor of Erich Fromm*. New York: Holt, Rinehart & Winston. Pp. 193–217.

Reprinted in *Journal of General Education* 23:81–110.

Reprinted as "Erich Fromm and the Reform of Education" in *Change*, Summer, pp. 24–31.

1972

"The Validity of Traditional Disciplinary Boundaries." In William E. Carter, ed., "Higher Education and Changing Population Patterns" (Senior Fulbright-Hays Scholars Conference, Uni-

versity of Florida at Gainesville, May). Gainesville: Council
for International Studies, University of Florida. Pp. 17–32.
Revised and reprinted as "The Scholar at the Border: Staying
Put and Moving Around inside the American University" in
Columbia Forum 8(1974):26–31.

1973

Academic Transformation: Seventeen Institutions under Pressure.
Edited with Verne A. Stadtman. Carnegie Commission Series.
New York: McGraw-Hill.
"Commentary and Epilogue." In *Academic Transformation* (1973),
pp. 409–69.
"Cultural Conflict in the University." In Alan Richardson et al., *Our
Secular Cathedrals* (1973), pp. 25–63.
"Education at Harvard." *Change*, September, pp. 24–37.
"Evangelism, Egalitarianism, and Educational Reform." With Gerald
Grant. *Minerva* 11:296–317.
Foreword to *Loneliness: The Experience of Emotional and Social Iso-
lation*, by Robert S. Weiss. Cambridge: MIT Press. Pp. ix–xxii.
"In the Mind of Man," a review of *The Anatomy of Human De-
structiveness*, by Erich Fromm. *New Republic*, 8 December,
pp. 24–26.
Our Secular Cathedrals: Change and Continuity in the University.
The Franklin Lectures in the Sciences and Humanities. Edited
with Alan Richardson, Walter W. Heller, Daniel Boorstin,
Philip Handler, and Leon Edel. Tuscaloosa: University of
Alabama Press.

1974

"Conversation with the Spice Committee." Simmons College, Bos
ton. 24 June.
"Educating Individuals As Citizens." Symposium on "The Urban
University in the 1970s." Dedication of the Harbor Campus,
University of Massachusetts at Boston. 27 April.
Revised and reprinted as "The Mission of the Urban Grant
Universities." *Journal of General Education* 27:149–56.
"The Future of Diversity in a Time of Retrenchment." Convocation
Address at Windham College, Vermont. 19 October.
Revised and reprinted in *Higher Education*, no. 4(1975:461–82.
"St. John's and the Great Books." With Gerald Grant. *Change*, May,
pp. 28–36.

1975

"An Ecology of Academic Reform." With Gerald Grant. *Daedalus* 104:166–91.

"Can We Maintain Quality Graduate Education in a Period of Retrenchment?" Second David Henry Lecture, University of Illinois at Chicago Circle. 28 April. Printed by the University of Illinois, with questions and responses.

  Revised and reprinted as "Thoughts on the Graduate Experience" in *Change*, April 1975, pp. 11–16.

Education and Politics at Harvard. With S. M. Lipset. "Part Two: Educational Reform at Harvard College: Meritocracy and Its Adversaries." Two essays prepared for the Carnegie Commission on Higher Education. New York: McGraw-Hill. Pp. 281–392.

Foreword to *Faces on the Campus: A Psycho-Social Study*, by Graham Little. Melbourne: Melbourne University Press. Pp. vii–xiii.

Introduction to *An Owl Before Dusk*, by Michio Nagai. Carnegie Commission Series. New York: McGraw-Hill. Pp. vii–xvii.

"New College." *Change*, May, pp. 34–43.

1976

"American Youth 1976." *World Magazine* (Japan) 18:42–44. Special issue on the Bicentennial.

"Liberation and Stalemate." *Massachusetts Review* 17:767–76.

"On Restraint." Commencement Address at Franklin and Marshall College, June.

  Excerpts published in *F & M Today*, no. 4, July 1976, pp. 1–2.

Preface to *A College in Dispersion: Women of Bryn Mawr 1896–1975*, edited by Ann Miller. Boulder, Colo.: Westview Press. Pp. xix–xxxiii.

"Some Questions About Discontinuities in American Society." In Lewis A. Coser and Otto N. Larsen, eds., *The Uses of Controversy in Sociology*. A publication of the American Sociological Association. New York: Free Press. Pp. 3–29.

"Student Attitudes at Harvard." *Forum*, no. 2, November. Pamphlet printed by the Harvard College Fund. Pp. 1–2.

1977

"Death of the Academic Heart," a review of *The Gamesman: The New Corporate Leaders*, by Michael Maccoby. *Change*, June, pp. 57–59.

"Human Rights and Human Prospects." Commencement Address at Williams College. June.

  Printed in Williams Alumni Review, no. 4, Summer, pp. 4–9.

  Excerpts reprinted as "Prospects for Human Rights" in Society 15(1977):28–33.

  Excerpts reprinted as "Human Rights: Conflicts Among Our Ideals" in Commonweal 104:711–15.

  Revised and reprinted as "The Danger of the Human Rights Campaign" in Carl Marcy, ed., Common Sense in U.S.-Soviet Relations. New York: W. W. Norton, 1978. Pp. 49–55.

  Revised and reprinted as "Human Rights versus Human Prospects," in Barry Rubin and Elizabeth Spiro, eds., Human Rights and U.S. Foreign Policy. Boulder, Colo.: Westview Press [forthcoming].

"Small Steps to a Larger Vision." In The Third Century: Twenty-Six Prominent Americans Speculate on the Educational Future. New Rochelle, N.Y.: Change Magazine Press. Pp. 24–32.

"Student Career Choice and the Anti-Organizational Syndrome." Commencement Address to the Advanced Management Program, Harvard Business School. August. Multilithed by the Advanced Management Program.

  Edited version reprinted as "The Anti-Organisational Syndrome: Of Generational Gaps" in Encounter, September 1978, pp. 52–68.

1978

"Beyond the Sixties." Wilson Quarterly 2, no. 4(Autumn).58–71.

"Capitalism, Socialism, and Democracy: A Symposium." Commentary 65.66–67.

"Community Colleges and Social Stratification: Some Tentative Hypotheses." Catalyst 8, no. 2, pp. 1–5.

"Ethical and Practical Dilemmas of Fieldwork in Academic Settings: A Personal Memoir." In Robert K. Merton, James Coleman, and Peter Rossi, eds., Qualitative and Quantitative Social Research: Papers in Honor of Paul F. Lazarsfeld. New York: Free Press [forthcoming].

"1968, Ten Years On: Spoilt American Heirs still Turn to Great Cathedrals of Learning." London Times Higher Education Supplement, 5 May, pp. 8–10.

  Abridged and reprinted as "Ten Years On." New Republic, July 1978, pp. 13–17.

"On Egocentrism." In the Year Book, supplement to Collier's Encyclopedia. New York: Macmillan Educational Corp. [forthcoming].

"Opportunities and Vicissitudes of a Curriculum of Attainments Program: A Case Study of the Florida State University, 1973–1977." In Gerald Grant, ed., *On Competence: An Analysis of a Reform Movement in Higher Education*. Report of the Educational Policy Research Center, Syracuse Research Corporation, to the Fund for the Improvement of Post-Secondary Education. Syracuse University. 2:14.1–14.96.

Reprinted in Gerald Grant, ed., *On Competence: An Analysis of a Reform Movement in Higher Education* [working title]. San Francisco: Jossey-Bass [forthcoming].

The Perpetual Dream: Reform and Experiment in the American College. With Gerald Grant. Chicago: University of Chicago Press.

"Social and Cultural Demands for Competence." In Gerald Grant, ed., *On Competence: An Analysis of a Reform Movement in Higher Education*. Report of the Educational Policy Research Center, Syracuse Research Corporation, to the Fund for the Improvement of Post-Secondary Education. Syracuse University. 1:1.2–2.25.

Rewritten and expanded in Gerald Grant, ed., *On Competence: An Analysis of a Reform Movement in Higher Education* [working title]. San Francisco: Jossey-Bass. [forthcoming].

This bibliography was, of necessity, prepared in haste and is incomplete. Any corrections or leads to citations omitted here would be appreciated and should be directed to Ms. L. McKay, Harvard University, 33 Kirkland Street, Cambridge, Massachusetts, 02138.

CONTRIBUTORS

(We asked the contributors to append, after their affiliation, a brief note about their relationships with David Riesman. The Editors)

BENNETT M. BERGER is Professor of Sociology at the San Diego campus of the University of California. "I never sat in any of David Riesman's classrooms, but I have been a student of his since *The Lonely Crowd.*"

THOMAS J. COTTLE is Lecturer on Psychology at Harvard Medical School. "My first encounter with David Riesman was in 1959, when I took his course, American Character and Social Structure, at Harvard. In 1967, I taught a section of the course. David Riesman's work, his teaching and his being, have deeply influenced my own research and teaching, and indeed the way I have chosen to live my life."

REUEL DENNEY is a Research Associate at the East-West Center, Honolulu, Hawaii. "I met Dave in the mid-1930s and we began to play tennis and talk about Romanticism and Puritanism in American life. I worked with him on *The Lonely Crowd* and taught with him at the University of Chicago. My friend Dave Riesman has been my greatest teacher."

JOSEPH FEATHERSTONE is a journalist and historian who teaches at the Graduate School of Education at Harvard. "I used to teach off and on throughout the 1960s in Dave's Harvard undergraduate course,

Social Sciences 136. Dave has taught me that teaching and writing about America has to be holistic, and rooted in one's own daily experience of American life; he has set, for me, an admirable example."

HERBERT J. GANS is Professor of Sociology at Columbia University and Senior Research Associate at the Center for Policy Research. "Like many others, I first met Dave by correspondence; while he was at Yale, he helped me develop my ideas on political apathy for my master's thesis. In 1949 I took his seminar on Popular Culture at the University of Chicago (which laid the groundwork for my later book *Popular Culture and High Culture*). Since then, Dave has been a teacher, adviser, and good friend, through his works, our periodic conversations, and frequent letters."

NATHAN GLAZER is Professor of Education and Sociology at Harvard University. "I first met Dave in 1948 when he asked me to work on the project that eventually became *The Lonely Crowd*. We then worked together on the materials that were published as *Faces in the Crowd* and on a number of joint articles, and we have met and talked together regularly over the years. Most recently we taught together in a course on higher education at the Harvard University Graduate School of Education."

GERALD GRANT is Professor in the Departments of Sociology and Cultural Foundations of Education at Syracuse University. "I took Riesman's course as a Nieman Fellow at Harvard in 1968, and Dave asked me to join the staff when I stayed on to do a doctorate in the sociology of education. We collaborated on *The Perpetual Dream: Reform and Experiment in the American College*, and more recently, with others, on a study of competence-based educational reforms to be published as *On Competence*."

JOSEPH R. GUSFIELD is Professor of Sociology at the University of California, San Diego. "I first met David Riesman when I was a teaching assistant in Social Sciences in the College of the University of Chicago in the late 1940s. Subsequently we collaborated, with Zelda Gamson, on *Academic Values and Mass Education* and several articles. Our friendship has existed over more than twenty years in meetings and in personal correspondence."

EVERETT C. HUGHES is Professor of Sociology Emeritus, Boston College. "Dave and I taught together at the University of Chicago; he has been a colleague and friend since 1944."

CHRISTOPHER JENCKS is Professor of Sociology at Harvard University and a Research Associate at the Center for the Study of Public Policy in Cambridge. "I was a student of Dave's in Social Sciences 136 at Harvard during its first year (1959). After that I collaborated with him on a lengthy study of American higher education, culminating in our joint book, *The Academic Revolution*, published in 1968. Since 1967 we have also been colleagues at Harvard."

HIDETOSHI KATO directs the Research Institute for Oriental Cultures, and is Professor of Sociology at Gakushuin University in Tokyo. "I was a graduate student of Dave's at the University of Chicago in 1954 and 1955; his seminar on Popular Culture was one of the most memorable experiences in my life. Since then, I have been corresponding and visiting with him. I translated *The Lonely Crowd* into Japanese in 1965."

ROLF MEYERSOHN is Professor of Sociology at Lehman College and the Graduate School, City University of New York. "When David Riesman received a grant from the Ford Foundation to establish the Center for the Study of Leisure, he invited me to become its research director. We worked together at the University of Chicago between 1955 and 1958."

MARTIN MEYERSON is President of the University of Pennsylvania. "I have known David Riesman since 1946. It was he who persuaded me to become a professor. We were colleagues at the University of Chicago and at Harvard; since that time—from Berkeley to the University of Pennsylvania—Dave's advice and knowledge have continued to be stimulating and extraordinarily helpful. For me, and for other university and college presidents, Dave has provided imaginative prodding to our consciences. My wife, Margy, and I relish the years of our close association with Evey and Dave."

RICHARD SENNETT is Professor of Sociology and Director of the New York Institute for the Humanities at New York University. "I was a student of Dave's at Harvard University from 1966 to 1968."

MARTIN TROW is Professor of Sociology in the Graduate School of Public Policy at the University of California, Berkeley, and Director of the Center for Studies in Higher Education. "I have known David Riesman, as scholar and friend, for nearly twenty-five years. During these years I have been a student of his in the 'invisible college' of people engaged in the study of higher education. His scholarly work and his personal qualities have had a strong and continuing influence on my own work and thought."

ROBERT S. WEISS is Professor of Sociology at the Boston branch of the University of Massachusetts and Lecturer in Sociology in the Department of Psychiatry of Harvard Medical School. "I have known Dave since 1957, when he invited me to join him as a member of the Center for the Study of Leisure at the University of Chicago. He has been a teacher, a model, a colleague on half a dozen projects, an advisor, and a friend."